Community Builders Handbook Series

DOWNTOWN DEVELOPMENT HANDBOOK
Second Edition

Sponsored by the
Members
of the
Urban Development/Mixed-Use Councils
of
ULI–the Urban Land Institute
1992

ULI–the Urban Land Institute, Washington, D.C.

About ULI–the Urban Land Institute

ULI–the Urban Land Institute is a nonprofit education and research institute that is supported and directed by its members. Its mission is to provide responsible leadership in the use of land to enhance the total environment.

ULI sponsors educational programs and forums to encourage an open international exchange of ideas and sharing of experiences; initiates research that anticipates emerging land use trends and issues and proposes creative solutions based on this research; provides advisory services; and publishes a wide variety of materials to disseminate information on land use and development. Established in 1936, the Institute today has some 16,000 members and associates from 40 countries representing the entire spectrum of the land use and development disciplines.

ULI Staff for *Downtown Development Handbook* Second Edition

Staff Vice President, Research	J. Thomas Black
Staff Vice President, Publications	Frank H. Spink, Jr.
Senior Director, Research	Michael D. Beyard
Project Director	Susanna McBee
Managing Editor	Nancy H. Stewart
Manuscript Editor	Barbara M. Fishel/Editech
Book Layout and Art	Helene Y. Redmond/HYR Graphics
Art Director	Betsy Van Buskirk
Production Manager	Diann Stanley-Austin
Administrative Assistant	Ronnie Van Alstyne
Word Processors	Laurie Nicholson, Renée Adams

This handbook is part of a series of publications based on the philosophy of the *Community Builders Handbook*, first published in 1947 and last published in the Fifth or Anniversary Edition, 1968.

Community Builders Handbook Series:
Industrial Development Handbook, 1975 (out of print)
Shopping Center Development Handbook, 1977; Second Edition, 1985
Residential Development Handbook, 1978; Second Edition, 1990
Downtown Development Handbook, 1980
Recreational Development Handbook, 1981
Office Development Handbook, 1982
Mixed-Use Development Handbook, 1987
Business and Industrial Park Development Handbook, 1988

Community Builders Handbook Supplement Series:
Working with the Community: A Developer's Guide, 1985
Project Infrastructure Development Handbook, 1989

Recommended bibliographic listing:
Susanna McBee et al. *Downtown Development Handbook*, Second Edition. Washington, D.C.: ULI–the Urban Land Institute, 1992
ULI Catalog Number D13

International Standard Book Number 0-87420-732-0
Library of Congress Catalog Card Number 92-60669
Printed in the United States of America

Principal Author

Susanna McBee, former Senior Associate, ULI

Contributing Authors

Ralph J. Basile, Principal, Basile Bauman Prost & Associates, Inc.
Robert T. Dunphy, Director, Transportation, ULI–the Urban Land Institute
John M. Keeling, President, Hospitality Counselors, Inc.
Ben C. Lin, former Associate, Transportation, ULI–the Urban Land Institute
David C. Petersen, Director, Development Advisory Services, Price Waterhouse
Patrick L. Phillips, Vice President, Halcyon/Ernst & Young
Richard D. Wagner, AIA, Partner, David H. Gleason & Associates, Inc.

With a Steering Committee
composed of the following
Urban Land Institute members

Clyde C. Jackson, Jr.
Steering Committee Chair
Chair & Chief Executive Officer
Wynne/Jackson, Inc.
Dallas, Texas

James M. "Mike" Davis
Director of Planning and Development Services
City of Aurora
Aurora, Colorado

Stephen F. Dragos
President
Somerset Alliance for the Future
Somerville, New Jersey

Harold S. Jensen
General Partner
Metropolitan Structures
Chicago, Illinois

John Kell Martin
Chair
First Fidelity Mortgage Corporation
Atlanta, Georgia

Joseph W. O'Connor
President
Copley Real Estate Advisors, Inc.
Boston, Massachusetts

Wayne Ratkovich
President
The Ratkovich Company
Los Angeles, California

James A. Ratner
President
Forest City Commercial Development
Cleveland, Ohio

Charles H. Shaw
Chair
The Charles H. Shaw Company
Chicago, Illinois

Nell D. Surber
City Council Member
City of Cincinnati
Cincinnati, Ohio

Acknowledgments

I'd always wanted to work for ULI. When circumstances brought me to Washington, D.C., for 18 months, I was delighted that Dave Stahl, Tom Black, and Michael Beyard gave me the opportunity. Completing this book was a challenge, a joy, and the highlight of that experience.

Michael Beyard provided guidance throughout the project. Before I arrived, he organized, with the help of LDR International's James A. Cloar a focus group to discuss the content of this second edition. The focus group's participants—Michael Beyard, James A. Cloar, Joseph R. Bender of Development Services, Lewis Bolan of Leggatt, McCall Advisors, M.J. Brodie of the Pennsylvania Avenue Development Corporation, Albert Copp of Charles Center–Inner Harbor Management, James F. Danusch of the Rouse Company, John Fondersmith of the city of Washington, D.C., Chip Newell of New Height Group, Robert Olson of Richmond Renaissance, and George Ray of the city of Charlottesville, Virginia—provided needed direction that resulted in a draft outline prepared by Michael Beyard and James Cloar. I developed a more detailed outline and am thankful for comments from the steering committee's members. Wayne Ratkovich's comments particularly helped this then-downtown-neophyte to head in the right direction.

I am thankful for the help of several individuals who helped me in my initial research to organize field trips to downtowns and who provided contacts as well as information: Joe O'Connor and Maureen McAvey in Boston, Tom Kohler in Orlando, John Gilmore and Carla Clark in Seattle, Patrick LaCrosse and Cynthia Catto in Portland, Jon Wellhoefer in Milwaukee, and Frank Perry and Ben Brewer in San Antonio.

The contributing authors provided current information and examples for the text. Most of the research was completed in 1990. Patrick Phillips wrote most of the chapter on retail development, and Ralph Basile, an author of the first edition of this book, wrote most of the chapters on financing and project initiation. Richard Wagner wrote the chapter on restoration and historic preservation and provided some of the information for the chapter on strategy and organization. He also made the National Main Street Center's files available for my review.

Robert Dunphy and Ben Lin wrote most of the chapter on transportation, and Cynthia Angell summarized information from David C. Peterson's *Convention Centers, Stadiums, and Arenas* for the chapter on entertainment facilities in this book. Petersen and his associates at Price Waterhouse also wrote the case studies on the Georgia Dome, America West Arena, and San Diego Convention Center. Angell compiled information on low-income and affordable housing, and John Keeling wrote the chapter on hotels. Tracy Casteuble conducted the telephone survey of downtown population and researched mixed-use projects. Sources from all over the country provided information through meetings or telephone interviews; I thank them. Also, as a juror for the 1990 International Downtown Association Downtown Achievement Awards, I gathered quite a bit of information about projects, and I thank Rich Bradley for the opportunity to serve in that capacity.

Besides those already mentioned, a number of ULI staff members were particularly encouraging and helpful. Terry Lassar provided ideas, contacts, and information. I appreciate her willingness to share! Scott Middleton and Andrea Keeny generously shared project reference and awards files. Dean Schwanke, Joan Campbell, Nancy Minter, and David Mulvihill were responsive information gatherers and sources. Diane Suchman gave me loads of background materials on downtown housing. Ronnie Van Alstyne coordinated the endless photographs, graphics, footnotes, and sources contained in the book. She and Renée Adams also provided administrative support; Tom Black, Frank Spink, and Michael Beyard provided insightful editorial comments. Steering committee members had the difficult task of reading a long rough draft and pointing out inaccuracies, misplaced priorities, and omissions while making sure the text had the true ring of experienced members.

Dozens of developers, architects, and other professionals contributed photographs; I'm especially grateful to Cy Paumier, Suzanne Long, Kenny Caldwell, Larry Davis, John Gilmore, Tom Kohler, Tom Miller, Brenda McClure, Jon Runstad, Jane Lantzy, Dave McGarry, and Lizbeth Richards. Artist Michael Woolson and *Planning* were generous to let us use the original comic strip that Woolson created for the June 1990 issue of the magazine. Chief planner Michael Harrison and graphic illustrator Judy Galantha allowed us to reproduce images from the Portland, Oregon, Central City Plan.

Much credit must be given to ULI's editing and production staff, particularly Nancy Stewart, managing editor, and Barbara Fishel, manuscript editor, for handling the book's monumental editing and production; Helene Redmond for developing the handbook's artwork and designing the book's layout; and Judith Hancock for generating the index.

Finally, I thank my husband Barry for his daily support. Amid his own incredibly intense work schedule, he encouraged me, gave suggestions, watched out for articles and resources, took numerous detours on vacations to see downtowns, and even helped with late-night deadlines. Thanks, Barry!

Susanna McBee

About ULI Councils

Within the Urban Land Institute, 25 councils represent 11 land use disciplines: Industrial and Office Park Councils—Blue Flight, Gold Flight, Green Flight, Silver Flight; Urban Development/Mixed-Use Councils—Blue Flight, Gold Flight, Green Flight, Silver Flight; Commercial and Retail Development Councils—Blue Flight, Gold Flight, Green Flight, Silver Flight; Community Development Councils—Blue Flight, Gold Flight; Residential Development Councils—Blue Flight, Gold Flight, Silver Flight; Recreational Development Council; Small-Scale Development Councils—Blue Flight, Gold Flight, Silver Flight; International Council; National Policy Council; Development Regulations Council; and Development Infrastructure and Services Council. Each council is comprised of active members drawn from ULI's membership. Appointment to a council is based on knowledge, experience, and a willingness to share. Developers, consultants, financial institutions, public officials, and academics are all represented on each council to provide a broad perspective and to encourage interaction among various disciplines.

URBAN DEVELOPMENT/MIXED-USE COUNCILS
1991–1992

URBAN DEVELOPMENT/MIXED-USE (BLUE FLIGHT) COUNCIL

Chair
Preston Butcher
President
Lincoln Property Company N.C., Inc.
Foster City, CA

Assistant Chair
Robert H. Lutz, Jr.
Executive Vice President
Cousins Properties, Inc.
Marietta, GA

Fred E. Arnholt
Vice President
Metropolitan Life Insurance Company
New York, NY

Edmund N. Bacon
Philadelphia, PA

Dan L. Beaird
President
Dan Beaird, Inc.
Dallas, TX

Gary J. Beban
President
CB Commercial
Los Angeles, CA

Wence F. Cerne
Vice President–Real Estate
Whitman Corporation
Chicago, IL

A. Larry Chapman
Executive Vice President
Wells Fargo Bank
Los Angeles, CA

Michael J. Choppin
Chairman of the Board
IDM Corporation
Long Beach, CA

Raffi Cohen
Chair & Chief Executive Officer
Raffi Cohen Industries
Los Angeles, CA

Charles L. Davidson III
Executive Vice President
Hines Interests Limited Partnership
Atlanta, GA

Thomas R. Delatour, Jr.
Chief Financial Officer
Keystone, Inc.
Fort Worth, TX

Rosalyn P. Doggett
Washington, DC

Thomas G. Eastman
Executive Director
Aldrich, Eastman & Waltch, Inc.
Boston, MA

Edward D. Fox, Jr.
Senior Partner
Maguire Thomas Partners
Santa Monica, CA

Stephen J. Furnary
Managing Director
Jones Lang Wootton Realty Advisors
New York, NY

Rene Gautschi
Vice President–Architecture
Marriott Corporation
Washington, DC

Peter Y. Gevalt
Managing Director
Wells Hill Partners, Ltd.
New York, NY

John W. Gilmore
President
Downtown Seattle Association
Seattle, WA

Christopher Gladstone
Executive Vice President
Quadrangle Development Corporation
Washington, DC

H. Patrick Hackett, Jr.
Managing Director
JMB Institutional Realty Corporation
Chicago, IL

John M. Hart
President
The Hart Companies
Hartford, CT

Henry W. Haunss, Jr.
Managing Director of Real Estate
UBS Asset Management (New York), Inc.
New York, NY

Leslie Wohlman Himmel
Partner
Himmel + Meringoff Properties
New York, NY

Stuart M. Isen
Chair & Chief Executive Officer
Heitman Financial Services, Ltd.
Beverly Hills, CA

Nita Kensington
N. Kensington & Co., Inc.
New York, NY

Neil C. Klarfeld
Executive Vice President
Park Tower Realty Corporation
New York, NY

A. Eugene Kohn
President
Kohn Pedersen Fox Associates
New York, NY

Masao Konomi
President
Konomi, Inc.
Tokyo, Japan

M. Thomas Lardner
President & Chief Executive Officer
Lehndorff Management, Ltd.
Dallas, TX

Ronald W. Lee
Executive Vice President
Security Pacific National Bank
Los Angeles, CA

Stuart Lipton
Chief Executive
Stanhope Properties
London, England

Daniel T. McCaffery
President
McCaffery Interests
Chicago, IL

Craig McCarty
Vice President, Eastern
Regional Manager
Bechtel Investments Realty, Inc.
Gaithersburg, MD

David K. Martin
Senior Vice President
Trizec Properties, Inc.
Houston, TX

Peter C. Moister
Los Angeles, CA

Frank J. Sullivan
Managing Director–Investment
Jones Lang Wootton, USA
New York, NY

Nell D. Surber
City Council Member
City of Cincinnati
Cincinnati, OH

Robert J. Sweeney, Jr.
Partner
Faison Associates, Inc.
Charlotte, NC

George L. Thorn
General Partner
Colorado Center Building Partners
Denver, CO

Nicholas V. Trkla
President
Trkla, Pettigrew, Allen & Payne
Chicago, IL

James M. Trucksess, Jr.
New York, NY

Sam L. Van Landingham
President
Van Landingham & Assoc.
Atlanta, GA

Robert C. Walsh
Deputy City Manager
City of Beverly Hills
Beverly Hills, CA

Michael J. Wechsler
Chief Operating Officer
  & Executive Vice President
The Related Companies, Inc.
New York, NY

Steven R. Wechsler
Partner/Managing Director
Tishman Speyer Properties
New York, NY

John A. Weisz
Managing Director
Jones Lang Wootton Realty Advisors
New York, NY

William A. White, Jr.
President
Charter Properties, Inc.
Charlotte, NC

William A. Worthington
Principal
BayGroup Property Advisory Services
San Francisco, CA

URBAN DEVELOPMENT/MIXED-USE (GREEN FLIGHT) COUNCIL

Chair
Joseph W. O'Connor
President
Copley Real Estate Advisors, Inc.
Boston, MA

Assistant Chair
Fredrick W. Petri
Executive Vice President
Wells Fargo & Company
San Francisco, CA

D. Gregory Baarson
Deputy Director
Washington State Investment Board
Olympia, WA

William S. Bahrenburg, Jr.
Rye, NY

Rex M. Ball, FAIA, AICP
Chair & Chief Executive Officer
HTB, Inc.
Oklahoma City, OK

Richard L. Beadles
President & Chief Executive Officer
CSX Realty, Inc.
Richmond, VA

Michael P. Buckley
National Director,
  Real Estate Consulting
Halcyon Real Estate Advisors
Hartford, CT

Robert J. Carey
President
Urban Centre Developments, Ltd.
San Francisco, CA

Elizabeth M. Conahan
Senior Vice President
United States Trust Company
Quincy, MA

John C. Cushman III
President & Chief Executive Officer
Cushman Realty Corporation
Los Angeles, CA

S. Gregory Davies
President & Chief Executive Officer
CPS, A Commercial Real Estate Co.
San Jose, CA

James J. Didion
Chair & Chief Executive Officer
CB Commercial Real Estate Group
Los Angeles, CA

Thomas J. Flynn
Chair
Blackman Flynn & Co.
San Francisco, CA

James E. Foley III
Vice President
J.P. Morgan Investment Management
New York, NY

Richard F. Galehouse
Principal
Sasaki Associates, Inc.
Watertown, MA

Drew Gibson
President
Gibson Speno Company
San Jose, CA

Susan L. Giles
President
Giles and Company
San Francisco, CA

R. Stevens Gilley
President
Swig Weiler and Dinner
  Development Company
San Francisco, CA

Sam M. Grossman
Chair & Chief Executive Officer
Grossman Company Properties
Phoenix, AZ

Claude Gruen
President/Principal Economist
Gruen Gruen + Associates
San Francisco, CA

John S. Hagestad
Executive Vice President
The Sammis Company
Irvine, CA

Douglas W. Hall
Executive Vice President
Homart Development Co.
Chicago, IL

William J. Hatch
Chief Executive Officer
Rockefeller & Associates Realty
San Francisco, CA

Stephen C. Hopkins
President
Hopkins Development Company
Newport Beach, CA

Glenn Isaacson
President
Bramalea Pacific, Inc.
Oakland, CA

Stuart M. Ketchum
Owner
The Ketchum Company
Los Angeles, CA

Donald A. King, Jr.
Managing Partner
The RREEF Funds
San Francisco, CA

James R. Knapp
President
The Brookhollow Group
Santa Ana, CA

James M. Luckman, AIA
President & Chief Executive Officer
The Luckman Partnership, Inc.
Los Angeles, CA

Maureen McAvey
Director
Coopers & Lybrand
Boston, MA

Christopher F. McGratty
Partner
The Linpro Company
New York, NY

Chase J. McLaughlin
Director
C. J. Segerstrom & Sons
Costa Mesa, CA

Donald E. Megathlin, Jr.
Assistant to the President
Worcester Foundation
Shrewsbury, MA

Stephen J. Meringoff
Senior Partner
Meringoff Equities
New York, NY

Edwin B. Morris III
Managing Director
Morris and Morse Company, Inc.
Boston, MA

Daniel M. Neidich
Partner
Goldman, Sachs & Co.
New York, NY

Richard A. Pogue
Division President
The Koll Company
Pleasanton, CA

Benjamin Pollock
Development Manager–
  Central Waterfront Project
Port of Seattle
Seattle, WA

URBAN DEVELOPMENT/MIXED-USE (SILVER FLIGHT) COUNCIL

Thomas B. Swift
Executive Vice President
Gerald D. Hines Interests
San Francisco, CA

Carl B. Tash
President
JMB Institutional Realty Corporation
Chicago, IL

Steven E. Wheeler
Chair & Chief Executive Officer
John Hancock Properties, Inc.
Boston, MA

Ray L. Wilson, Jr.
President
CB Commercial Real Estate Group
  of Hawaii, Inc.
Honolulu, HI

Hiroharu Yamada
Executive Vice President
Mitsubishi Estate NY, Inc.
New York, NY

URBAN DEVELOPMENT/MIXED-USE COUNCIL AFFILIATES

Joseph C. Canizaro
Chief Executive Officer
Joseph C. Canizaro Interests
New Orleans, LA

Lawrence M. Cox
Real Estate and Urban
  Development Counselor
Hilton Head, SC

Henry J. Faison
President
Faison Associates
Charlotte, NC

Robert M. Gladstone
President
Quadrangle Development Corporation
Washington, DC

Bruce P. Hayden
Chairman
Hayden, Tolzmann & Associates, Inc.
Bloomfield, CT

E. Eddie Henson
President
Henson-Williams Realty, Inc.
Tulsa, OK

Gerald D. Hines
Owner
Hines Interests Limited Partnership
Houston, TX

Clyde C. Jackson, Jr.
Chair & Chief Executive Officer
Wynne/Jackson, Inc.
Dallas, TX

Harold S. Jensen
General Partner
Metropolitan Structures
Chicago, IL

Raymond D. Nasher
Chair
Raymond D. Nasher Company
Dallas, TX

I. Rocke Ransen
Chair & Chief Executive Officer
Mondev International, Ltd.
Montreal, Quebec

Wayne Ratkovich
President
The Ratkovich Company
Los Angeles, CA

Contents

1. The Rationale for and History of Downtown Revitalization   1

Why Revitalize Downtowns?   1

The CBD in the 20th Century   2

2. Strategy and Organization of Downtown Redevelopment   9

Strategies Defined   9

Organization as Strategy   13

Widespread Support, 14 • Management by One Entity with Full-Time Staff, 15 • The Downtown Plan and Guidelines for Its Successful Development, 19

Downtown Zoning   25

Incentive or Bonus Zoning, 25 • Mandated Design Features, 27 • Transfer of Development Rights, 27 • Inclusionary Zoning, 28 • Design or Development Review, 28 • Zoning Changes in the 1990s, 29

Downtown Orlando: A Successful Strategy for Revitalization   30

Organizing for Revitalization, 30 • Project Review: No Mystery, 30 • Development, 31

3. Initiation of the Project and Options for Development   37

Project Conception   37

Management Options for Public/Private Ventures   38

Private Management, 38 • Public/Private Joint Venture, 38 • Public Management, 39 • Public Implementation without Direct Private Involvement, 39

Development Prospectus and Selection of a Developer   40

What Developers Should Ask, 40 • What Cities Should Ask, 41 • The Request for Qualifications or Request for Proposal, 41

Development Analysis   43

The Rationale for Professionally Prepared Studies, 44 • Market Studies, 44 • Feasibility Analysis, 44

Obtaining Public Approvals   45

4. Financing   49

The Effects of Tax Reform   49

Private Sources of Capital   50

Commercial Banks and Thrift Institutions, 50 • Bank Community Development Corporations, 51 • Insurance Companies, 52 • Pension Funds, 53 • Real Estate Securities, 53 • Foreign Capital, 53 • Corporations, 54 • Financing Vehicles, 54

Public Sources of Capital: City Deal Makers 54

Public Financing Techniques 55

Indirect Measures, 55 • Direct Measures, 58

5. Design 71

Principles of Urban Design for Downtown 71

Develop According to an Organized Plan, 71 • Accentuate the Downtown's Distinctive Identities, 72 • Foster Variety, 73 • Keep It Tight, 73 • Create "People Places" by Enhancing Street-Level Activity, 74 • Encourage Visual Continuity, 74 • Stress Quality, 77

Architectural Guidelines for Downtown 77

Historic Preservation and Infill Development, 77 • Major New Developments, 80 • Megastructures, 81 • Parking, 82

6. Transportation and Parking 85

Misperceptions about Commuting and Congestion 85

Solutions to Downtown Transportation Problems: Getting There 86

In Search of the Holy Rail, 86 • High-Caliber Bus Service, 88 • New Roads and Improved Highways, 88 • Transportation Management Programs, 89 • Site Access Planning, 93

Pedestrian and Vehicular Circulation: Getting around Downtown 94

Catering to Pedestrians, Not Cars, 94 • Downtown Skywalks, 97 • Banning Cars: Streets for People and Transit, 99

Downtown Parking: How Much Is Too Much? How Much Is Not Enough? 100

Parking Reduction Ordinances, 101 • On-Site Parking, 102 • Shared Parking, 102 • Parking in Historic Areas, 102 • Public Parking Downtown, 102 • Free Parking Downtown, 103 • More Productive Use of On-Street Parking, 104

7. Mixed-Use Development 105

Planning and Design 107

Zoning 108

The Future of MXDs Downtown 109

8. Downtown Office Buildings 111

Factors Affecting the Downtown Office Market 111

The Future Need for Office Space 113

Estimating Supply and Demand 114

Designing Downtown Office Space 119

Marketing Downtown Office Space 120

Managing Downtown Office Space 126

9. Downtown Retailing ... 127

Challenges to Downtown Retailing ... 128

A Migrating Market, 128 • Downtown's Physical Setting, 130 • Decentralized Management, 130 • Other Hurdles for Development, 130

Opportunities for Downtown Retailing ... 132

A Changing Work Force, 132 • Attractions for Visitors, 133 • Public/Private Cooperation, 133 • New Organizational Resources, 133 • Downtown Is Different, 134

Defining the Downtown Retail Market ... 134

Market Segments, 134 • Competing Retail Centers, 138 • Downtown's Drawing Power, 139

Market and Development Feasibility ... 140

Estimating Market Support for a Downtown Retail Project, 141 • An Example of Estimating Demand, 142

Strategies for Downtown Retailing ... 145

Basics of Retail Design, 146 • Strategies for Specific Types of Projects, 149 • Centralized Retail Management, 166

10. Downtown Housing ... 173

Socioeconomic Changes Affecting Downtown Housing ... 173
Difficulties in Developing Housing Downtown ... 174
What Creates a Livable Downtown? ... 175
Downtown Housing Plan ... 177
Market and Feasibility Analysis ... 177

Site Potential and Evaluation, 183 • Market Potential, 183 • Project Feasibility, 185

Downtown Housing Strategies ... 185

Financial Incentives, 185 • Zoning Incentives, 186

Strategies for Low-Income Downtown Housing ... 189

Federal Programs, 189 • State and Local Programs, 190 • Public/Private Partnerships, 196 • Opposition to Affordable Downtown Housing, 198

11. Hotel, Convention, Entertainment, and Cultural Facilities ... 199

Downtown Hotels: A Crucial Component of a Successful Strategy ... 199

Convention Hotels, 201 • Commercial Hotels, 202 • Luxury Hotels, 202 • Public Incentives for Downtown Hotels, 203

Convention and Entertainment Facilities ... 204

Types of Public Assembly Facilities, 205 • Determining Need, 205 • Planning, Design, and Construction, 206 • Financing Development Costs, 208 • The Operating Budget, 209 • Management, 211 • Marketing, 214

Cultural Facilities ... 215

Projects that Include Cultural Facilities, 218 • Cultural Districts, 219 • Cultural Planning, 221 • The Economics of Culture, 221

12. Restoration and Reuse ... 223

Federal Incentives for Rehabilitation ... 224
Preservation Easements ... 232
Managing Historic Preservation Downtown ... 233
Conclusion and Trends ... 236

13. Waterfronts ... 237

Geographic Location ... 238
Functions of the Waterfront ... 239
The Regulatory Process ... 241
Access to the Waterfront ... 242
Design ... 242
Financing ... 243
Opportunities for Waterfront Development in the 1990s ... 245

14. Future Trends in Downtown Development ... 247

Planning the Work and Working the Plan ... 247
Proven Strategies ... 248
For Plan Development, An Inclusive Process, 248 • For Plan Implementation, E Pluribus Unum, 248 • Incremental versus Catalytic Approach, 249 • Zoning—No New Taxes, 249
The Shift from Creating Buildings to Creating Quality of Life ... 249
Management versus Development, 249 • Creating People Places, 249 • Management Trends in Transportation, 250 • Outlook by Type of Product, 251 • Tomorrow's Design, 254
Public/Private Partnerships—Still Crucial ... 254

Selected References ... 259

Index ... 263

Illustrations

1- 1	Vancouver Art Gallery, B.C.	1
1- 2	Pike Place Market, Seattle	2
1- 3	Landscaped downtown pedestrian environment, Washington, D.C.	2
1- 4	Historic downtown streets	3
1- 5	Early suburban shopping center—Northland Center near Detroit (1954)	4
1- 6	Vacant land from urban renewal, Baltimore	4
1- 7	Light rail, Portland, Oregon	5
1- 8	Faneuil Hall, Boston	5
1- 9	Sculpture in Portland, Oregon	6
1-10	Poster from Citizens for a Better Downtown, Seattle	6
1-11	J.P. Morgan & Co.'s headquarters on Wall Street, New York	7
2- 1	Feature box—Milwaukee Redevelopment Corporation	10
2- 2	Grand Avenue shopping center, Milwaukee	10
2- 3	Feature box—Missouri 353 Corporations	11
2- 4	Family living in affordable housing project in Toronto, Ontario	11
2- 5	Feature box—Downtown revitalization, Shelby, North Carolina	12
2- 6	Historic structures awaiting renovation, Dubuque, Iowa	13
2- 7	Underground Atlanta, Georgia	13
2- 8	City Hall, Milwaukee	14
2- 9	Historic City Market, Raleigh, North Carolina	15
2-10	Detail from renovated South Station, Boston	15
2-11	Feature box—Lakewood Center, Colorado	19
2-12	Illustration—Central City Plan, Portland, Oregon	20
2-13	Graphic—Citizens' participation, Portland, Oregon	20
2-14	Police patrolling street	21
2-15	Security Pacific Plaza, Bellevue, Washington	21
2-16	First Interstate Center, Seattle	21
2-17	Feature box—Transportation goals, Portland, Oregon	23
2-18	Transportation plan for downtown Portland, Oregon	23
2-19	Chart—Portland, Oregon	24
2-20	Chinatown, Vancouver, B.C.	25
2-21	Graphic—Cover of Central City Plan, Portland, Oregon	25
2-22, 2-23	Artwork in and around office buildings	26
2-24	Bank One Center, Dallas	27
2-25	Low-cost housing in Boston's Tent City	28
2-26	Streetscaping in Orlando	31
2-27	Children's play area, Orlando	31
2-28	Feature box—Affordable housing, Orlando	32
2-29	Feature box—Downtown Orlando's required retail space	33
2-30	Feature box—Public/private deal making, Orlando's City Commons	34
2-31	Model of City Hall, Orlando	34
3- 1	Chart—Downtown development process for public/private projects	38
3- 2	South Station, Boston	39
3- 3	Willard Hotel, Washington, D.C.	40
3- 4	Comic strip—Dirk Tracer	42
3- 5	Feature box—Analyzing financial returns to the city	46
4- 1	Feature box—Low-interest loan pools	51
4- 2	Feature box—The NCNB CDC: An early, but still working model	52
4- 3	The Poplar condominiums, Charlotte, North Carolina	52
4- 4	Fourth Ward redevelopment area, Charlotte, North Carolina	52
4- 5	225 West Wacker Drive, Chicago	53
4- 6	TDRs sold to another developer	56
4- 7	Skywalks—An example of air rights transfer in Orlando	56
4- 8	Aerial view—Arizona Center, Phoenix	57
4- 9	Audubon Court, New Haven, Connecticut	58
4-10, 4-11	The Adler Block in Asheville, North Carolina, before and after restoration	60
4-12	Jacksonville Landing, Florida	61
4-13	Old Town Square, Fort Collins, Colorado	62
4-14	Arizona Center, Phoenix	63
4-15	Feature box—COPs: An emerging financing technique	65
4-16	Table—Certificates of participation by unit of government, January 1985 to May 1990	65
4-17	Table—Certificates of participation by specific use of proceeds, January 1985 to May 1990	66
4-18	Feature box—Participation ground leases	67
4-19	National Theatre, Washington, D.C.	68
4-20	Site plan—Dallas Arts District	68
4-21	Feature box—Downtown retail center financing tools, Manhattan, Kansas	69
4-22	Manhattan Town Center, Kansas	69
5- 1	Downtown Seattle from Lake Union	72
5- 2	Boston's distinctive downtown identity	72
5- 3	Lake Eola, Orlando	73
5- 4	Downtown Vancouver, B.C.	73
5- 5	Festival in St. Louis	74
5- 6	Playground for daycare center, Boston	74
5- 7	Downtown setting, Milwaukee	75
5- 8	Shaded public spaces	75
5- 9	Seasonal plantings	76
5-10	Coordinated signage	76
5-11	Billboard in downtown St. Paul	77
5-12	Marketing materials	77
5-13	Downtown historic preservation	78
5-14	South Station, Boston	78
5-15	Liberty Place, Washington, D.C.	79
5-16	343 Sansome, San Francisco	80
5-17	712 Fifth Avenue, New York	81
5-18	Bank One Center, Dallas	81
5-19	Worldwide Plaza, New York	82
5-20	Landscaped buffers used to screen parking	83
5-21	Display windows in parking garage	83
5-22	Landscaped garage	84
6- 1	Table—New light-rail systems in North America	87
6- 2	Trolley in Baltimore's Inner Harbor	87
6- 3	Feature box—San Diego Trolley	88
6- 4	Transit hub at Westlake Center, Seattle	88
6- 5	Transit corridor and waiting area	90
6- 6	Table—Selected downtown organizations operating commuter transportation services	90
6- 7	Feature box—The Gallery at Market East, Philadelphia	92
6- 8	The Gallery at Market East entrance, Philadelphia	92
6- 9	Feature box—Access planning in downtown Boston	93
6-10	Bus-only lane and sidewalks	94
6-11	Improved sidewalks along Ocean Drive, Miami	95
6-12	16th Street Mall, Denver	96
6-13	Feature box—Hartford's downtown Scooter	96
6-14	Table—Grade-separated pedestrian networks in North American cities	97
6-15	Skywalk—Boston	98
6-16	Skywalk parade, Edmonton, Alberta	98
6-17	Transit mall, Vancouver, B.C.	99
6-18	Transit mall, Portland, Oregon	100
6-19	Feature box—Parking incentives in Seattle	101
6-20	Pedestrian walkway, Orlando	102
6-21	Feature box—Parking validation programs	103
7- 1	Charleston Place, South Carolina	105
7- 2	Warehouse Row, Chattanooga, Tennessee	106
7- 3	Feature box—Key features of mixed-use development	106
7- 4	Arizona Center, Phoenix	107
7- 5	Rowes Wharf, Boston	108
7- 6, 7- 7	Rockefeller Center, New York	108
8- 1	Fifth Avenue Place, Pittsburgh	112
8- 2	Chart—Growth rate of labor force, 1900 to 2000	112

XV

8- 3	Seattle's downtown bus tunnel	113
8- 4	Feature box—West Virginia recycles department stores	114
8- 5	Feature box—Metering office space	115
8- 6	San Francisco skyline	115
8- 7	Feature box—Kids Building Boston	116
8- 8	Woodworking laboratory at Wentworth Institute, Boston	116
8- 9	On-site construction class for Kids Building Boston	117
8-10	Pedestrian bridges at Copley Place, Boston	118
8-11	Plaza with landscaping and seating, Seattle	119
8-12	Interior finish for Security Pacific Plaza, Bellevue, Washington	119
8-13	Downtown city park and lake	121
8-14	Feature box—Downtown daycare	122
8-15	Children at a downtown project with daycare	122
8-16	Security in daycare center in CBD	123
8-17	Infant care at a downtown daycare center	123
8-18	Commercial kitchen in daycare center	124
8-19	Playground for daycare in CBD	125
9- 1	Table—Operating characteristics of downtown/intown shopping centers: 1990	128
9- 2	The Galleria regional shopping center, suburban Dallas	129
9- 3	Church Street Market, Orlando	129
9- 4	Feature box—The Grand Avenue, Milwaukee	131
9- 5	The Grand Avenue, Milwaukee	131
9- 6	The Grand Avenue, Milwaukee	131
9- 7	Market at Citicorp Center, New York	132
9- 8	Food market advertising	132
9- 9	Entertainment and restaurant district, Dallas	133
9-10	Underground Atlanta	133
9-11	Conventional downtown retail district	135
9-12	North Michigan Avenue, Chicago	135
9-13	Suburban shoppers downtown	136
9-14	Harborplace, Baltimore	137
9-15	Feature box—Making street vending successful	138
9-16	Street vendor with pushcart	138
9-17	Downtown parking	140
9-18	Downtown cultural event	140
9-19	Table—Analysis of retail demand	143
9-20	Pioneer Place, Portland, Oregon	146
9-21	Continuous retail frontage	147
9-22	Retail display windows designed by an artist	147
9-23	Repeating storefronts	148
9-24, 9-25	Merchandise displays	148
9-26	Retail signage	149
9-27	Oktoberfest, Larimer Square, Denver	150
9-28	Church Street Marketplace, Burlington, Vermont	151
9-29	Festival Center in Underground Atlanta	151
9-30	Festival marketplace, Boston	152
9-31	Festival marketplace	152
9-32	Feature box—Cityfair, Charlotte, North Carolina	153
9-33	Tryon Street entrance to Cityfair	153
9-34	Feature box—Escondido Farmers' Market	154
9-35	Farmers' market, Escondido, California	154
9-36	Horton Plaza, San Diego	155
9-37	Stamford Town Center, Connecticut	156
9-38	Feature box—Rivercenter, San Antonio	157
9-39	River walk at Rivercenter, San Antonio	157
9-40	Commerce Street at Rivercenter, San Antonio	158
9-41	Project data—Rivercenter, San Antonio	159
9-42	Water Tower Place, North Michigan Avenue, Chicago	160
9-43	Feature box—Multilevel retailing	161
9-44	Feature box—San Francisco Shopping Centre	161
9-45	San Francisco Shopping Centre	161
9-46	Garden park at Arizona Center, Phoenix	163
9-47	Market at Citicorp Center, Manhattan	163
9-48	Specialty stores in an MXD	164
9-49	Union Station, Washington, D.C.	164
9-50	Union Station, Hartford, Connecticut	165
9-51	Pioneer Place, Portland, Oregon	166
9-52	Feature box—New hat for developers?	167
9-53	Occidental Grill, Willard Hotel, Washington, D.C.	167
9-54	"Adult" bookstore	168
9-55	Display windows	168
9-56	Downtown park, Orlando	169
9-57	Police officers patrolling on horseback	170
9-58	Outdoor concert in Westlake Park, Seattle	171
9-59	Downtown Partnership of Baltimore	172
10- 1	Arbor Place apartment complex, Seattle	174
10- 2	Quality Hill, Kansas City, Missouri	174
10- 3, 10- 4, 10- 5	Downtown housing	175
10- 6	Whitney Grove, New Haven, Connecticut	176
10- 7	Public park downtown	176
10- 8	The Meridian, Dallas	177
10- 9	Yankee Hill, Milwaukee	177
10-10	Bice restaurant, Washington, D.C.	177
10-11	Feature box—Portland's downtown housing strategy	178
10-12	University Park Apartments, Portland, Oregon	179
10-13	South Park Square, Portland, Oregon	179
10-14	Table—Characteristics of Portland's downtown/close-in middle-income housing	180
10-15, 10-16	Riverside esplanade and marina—Portland, Oregon	180
10-17	Residential buildings, Portland, Oregon	181
10-18	Portland Center for the Performing Arts	181
10-19	Pioneer Place, Portland, Oregon	182
10-20	View from residential units	183
10-21	Table—Calculating market potential for downtown housing	185
10-22	The Paperworks, Memphis, Tennessee	186
10-23	Riverset, Memphis, Tennessee	186
10-24	Close-in residential neighborhood	186
10-25	Feature box—Downtown Columbus housing incentives	187
10-26	The Waterford, Columbus, Ohio	187
10-27	Market Mohawk, Columbus, Ohio	188
10-28	Wall Street condominiums, Columbus, Ohio	188
10-29	Resident in renovated low-income building, Seattle	189
10-30	Feature box—Tax credit investment	191
10-31	Assisted-living housing project	191
10-32	Low-income housing—The Genesis, Los Angeles	192
10-33	Feature box—Lenders' learning curve on SRO units	193
10-34	Table—Annual income and expenses per SRO unit	193
10-35	Serving people with special needs with SROs	194
10-36	Feature box—The San Diego solution	196
10-37	Sara Frances "Hometel," San Diego	196
10-38	Feature box—Seattle business community initiates low-income housing	197
10-39, 10-40	The Oregon in Seattle—before and after renovation	197
11- 1	The Mission Inn, Riverside, California	200
11- 2	Table—Location of hotels by size	201
11- 3	Stouffer Harborplace Hotel, Baltimore	201
11- 4	Chart—Houston hotel occupancies, 1978 to 1990	202
11- 5	The Ritz-Carlton Cleveland	203
11- 6	Table—Market mix of downtown hotels	203
11- 7	The Fairmont Hotel and surrounding area, San Jose, California	203
11- 8	Holiday Inn Crowne Plaza, Memphis, Tennessee	204
11- 9	Table—Hotel sales per guest-day, 1988	204
11-10	Tampa Convention Center	206
11-11	Water features	207
11-12	Washington State Convention and Trade Center, Seattle	207
11-13	The Orlando Arena	208
11-14	Feature box—America West Arena, Phoenix	210
11-15	America West Arena, Phoenix	210
11-16	Project data—America West Arena, Phoenix	211
11-17	Table—Recent concession agreements	212
11-18	Table—Advantages and disadvantages of alternative management structures	212
11-19	Feature box—San Diego Convention Center	213
11-20	San Diego Convention Center	213
11-21	Project data—San Diego Convention Center	215

11-22	Feature box—The Georgia Dome	216
11-23	Georgia Dome, Atlanta	216
11-24	Project data—Georgia Dome, Atlanta	217
11-25	"Arts in the Park," Fort Myers, Florida	218
11-26	Fairfield center for creative arts, Fairfield, California	219
11-27	California Plaza, Los Angeles	220
11-28	Morton H. Myerson Symphony Center, Dallas	220
11-29	International district in Vancouver, B.C.	221
12- 1	Contrasting architectural styles	223
12- 2	Woolworth building	224
12- 3, 12- 4	Greyhound Bus Terminal, Washington, D.C.—before and after restoration	224
12- 5	Feature box—Union Station, St. Louis	225
12- 6	Interior of Union Station, St. Louis	225
12- 7	Water feature at Union Station, St. Louis	225
12- 8	Feature box—Union Station, Washington, D.C.	226
12- 9	Union Station, Washington, D.C.	227
12-10	Feature box—Hillsboro, Texas	228
12-11	Downtown Hillsboro, Texas	228
12-12	Feature box—The National Register	229
12-13	Feature box—Secretary of the Interior's Standards for Rehabilitation	230
12-14	Feature box—Tax credits for historic and older buildings	231
12-15	Architectural detailing at South Station, Boston	232
12-16	Preservation of historic facades	232
12-17	Mission Inn, Riverside, California	234
12-18	Facade-ectomy	235
12-19	Refurbishment in San Luis Obispo, California	235
13- 1	Waterfront development	237
13- 2	Paseo del Rio, San Antonio	237
13- 3	Banners add color and interest.	238
13- 4	Waterfront development	239
13- 5	Feature box—Federal regulation of waterways	240
13- 6	Feature box—How Section 10 and Section 404 permits are processed	241
13- 7	Battery Park City's esplanade, New York	242
13- 8	Foster's Court, Rowes Wharf, Boston	243
13- 9	River walk in Milwaukee	243
13-10	Feature box—Granville Island, B.C.	244
13-11	Restaurants at Granville Island, B.C.	244
13-12	Water-taxi connecting Granville Island to downtown Vancouver, B.C.	244
14- 1	Trees along Pennsylvania Avenue, Washington, D.C.	248
14- 2	Affordable housing	248
14- 3	People-oriented downtown	250
14- 4	An urban forest	250
14- 5	The shops at Arizona Center, Phoenix	251
14- 6	Market Square, Washington, D.C.	253
14- 7	New downtown housing	253
14- 8	Whitney Grove, New Haven, Connecticut	254

A Brief History of the Community Builders Handbook Series

The Community Builders Handbook Series came into being when the *Industrial Development Handbook* was published in 1975. The series replaced the *Community Builders Handbook*, first published in 1947.

The original handbook was intended as a medium through which to share the experience and knowledge of developers and to encourage the improvement of land use and development practices. The handbook was sponsored by the Community Builders Council (now the Residential Development Council), which had been formed in 1944. Although the first edition contained only 205 pages and was sparsely illustrated, it represented a major achievement: for the first time, a book was available that described the development of residential communities and shopping centers.

The second edition, the J.C. Nichols Memorial Edition, published in 1950, was a modest revision and update of the original text. In 1954, the third or Members Edition, with 315 pages, significantly expanded the scope of the work. The fourth or Executive Edition, published in 1960, continued this expansion in response to the increasing complexity of development practices. With this edition, the handbook grew to 476 pages, but it continued to focus on residential and shopping center development. The fifth or Anniversary Edition, published in 1968, jumped to 526 pages, and its coverage was once more broadened. In addition to sections on residential and shopping center development, new material discussing a variety of special types of land development was included. Also added was a section on industrial development, drawing on the experience of ULI's Industrial Council, which was formed in 1951. The Industrial Council had previously sponsored other ULI publications, but the 1968 Anniversary Edition marked its first contribution to the handbook.

The *Community Builders Handbook* became widely recognized as a major reference source and textbook on land use and development practices based on the practical experience and accumulated knowledge of leading practitioners in the field. In 1965, as work on the 1968 edition was beginning, ULI was growing rapidly in membership and in areas of interest. The development industry was maturing, and the Institute was examining new directions it might take. By 1970, the Institute had decided to publish future editions of the *Community Builders Handbook* in separate volumes to provide expanded and more comprehensive coverage of each topic.

Following the publication of the *Industrial Development Handbook*, successive volumes were added on shopping center, residential, downtown, recreational, and office development from 1975 through 1982. Then, in 1985, renewal of the series began with the publication of the second edition of the *Shopping Center Development Handbook*, completely rewritten to cover the dramatic changes that had taken place since 1977, when the first edition was published.

In 1985, the need to deal with a topic that crossed the boundaries of specific types of development covered in each handbook resulted in the publication of *Working with the Community: A Developer's Guide* as the first volume in the Community Builders Handbook Supplement Series.

In 1987, mixed-use development had reached sufficient maturity as a type of development to become the subject of the seventh volume in the handbook series. In 1988, the *Industrial Development Handbook* was completely rewritten as the *Business and Industrial Park Development Handbook*, reflecting the changed character of industrial development in America. That book was followed in 1989 by the *Project Infrastructure Development Handbook* and in 1990 by the second edition of the *Residential Development Handbook*.

This second edition of the *Downtown Development Handbook* represents another refinement in the evolution of the handbook series. This volume addresses the dramatic changes in the nature of downtown development, the levels and type of support from federal, state, and local governments, and expanded coverage of the downtown development process.

The handbook series now contains over 3,000 pages, compared to the 205 pages of the first single-volume edition. The compilation of the knowledge and experience of ULI's members can thus be shared with both the knowledgeable and the novice in land use and development.

Frank H. Spink, Jr.
Managing Editor
Community Builders Handbook Series

Foreword

Having produced over 30 resources in books, infopackets, PRFs, videos, tour booklets, and continuing education programs covering downtown development and revitalization, the members of the Urban Land Institute have evidenced a strong commitment to the responsible use of land in central business districts. In no single resource, however, have users been able to find the how-to of downtown development—with an emphasis on strategies for revitalization—except in the original edition of the *Downtown Development Handbook* published by ULI in 1980. Since that time, however, the way in which downtowns are built has changed dramatically. New strategies for redevelopment, new roles for local governments, new financing sources and mechanisms, and less assistance from the federal government represent some of these changes. Over the past decade, we also have had an opportunity to assess just how successful earlier redevelopment has been, helping us to understand what works and what does not work in a downtown setting.

This second edition of the *Downtown Development Handbook* is a completely rewritten volume covering not only the process of developing downtowns in the 1990s—which often requires codevelopment between business and government and includes their working together on zoning, design, financing, and transportation planning—but also the products often seen there, including office, urban specialty and department store retailing, housing, mixed-use development, hotels and convention centers, and entertainment and cultural facilities. Development in unique settings, on waterfronts or in historic buildings, is also covered.

Though the handbook provides considerable detail as to current and recommended strategies and practices in downtown development and revitalization, it also serves as a jumping-off place by providing examples and lists of other resources for even more in-depth information on the many subjects covered, such as low-income housing or historic preservation.

The *Downtown Development Handbook* has been the commitment of a ULI steering committee for nearly three years, starting with a review of a draft outline in fall 1989 through the review of the draft manuscript in spring 1991. During that time, markets continued to suffer from the effects of overbuilding, financial institutions restructured themselves, limiting credit for real estate projects, and states, cities, and towns attempted to cope with dwindling funds. In some cities, resources continued to shift away from downtown. In others, work continued, producing in some cases stunning results. As in other ULI handbooks, this text focuses on these success stories.

The Urban Land Institute and the members of the steering committee who represent its Urban Development/ Mixed-Use Councils offer this latest entry in the Community Builders Handbook series in the hope that it will provide further stimulus for the revitalization of North American downtowns.

Clyde C. Jackson, Jr.
Chair
Downtown Development Handbook
Steering Committee

Introduction

Twelve years ago, ULI published the first edition of *Downtown Development Handbook*, which focused on the development process. Three other handbooks in the same series, those about industrial, shopping center, and residential development, had preceded it. Since then, ULI has published handbooks on mixed-use developments (MXDs), business and industrial parks, office buildings, recreational facilities, and infrastructure as well as a second edition of the original handbooks on shopping center and residential development. Companion books on hotels and motels, urban waterfronts, adaptive use, and convention centers, stadia, and arenas have been published, as have studies on public/private partnerships, downtown zoning, and downtown design. Clearly, the development process in general and most specific real estate products that make up a downtown (although not necessarily in a downtown setting) have been thoroughly covered. Those interested in the basics of downtown development as well as the fine points of developing in locations outside downtown should refer to those texts.

This second edition of *Downtown Development Handbook* focuses on the distinctive aspects of developing downtowns, emphasizing strategies for revitalization in particular. For example, most of ULI's development handbooks are project oriented. While this handbook is also, it looks as well at entire downtowns, for the success of individual projects hinges on the success of downtown revitalization. Toward that end, the strategy and organization for downtown revitalization are emphasized, along with other aspects of downtown development: public/private financing techniques, downtown retail space, and downtown housing, all of which differ depending on whether they are downtown or not. The handbook also covers products that are more often found in downtowns, convention centers, for example. Examples and case studies are woven into the text to illustrate the points made.

Furthermore, the focus of this handbook is the traditional U.S. downtown, not suburban or urban growth centers, such as the Post Oak/Galleria area in Houston. Though many of the techniques applied in downtown settings are being used in these growth centers and in neotraditional town planning like that for the Town Center in Reston, Virginia, many of the problems and opportunities facing central cities are distinctive. Finally, the changes in downtown development during the 1980s warrant a study of that topic by itself.

This handbook is divided into two major sections, one process oriented and the other product oriented. The final section (also the final chapter) discusses future trends to expect in downtown development.

Part One, the downtown development/revitalization process, includes Chapters 1 through 6:

Chapter 1 presents a rationale for and a brief history of downtown development in the 20th century.

Chapter 2 classifies and describes strategies for revitalizing downtowns and sets forth a model strategy that includes three key features: 1) widespread support, 2) management of the program by one entity, and 3) the downtown plan. Because the creation of a downtown plan often necessitates changes in the zoning ordinance, the chapter also includes a section on new downtown zoning techniques.

Chapter 3 focuses on a project's conception and approval for public/private ventures, also discussing the processes by which developers are selected and choose to participate in public/private projects, requests for qualifications and proposals, initial analysis of a project, and a city's approval of development.

Chapter 4 sets forth the host of federal and local, public and private financing mechanisms that have been successfully applied in revitalizing downtowns.

Chapter 5 puts forth principles of urban design for downtowns and guidelines for the architecture of downtown structures.

Chapter 6 discusses options for managing and reducing traffic congestion, including rail and bus systems, "transportation management," vehicular and pedestrian circulation, and downtown parking.

Part Two, components in revitalization strategies, includes Chapters 7 through 13:

Chapter 7 introduces a theme for the next five chapters, that is, the importance of a variety of land uses downtown, and presents key development considerations for downtown MXDs.

Chapter 8 recognizes office development as the engine of downtown revitalization but suggests that reduced demand for new development will shift the emphasis from developing buildings to retaining tenants; it thus focuses on marketing and management. Because new office development will occur no matter what, it also presents arguments for a managed supply of new space, tools for accurately estimating supply and demand, and guidelines for designing downtown office buildings.

Chapter 9 discusses the challenges and opportunities facing downtown retailers and retail developers and describes strategies for meeting them: restructuring and renovating current buildings, developing regional centers and mixed-use projects, and centralizing downtown retail management. A section on defining the retail market is presented as well.

Chapter 10 focuses on the factors contributing to a livable downtown and strategies for creating a downtown that can support residential development and describes the nuances of market and feasibility analysis for downtown housing, with special attention to the production of low-income and affordable housing.

Chapter 11 describes the means to implement a strategy for capturing meetings and tourism; the development features of convention, commercial, and luxury hotels, convention centers, stadia, and arenas; and a rationale for cultural planning downtown.

Chapter 12 aims to encourage preservation, restoration, and adaptive use as part of a strategy to accentuate a downtown's positive attributes and to recycle existing assets.

Chapter 13 provides development details for waterfronts, one of the most complex but potentially most successful types of downtown development.

Part Three, which is also Chapter 14, assimilates activities seen in the downtowns studied for this book into strategies that can be expected to be used in the 1990s.

New downtowns are rising from the old to become economic, cultural, and political city centers. Boston, Baltimore, Washington, D.C., Denver, Portland, and Seattle, among others, stand as testaments to the determined efforts by public and private sectors to remake the traditional downtown into "people places" of the next century. Other cities, it is hoped, can use the information in the remainder of this text to remake their downtowns as well.

Metric Conversions

meters = feet x 0.305
kilometers = miles x 1.609
square meters = square feet x 0.093
hectares = acres x 0.405
(1 hectare = 10,000 square meters)

1.
The Rationale for and History of Downtown Revitalization

Why Revitalize Downtowns?

The image that citizens and visitors have of a city is usually created by its downtown; it is a powerful symbol of the city's vitality or lack of it. A city's downtown is a center of its history, culture, and heritage. Seattle's Pike Place Market reminds us of that city's history as a seaport, while its skyscrapers reflect its transition to a more diverse commercial economy. Cleveland's Playhouse Square, which hosts resident ballet, opera, and Shakespeare companies, confirms that the city center is the area's performing

1-1   A city's downtown is its cultural center.

arts center. The storefronts and buildings in downtown Hillsboro, Texas, preserve a rich decorative tradition of historic architecture. The pueblo-style buildings in downtown Taos, New Mexico, remind us of the historic culture of the Taos-Tiwa Indians, there since 3000 B.C.

The same factors that give a downtown its sense of place also contribute to the central business district (CBD) as an effective place to conduct business. The high visibility and in many cases prestige of a downtown location are attractive to businesses that are pillars of the community—banks, courts, government agencies, power companies, major accounting, law, and insurance firms. The projected labor shortage of the 1990s[1] is expected to render the quality of the workplace even more important. An increasingly service-oriented, white-collar work force is attracted to the history, culture, and heritage a downtown location offers. Downtown as the transportation hub, with access to in-city airports as well as to all parts of the metropolitan area, and downtown as its own mixed-use development with office buildings, hotels, and restaurants all within walking distance support the central city as a business address. Though technology

[1] David L. Birch et al., *America's Future Office Space Needs: Preparing for the Year 2000* (Arlington, Va.: National Association of Industrial and Office Parks, 1990), p. 12.

1

has lessened the need to locate in a central place—computers do not care about location—a need remains for face-to-face meetings, carried out most efficiently in a downtown setting.

Revitalized downtowns are good for the city as a whole. Downtown development increases the city's tax base and creates jobs, and even low-paying, unskilled jobs as office and hotel housekeepers, restaurant cooks, and retail clerks are in great demand. The finance and business service sectors added some 154,000 jobs to New York City between 1977 and 1984; only one-third were in high-paying professional, technical, and managerial positions, while half were clerical and one-sixth were blue-collar and service positions.[2] Minorities in New York registered support—not opposition—for this trend by reelecting the mayor who had promoted a development agenda. In other cities, Boston and Baltimore, for example, providing permanent jobs for minorities became one of the points for negotiation in public/private efforts to redevelop

1-3   Trees, plants, and sculpture all enhance the downtown for pedestrians.

downtown. In markets with strong development climates, developer fees funded affordable housing, job training programs, and daycare facilities.

The fact that downtowns represent a tremendous existing investment in buildings, infrastructure, and public space makes their maintenance and enhancement a prudent and efficient use of resources. The negative impact of suburban sprawl provides additional impetus for encouraging rehabilitation of and development in the central city. Stewardship is back: moving into the 1990s, a use-what-you-have mentality is replacing the get-what-you-want attitude of the 1970s and 1980s.

The CBD in the 20th Century

Like all dynamic entities, the CBD is still evolving. Before World War II, downtown was the hub of economic, social, and residential life in metropolitan areas. Proximity to transportation and labor centers rendered manufacturing and commercial economies best realized in a downtown location. Movement within the CBD was on foot or in horse-drawn vehicles, so services and public facilities—schools, markets, and courts—were located in concentrated areas that in turn spurred growth of more supporting businesses and activities.

The arrival of the streetcar undermined the concentration of residential neighborhoods, for residents had a way to move away from the central city where most

1-2   Seattle's historic Pike Place Market attracts not only downtown workers and residents but also suburban residents and tourists.

[2] Bernard J. Frieden and Lynne B. Sagalyn, *Downtown, Inc.: How America Rebuilds Cities* (Cambridge, Mass.: MIT Press, 1989), pp. 300–301.

jobs were located. The wealthy, in particular, left their 18th and 19th century mansions, located near manufacturing plants, breweries, and other symbols of the industrial age, for the fresh air and open space of the suburbs. After World War II, the Veterans Administration housing insurance program and the rapidly rising incidence of car ownership combined to increase the number of city dwellers moving to the suburbs. Continued improvement and construction of roads through federal highway programs compounded the trend, and growing numbers of affluent and middle-income households moved out of the city. Passage of the Interstate Highway Act in 1956 further stimulated growth in suburban areas.

Following the exodus of downtown residents, downtown retailing declined. The 1950s saw the first suburban regional shopping centers, which evolved into the modern mall. Northland Shopping Center in Detroit, for example, developed in 1954, served as a model for new shopping centers throughout the country. Though downtown retailers began giving face-lifts to storefront shops, results were unsuccessful because the core problems—exiting anchors and customers—were not addressed. Some downtowns widened streets to accommodate burgeoning traffic, but doing so further eroded the quality of pedestrian life, long a hallmark of downtown. Others closed off streets entirely to create a kind of downtown mall, but it too met with mixed success.

In addition to the significant losses in residents and retailers, manufacturers began to move out of the urban core as highways enabled them to transport goods by truck instead of rail and waterway. Though railroads remained a means of moving goods and

1-4 Historically, movement within the CBD was on foot or in horse-drawn vehicles, so the downtown was compact and its uses interactive.

1-5 With the streetcar came the beginning of the exodus of downtown residents, followed by a decline in downtown retailing. The 1950s saw the first suburban shopping centers.

people into and out of the CBD until the second half of the 20th century, transportation by truck continued to garner a larger and larger market share. Cheap available land and labor in the suburbs added to the comparative advantage of a suburban location. During the 1970s and 1980s, the movement of offices to the

suburbs accelerated dramatically as employers followed workers and retailers to rapidly growing outlying areas.

The effects of this dramatic change in patterns of living and working on downtowns meant declining tax bases, changing demographics of downtown residents, deteriorating public services and retailing, and, overall, the transformation of downtown into a daytime-only environment. Even cultural facilities that did remain downtown suffered from declining attendance, although they were bolstered by support from corporations and wealthy individuals. Beginning in the late 1940s, planning schemes, federal programs, and local incentives were devised to combat these problems.

The Housing Act of 1949, an early urban renewal program, promoted the clearing and sale of residential land to developers. In 1954, the act was amended to allow commercial urban renewal and to require renewal to be part of a comprehensive city plan. This change encouraged cities to deal with the entire CBD, not just the areas where "blighted" or "economically obsolescent" housing existed. Still, with too few incentives to attract builders to downtown, the initiative stalled. Huge tracts of land remained vacant for years and contributed to the decline of downtown. The Community Development Block Grant (CDBG) program, started in 1974, gave grants to cities to

1-6 Vacant tracts of land left over from urban renewal contributed to downtown's decline.

1-7 Improvements in transportation, like light rail, made getting to downtown easier.

implement their own revitalization strategies, but it alone was insufficient to attract a significant amount of new development.

Starting in 1977, the Urban Development Action Grant (UDAG) program introduced a new solution: public entities and private companies working together as partners. The public sector generally remained involved in a project from beginning to end, awarding grants for demolition of old buildings only if new projects were planned in their places. Though the UDAG program has been terminated, it served as the forerunner of today's public/private partnerships. And the program continues to positively affect downtown revitalization as UDAG repayments are recycled into new projects.

Federal tax incentives to revitalize downtown areas began with the Tax Reform Act of 1976. Private companies were awarded accelerated depreciation for rehabilitating commercial buildings. The Economic Recovery Tax Act of 1981 bolstered this incentive with investment tax credits for rehabilitating historic properties. The Tax Reform Act of 1986 reduced those credits, but tax incentives for historic preservation continue to spur revitalization.

Though the case can be made for the benefits of federal funding and tax incentives on downtown revitalization, another case can be made for the detrimental effects of overreliance on financing mechanisms. Tax benefits and easy federal money caused some to lose sight of the fact that financing alone builds temporary success at best—and in some cases instant failure. Unsuccessful festival marketplaces across the country—long on creative financing but short on market justification—illustrate this point.

Still, by the late 1970s and early 1980s, the results of successful federally and locally funded programs began to show. Infill projects had replaced rubble

from urban renewal. An appreciation for historic architecture had resulted in renovated storefronts and rehabilitated buildings, paving the way for a later shift in architectural style toward fitting in rather than standing out. Improved transportation, including mass transit and superior bus systems, made getting to, from, and around downtown easier—even easier than getting around in some suburbs. Suburban gridlock began to affect downtown positively.

Besides the physical improvements, the success of UDAG and CDBG projects primed public and private entities for the partnership that would be required in the 1980s in the wake of reduced federal funds. Confidence grew, not only among developers and city deal makers but also among lenders, as pioneering projects like Harborplace in Baltimore and Faneuil Hall/Quincy Market in Boston performed beyond expectations.

It was against this backdrop of improved physical conditions and heightened confidence that the dramatic economic boom of the 1980s occurred. Baby

1-8 The success of pioneering projects like Faneuil Hall in Boston encouraged development not only in Boston's financial district but also in downtowns across North America.

1-9　Art has enhanced the downtown for pedestrians.

abatements and deferrals, tax-exempt, tax increment, and industrial development bond financing, mortgage guarantees, land writedowns, and low-interest loan pools. For easier deals, banks, foreign lenders, insurance companies, and pension funds provided plenty of capital.

The flip side of strong downtown development in the 1980s was the imposition of growth controls in cities like San Francisco and Seattle. These rapidly growing cities, concerned about the changing character of their downtowns, imposed moratoriums or limits on building and hefty fees on builders. Not many areas faced this kind of rampant growth, however, and the use of such restrictions for the downtown area was not widespread. (Many more cities imposed growth

[3] Birch et al., *America's Future Office Space Needs*, p. 5.

boomers joined the workforce, signing on primarily for white-collar work. Almost 45 million jobs have been added to the economy since 1967, a 68 percent gain, not one of them in manufacturing. Advances in technology fueled economic growth as well, as computers and telecommunications equipment allowed more business transactions to be completed. It was the decade of the deal. The result: almost 50 percent of all the office space built in the entire history of the United States was built in the 1980s.[3] Huge increases occurred in both suburban and downtown markets.

Office development spurred further downtown revitalization in the 1980s. Strong markets fostered the creation of design guidelines, bonus systems, and linkage fees to encourage and discourage targeted building types and features. The pedestrian became at least as important as the automobile, and requirements for active uses at ground level, streetscaping, and building to property lines surfaced. Bonus systems encouraged the development of mixed-use projects, open space, neighborhood retail services, and daycare centers. Linkage dollars built affordable housing. Single-room-occupancy hotels were saved with transfers of development rights.

One way or another, financing was readily available to fund the development boom of the 1980s. For pioneering downtown projects, public professionals fine-tuned the art of negotiating and real estate skills in working with developers to create new financing mechanisms. Enterprise zones gained popularity as redevelopment districts were created using former UDAG eligibility and other criteria for "distressed" property. Local incentives for downtown investment included the provision of public improvements, tax

Crowley Associates

1-10　Shown is a poster from Citizens for a Better Downtown.

controls in suburban jurisdictions, hoping to slow suburban sprawl and use existing city infrastructure more efficiently.) Increasing payments from developers for downtown park space, sidewalks, utilities, and streets, however, have become more common as cities meet budget challenges.

Other problems remain or have surfaced in many downtowns; some cities are farther along in the revitalization process than others. Despite a decrease in demand for office space, land prices continue to reflect development only as high-rent office space, even though the development many cities want downtown is residential. Ironically, downtown office development of the 1980s was, in some cases, both the ammunition for eliminating blight and the friendly fire of revitalization. Office development improved the investment environment downtown, but in many cities it deadened rather than enlivened downtown after dark.

Crime remains a problem in many downtowns, if only in the perception of suburbanites; the highly visible homeless population has an unsettling impact on those who live and work downtown, even in small cities; deteriorated low-income neighborhoods often abut glitzy skyscraper precincts; infrastructure, including streets, sidewalks, bridges, water and sewage systems, are often decaying; and power and telephone lines still clutter many downtown streetscapes. Retailing continues to atrophy in many downtowns as it is pushed out by land assembly for new office space or for parking lots to support other commercial activity. The rubble from urban renewal still exists in some downtowns, where assembled but vacant land and boarded-up buildings disrupt the continuity of revitalization.

In most downtowns, these problems are being attacked rigorously. This handbook is designed to document how it is occurring and to highlight what the results have been. Many cities made dramatic progress in the 1980s, with revitalization having placed some downtowns on a level with other markets in the metropolitan area. In those cities, the relocation of back-office operations is no longer a given, and some of the major tenants that moved to the suburbs in the 1970s and 1980s are now returning. J.P. Morgan & Co., for example, has rejected the notion of splitting its staff into headquarters and back-office operations by moving all executives, traders, and support personnel into a new headquarters building on Wall Street. "We want people close together," said A. Bruce Brackenridge, a group vice president.[4] In Boston, Cabot Corporation and Touche Ross, two major downtown tenants that had moved to suburban locations, have returned downtown. In other downtowns where revi-

1-11   J.P. Morgan & Co. is staying downtown. Its new headquarters is located at 60 Wall Street in New York.

talization has been implemented successfully, Portland, Oregon, for example, retail and residential development is flourishing. In fact, a ULI survey of 20 metropolitan downtowns indicates that downtown population in metropolitan cities has increased over

---

[4] Thomas J. Lueck, "Corporations Demand Flexibility in New Offices," *New York Times*, May 20, 1990.

the last 10 years.[5] In another encouraging sign, tenant sales, total operating receipts, total rent, total expenses, and net operating balances at super regional/regional and neighborhood-type centers in metropolitan downtowns were all higher per square foot than those for their suburban counterparts. Community centers in downtown/intown locations performed about the same as those in suburban neighborhoods.[6]

Planners now understand better what makes a downtown desirable and attractive. With innovative incentives, public/private partnerships, design and use criteria, and improved mass transit, a wider array of cities and towns are experiencing resurgence. Using the lessons learned from the last 30 years, the downtown renaissance will become even wider and deeper in the 1990s.

---

[5] ULI telephone survey, 1991.
[6] ULI–the Urban Land Institute, *Dollars & Cents of Downtown/Intown Shopping Centers: 1990* (Washington, D.C.: Author, 1991).

2.
Strategy and Organization of Downtown Redevelopment

Many towns and cities now have a broad range of overlapping public and private organizations or blue ribbon commissions that are attempting to manage or redevelop downtown through one major project or several smaller ones, hoping to revitalize the center city. Policies and priorities can be inconsistent, key players can be stretched thin by meeting schedules, and funding can wax and wane. Often, no good, single source exists for credible information on downtown. The result is occasional progress amid a flurry of memos, meetings, and reports, and general frustration.

This handbook provides models for more effective downtown revitalization. It describes potential strategies, focusing on those that have been successful, and, based on the research of the authors and the experiences of the steering committee, sets forth preferred strategies.

Strategies Defined

Strategies for revitalizing downtown can be described in a number of ways.[1] First, *who* initiates and implements the revitalization program is one way of describing the strategy, whether public agencies, private business owners or associations, or a public/private partnership. In most cities, all three types of groups are involved, with no lead organization accountable for steady progress (see "Organization as Strategy" later in this chapter).

The method for accomplishing revitalization—the *what* of management or development—is another way of defining the strategy. In Orlando, after a decade of strong development, the Downtown Development Board now focuses on management, particularly important in a city with Disney as a competitor. Centralized retail management and a tenant retention program for the office market are two of the programs it now employs. In Milwaukee, a development strategy continues to be used (see Figure 2-1).

How revitalization is completed, either by a catalytic or incremental approach is a third way of defining strategy. Development with a catalyst usually relies on a major development to revitalize the downtown, a festival shopping center or an arena, for example. An incremental strategy might include the development of an arena or festival center, but it would also include other plans for addressing problems downtown: specific financial programs aimed at attracting investment, concern for the overall design, appearance, and security of downtown, and promotions aimed at attracting consumers for downtown's goods and services. An incremental strategy is typically implemented over a long period of time.

---

[1] This basic typology is set forth in Richard Wagner and Ted Miller, *Revitalizing Downtown, 1976–1986* (Washington, D.C.: National Trust for Historic Preservation in association with The Urban Institute, 1988), pp. 15–19.

The Milwaukee Redevelopment Corporation (MRC) is a private nonprofit corporation whose board of directors is made up of chief executive officers of major area corporations. Beginning in 1973 as a limited-profit development corporation, MRC raised $3 million in donated seed money for planning and operations and another $16 million for investing in projects by selling stock to over 40 Milwaukee-based firms. Though shareholders were told not to expect a quick or market rate of return on their investments, MRC reconstituted itself as a nonprofit corporation in 1983 to reflect its actual performance. Operating funds now come from membership dues rather than from the sale of stock.

In its first two years of operation, MRC met with business and government to identify priorities and to establish a development agenda for the revitalization of downtown. Priority districts were targeted; the first was the central retail area west of the Milwaukee River. A three-pronged strategy involved the development of a hotel, a regional shopping center leased to the Rouse Company, and an office building partially leased to the federal government.

For the hotel, MRC made a cash equity investment in the project, while the city participated in landscaping and in the construction of a skywalk. For the office building, MRC optioned much of the land at risk to ensure the building's location between the retail center and the hotel. The city also assembled a portion of the land. For the retail center, MRC forged a coalition with the city and the Rouse Company and developed all of the $70 million project except for two parking garages. It pro-

2-2　　MRC forged a coalition with the city of Milwaukee and the Rouse Company to develop the $70 million Grand Avenue.

vided more than $16 million in equity and owns the private sections of the project.

Since the completion of its first three projects, MRC has continued to check off its priority list of work downtown. It initiated and later became a joint venture partner in the development of the 354-unit Yankee Hill, the first major housing development in downtown Milwaukee in 20 years. Completed in 1988, Yankee Hill is a market-rate rental project. MRC is also working with the Trammell Residential Company to develop a 20-acre project on the edge of downtown that will include more than 700 units of housing and 20,000 square feet of commercial space. In another partnership with the Crow organization, MRC initiated and participated in the redevelopment of a historic building that is now the new home of the Milwaukee Repertory Theatre as well as an adjoining hotel and office complex.

As compensation for its involvement in projects, MRC negotiates a percentage of the cash flow from the project as well as a percentage of the residual proceeds of sales. A negotiated fee is also sometimes part of its share in the deal.

MRC has used both informal and formal processes in initiating deals, and both have worked well. The Grand Avenue project exemplifies the informal process. Stephen Dragos, the founding executive vice president of MRC, had contacted more than 10 developers about the project to no avail; the Rouse Company was the 11th, and it ultimately became one of the partners in the project.

A similarly informal process had been used to work with Trammell Crow on the development of Milwaukee Center, the mixed-use project that includes the Milwaukee Repertory Theatre. MRC had already initiated the redevelopment of the theater building, formerly a power plant, and design had begun. A development partner for the other components, however, had not been located. Jon Wellhoefer, the current (1990) MRC executive vice president but then with the city, recalls phoning Crow. "I'd just returned from a ULI meeting where I'd heard Trammell Crow speak on Dallas's downtown arts district." Wellhoefer thought the company might be interested in the Milwaukee project as well. It was, and the company later became a partner in the project.

A more formal request for proposals was used for the 20-acre residential project. Letters to more than 60 local and national developers resulted in "something of a beauty contest," with finalists submitting plans for the project in competitive selection.

How revitalization is being accomplished can also be centered around the types of financial incentives or regulatory authority used. In St. Louis, Missouri, the Missouri 353 corporation defines the revitalization strategy. Such corporations are privately held but have authority usually associated with the public sector, such as eminent domain (see Figure 2-3).

Finally, *why* the revitalization program is being undertaken defines the strategy in some cities. In downtown Toronto, for example, social equity is a guiding principle of its Toronto Cityplan 1991. To increase affordable housing, to provide safety and freedom from discrimination, and to empower and enable participation in policy making drive revitalization policy.[2] Taking a more traditional tack, the strategy for Cleveland's downtown plan is designed to stimulate new growth and to reinforce the downtown as the financial, administrative, and entertainment center for the metropolitan area.[3]

This handbook promulgates a strategy that combines some of all the strategies described in the preceding paragraphs. It presents a comprehensive incremental strategy as most effective, as it has proven itself in both declining and prospering downtowns. According to a 10-year study of downtown revitalization programs, the catalytic strategy was successful only when applied to areas with fairly stable economies.[4] In cities where the downtown was declining sharply and was located in a region of poor economic performance, the catalytic approach failed. A compre-

2-4 Toronto's downtown revitalization is driven by five basic urban rights, including affordable housing.

hensive incremental strategy, however, was found to be more effective in cities with declining downtowns. Most of the cities highlighted in this text employ an incremental strategy. "The Downtown Plan and

---

[2] W. Dennis Keating and Norman Krumholz, "Downtown Plans of the 1980s: The Case for More Equity in the 1990s," *Journal of the American Planning Association*, Spring 1991, p. 150.
[3] Ibid., pp. 143–44.
[4] Wagner and Miller, *Revitalizing Downtown*, p. 17.

2-3   MISSOURI 353 CORPORATIONS

The state of Missouri allows a certain form of development corporation that operates as a private corporation but has the power of eminent domain. Developers may apply to a municipality to create a so-called "353 corporation" (after the legislation that created it); if approved, it can operate for 99 years. The limited-profit corporation may engage in the redevelopment of "blighted" areas by raising funds from investors and by applying for public funds, such as CDBGs or repayments of UDAGs. In addition, the 353 corporation is granted an abatement on property taxes for up to 25 years on improvements made. The most unusual feature of a 353 corporation, however, is its power of eminent domain. The corporation may "take" property within its project area in exchange for fair market value if the owner does not bring the property into compliance with the project's development plan within a specific period of time.

To establish a 353 corporation, a developer must target a "blighted" area as defined by the legislation—a definition that is fairly broad and recognizes both economic and social factors. The developer must also prepare a development plan for the area, describing design standards and detailed plans for rehabilitation, new construction, and improvements to infrastructure. Typically, the development plan is phased over a number of years and encompasses a fairly large area. The developer must also agree to adhere to the completion schedule set forth in the plan or risk having the corporation dissolved.

Though the 353 legislation was passed in the early 1940s, it was not until the 1960s, when Lacledes Landing in St. Louis was revitalized, that the tool was used extensively. Since then, 353 corporations have been established to assist in the redevelopment of St. Louis's Union Station, Kansas City's Quality Hill, and other projects around the state.

Founded in 1843 as the county seat, Shelby is located in rural southwestern North Carolina. Until the 1950s, the town's economy was based on cotton and government, but a shift in cotton growing and textile manufacturing to overseas locations in the 1950s and 1960s began a slow decline in the town's economy and population. The community's downtown, however, remained the center of retail trade until the early 1980s, when the county's first regional mall was constructed.

Recognizing that a strong public/private response was needed to direct the future of its downtown, this town of 18,000 residents formed Uptown Shelby Association (USA) in 1982. The nonprofit organization was directed by a board of local downtown property owners, merchants, and businesspeople; it employed one full-time staff person. Working with the Shelby Economic Development Commission (EDC), a branch of the municipal government, USA implemented an incremental downtown revitalization program with assistance from the North Carolina Main Street Center (part of the state's Department of Community Assistance) and the National Main Street Center.

In its first three years of operation, USA was funded by a mix of city general funds and private donations. In 1985, however, the organization recognized its emerging role as an ongoing management entity and the corresponding need for an ongoing source of funds. A special assessment district was established, and, as of 1990, assessments account for 78 percent of the organization's budget. Private sources and the city contribute the balance.

Business development and retention were major goals of Shelby's strategy for revitalization. Responding to a mix of programs, including open houses for new businesses and direct mail, 124 businesses located downtown between 1983, when the program began, through 1990. Additionally, 22 existing businesses expanded in the downtown. Over the seven-year period ending in 1990, the equivalent of over 300 full-time jobs was created, the vacancy rate for downtown buildings fell from 65 percent to less than 20 percent, and almost no vacant ground-floor space exists.

Early in the process, USA, EDC, and the city's four financial institutions created a $1 million tax-exempt loan pool, the first in North Carolina. In its six years of operation, the pool leveraged an additional $3.7 million in investment in downtown buildings. To further strengthen the identity of the CBD as well as to assist property owners in taking advantage of investment tax credits for rehabilitating historic buildings, USA and EDC also nominated the commercial district for the National Register of Historic Places. The National Park Service granted the historic designation in 1983, and, as a result, developers undertook a number of historic restorations, including North Lafayette Square, a $1.4 million storefront rehabilitation that has remained almost 100 percent occupied since completion; the Gheen Building, a $150,000 renovation of an about-to-be-demolished building into office space; the Post Office Building, modification of the old central post office to offices for county government; and Mason Square, a $1.2 million adaptive use of the 1920s Masonic Temple into offices and housing. Other office expansions include the 1988 move of municipal offices into a rehabilitated building near city hall and the construction of a new building for the county, to be completed in 1992.

With the renovation of buildings like Mason Square and the overall improved livability in the downtown, downtown Shelby has also begun to attract residents. During the past decade, a number of vacant upper floors have been converted to apartments. In 1987, a 41-unit housing complex for elderly residents was built, and in 1990, a 15-unit market-rate complex opened. Increased numbers of downtown residents and office workers have also resulted in the first new retail building built since the 1950s. Completed in late 1990, the new building reinforces architecturally the existing character of the downtown.

Another component of Shelby's incremental strategy has been the introduction of centralized retail management (CRM). Selected in 1986 by the International Downtown Association as a pilot city for its CRM program, Shelby developed a target market study for downtown retail opportunities. The information from the study directed USA's efforts toward business recruitment, retention, and expansion.

A former president of USA attributes the success of Shelby's revitalization to the "realistic, comprehensive" strategy that USA undertook. The current executive director cites the organization's ability to work with both the public and private sectors as well as its maturation into a management organization as keys to its success.

Source: National Main Street Center, National Trust for Historic Preservation.

2-6   Renovating historic structures was part of the revitalization strategy in Dubuque, Iowa. Since 1985, almost $15 million has been invested in new or rehabilitated projects, with an additional $35 million committed through 1991.

Guidelines for Its Successful Development," later in this chapter, describes the process of developing a downtown plan, using an incremental approach as a guiding principle.

The cooperation of public and private groups is another principle guiding the strategies presented in this book; such an approach is even more important in this decade as demand for new real estate and the supply of public monies level off. Public and private sectors working together are a necessity more than an option.

Both development and management are crucial parts of an effective strategy. Office and retail space, housing, hotels and convention centers, stadia, arenas, and cultural facilities, whether their development is part of a mixed-use project or part of the mix of uses needed for a vital downtown, are all potential components of a strategy for revitalization. At the same time, the importance of having one entity whose primary function is to manage downtown revitalization is recognized, specifically in "Organization as Strategy," later in this chapter. Centralized retail management is a key revitalization strategy for downtown retail stores presented in Chapter 9. And, as a result of the oversupply of development projects and the leveling off of demand, a strategy of managing and retaining tenants is a theme of this text.

The reasons for the revitalization strategies discussed in this handbook become evident with a little more examination of the text. Devoting entire chapters to the development and management of office buildings, retail space, hotels, and convention centers/stadia/arenas reinforces economic development and business retention as primary goals. The chapter on housing presents the provision of not only market-rate but also low-income and affordable housing as key objectives. The section on cultural facilities promotes the downtown as the cultural center of a metropolitan area. And the chapters on historic preservation/restoration and waterfronts recognize the historical precedence and natural resources of many downtowns. Chapters on organization, design, and financing present tools to support those goals. Throughout, the who, what, how, and why of successful strategies are woven into the discussion.

Organization as Strategy

The way downtown revitalization is organized is part of the strategy. Support from only the business community can prevent the inclusion of public incentives in a program. On the other hand, management of the program by a department within city government that already has other responsibilities could result in a

2-7   The development of Underground Atlanta was part of a modified catalytic strategy; the 220,000 square feet of shops and restaurants supports Atlanta's image as a convention city.

lack of the single-minded intensity needed to get the job done. Working without a plan for downtown can dilute efforts, but a plan that is not comprehensive will also be ineffective.

Based on the research for this handbook, three features are essential components of the organization behind successful downtown revitalization: 1) widespread support, 2) management of the program by one entity with full-time staff, and 3) the downtown plan itself. In Portland, Oregon, for example, all three components have been used. About 10,000 people, including citizens, professionals, and officials, participated in the planning that resulted in Portland's 1988 Central City Plan,[5] the plan that will direct Portland's next 20 years of development.[6] Revitalization of downtown is carried out by the Portland Development Commission. This quasi-public entity alternates among being developer, planner, and financier in implementing the plan.

Widespread Support

The trend toward inclusiveness in public policy making gathered steam in the 1980s and continues to accelerate in the 1990s. In successful downtowns, widespread support has been obtained from at least the following constituencies:

- *City and county governments,* with the leadership and support of their officials and staff, can help ensure the downtown organization is effective. Local governments can provide financial resources and information, authority not available to other nongovernmental entities, political accountability, and leadership in the revitalization. Regional planning commissions and councils of government are also excellent sources of technical information needed to analyze a downtown and develop a plan. They can also act as liaison between the downtown organization and other state, regional, and federal resources.
- *Property owners* have a vested interest in downtown's success and are often willing participants in revitalization.
- *Retailers,* like property owners, have a vested interest in downtown. Securing their support is vital in organizing any sort of centralized program of promotions, management, and maintenance.
- *Major employers* can also be major property owners with a built-in interest in downtown. They are also interested in the quality of downtown as it affects their employees. The smaller number of workers, caused by decreasing birthrates in the wake of the baby boom, have become

2-8   Milwaukee's City Hall, built in 1895, is the city's most important landmark. Without the city's partnership, most of Milwaukee's downtown redevelopment would not have occurred.

more conscious of amenities. If downtown is not a good place to work, they leave for the suburbs. Financial institutions are particularly affected by a healthy downtown, for they benefit from the opportunity to lend money to new or growing businesses. Sagging returns on assets resulting from the havoc in the industry of the 1980s make new business opportunities even more important. Further, participating in a downtown program helps banks satisfy their obligations under the Community Reinvestment Act.
- *Chambers of commerce* are natural partners in downtown development because of their mission to develop business. Because of their communitywide focus, however, chambers often can contribute to but not lead downtown revitalization.

[5]Keating and Krumholz, "Downtown Plans of the 1980s," p. 148.
[6]Portland Development Commission, "Moving into the Fourth Decade," 1989.

2-9　NCNB, through its Community Development Corporation, agreed to manage the historic City Market in Raleigh, North Carolina, with the help of York Companies. A farmers' market that had fallen into disrepair, City Market now houses 55,000 square feet of retail space and restaurants and 17,000 square feet of office space.

- *Historic preservation organizations*, using a building's distinctive architectural features for economic benefit, have contributed expertise regarding local history and techniques for preservation. In many cities, they are also involved in the review process for redevelopment.
- *Citizen or neighborhood groups*, like historic preservation organizations, came of age in the 1980s. While some might argue over the right of neighborhood groups to be involved in downtown development, the fact is that they are increasingly influential. So that planning is not interrupted or delayed at critical stages, citizen and neighborhood groups should be involved early in the process (a procedure some cities encourage more than others). The Boston Redevelopment Authority, for example, will not even

meet with developers seeking variances until the developers have met with, sometimes, dozens of citizen groups.

A study of downtown Centralia, Washington, demonstrates the need for widespread support of a downtown plan.[7] Centralia is a town of approximately 12,000 people located on I-5 halfway between Seattle and Portland, Oregon. The case study suggests that, particularly in a small town, the community at large, not just city staff and downtown activists, must believe in the plan's long-term nature.

In Centralia, the city council approved a three-year downtown plan during the mid-1980s. After three years, during which owners of several significant downtown buildings rehabilitated them, a promotional team initiated a historical mural program, and retail sales increased almost 10 percent, public funding for the program was terminated because the public sector believed the program should have accomplished more. Without public funding, private funds could not be raised, leading to the entire program's demise. Widespread support for the long-term nature of downtown revitalization is critical to success.

Management by One Entity with Full-Time Staff

In one Texas city, over 25 organizations are working to improve some aspect of downtown. No one single group coordinates the work, and, as a result, efforts are splintered. Management of the revitalization program primarily by one organizational entity with full-

---

[7] Wagner and Miller, *Revitalizing Downtown*, pp. 65–69.

2-10　Historic preservation is now an important part of downtown development.

time staff is essential. A variety of groups should be responsible for implementing different portions of the plan; however, one organization must be responsible for coordinating the plan's implementation.

The types of groups enveloping downtown organizations are difficult to categorize. A myriad of different organizations have been formed to respond to specific needs and varying local and state laws. Generally, however, three types of organizations have been formed to work downtown: public organizations, quasi-public organizations, and private organizations.

Public Organizations

Public agencies or corporations have important powers that can be used to initiate downtown projects—the power of eminent domain, the power to sell bonds, the right to receive revenues from the sale or lease of property, and the authority to levy property taxes, special assessments, or fees for specific public improvements, for example. They could include agencies within the city government or development authorities or commissions.

City Government. Some cities have established downtown planning departments; others have designated one or more individuals from planning or other departments to handle downtown development. While it is desirable to designate an agency, problems can occur if that department is the lead organization involved in revitalization. Often the group within city government responsible for redevelopment has other responsibilities so that the necessary focus is lost. The city department's constituency might be jeopardized or the mandate for revitalization lost when elected officials change.

On the other hand, the political nature of city government can work in favor of a downtown program, because it adds the element of political accountability to the plan. Further, housing a downtown program within city government ensures full access to all public funding mechanisms and powers. And the demonstration of a strong public commitment to downtown revitalization by housing the downtown organization in the city government can attract an even greater level of private initiative and investment (although the same statement could be made of any public/private organizational structure).

Downtown Development Authorities or Commissions. Often created by state enabling legislation, downtown development authorities or commissions are agencies independent of the city or county government. A board of directors, usually appointed by the mayor and approved by the city council, oversees the work of the authority. Funding might come from a variety of sources, including the city or county, tax increment financing, special assessments, and state and federal grants.

While some of the drawbacks of housing a downtown organization within city or county government also apply to development authorities, they can be minimized by establishing a broad-based board of directors. In this case, being associated with the city offers the city's resources—including political accountability—but with a much larger constituency.

Orlando's Downtown Development Board is an effective downtown development authority. Reporting to a board of directors and ultimately to the city council, the board has developed a downtown plan and a downtown land development code, both of which the city council has adopted. It reviews and approves all proposed downtown development, redevelopment, and demolition and is funded by a special taxing district and tax increment financing, the latter administered by a separate organization, the Community Redevelopment Agency. Staff for the agency come from the development board; city council members serve as its officers. Thus, all downtown planning and financial resources are administered by the same staff.

Quasi-Public Organizations

Quasi-public organizations take a variety of forms. Often they receive some form of public money but do not have the authority of a public organization to levy taxes or condemn land by eminent domain. In an era of declining public funds for downtown revitalization, a quasi-public organization using private money applied to visionary planning and privately organized renewal can supplement the public sector's activities.

One particularly important benefit of a quasi-public organization is the ability to conduct negotiations in private. Having to negotiate on the record can result in a less competitive deal, particularly if the terms of other offers are revealed. Many qualified developers might resist entering the competition if their financial conditions are made public.

Nonprofit Development Corporations. Development corporations can be incorporated as nonprofit or for-profit organizations and as private or quasi-public or public entities. Most downtown development corporations are nonprofit. The New Rochelle (New York) Development Council is an example of a quasi-public corporation.[8] With one-third of its reve-

[8] Laurence A. Alexander, *How Downtowns Organize for Results: 24 Case Studies* (New York: Downtown Research and Development Center, 1987).

nues coming from a contract with the city and the remaining two-thirds from members' dues, this nonprofit organization "cloaks itself with the power of the public sector while offering clients the confidentiality, consistency, and efficiency of a private company."[9] The council provides development services, such as site selection, planning, and design, and financing by seeding new projects, packaging tax abatement programs, and providing permanent financing. It also acts as a liaison with government officials.

Fayetteville (North Carolina) Progress, Inc., is another nonprofit downtown development corporation. Among other accomplishments, it identified a surplus school site as the likely location for in-town market-rate housing and arranged, with the help of a consultant, a joint venture between the corporation and North Carolina National Bank's Community Development Corporation. The joint venture secured the site and developed the 24-unit project, which sold out in one day.

Ad Hoc Committees. Such committees often form as the first step toward revitalizing a downtown. If they include representatives from both the public and private sectors, ad hoc committees can unite public and private leadership to determine an initial strategy. The committee might later be converted to some sort of advisory board or evolve into a nonprofit development group.

Private Organizations

Downtown Owners' or Merchants' Associations. Owners and merchants are key participants in the development and implementation of any downtown plan; however, they might be too narrowly focused to be able to coalesce the varied interests in a downtown revitalization effort. An organization with a history and reputation of broad community representation, however, could be an appropriate place to house the program.

Nonprofit Development Corporations. Private, nonprofit development corporations are another vehicle that can involve local public and private leadership in downtown revitalization. Used quite successfully in the 1980s, such corporations produced visionary downtown plans under the guidance of the private sector working with the public sector, assembled property (usually before the project's announcement), established joint ventures with private developers, and provided risk capital often not available from federal or local governments. Private nonprofit corporations have a number of advantages.

Private corporations are not restrained by limitations often imposed on public or quasi-public agencies, such as lengthy reviews and hiring processes, uncertain budgets, bureaucracy, and public negotiations. As well, private institutions can acquire property and finance real estate ventures using techniques for negotiating, contracting, and financing that might not be permissible for a public agency.

In response to different tax provisions for fund raising and operations, many private downtown organizations are organized along double lines: a nonprofit membership association with nonprofit development or operation organizations, usually with overlapping boards. In Tulsa, for example, the focus of downtown management is Downtown Tulsa Unlimited, Inc. (DTU), a membership organization that pursues a broad operating agenda and receives funds from dues, contract services, and parking fees. DTU is run by a professional staff overseen by a board of directors and executive committee encompassing the city's top business leadership. In addition, a nonprofit development corporation, Tul-Center, Inc., manages and operates the Downtown Tulsa Improvement District, an effort funded principally by special assessments on businesses within the district. Tul-Center, Inc., has also acquired and developed property to support DTU's program, and DTU's executive committee serves as the board for Tul-Center, Inc.

This sort of companion organization structure is common. In many cases, the operating organization is a Section 501(c)(6) corporation with a companion 501(c)(3) entity that may accept tax-deductible charitable donations to support downtown projects. In most cases, the organization presents a united front, for example, The Denver Partnership, Downtown Norfolk Council, and Central Atlanta Progress.

Chambers of Commerce. Chambers often pose different problems for housing potential downtown organizations: their interests, while oriented toward business, can be too broad and thereby dilute the effectiveness of the downtown organization. While they should participate in downtown revitalization, they should probably not house the downtown organization.

Organizational Structure and Role

Once the entity that will house the downtown organization is chosen, the structure of the organization can be determined. If the organization is independent

---

[9] Ibid., p. 17.

or quasi-independent, a board of directors will be needed. The success of downtown revitalization depends largely on the board's ability to identify and mobilize resources, build volunteer support, develop new leadership, and maintain a united focus on the downtown's needs and opportunities.

The board should be decisive and action-oriented, small enough to easily establish a quorum and large enough to include broad representation from the community. In a study of 201 downtowns in communities ranging in population from 2,500 to 500,000, programs with appointed boards tended to be more successful than those with elected boards or those without boards. Appointed boards were more likely to include influential community leaders with a variety of different perspectives and substantial expertise. Appointed boards were also more willing to take risks or make potentially unpopular decisions than boards elected by the members of the revitalization organization. Furthermore, board members who were appointed for a fixed term appeared to be less prone to infighting and stalemates.[10]

Ideally, the board should contain five to 11 members chosen from several groups: city and/or county government officials, downtown property owners, downtown retailers, professional and other business people, lenders, the board of the chamber of commerce (not the staff), heads of neighborhood organizations, and community leaders. The top-ranking person from these groups should be the board candidate—the president or chairman of the board of a bank, for example—because they are the individuals who typically have the influence and the time necessary to work at revitalizing a downtown. Other people who are interested or should be involved can be appointed to a committee or advisory board.

While the board of directors is a volunteer group, the staff should be full time and paid. Almost 75 percent of the cities in one study employed a full-time manager for their downtowns. Even in the smallest communities, those ranging in size from 2,500 to 10,000, 76 percent had full-time managers.[11]

Staff for the most productive downtown organizations are skilled in planning, design, development, and finance. They have several responsibilities:

- *Developing a yearly work plan.* Using the priorities set in the downtown plan, the staff develops a specific one-year plan and budget.
- *Simplifying the regulatory process.* As much as possible, the downtown organization acts as an umbrella organization to consolidate development review, reduce red tape, and act as an advocate—an honest broker—for private devel-

opers by working out agreements with government agencies. The ideal arrangement is for the organization to act as a one-stop destination or advocate for all necessary approvals. In the District of Columbia, for example, developers have to deal with approximately 25 reviewing agencies, whose functions frequently conflict and overlap with federal agencies. The Pennsylvania Avenue Development Corporation, through a combination of written agreements and staff coordination, has centralized the process and enabled some developers to obtain approvals in half the time normally required.[12]

- *Managing development projects.* Each project should have one primary contact at the organization. This deal maker will be responsible for all aspects of the project, including design, financing, and construction. If the organization can afford only a minimum permanent staff, this position should be filled first with a consultant assisting in other areas.
- *Providing technical support.* Staff will prepare market and financial analyses. Market studies of the entire downtown will be needed to respond appropriately to developers' proposals and to amend the downtown plan when necessary, though third-party studies will be needed for individual projects. Financial analyses will be needed to evaluate the organization's financial stake in projects and to assist developers as they prepare feasibility studies. A thorough knowledge of public financial incentives is required to assist developers in incorporating them into pro formas. Other technical support might include planning or architectural services.

If the organization cannot afford an adequate staff, the use of consultants, either for-profit or nonprofit, can be an appropriate alternative. Nonprofit organizations like the International Downtown Association, the National Trust for Historic Preservation's Main Street Center, the American Planning Association, the American Institute of Architects, the Council on Urban Economic Development, and ULI–the Urban Land Institute offer advisory services to assist communities with special problems. Usually, for-profit consultants participate in one of three ways:

---

[10] Wagner and Miller, *Revitalizing Downtown*, p. 38.
[11] Ibid., p. 25.
[12] W. Anderson Barnes, *Downtown Development: Plan and Implementation* (Washington, D.C.: ULI–the Urban Land Institute, 1982), p. 6.

- *As the organization's negotiator.* In effect, the consultant acts as the designated third-party negotiator representing the organization's interests with a developer. In this approach, little or no contact occurs between the developer and the organization while the deal is being negotiated.
- *As the technical support to the organization's chief negotiator.* In this role, consultants take a back seat but assist the organization as a technical analyst, providing support during planning and negotiations.
- *As a resource as needed.* Consultants are not intricately involved in the negotiations but are only a resource called upon to perform assignments as needed, perhaps a market study or cost-benefit analysis. The consultant has no responsibility for representing the organization in negotiations with developers.

The Downtown Plan and Guidelines for Its Successful Development

Once widespread support and a downtown organization have been established, work on the plan for downtown can begin. Such a plan describes a clear, shared vision for downtown supported by measurable objectives and action plans. It is an official public document, adopted to guide the physical and economic development for the downtown and to provide a standard against which individual proposals can be measured. Given limited resources, it should set priorities regarding physical and economic development goals and projects, considering, for example, the generation of jobs and taxes, housing, and revitalization of retailing. Furthermore, should several opportuni-

---

2-11   LAKEWOOD CENTER

The formation of the Lakewood Center Plan in Lakewood, Colorado, offers several perspectives on downtown revitalization. Lakewood Center had been a source of controversy in the community, with various lawsuits between the city, community organizations, and major property owners concerning potential development. To overcome these organizational constraints, an advisory committee was established to work with local community leaders to create a realistic and detailed implementation and financial plan to allow revitalization to proceed.

The plan, which won the 1990 Gold Nugget Award from the American Planning Association as the best master plan/community site plan in the West, had several important characteristics:

- Consensus was derived and a community focus created through active discussions, open-door public meetings, creation of a local newsletter, a series of on-site design workshops, and the maintenance of a storefront drop-in office.
- A balance between the developer's and the community's interests allowed expansion of open space while doubling the existing development capacity of the area.
- A portion of a special citywide sales tax was designated for an infrastructure fund that would be used to create an image and identity for the center and to help finance improvements for specific projects. In return for the city's designating its revenue in this manner, the city is to be paid back through a series of mechanisms,

including development agreements containing specific formulas for repayment and the city's participation in the cash flow of selected private projects.
- The agreement between developers and community interests did not bind developers to a building timetable. Instead, it designated where development would occur and in what maximum amount. The plan was designed to allow additional quality improvements as tax revenues, unrelated to specific projects, were generated.
- A new public/private organization, Lakewood Center Civic Vision, was created as a private nonprofit corporation with an independent board. Charged with promoting new development, negotiating projects with developers, and serving as an investment/construction manager for the city regarding public facilities, Lakewood Center Civic Vision will serve as an independent body; the city, however, will maintain financial and audit control over its infrastructure funds.
- A business improvement district was created to build and operate public facilities and raise money with special taxes or service fees within the district.

As a result, a strong consensus for development was created among all parties, and the advisory committee, the planning commission, and the Lakewood City Council all adopted the plan.

ties present themselves, the plan should establish criteria for participation by the city. Will the creation of jobs be viewed more favorably than the development of housing? Will market-rate housing be given greater emphasis than low-income or affordable housing? Addressing these questions in advance will result in a more substantive plan and aid in streamlining the plan's implementation.

The downtown plan must also reflect present community values and project future desires, melding the community's cultural, economic, social, architectural, and geographic conditions and values. While it forecasts the future, however, it should not be unalterable. The downtown plan must be structured so that it can be adapted to changing conditions.[13]

2-13 The development of a downtown plan will involve numerous meetings and hearings to consider the city's future. *Source:* Central City Plan, Portland, Oregon (1988), p. 3.

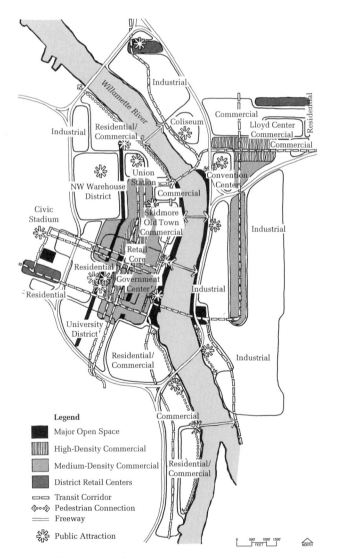

2-12 Illustration for the concept plan in Portland, Oregon's, Central City Plan (1988), p. 27.

Many communities have successfully used a task force of representatives from key constituencies or perhaps an ad hoc committee to organize and oversee the plan's development. The task force can then organize additional groups to work on specific sections of the plan, and a series of community meetings to obtain initial input and, eventually, to review the plan. Preparing a downtown plan involves several steps.

1. **Inventory Existing Conditions**
   Existing buildings and conditions must be inventoried to assess the downtown's strengths and weaknesses and to prepare a property base map. Land use maps of existing conditions should include information concerning available parking, mass transit, waterways, railroads, street rights-of-way, easements, existing structures, vacant land, historic buildings or districts, community assets like museums, theaters, and other public buildings, landownership, pedestrian routes, and topography. Aerial photos and maps indicating points of interest are also useful.

2. **Identify Problems and Opportunities, Complete Market Studies**
   A downtown might have several problems:
   • Inappropriate uses, such as wholesaling, warehousing, manufacturing, pornographic retailing, or surface parking;
   • Vacant or dilapidated structures, contributing to a decline in property values and the tax base;
   • A lack of pleasant public open space;
   • An insufficient number of retail establishments and a lack of their use during evenings and weekends;

---

[13] Ibid., p. 7.

2-14 A perceived or actual unsafe downtown is a typical problem to be addressed in the downtown plan. Many downtown organizations work with city police departments to secure dedicated patrol officers.

- Unpleasant pedestrian spaces resulting from too much emphasis on routing vehicular traffic efficiently, or an unsightly streetscape;
- A perceived or actual unsafe environment;
- A lack of daycare for children or elderly adults;
- A lack of low-income, affordable, and/or market-rate housing;
- Inadequate transit; and/or
- A lack of parking.

The downtown might also face certain opportunities:

- Potential new or increased sources of demand for retail and business activities, such as untapped tourism and convention markets. Orlando's Church Street Station, for example, the third largest tourist attraction in the state, became an important source of demand for the development of an urban shopping center totaling 120,000 square feet in the same downtown block;
- Historic buildings for restoration or adaptive use. In Hillsboro, Texas (population 8,500), 107 buildings were rehabilitated downtown between 1980 and 1988, representing a total investment of $5 million;
- Underused natural resources, such as a waterfront. Portland, Oregon, for example, ripped out a freeway separating its downtown from the banks of the Willamette River and replaced it with a riverfront park, presenting an additional opportunity to develop a mixed-use project that includes retail, residential, hotel, and office space at one end of the park.

James F. Housel

2-15, 2-16 Creating comfortable and inviting public spaces is an opportunity for most downtowns.

The basis for fleshing out any potential opportunity for development is sound market analysis. Studies focusing on each existing type of downtown development—offices, stores, and hotels—plus desired types, such as housing, will determine the level of existing and potential demand for these uses. These studies must be the foundation of the downtown plan and should be updated to stay abreast of changing conditions.

3. **Determine the Boundaries of the Plan Area**
Delineating the boundaries of the plan area is a crucial step in the development of a downtown plan. The plan should incorporate sufficient scale and magnitude to significantly affect the area. At the same time, it should concentrate on an area that makes sense economically and can be organized, managed, and funded. In other words, the defined area of the plan needs to be big enough to make a difference but small enough to succeed.

The 110-acre Pennsylvania Avenue Development Corporation (PADC) plan area in Washington, D.C., was designated to tie diverse elements together so that it was large enough to make a difference but remained small enough to be manageable. Because buildings are limited in height in Washington, more land was needed to produce the same amount of square footage obtainable in a city with greater permitted heights. The World Trade Center in New York, for example, contains more square feet of office space than that planned for all of the PADC area.[14]

The PADC area's boundaries and proximity to existing activity centers in the downtown were important factors in determining the ultimate size and development limits of the plan area. The Hecht's and Woodward & Lothrop stores, the F Street shopping corridor, and the Washington Convention Center served as strong area anchors to the north. Natural boundaries were set by the White House to the west, the Capitol to the east, and the Federal Triangle and the Smithsonian museums to the south.

4. **Develop Goals, Objectives, and Action Plans**
One of the most important steps in development of the plan is setting forth specific functional objectives and action plans to accomplish the objectives for the downtown. The overall steering committee should develop the initial range of action plans needed, which includes:

- Economic development and business retention
- Housing

- Transportation
- Human services
- Public safety
- Parks and open spaces
- Culture and entertainment
- Historic preservation
- Urban design
- Education
- The natural environment
- Infrastructure
- Development and maintenance of retailing
- Marketing, conventions, and tourism
- Plan review.

To the extent that functional objectives do not cover specific districts downtown, such as a waterfront, a market, a convention center, a government center, the office core, an international district, or a historic train station, specific plans for these areas also need to be developed. In the PADC plan, for example, 21 "squares" were designated and specific plans developed for each. After the appropriate list for the downtown is developed, additional task forces can develop the proposed objectives and action plans.

Objectives should be as specific as possible, measurable so that accomplishment can be tracked, and ranked in order of importance. For example, one of Atlanta's objectives for downtown housing is to increase the downtown population fourfold, to 40,000 by 2000. Specific action plans for accomplishing that objective are presented in the downtown plan.

Zoning might also need to be reviewed and revised with the downtown plan in mind. Whether downtown has a separate code or zoning for downtown is incorporated into the overall zoning ordinance, incentives and disincentives for achieving the objectives of the plan should be an integral part of the city's zoning (see the following section).

5. **Describe the Financing and Management Needed to Implement the Plan**
A good downtown plan sets forth who will be responsible for specific action programs and by what dates. It should also describe financing options, including the investment the public sector is willing to make to see the plan implemented. Financing strategies and tools that

---

[14] Ibid., p. 13.

could be used by both the public and private sectors in implementing a downtown plan are described in Chapter 4.

6. **Formalize the Plan**
So that the plan will have clear authority and an accountable sponsor, the local legislature or other appropriate body should formally adopt it. While citizens would have already been involved in the plan's development, public hearings might still be held, giving opportunities to modify the plan. After the plan's approval, regulatory changes, such as zoning revisions or the introduction of design reviews, are necessary.

2-17   GOALS AND ACTION PLANS FOR TRANSPORTATION
IN DOWNTOWN PORTLAND, OREGON

Improve the central city's accessibility to the rest of the region and its ability to accommodate growth by extending the light-rail system and by maintaining and improving other forms of transit and the street and highway system, while preserving and enhancing the city's livability.

FURTHER:

A. Develop the central city as the region's transportation hub through construction of a regional light-rail transit system.

B. Work with Tri-Met and other metropolitan area jurisdictions to locate and obtain funding to complete the regional light-rail transit system.

C. Support transportation facility improvements that improve the flow of traffic to, within, and through the central city.

D. Recognize that parking is an important element in the transportation system that supports growth and ensure that each district has adequate parking while improving air quality and traffic flow.

E. Encourage the use of bicycles and other alternative modes of transportation for general access into and within the central city by improving the pleasure and safety of the transportation system.

F. Separate bikeways and pedestrianways wherever it is both practical and possible, especially in parks and open spaces.

G. Protect residential neighborhoods from auto and truck through traffic.

H. Develop new systems and better utilize the existing transportation system to promote tourism by connecting the city's hotel, retailing, recreational, cultural, and entertainment attractions.

I. Improve the movement of goods to, from, and within the central city.

2-18   DOWNTOWN PORTLAND

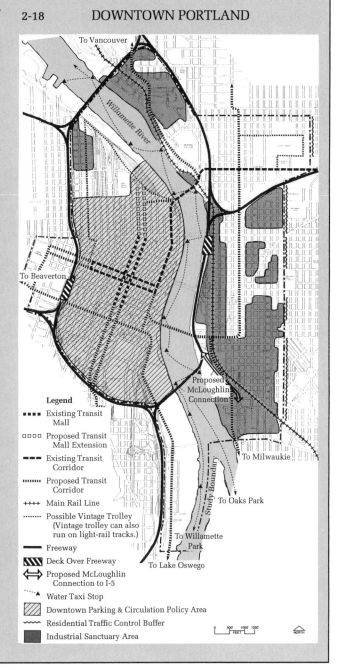

Legend

■■■■ Existing Transit Mall

□□□□ Proposed Transit Mall Extension

▬ ▬ ▬ Existing Transit Corridor

▪▪▪▪▪▪ Proposed Transit Corridor

++++ Main Rail Line

······· Possible Vintage Trolley (Vintage trolley can also run on light-rail tracks.)

▬▬▬ Freeway

◥◣◥◣ Deck Over Freeway

⇔ Proposed McLoughlin Connection to I-5

- - -▲ Water Taxi Stop

▨ Downtown Parking & Circulation Policy Area

〜〜〜 Residential Traffic Control Buffer

▓ Industrial Sanctuary Area

2-17 (continued)

J. Develop an integrated transportation system where each mode and the system as a whole are both efficient and practical.

K. Preserve access for all transportation modes on rights-of-way that lead directly to and from bridges.

2-19   ACTION CHART

#	PROPOSALS FOR ACTION	TIMING			POSSIBLE IMPLEMENTING AGENCY	INDEX TO ACTION DETAIL
		ADOPT WITH PLAN	NEXT FIVE YEARS	SIX TO 20 YEARS		
	PROJECTS					
T1	By January 1, 1989, finish a feasibility and engineering study for the two-mile stretch of Eastbank Freeway.	■			Planning/PDOT/ ODOT	P 88
T2	Engineer and construct the west-side light-rail line.	■			Tri-Met	P 88
T3	Plan and construct the remaining portions of the regional light-rail system.			■	Tri-Met	
T4	Plan and construct an inner-city transit loop (possibly on Grand Avenue).			■	Tri-Met	P 88
T5	Allow the use of some local service streets in industrial areas for angled parking for employees and for loading.		■		PDOT/PDC	P 89
T6	Develop informational guides, directional signs, and maps explaining the location and operation of auto and bike parking within the central city.		■		Planning/Pvt.	
T7	Design and install traffic control devices to keep auto and truck through traffic from infiltrating residential neighborhoods.		■		PDOT	
T8	Clearly designate and sign truck routes to and within industrial areas.		■		PDOT	
T9	Further study the proposed connection from McLoughlin to I-5.		■		ODOT/PDOT	
T10	Create a safe, clear, and pleasant system of walkways and bikeways.		■		PDOT/PDC	P 89
T11	Reinforce the Union Station area as a transportation center.		■		PDC/PDOT/Pvt.	
T12	Develop a system of short-term parking facilities in the central city.		■		PDC/PDOT/Pvt.	
T13	Develop an improved parking data system.		■		PDOT	
T14	Develop a parking strategy for each central city district and for specific sectors within the downtown; review and make recommendations on the parking needs of each district. Update this information regularly.		■		PDOT	
T15	Encourage the development of Bike Central bicycle commuter facility near employment centers.		■		Parks/Pvt./PDOT	
	PROGRAMS					
T16	Encourage reduced parking rates on weekends and at night.		■		Gen. Serv./ Planning/Pvt.	P 89
T17	Encourage new parking facilities to stay open in the evenings/ on weekends.		■		PDOT/PDC/Pvt.	

Note: Proposals for actions shown on the Action Chart and map were adopted through City Council Resolution. The projects, programs, and regulations listed are a starting place. As studies are undertaken, some actions will need to be amended or, in some cases, replaced with other proposals found to be better or more feasible.
Source: Central City Plan, Portland, Oregon (1988), p. 44.

2-20 Goals for a specific district—like a Chinatown—can be included in the downtown plan.

Procedures for amending the plan should also be approved, as its implementation period is likely to require several years. The approved plan should be the *only* comprehensive downtown plan. While different entities within a city might need other subplans, only one overall plan should be prepared. The existence of multiple plans creates confusion and lack of focus. And the plan should be published and available upon request to the public.

Downtown Zoning

As described earlier, cities might need to revise their zoning ordinances to contain specific encouragements or requirements aimed at implementing the downtown plan.[15] This section briefly summarizes the tools the most progressive downtowns use.

Incentive or Bonus Zoning

Incentive zoning allows the developer to build a bigger project—either in terms of the building's height or the project's density—in return for certain pre-stated amenities.[16] Bonus programs are discretionary (in New York and Los Angeles, for example), as-of-right (Bellevue, Washington), or a hybrid of the two (Seattle). Which amenities are granted depends on the community's goals and can include a variety of features:

- *Building amenities*—ground-floor retail space, retail arcades, artwork, water features, sculptured rooftops, rooftop gardens, atria, and daycare facilities. In New York, the Real Estate Board has proposed creating a bonus for providing

space not only for selected nonprofit organizations like daycare centers, but also for desirable for-profit users that have difficulty paying rent, such as grocers;
- *Pedestrian amenities*—wider sidewalks, canopies and other overhead devices to protect pedestrians from inclement weather, through-block con-

[15] See Terry Jill Lassar, *Carrots and Sticks: New Zoning Downtown* (Washington, D.C.: ULI–the Urban Land Institute, 1989) for extensive detail on the advantages and disadvantages of zoning techniques used downtown.
[16] Robert Cook, "Innovative Zoning Tools for Downtowns," in *Managing Design and Development Downtown* (Washington, D.C.: National League of Cities, 1981), p. 9.

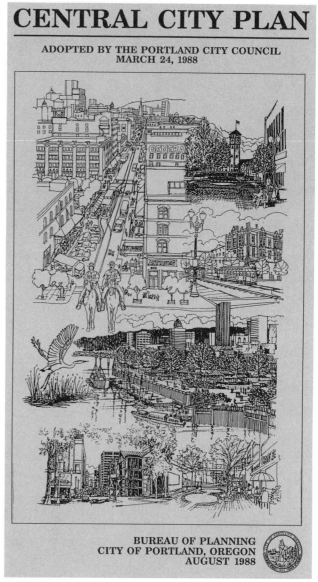

CENTRAL CITY PLAN

ADOPTED BY THE PORTLAND CITY COUNCIL
MARCH 24, 1988

BUREAU OF PLANNING
CITY OF PORTLAND, OREGON
AUGUST 1988

2-21 To give it authority and accountability, the downtown plan should be formally approved by appropriate legislative bodies.

2-22, 2-23 Artwork in and around office buildings is encouraged through zoning in many cities.

nections, landscaping, multiple building entrances, plazas, and urban parks and open space;
- *Housing and human services*—employment and job training, low-income health clinics, and low-income, affordable, and market-rate housing;

- *Improved transportation*—transient parking, below-grade parking, and access and upgrading for transit stations;
- *Cultural amenities*—cinemas, performing arts centers, art galleries, museums, and live theaters;
- *Preservation*—historic structures, theaters, and low-rent housing stock.[17]

The quid pro quo for the amenity differs from city to city, but one common method for determining it is to describe the bonus in terms of a given number of square feet that can be added to the building for each square foot of amenity provided. In Hartford, for example, the bonus ratio for providing performing arts space is 1 to 4: for each square foot of performing space provided, the developer can add four more square feet of commercial space. Cincinnati, on the other hand, expresses the bonus as a percentage of the project's size, say, 20 percent more density. Most second-generation bonus programs include a cap on the bonus. For example, in Hartford, no additional square footage for the performing arts space is granted beyond a floor/area ratio (FAR) of 1.

The effectiveness of incentive zoning in achieving objectives for urban design depends on market demand. If demand for office space is low or nonexistent, so will demand for incentives be. A system that incorporates not only incentives like those described above but also economic incentives might be appropriate for the 1990s to encourage specific types of development. In Portland, Oregon, for example, tax abatements were used to support the residential component of RiverPlace, a mixed-use project along the Willamette River downtown. Taxes will be abated for 10 years for the 108-unit rental housing portion of the project. Two-thirds of the project will rent for $500 to $650 per month. In Portland, Maine, a host of new financial incentives have recently been proposed, including special funds, aggressive use of the city's bonding authority, and tax increment financing for smaller projects.

Where demand is higher than zoning allows, incentive zoning can be a very effective tool for linking public amenities to private development at little cost to the city. It is important to note, however, that density bonuses must be managed to ensure that they do not overburden infrastructure and that the amenities accompanying them in fact achieve desired goals. Plazas that do not invite people to use them and ground-floor retail space that is inappropriately located and therefore vacant can be detrimental to both the public and the developer.

---

[17] Lassar, *Carrots and Sticks*, pp. 14–15.

Mandated Design Features

Requiring certain features to be incorporated into a project's design is not a new concept. What is new is the ever-expanding scope of the requirements for downtown projects, including required retail space at street level, transparent facades at street level (that is, no blank walls), open space, space for light to penetrate, and wind mitigation. Though many of these requirements were created in the boom development climate of the early to mid-1980s, most cities as yet are not planning to change them, in light of decreased demand for office development.

In Boston, for example, assistant zoning director Linda Bourque believes zoning has only a marginal effect on the economics of development. "What we do at the margin doesn't make or break a development," she says. In the recently rezoned Midtown Cultural District between Boston's Back Bay and its financial district, it is the lack of available financing, not restrictions on ground-floor uses or even linkage fees, that has put planned projects on hold, according to Bourque. In fact, even more aggressive requirements were recently finalized for Boston's waterfront district. In that area, 40 percent of the ground floor must consist of uses that are publicly accessible, and 50 percent of a project must consist of open space. Cultural and water transport facilities are required, and height is limited to 55 feet in most areas.

Not surprisingly, San Francisco, known for its highly restrictive development climate, also has not relaxed standards, according to land use attorney Harry O'Brien. The city is beginning to see some of the effects of its highly detailed development regulations, however. In 1990, when the four projects approved in the 1988 beauty contest requested extensions for permits, they were denied. Proposition M clearly stated that rights to build would be lost if they were not exercised within 18 months, a very narrow window in a competitive or overbuilt market. Regulations that are too specific can be self-defeating.

In light of market conditions, however, some cities are easing up on enforcement or speeding the approval process. In Cincinnati, for example, the prohibition against tearing down buildings and replacing them with surface parking to save on property taxes and also to generate income has been relaxed. Three new surface lots were recently approved, one on the edge of downtown that did not result in a hole in the streetscape, one with a significant difference in grade between street level and the lot, and another in a block with a number of other lots. In Orlando, city planners are considering shortening the distance where ground-level retail space is required. And even in Boston,

2-24 The bland granite walls of the lower level at Bank One Center in Dallas alienate pedestrians.

developers have noticed that the city is actively attempting to make the approval process easier for them to navigate.

Transfer of Development Rights

In more and more cities, the right to develop a lot to a certain density is viewed as a transferable commodity. Most often used in conjunction with historic buildings and low-income housing, unused density from such buildings is transferred to another site. When little demand exists for office space or by-right FAR limits are generous, the market for transferable development rights (TDRs) could be limited. Of the approximately 50 jurisdictions with TDRs, actual transfers have transpired in no more than a dozen.[18]

---

[18] Ibid., p. 186.

27

Inclusionary Zoning

Inclusionary zoning ordinances require or encourage developers of new residential (or commercial) projects to include a certain amount of low-cost, subsidized housing in their projects or to contribute to a fund to be used to develop, finance, or subsidize housing. This type of zoning can be voluntary, incorporating incentives like density bonuses and fast-track approval procedures, or mandatory, offering the same incentives or state and federal financing. Whether voluntary or mandatory, most inclusionary programs contain the following elements:

- Inclusionary requirements
- Income-eligibility criteria for defining affordability
- Provisions for in-lieu fees
- Pricing criteria for affordable units
- Restrictions on the resale and rerental of affordable units and
- Miscellaneous requirements regarding on-site versus off-site construction, transfers of excess affordable housing credits, and the like.[19]

Inclusionary zoning programs and the related linkage or exaction systems—where cities assess fees on commercial development and develop housing with the funds collected—have sparked controversy wherever they have been tried and, in many cases, legal challenges. In an era of scarce public resources, however, these tools have been effective in helping to meet the need for housing.

Design or Development Review

The increased use of community-based approval processes, the growth of concern for environmental conservation and historic preservation, and greater awareness of urban design have all contributed to an increase in design, site plan, or development review for downtown projects. Cities take a variety of tacks in incorporating design review into the zoning process, including the development of special district guidelines and design criteria for incentive bonuses. Design review as a means to density bonuses is another variation of this tool.

---

[19] Michael A. Stegman and J. David Holden, *Nonfederal Housing Programs: How States and Localities Are Responding to Federal Cutbacks in Low-Income Housing* (Washington, D.C.: ULI–the Urban Land Institute, 1987), p. 51.

2-25 Inclusionary zoning requires or encourages developers of new residential housing to include a certain amount of low-cost housing, like these structures in Boston's Tent City.

Special Districts

Special districts come in all kinds of combinations. They are overlay districts, superimposed on one or more existing zoning districts to protect or enhance an area's special qualities. The common characteristic is governmental review of virtually all development, with the power to approve design according to standards contained in the ordinance or in a district plan or design guidelines.[20]

Downtown Seattle, for instance, has 11 special districts, including two for office buildings, one for retail space, two "international" districts (one for mixed-use developments and one for residential development), two for the harborfront, and one for the Pike Place Market area. In the retail district, shopping, entertainment, and service uses are designated the primary uses at street level, with compatible office, hotel, residential, and commercial uses in the upper floors of buildings. Maximum base FARs are stated, with bonuses for certain amenities and for housing, a major retail store, or a performing arts theater.

Design Review of Bonus Features

In some cities, a dissatisfaction with the actual amenities granted as bonuses has resulted in design review's becoming an integral part of the bonus program. In other, newer bonus systems, design review has been incorporated from the very beginning as a safeguard. In Hartford, after architects and developers complained about rules that were not spelled out in advance, specific guidelines were developed setting forth precise elements that needed to be included to qualify for a density bonus.[21]

Design Review as a Bonus Feature

A number of cities, including Cincinnati and Boston, award greater density in return for submitting to design review. In Cincinnati, for example, density is increased 20 percent when the design of a building has been reviewed and approved according to the design review process.

Vertical Zoning

Several cities have mandated certain uses on the ground floor and other uses on upper floors. Most often, this tool is used to require some or all of the ground level to be retail space. This tool can be effective if demand exists for the amount of retail space that would be required and if the area where the requirement applies is compact enough to support rather than dilute retailing (see Chapter 9).

Zoning Changes in the 1990s

The cities that overhauled their zoning in the 1980s will fine-tune it in the 1990s, particularly encouraging certain uses that draw people downtown after work, such as housing and entertainment. In Bellevue, Washington, for example, senior planner Dan Hardin says the city is considering expanding the coverage of residential lots downtown from 75 percent to 100 percent to encourage housing downtown. Further, developers' interest in using pitched roofs in downtown residential projects has resulted in a more flexible attitude regarding calculations of height. In a nod to the increased importance of the timing of development, Bellevue also now allows developers to choose, at their expense, from a stable of approved consultants to expedite design review. In one particularly time-sensitive project, the city allowed the developer to pay staff overtime to finish the necessary design review.

Hartford, another city that overhauled its downtown zoning in the 1980s, is also fine-tuning its regulations. According to chief staff planner Peter Spitzner, the city's desire to encourage entertainment downtown has caused it to permit "brewpubs" no larger than 2,000 gross square feet where beer is brewed and served for on-premise consumption. The old zoning would have considered it a manufacturing use and therefore not permissible. Also being added is a bonus for off-site improvements, which is meant to encourage developers to extend improvements to the streetscape beyond their developments to the end of the block.

Another amendment Hartford is considering could signal a trend in the 1990s. With developers now holding sites downtown for which there is no immediate demand for new development, some are scrapping them to lower tax assessments and/or building surface parking lots to generate income. To avoid the look of Berlin after the Blitz, a proposed amendment places a moratorium on new surface parking lots in certain downtown areas. Waivers include the requirement for specifically described, landscaped buffers that range from 15 feet to 50 feet, depending on the location of the lot, its width, and the width of the adjacent right-of-way.

Fine-tuning in the 1990s is also occurring in cities not requiring the host of benefits they used to be able to get in a strong market. The Boston Redevelopment Authority, for example, still requires linkage fees,

---

[20] Cook, "Innovative Zoning Tools," p. 8.
[21] This paragraph and the next one are summarized from Lassar, *Carrots and Sticks*, pp. 55–57.

which it claims are not deal breakers. But even the authority realizes that, in a soft market, it is unrealistic to require benefits like daycare facilities, new parks, free shuttle transportation, or extra parking. The city government is searching for effective new financial incentives to spur development. Other cities should take a serious look at any requirements in their current zoning codes that would inhibit development in the 1990s.

Downtown Orlando: A Successful Strategy for Revitalization

"To be in the shadow of the mouse ears has made it somewhat difficult for Orlando to establish its identity," says Thomas R. Kohler, executive vice president of the city's Downtown Development Board (DDB).[22] Indeed, while retailers were exiting downtown beginning in the 1960s and continuing through the 1980s, Walt Disney World and other large-scale tourist attractions captured tourist, hotel, and meetings business that might otherwise have gone downtown.

Yet even as Disney World grew, Orlando participated in its growth as well as the growth Florida as a whole experienced, and all of it benefited the downtown. Metropolitan Orlando remains one of the fastest-growing major markets in the nation, having grown 41 percent from 1980 to 1989. Over 1 million people now live in the Orlando metropolitan statistical area (MSA). Employment grew more than 70 percent during that same time.

With that kind of growth, expectations for development are high, even for downtown. How did downtown Orlando ensure its fair share of the magic? It started planning early. In 1972 through state enabling legislation, the DDB was created to revitalize downtown. Committing the resources to fund an organization whose sole purpose was to revitalize downtown resulted in more than $1 billion of new investment downtown between 1981 and 1989.

Organizing for Revitalization

The DDB's organizational structure has not always been effective. During its first seven years, five different directors came and went. Each tried to separate the organization from city government, emphasizing the private sector's involvement. Kohler saw the need for a public/private partnership and reorganized the structure.

The fact that Kohler had been a senior staffer with the city of Orlando certainly helped. The relationship between the city and the DDB is quite close, with the DDB viewed as a quasi-city department. Kohler attends senior staff meetings on behalf of the DDB. And with a staff of seven, the DDB is able to focus on downtown revitalization, unlike many downtowns where revitalization is the responsibility of overworked city staffers. The DDB's board of directors ensures that the private sector and the community are also represented. Five community leaders serve on the board by mayoral appointment.

Rounding out the DDB organizational structure is the Community Redevelopment Agency (CRA), whose role is implementation. Evidencing a high level of commitment to downtown development, the city council serves as the CRA, and the mayor is its chair. The agency is staffed by the DDB and funded by a tax increment trust fund.

The DDB's and CRA's responsibilities include:

- *Project review.* The DDB reviews projects within in the tax district's boundaries requiring a building permit;
- *Downtown plan.* An overall downtown marketing program to enhance downtown's use by a broad cross section of Orlando's community is also part of the DDB's responsibilities. The DDB also assists in coordinating the activities of other public and private organizations interested in downtown, for example, the Historic Preservation Board;
- *Development.* The DDB also assists in planning and completing public projects, such as streetscaping, parking facilities, affordable housing, open spaces, improvements in traffic circulation, and retail development.

Project Review: No Mystery

To accomplish the first task, reviewing all proposed downtown projects, the DDB appointed a seven-member development review committee. The majority of the committee must be chosen from real estate professions, such as planning, architecture, landscape architecture, signage/graphic design, or real estate law. The committee meets once a month and considers site plans, building elevations, exterior materials and colors, signage and graphics, lighting, landscaping, awnings and canopies, and other items requiring

---

[22] The remainder of this chapter discusses the successful strategy employed in Orlando, Florida, to revitalize its downtown, from organization through implementation.

2-26 The Community Redevelopment Agency undertook street-scaping of two major downtown streets in Orlando, leading to dramatically increased retail sales.

building permits or involving exterior alterations visible from the public right-of-way. Though the city has to grant final approval, disagreements are unusual because of the coordinated organizational structure.

Developers seem to like the organization of the DDB and the review committee. Though not quite the one-stop approval system other cities have devised, developers find they get more attention and responsiveness from the DDB team than they would if they worked directly with the city staff. With one exception, developers interviewed believed that the approval process was clearly defined. "The city knows what it wants; there is no mystery about what its decisions will be," says developer Peter Fox, a partner with Pillar-Bryton Properties, which developed the 450,000-square-foot duPont Centre downtown.

Development

Given Orlando's strong climate for development during the 1980s, some experts have taken for granted the

projects initiated by Orlando's DDB. Even in a strong market, however, the commitment to downtown is impressive.

Streetscape

In 1984, the Community Redevelopment Agency undertook one of the first, highly visible projects downtown, the streetscaping of Orange Avenue and Pine Street, two major downtown streets. While streetscaping is no longer novel, what is special about Orlando's program is the short amount of time it took to complete the project and the promotions supporting retail sales during construction. Originally estimated to take 18 months, the CRA allocated extra funds to complete the redevelopment in seven months, the maximum period retailers believed they could withstand the disruption without jeopardizing the viability of their businesses. Press coverage and promotions abounded during this time, and retailers reported an 18 percent increase in sales during the construction period. Since then, the CRA has streetscaped portions of eight other streets, providing a total of 12,657 linear feet of paved sidewalk, 304 street trees encased in grates, 181 street lights, and 23 benches.

Housing

With no industrial district downtown or at its perimeter, residential neighborhoods surround Orlando's CBD. To prevent commercial development from overtaking the area, the city downzoned some of it in the mid-1980s. Loan programs were offered to update the charming but old housing stock.

To meet a need for affordable housing, the CRA teamed with Orlando Housing Authority Properties,

2-27 A children's play area was provided in two affordable housing projects adjacent to Orlando's downtown.

Jackson Court

Description: Forty-two units of low-income housing for senior citizens. The one-bedroom/one-bathroom units total 610 square feet each and rent for $240 per month. The site totals 1.45 acres, and parking totals 0.33 space per unit. Started in May 1988, the project opened seven months later.

Project Costs:

Land	$ 625,000	($10,593 per unit)*
Hard Costs . . .	1,700,000	($40,476 per unit)
Soft Costs	525,000	($12,500 per unit)
Total	$2,850,000	($63,569 per unit)

Financing Method: Joint venture between the Orlando Community Redevelopment Agency and Orlando Housing Authority Properties, Inc. Sources of funds include tax increment funds contributed by CRA and nonfederal dollars contributed by OHAP.

---

*Including 17 units in Phase 2.

Callahan Oaks

Description: Forty-unit complex of stacked flats completed in March 1989. A low- and moderate-income project for families, the project includes 32 three-bedroom/two-bathroom, 1,150-square-foot units renting for $330 to $370 per month and eight two-bedroom/two-bathroom, 1,000-square-foot units renting for $290 to $315 per month. Located on 2.19 acres, the parking ratio for the project is 1.95.

Project Costs:

Land	$ 250,000	($ 6,250 per unit)
Hard and		
Soft Costs . . .	1,231,800	($30,795 per unit)
Total	$1,481,800	($37,045 per unit)

Financing Method: After purchasing the land for $250,000, the CRA leased it to the Orlando Neighborhood Improvement Corporation for 50 years. The city of Orlando contributed $300,000, and the Florida Affordable Housing Demonstration program provided a $240,000 loan at 3 percent. Local banks provided the balance of project costs.

Inc. (OHAP), and Orlando Neighborhood Improvement Corporation, Inc. Two low- and moderate-income housing projects, Jackson Court and Callahan Oaks, have now been developed in neighborhoods surrounding Orlando's downtown. Close to $4.6 million was made available to fund these projects, about half of which came from tax increment bond revenues.

Parking

Orlando's proposed DRI (development of regional impact) plan calls for the formation of a downtown transportation management association. As a private, nonprofit group, the association will work with employers and employee groups on alternative modes of transportation and the easing of peak-hour traffic congestion.

The plan sets forth new parking policies, including a cap of three parking spaces per 1,000 gross square feet of commercial office space. Of those three spaces, only two may be on site. The third space is available only with a payment (the cost of building one parking space) by the developer to the city. The city provides the third space as part of the public parking system in remote facilities. Those sites are linked together with an expanded shuttle service.

The opening of three attractive garages downtown or on the edge of downtown has added 2,100 new spaces. The use of brick columns, accent tiles, period light fixtures, and retail storefronts in one garage makes the $11 million Church Street Garage complementary to nearby Church Street Station, the historic entertainment complex. And with the garage located on the west side of the elevated I-4, which denotes the edge of downtown, the city developed Church Street Walk, a pedestrian walk connecting the garage with Church Street Station. Church Street Walk features streetscaping, light fixtures, landscaping bollards, a telephone booth, a fountain, and kiosks.

The $3.6 million Market Garage, attached to Church Street Market, is another attractive downtown garage. Its brick construction, retail display windows on the ground floor, period light fixtures, and decorative banners make it especially attractive. The city will build four new garages on the perimeter of downtown to intercept drivers entering downtown, one in each direction. Once drivers park their cars, they can use a shuttle to get to the office.

Omni International Hotel

Because Orlando's major convention center is not located downtown, one of the DDB's goals was to develop a competitive entertainment, meeting, and recreational complex. An old exhibition facility, located next to a 2,500-seat auditorium, was renovated and expanded in 1982; however, a hotel was needed in the immediate area to establish downtown as a regional conference and convention destination.

The DDB/CRA targeted a 3.5-acre tract of publicly opened land for the hotel. After preparing a prospectus to solicit a hotel developer and choosing Py-Vavra Development, Inc., it became apparent that the developer would need financial incentives to make the project feasible. The CRA negotiated a 75-year ground lease in which it received a $50,000 base fee, subordinated only to primary debt, a stepped percentage of the gross room rent (up to 3.5 percent), and a 10 percent return on investment. The city also retained a residual payment of 12 percent of net refinancing or sales proceeds. In exchange, the city cleared the site and paid for underground stormwater facilities, widened an important street, and improved the entrance to the convention center.

The Omni International Hotel is a 15-story glass and concrete building physically connected to Expo Centre; it has exclusive catering rights for all functions held there. With 289 rooms, the hotel provides 250 on-site parking spaces; an additional 1,500 spaces are located immediately adjacent to the hotel. The Omni was completed in March 1986 for $25.5 million.

Since then, the Orlando Arena, a 15,500-seat facility that grossed almost $16 million in ticket sales in its first year, has been developed across from the convention center and hotel.

Church Street Market

Another of the DDB's goals was to revitalize retailing in downtown Orlando. Downtown's Church Street Station had long been a popular attraction. Conceived in 1973 by developer Robert Snow, the Station is a 100,000-square-foot entertainment and shopping center that includes restaurants and bars featuring live music and promotional events. Over 70 percent of Church Street Station's business comes from tourists; it is the third largest tourist attraction in the state. Seeing an opportunity, Walt Disney World recently opened a center with a similar theme.

Hoping to build on the popularity of Church Street Station, the DDB planned additional retail shops adjacent to it based on a target market of local residents, particularly downtown workers, and tourists. Church Street Market is a three-level shopping center with specialty retail shops on levels one and two and a food court and entertainment arcade on the third level. To facilitate the project, the CRA purchased from the city the property next to Church Street Station to lease to a developer, Lincoln Property Company, which was selected through a competitive process.

Over the 75-year term of the lease, Lincoln pays the CRA $100,000 per year for ground rent plus 20 per-

---

2-29   DOWNTOWN'S REQUIRED RETAIL SPACE

One of Orlando's downtown zoning features has resulted in mixed success. Within an eight-block corridor of Orange Avenue, at least 50 percent of ground-floor street frontage must consist of eligible commercial uses, including retail shops (but not banks or S&Ls), personal services, entertainment, or restaurants and bars. The regulation applies not only to new development, but also to the re-leasing of existing space. A bonus FAR of 1:1 is granted as part of this mandatory requirement, with FARs of 1.5:1 and 2:1 granted for leasing 70 percent and 90 percent, respectively, of ground-floor street frontage for eligible commercial uses.

A little over half of the new space created to meet this requirement is leased. DDB officials say that the space will eventually be leased, but developers are skeptical of legislating demand. They also point to the overly long distance to which the regulation applies, and the DDB is considering shortening the distance to about 1,500 feet, or the average length between one end of a shopping mall and the other.

The regulations for parking garages face similar challenges. Garages on primary pedestrian streets or pedestrian malls must have at least 75 percent of ground-floor frontage as "active uses," including office, retail, or entertainment space. On secondary streets, landscaped pedestrian-oriented setbacks of at least 20 feet are required, except where active uses are included.

cent of net cash flow from the 73,000-square-foot urban specialty retail center. The ground rent is sub-

ordinated to operating expenses, debt service, and any guaranteed returns to equity investors; however,

By spring 1988, Orlando city officials could no longer put off building a new city hall. The current one had outgrown its 1950s-vintage building years earlier, and operations were spread all over downtown. Building a new city hall on the current site, at the southern edge of downtown, would provide needed space and give the city the opportunity to enhance the entrance to the CBD.

To realize their vision of a modern government complex, officials planned to package the seven acres of land occupied by the existing city hall and ancillary buildings. In two recent public/private redevelopment projects downtown, the city had used the value of land it owned to subsidize the private construction of a hotel and a specialty retail center. If city-owned land could be used to subsidize private development, why not use it to finance public development?

To sell the land not needed for construction of the new city hall would yield only enough money to cover about half the costs of the new building and associated public improvements. Instead, the city chose to lease its land to a private developer who would develop a project designed to include significant commercial elements. A new 245,000-square-foot city hall, a public park/plaza, associated parking, and the planned 1 million square feet of commercial office space and ancillary retail space would certainly strengthen the downtown's southern gateway.

The city chose two types of consultants to guide them through planning and negotiations: 1) a planner to help create a vision for the public spaces and the project's interaction with the downtown, and 2) a financial/real estate adviser to help profile the economic alternatives and structure a favorable business deal. Once design guidelines and financial goals were developed, officials developed a prospective list of qualified national developers and sent requests for proposals. Eight developers sent written proposals, and four of them were invited to make presentations to a specially created selection committee. Three were chosen for final consideration.

To maximize each developer's financial offer, the city chose to negotiate simultaneously with all three finalists. Each was required to fill in the blanks of a form development contract and lease document.

2-31   Orlando's City Hall, developed through a public/private partnership.

This approach forced an apples-to-apples comparison of competing offers, prompted the developers to make their best possible offers, and exerted pressure on the developers and the city to make decisions early that proved time-saving.

Over the six months it took to strike a final deal, the city's assessment of the relative merits of the different competitors and its choice of a front-runner changed several times. In the end, the financial offers of the finalists were nearly identical. Lincoln Property Company was chosen because the other front-runner insisted on a six-month study period after execution of the development contract, during which time it would have the right to withdraw from the deal without penalty.

The Deal

The final deal between the city and Lincoln was complex:

1. The city would retain fee simple title to approximately 2.5 acres of land (of the total seven-acre site), where the new city hall and a park/plaza would be constructed. Although the city would have been willing under cer-

the agreement does provide for the recapture of un-paid base rent. Upon sale or refinancing, 15 percent of the cash remaining after payment of certain items (debt, for example) goes to the CRA. Lincoln also has

tain conditions to rent the city hall from the developer to facilitate financing the private portion of the project, the final deal called for the city to own the building outright and to finance its construction with tax-free munic-ipal bonds.

2. Lincoln would be paid a negotiated develop-ment fee on performance of a guaranteed fixed-price contract to demolish the old and construct the new city hall and park/plaza. Lincoln, then, would act as the general con-tractor for the city.

3. Lincoln and the city would jointly plan and design the project, but Lincoln would take the lead role in paying planning costs and managing the process to satisfy private fi-nancing requirements, control construction costs, and enhance the overall project's mar-ketability should Lincoln have to withdraw from the contract for whatever reason.

4. Lincoln will rent the remainder of the site from the city in two phases, one beginning in 1992 and the other in 1996. Lincoln could delay the commencement dates for the ground lease for a limited number of years in the event that vacancy rates in downtown Orlando for Class A space exceed 20 percent or the prime interest rate exceeds 12 percent. After a set amount of delay, however, failure to begin would result in termination of the ground lease and Lincoln's forfeiture of a $750,000 deposit and its other investment in soft costs.

The term for each phase of the ground lease totaled 75 years. The unsubordinated ground rent was fixed at the time of building con-struction and would escalate by 4.5 percent per year on a 1989 base of $750,000. The city's participation in future value came from its receipt of 20 percent of net proceeds from the office/retail rents over stabilized income or from the project's sale or refinancing. In-come from Lincoln over the 30-year life of the bonds is expected to pay for the new city hall, even in present-value dollars.

At the end of the leases, ownership of the entire project, including both private office towers, reverts to the city in fee simple, thus creating the opportunity for long-term growth and income.

5. Upon execution of the ground leases for the private phases, Lincoln will reimburse the city for the cost of the park/plaza and for two-thirds of the cost of demolishing the existing city hall. Structured parking would not be required until the private office towers occupy the site's interim surface parking area. Although the city would pay its share of the garage, the timing of this payment would coincide with Lincoln's reimburse-ment for the park/plaza and demolition.

Experience Gained

1. In a retrenching market, government busi-ness is good business. With government still growing and/or replacing outdated facilities, projects like Orlando's City Commons pro-vide the opportunity for developers to go where anchor opportunities exist, even if the opportunities are only fee-based ones in the near term. Downtowns, as the centers of city and often county government, offer prime opportunities for this kind of business.

2. A full-time contact in government must be responsible for the project. Furthermore, this manager must have access to and the support of key government decision makers so that decisions can be made expeditiously.

3. For a developer to be interested in a project like Orlando's City Commons, the real estate must have potential for development and the financial structure must be attractive.

4. If the city lacks in-house resources to put together a project of this kind, qualified and compatible consultants should be integrated into the process early. Just as the search for the best developer should be a national one, so should the search for consultants.

Source: Lewis Oliver and Eric Smart, "Orlando's City Commons: A Model Public/Private Venture," *Urban Land,* January 1990, pp. 21–25.

an option to purchase the land under certain conditions at a set price. Finally, Lincoln built a garage as part of the project, which it leases to the city. As of February 1990, the center was 77 percent leased, with sales from restaurant tenants totaling about $300 per square foot and from nonrestaurant tenants $200 per square foot.

Knowing that government entities were primary prospects for tenants in light of the languishing commercial and office market and buoyed by the success of the previous two public/private ventures, the city of Orlando embarked on another public/private deal in negotiations for the development of a new city hall (see Figure 2-30).

3.
Initiation of the Project and Options for Development

With a downtown organization in place, developers have a framework within which to evaluate prospective projects, and downtown constituents have a structure by which they can judge whether proposed projects meet the community's objectives as embodied in the downtown plan. Because of the structure of downtown, however, the process of developing projects there can be different from, say, suburban locations. This chapter reviews that process and highlights those differences.

Project Conception

A private developer, a major corporation acting as a developer of a building where it will occupy space, the downtown organization or another public/private organization, or the city could initiate a project. When the city initiates development, for a public park or meeting space, for example, the city could sponsor a competition, providing stipends to teams of competitors (developers, architects, and so on) to design/build the project for an agreed-upon price. The city establishes strict criteria within which the teams must work. When a team is selected, a contract is negotiated and executed. This type of competition can also be sponsored for a critical site within the downtown that is developed for purely private use, such as a mixed-use project on city-owned or -controlled land.

If the developer initiates the project, one of two approaches is usually possible. In a primarily private development, the developer or corporation purchases land directly and proposes development in conformity with the downtown plan. Assuming the project is feasible without public participation, the public sector's role in organizing the project is limited to approval processes that have been established as part of any downtown development. The public sector is involved in zoning approvals, permitting, and any other project reviews as part of the downtown plan, but little else.

If the preliminary analysis of the project indicates that more significant public involvement is necessary, however, organizing a project becomes more complex and will probably require either public initiation and management or a public/private venture, a hallmark of downtown development and the focus of the rest of this chapter. The term "public/private" is often loosely used. A venture might actually be a private/private/public venture, as is the case of the Milwaukee Redevelopment Corporation, Milwaukee's private but civic-oriented downtown developer that joins with a private developer and the city—or several public and private entities might be required to get the project done.

PROJECT CONCEPTION	SELECTION OF DEVELOPER	ANALYSIS OF DEVELOPMENT	IMPLEMENTATION (LATER CHAPTERS)
Initiators can be city, developer, or downtown organization	Prepare development prospectus	Complete final feasibility studies	Obtain financing • Prepare financing package • Secure construction and permanent loans
Compare concept to Downtown Plan	Develop prospect list of developers	Complete approval process with city, including meeting with neighborhood and citizen groups	Complete design • Final illustrative site plans • Final plans • Final site and building engineering
Preliminary analysis includes: • Public and private use, supply and demand • Potential sites • Potential problems • Potential costs and funding	Send RFQs Send RFPs Select preferred developer and plan based on: • Urban design and project design • Public and private development program and schedule • Cost estimates and guiding sources • Overall feasibility • Degree to which established priorities met	Negotiate agreements with public entities for funding Negotiate development agreement Negotiate operating agreements Continue land and/or building acquisition	Construction Marketing Management
Decision to proceed or withdraw	Begin (or continue) land acquisition	Begin tenant pursuit in earnest	

Management Options for Public/Private Ventures

Whoever initiates the project will need to have some idea of how the public/private venture should be managed. Basically, four alternatives exist.

Private Management

In a project that combines the public and private sectors, a private development entity can be responsible for overall project development. In this case, a developer and a public entity sign a contract to develop specified public facilities as part of the total project. The advantages of this approach include assurances that predevelopment and development activities are coordinated and that public facilities are designed and constructed as part of the total project.

Public/Private Joint Venture

When significant public incentives are required to make the project feasible, this approach is often chosen.

Through a legally binding agreement, both partners agree on a specific formula for each one's contribution of financial resources and share of the proceeds from the project.

An example is the restoration and renovation of South Station at the junction of the financial and retail districts in downtown Boston. Located within a five-minute walk of more than 6 million square feet of office space, the project has undergone an $80 million redevelopment through a three-way public/private partnership of Amtrak, the Massachusetts Bay Transportation Authority (MBTA), and the Beacon Companies. Approximately $55 million in development costs have been covered using public funds, which have transformed the historic building into a restaurant, retail destination, office building, and state-of-the-art transportation facility.

MBTA, the owner of South Station, is restoring the structure and has entered into a 65-year lease with Beacon South Station Association for development, leasing, and management of over 150,000 square feet of commercial space in South Station. MBTA receives fixed rent through the development period, offsetting commuter rail obligations; after that, it receives 50 percent of all net available income for the first five years of operation. After this initial period, MBTA continues to receive a percent of rents but will also receive a guaranteed minimum annual payment, which escalates on a continuing basis throughout the term of the lease. When certain percentage rents are achieved, the base rent is bumped to a higher level and continues to escalate throughout the term of the lease. The developer, MBTA, and Amtrak share operating costs according to the following formula: developer – 50 percent, Amtrak – 35 percent, and MBTA – 15 percent.

Public Management

Like traditional urban renewal, this approach involves the public sector alone carrying out predevelopment to the point where it offers a specific site on the market for development. The lessons learned from urban renewal and the success of public/private joint ventures, however, have contributed to the decline in the use of this approach. (A notable exception is Battery Park City in New York City.) Since the days of urban renewal, cities have learned the importance of analyzing market conditions and of using developers' expertise in formulating the project from the very beginning.

Public Implementation without Direct Private Involvement

The private sector is usually not involved when public entities construct buildings for their own or for public use—parks, convention centers, city halls, libraries, public office buildings, and fire stations, for example.

3-2   A public/private partnership transformed Boston's historic South Station into a restaurant, retail destination, office building, and state-of-the-art transportation facility.

The local government hires the project architect and retains a contractor to construct the building; thus, involvement of the private sector is necessary only to design and construct the building. Funding comes directly from public monies or from a publicly secured source.

The roles of the public and private sectors can overlap. It can be a mistake, however, for the city government and the developer to exchange roles. The private developer is the source of entrepreneurial and managerial skills and financing; the public sector is the principal source of political and public support for downtown development. Each participant in a productive partnership must clearly define mutually agreeable roles for a specific undertaking.

Development Prospectus and Selection of a Developer

When a project has been conceived but a specific site is not already owned or selected, the next step is to invite proposals to develop or redevelop one or more priority sites. Before initiating this step, however, both the public and private sectors should enter the process without misconceptions about each other.

Developers should realize that public officials do not have the power to deliver the deal. Public officials should not presume that developers have analyzed the project fully. Both sides should recognize that changes will occur in the original project because of market conditions, financing requirements, and the needs of major tenants and operators. Both sides should recognize that delays, bureaucratic obstacles, and changes in both parties' priorities are likely occurrences. And both sides need to understand the other side's expectations and concerns about the project.

What Developers Should Ask

When considering whether to pursue an opportunity for development with a public entity, developers should look for the following factors:

- *Market feasibility.* Have market studies been completed, and are they available for review? Is the economy diversified? Is the project located in a growing, or at least a stabilized, area? Are other businesses or employers deciding to expand? What is the existing and projected amount of square footage of competing projects to be developed in the market area? Does demand exist for the project? Are any major tenants or operators interested in the location?

3-3   In 1978, the Pennsylvania Avenue Development Corporation acquired the closed Willard Hotel and adjacent properties and conducted a national design competition for redevelopment of the hotel. The Oliver Carr Company completed structural renovation of the Beaux Arts building and built an accompanying mixed-use project. The PADC restored the historic interior of the hotel.

- *Physical feasibility.* Does the site have any unusual problems? Is it large enough? Would the site's topography, access, or visibility increase the project's costs? Is site assembly uncomplicated? Does the agency want to force the developer to sign an agreement regarding the disposition of the site earlier than desired?
- *Financial feasibility.* Do initial pro formas indicate that the project is financially feasible? Is the city prepared to minimize the developer's initial costs until the project is more certain? Will the property be sold or leased? Have land values been determined fairly? Does the city offer a

cache of tools to aid development of the project? What types of return on investment is the city likely to negotiate? Are local or other investors likely to be interested in the project?

- *Community consensus and clear objectives.* Is the city committed to the project? What is the likelihood of the developer's receiving favorable reviews and approvals? Is the city willing to expedite project approval? Are one-stop permitting and approvals available? Has the city evaluated the need for short- or long-term income versus its need to achieve goals for downtown? Is the city interested in achieving social goals, such as affordable housing, employment of minorities, or child care? Have any local groups opposed the project? Will the public be involved in design? If so, how? The city's downtown plan should ideally answer many of these questions.

- *The staff's sophistication.* Is the city adequately staffed with qualified people focused on real estate development? Has the city retained experienced professional consultants to augment its staff? Does the city have a successful track record in undertaking public/private ventures? Has it evidenced a patient commitment to complete the project and to stick to originally defined ground rules with the developer?

- *The deal.* Does the city plan to sell or lease the property? Has a fair value for the property been determined? Will the developer be permitted to stage development according to market conditions? Will it retain the ability to proceed with separate stages without being committed to later stages? Is the process of selecting a developer protracted and expensive? Will political contacts outweigh merit in selection of a developer?

- *The unknowns.* What is the likelihood of key city staff leaving or current elected officials being replaced during the course of development? What other agencies will require approval of the project? Will an environmental impact report be required? What is the likelihood of significant opposition from citizens?

What Cities Should Ask

The public sector has a similar checklist to incorporate into any solicitations for development partners.

- *The developer's expertise.* Has the developer successfully built and operated similar projects? Has the developer entered into other public/private ventures? Was the project completed on time and within budget? If delays occurred, who

was responsible? Do the developer and his team have a good reputation in the business and financial communities? What is the developer's availability? Does the developer have the capacity to handle the project?

- *The developer's financial capability.* Has the developer demonstrated an ability to secure financing? Have equity investors joined with the developer in other, similar projects? Could the developer's financial position be described as "liquid"? Does the developer have the financial resources to fulfill all commitments on the project?

- *The developer's management experience.* Has the developer organized the appropriate teams in the past to execute similar projects? Once the project is built, is the developer capable of marketing and managing it properly?

The Request for Qualifications or Request for Proposal

With this understanding in mind, agencies can market a prospective project by publicly soliciting the development community in general or by soliciting only a handful of developers. Under the former, more public approach, developers are solicited from pre-screened lists, through general advertisements and publications, or both. Or, if they are not prohibited by statutes or public policy, agencies can directly approach two or three developers to solicit their interest in a project. Most solicitations from agencies use the former approach, which exposes the opportunity to a significantly greater number of developers and avoids perceptions of favoritism for past work.

The advantages of approaching only two or three highly qualified developers, however, include a savings in time and cost. By approaching the general development community, agencies can end up with the same two or three highly qualified developers but spend far more time and money reaching that conclusion. Depending upon the size, complexity, and visibility of the project as well as the legal and political constraints associated with offering the project to a limited number of parties, agencies could streamline the process of soliciting developers or could adopt an approach asking for bids from numerous developers, a more public approach.

Procuring proposals from developers through the latter approach can be accomplished through one of two ways: a two-stage process, issuing a Request for Qualifications (RFQ) followed by a Request for Proposal (RFP), or a one-stage process, issuing an RFP only. The two-stage process is recommended when the city perceives that desirable developers might not respond to an RFP open to all competitors regardless of qualifications or when the city has not already determined the specific use or size of the project. In this case, the developer provides recommendations about the development of the site. The one-stage process is recommended when the agency has specifically determined the use and parameters of development and is certain that the developers it wants to attract will submit proposals in an open competition.

The document the city issues in the two-stage process should be comprehensive and include the following sections:

- *Background.* The site's location, key participants, completed studies or plans, and the city's goals for the project.
- *Site description.* The exact location and boundaries of the site, existing zoning and any other restrictions on and guidelines for development, and an idea of what type of development program should be considered.
- *Criteria for selection.* The development concept, strength of the developer's organizational and management structure, related experience, financial capacity, team members and their qualifications.

Once developers have submitted their qualifications, the agency evaluates the packages and prepares a short list of those developers that will be requested to respond to an RFP. The RFP is designed to solicit specific terms and conditions from developers, including desired financial propositions to the city, more specifics on the project's design (site plans, conceptual design, and/or simple models), and a detailed development schedule that indicates projected times of completion for key activities.

The RFP could stand on its own or could be accompanied by supporting documentation. A weak market and an untested site might require a detailed prospectus and thorough feasibility study to attract qualified developers. A strong market, on the other hand, could call for less documentation. In either case, supporting documentation might also include legal and regulatory materials, such as pertinent sections or all of the downtown plan and downtown zoning ordinance, information on tax considerations (tax credits for historic preservation, for example), or affirmative action guidelines. The RFP might also request developers to submit additional financial information verifying their capacity to carry out the project.

Many developers are reluctant to submit sensitive financial information that can be made public under local and state public disclosure statutes, especially when the developer is only one of many business organizations being considered for the project. Cities have found that public disclosure laws are not violated if the developer's financial information is presented to the city's consultant for review and recommendation to agency officials. Confidentiality can thus be maintained for all submissions until finalists are selected, when financial information might or might not be required to be made publicly available for inspection.

3-4 "Dirk Tracer," maker of no small plans.

Mike Woolson, owner and artist, and Camille Severinsen, letterer

In addition, cities usually employ ranking and weighting schemes to evaluate developers' qualifications and proposals. This approach assumes that among the many goals and objectives of the downtown plan, some specific objectives have been targeted to be achieved by the development of the specific project. In the review of qualifications, then, more weight is sometimes given to the features of the proposal that accomplish the objectives to be achieved. If, for example, affordable housing is an objective, more weight would be assigned to this feature than to the market-rate housing of a competing project. Other features of a proposal that might be more heavily weighted include the developer's track record and experience or financial capacity. Evaluation systems can be tailored to fit local preferences. Regardless of which system is adopted, however, to make the system fair and open, developers should be made aware of the criteria and their relative importance to the city from the outset of solicitation.

Cities or their organizing vehicles usually establish evaluation committees to review developers' qualifications and proposals. An evaluation committee with expertise in real estate finance, real estate law, appraisal, development, and property management is usually assembled with professionals from city staff and from the private sector.

After the proposals are evaluated and scored, the evaluation groups reconvene, recommend a winner to the governing body, and suggest entering into development agreements securing the developer's and the city's commitment to the project. The terms of development agreements can vary. In some instances, developers merely secure an exclusive right to negotiate for the proposed project within a stated time period. They might be asked to post a deposit or pay for the privilege of being granted this exclusive right to negotiate. Other cities do not require a deposit at this juncture but often require financial commitments after more binding development agreements are executed. Cities are usually quick to point out that acceptance of a developer's proposal and designation of that developer do not create any rights on the part of the developer or the city until final approval is received and contracts are executed.

Development Analysis

Once a strategy for downtown development has been formulated and an approach to accomplish that strategy adopted by the city and its political leadership, a more rigorous process of analysis ensues before a final deal is negotiated. Market and financial feasibility studies furnish decision makers with the information necessary to determine economic use of properties downtown.[1] The following paragraphs summarize this process.

---

[1] See the discussions of market and feasibility studies later on specific types of development and more detailed presentations by type of land use in ULI's other handbooks on residential, office, hotel, mixed-use, and shopping center development.

The Rationale for Professionally Prepared Studies

Because many downtown real estate projects are large and complex, developers do not commit themselves and their resources without adequate market and financial justification. Furthermore, limited opportunities and narrow market niches can be overlooked if developers must first be convinced to spend their time and money investigating opportunities for development. For this reason, cities willing to spend the relatively small sums of money for market and financial feasibility assessments enjoy a competitive edge over those that do not.

Most developers and virtually all lenders require objective, third-party market and financial feasibility studies for individual projects. Studies prepared by agency personnel responsible for managing public real estate assets are often construed as less than impartial. They might not contain the level of analysis and depth of information required by investors and lenders. And the data contained in market and financial feasibility assessments prepared by an agency might not be presented according to the increasingly stringent requirements of banks and S&Ls.

Market Studies

Market studies analyze the potential for development at a specific location or in the downtown as a whole. Whatever the location, a market study contains three general areas: *indirect economic factors*, such as zoning, soil conditions and topography, utilities, transportation, parking, environmental impact, and prevailing attitudes; *direct economic factors*, including demand (population, income, employment, and factors affecting demand, such as tax and financing policies) and supply (existing and planned); and *data synthesis and recommendations*. This last step of the market study presents a determination of the viability of the development program. In addition, if development appears viable, suggestions regarding the type of product and its phasing should result. Final recommendations should also reflect the compatibility of the development program with surrounding neighborhoods, the preservation of environmental features, and the assimilation of local political concerns.

Feasibility Analysis

The next step in analyzing a project is to perform a financial feasibility analysis, which includes an examination of public incentives. Financial feasibility studies are conducted for two reasons. First, they assess whether the proposed project might be attractive to a developer. Second, they are a useful preparation for the negotiations once the developer has been selected, and they can be used to test the viability of suggested terms during negotiation.

The components of a typical pro forma calculation for a project include an examination of income, operating expenses, and debt service, factoring in absorption, vacancy, and turnover. To determine expected rents, adjustments are made to comparable projects to

3-4   (continued)

account for differences in the location, design, layout, construction, age, condition, and amenities provided. While specific building rents are usually easily obtained, information on average expenses and other data usually require the assistance of professional organizations, local property managers, private consultants, or brokerage firms.

Once these factors have been determined, net operating income (NOI) can be calculated. If the operating ratio is too low, the project could appear unattractive to developers without incentives, and the public sector might be required to be more flexible in negotiations. NOI is usually capitalized to determine the amount of mortgage loan the project is likely to receive. Or NOI can be multiplied by the debt service coverage ratio lenders are likely to require to back into the amount of debt service a project can handle and, consequently, the amount of the loan.

A final step in determining a project's financial feasibility is to calculate return on equity, net present value, and internal rate of return. They are calculated not only to assess the project's feasibility but also to determine the level of public subsidy that will be required and the returns the city can expect. Projecting internal rates of return allows all of the parties to analyze the effects of the project's stabilized operating performance as well as its potential for gain upon the resale or refinancing of the deal.

Once the developer has completed its feasibility and financial studies, the public partner conducts an economic assessment of public costs and benefits associated with the project if it is developed. The aim of an impact study is to understand any net benefits to the community if it participates in the project and amounts to the public's technique for evaluating profit to the community from public investment. Such profit to the public sector could include direct benefits (jobs, tax revenues, or a share in the profit from the project) and indirect benefits (stimulation to the economy of existing local businesses from new visitors or induced effects from wages spent by new employees, for example).

Economic impact assessments also are used to evaluate policies affecting downtown infrastructure and public services provided to property owners. Many cities, for example, do not know how to improve parking for downtown employees, visitors, and shoppers while maintaining equitable pricing policies and promoting a positive environment for development. In Syracuse, New York, the city, as the primary provider of downtown parking, was losing over $2 million (or $1.86 per space) annually in parking operations and debt financing. Its bond credit rating was suffering as a result. An economic impact study helped Syracuse develop more realistic parking policies.

Obtaining Public Approvals

Being a partner with the city does not eliminate the need to receive the required public approvals. Once the parties have agreed to a conceptual development plan and the business deal, the developer must obtain zoning approvals and permits. Presumably, the partnership would already have consulted the downtown

To accomplish goals for revitalization, cities are increasingly bargaining for better terms on paying back loans, lease arrangements, and land write-downs, and are requiring higher percentages of net cash flow for the risk they are taking in development. Their negotiating prowess, however, has resulted in increasingly complex deals, rendering financial analysis more complex as well.

Arizona Center, for example, is an 18.5-acre, $515 million mixed-use development in downtown Phoenix that will ultimately feature 1.9 million square feet of office space, 450,000 square feet of retail shops, a 600-room hotel, a three-acre garden park, and parking for approximately 5,400 vehicles. Phases 1 and 2, already completed, include two office buildings totaling about 750,000 square feet, 150,000 square feet of specialty retail shops, the garden park, and two parking structures. Completion of these portions of the project in November 1990 followed the city's RFP in May 1986 and selection of the Rouse Company of Columbia, Maryland, and the Phoenix Community Alliance, a private, nonprofit developer, in August 1986 as the entities with whom the city would enter into exclusive negotiations. By December 1986, the city council was requested to approve the right to negotiate a Disposition and Development Agreement with the developers based on the following terms. (The terms are as described in a memorandum of understanding between the city of Phoenix and the Rouse Company dated December 19, 1986, and might not reflect the terms of the final deal.)

Terms of the Agreement

1. *City's contribution:* Acquiring 1.85 acres through eminent domain. Vacating 4.71 acres of public right-of-way (streets and alleys). Subordinating its interest in the land and buildings to any project financing.
   City's return: Land to be leased to developer for 60 years for rental payments totaling the sum of 1) debt service required to retire land

acquisition bonds for the 1.85 acres; and 2) participation in cash flow as follows: 8 percent on any cash invested by the city in the 600-space garage plus 7 percent on the value of the 4.71 acres in vacated streets and alleys, so long as that amount does not exceed 17 percent of operating cash flow after certain defined expenses and returns to the developer and the city (the 8 percent on the garage). After the 15th year, the developer has the right to purchase the city's fee interest, in which case the 17 percent return would increase to 27 percent. If the developer does not exercise this right, however, the percents remain the same.

2. *City's contribution:* Abating all real estate property taxes for eight years. Making best efforts to obtain tax-exempt bonds or certificates of participation to finance the developer-funded garden park as well as certain improvements to traffic, sewer, water, and storm sewer systems to be built by developer with tax abatements.
   City's return: Upon the sale or refinancing of office buildings other than those built during Phases 1 and 2, city receives an amount equal to the capitalized tax abatement provided on those buildings after the payment of defined expenses and returns. Further, the project is to be completed according to the approved development plan, with developer to fund the garden park as well as certain improvements to off-site traffic, sewer, water, and storm sewer system and dedicating tax abatements toward repayment of bond obligations if the city does obtain financing. Developer is also to work with the Public Transit Department to develop an incentive program encouraging ridership on public transit and carpools, and to develop a participation plan for including minority and women business owners in the project. Future abatements are to be used to fund additional parking, maintenance of the

plan to determine the project's adherence to it. In some states, statewide growth management plans must also be followed. In Florida, for example, Orlando's Downtown Development Board has developed a fast-track procedure to streamline the state's application process for developers that complies with growth management.

The next step in most cities is obtaining zoning and, for superblocks or even mixed-use developments, subdivision approval. In cities where as-of-right zon-

garden park, and incentives for hotel and department store development.

3. *City's contribution:* Making best efforts to obtain financing for the 600-space garage to be owned and operated by the city. (The parking requirement has been reduced based on calculations of shared parking.)
City's return: Eight percent return on any cash invested if the city obtains financing (see no. 1 above).

4. *City's contribution:* Making best efforts to ensure certain traffic improvements, including the maintenance of two key streets as high-volume, two-way arterials, relocation of certain diagonals, and modification of travel on key avenues to improve public transit. Making best efforts to extend streetscaping.
City's return: No specific return.

5. *City's contribution:* Conveying ownership of the garden park.
City's return: Developer builds and maintains garden park.

6. *City's contribution:* Rezoning the entire parcel, permanently waiving the permit requirements for outdoor activities and changing the High-Rise Residential Incentive Overlay Zone, among others.
City's return: No specific return, but on an overall basis, the project is expected ultimately to employ 10,500 people and be valued at $515 million.

A careful reading of these terms, even summarized as they are, indicates the deal's complexity. In fact, the cover memo that accompanied the memorandum of understanding appears to have misstated the deal in assuming that, for example, the city's participation in cash flow would automatically increase to 27 percent in the 16th year, when in fact that event would occur only if the developer chose to exercise its option to purchase.

Analysing Potential Returns

A city should consider several questions when analyzing the potential returns on a deal like this one:

- What are the opportunity costs associated with the tax abatement on property of potentially rising value? Can increases in property values for areas surrounding the subject property be projected?
- How does the city account for its costs related to the project, including soft administrative costs?
- How critical to the city is the developer's purchase of the property? (It is the purchase that triggers an increase in the percentage of participation in cash flow.)
- Not counting the value of social goals, such as minority employment, what is the net present value of the city's investment in the project? Have long-term financial pro formas been developed so that such value can be calculated? What discount rate should be used in calculating the net present value of the city's investment?
- What value should be placed on the projected new jobs to be generated by the project?
- What is the procedure, if any, for renegotiating any portions of the deal in the event of unforeseen circumstances?

Cities like Phoenix—and many others—are fine-tuning their skills in analysis and negotiation to leverage public dollars for revitalization. As the competition for public money increases, however, and as deals become more complex, they will need to hone these skills even more to use resources as wisely as possible.

Sources: Phoenix Community Alliance, "Central Phoenix Project Update, Summer 1990"; "City Council Report," cover memorandum, December 19, 1986, describing the memorandum of understanding for the project; and memorandum of understanding between the city of Phoenix and the Rouse Company, December 19, 1986.

ing is generous, clearly the process is easier. In downtown Cincinnati, for example, the maximum FAR is 13, and, if all bonus options are exercised, the allowable FAR jumps to 30. In contrast, zoning regulations in downtown Seattle and Hartford limit as-of-right projects to a FAR of 10.[2] Other complications might include seeking a change in zoning when, for exam-

---

[2] Terry Jill Lassar, *Carrots and Sticks: New Zoning Downtown* (Washington, D.C.: ULI–the Urban Land Institute, 1989), p. 9.

ple, specific zones for mixed uses or for a particular use, say housing, are not set forth in the code. The entire application process for rezoning is complicated by the sometimes multiple agencies involved, the lack of uniform standards for changing zoning, and the participation of citizens or neighborhood groups in the process. For these reasons, zoning administrations that offer a fast track or at least provide an advocate can go far toward encouraging developers to become involved in a downtown project.

Following these approvals, public agencies issue a variety of permits that usually hinge on conformance to the final map. Permits for demolition, grading, building, and other phases of construction commonly require detailed technical documentation and are typically issued at the end of the regulatory process. Permit approval is often the most difficult, time-consuming, and frustrating part of development.[3]

---

[3] Michael D. Beyard et al., *Business and Industrial Park Development Handbook* (Washington, D.C.: ULI–the Urban Land Institute, 1988), p. 107.

4.
Financing

Significant changes will continue in the types and methods of financing available to development projects, whether downtown or not. Sources of private capital continue to be restructured and to undergo regulatory changes in an effort to rectify many of the ills that surfaced in the banking and thrift industries in the 1980s. The public financial arena also is changing significantly, primarily because of severely reduced—or eliminated—federal funds to support real estate development.[1] In their places, cities have used creative financing mechanisms—tax increment financing, ground leasing, and tax abatement, for example—to continue the work formerly financed with federal dollars.

The Effects of Tax Reform

Changes in tax laws embodied in the Tax Reform Act of 1986 have also dampened downtown real estate. Many of the favorable tax credits for rehabilitation developers used in the preservation of historic properties and adaptive use of older buildings were stripped away and replaced with more stringent, less lucrative provisions.

Limitations on an investor's income when using rehabilitation credits changed the base of targeted investors available to contribute equity to projects. Depreciation schedules were lengthened and opportunities for tax deferral limited by new rules governing passive losses. The tax changes also eliminated opportunities for conversion of ordinary deductions into tax-favored capital gains and further restricted the use of tax-exempt bonds in real estate projects.

The Tax Reform Act of 1986 also affected the public sector's ability to facilitate private development. It reduced the state caps on the volume of tax-exempt bonds and lumped many other types of bonds under the cap, thus making it more difficult to find capital for real estate projects. The bonds placed under the cap included industrial revenue bonds, multifamily housing bonds, and tax increment financing bonds, all used frequently in downtown development.

The changes in the tax act therefore hurt almost all downtown development but particularly that in small and medium cities. Those communities had a more difficult time absorbing the limitations imposed by the changes, because they have fewer resources than larger cities to offset the effects of tax reform. Thus, the remainder of this chapter more closely examines private and public sources of financing for downtown development within the context of these shifts and changes in the financial environment.

---

[1] For example, the UDAG and CDBG programs administered by the U.S. Department of Housing and Urban Development and financing for infrastructure provided by the Urban Mass Transportation Administration.

Private Sources of Capital

Most analysts would agree that, in the near term at least if not the intermediate term, financing from private sources will be more difficult to obtain. Some, however, including ULI's Real Estate Credit Task Force, contend that the withdrawal of financing for most new construction is generally desirable, given the oversupply of space in most markets. In fact, in its 1991 report, the task force recommended a halt to lending for speculative commercial development.[2]

Desirable or not, halt or no, one fact that most people agree on is that financing terms have changed for downtown development projects (as well as for other projects). Equity and the borrower's personal liability (recourse) are required where once they were not, extensions are being shortened to keep the pressure on owners to secure long-term financing, and rates as well as fees have inched up, increasing profit margins for lenders significantly. Further, tenants' creditworthiness is being examined much more closely. Though some developers and owners have been shut out of the market, those seeking new loans for land development or speculative construction, for example, most others have been able to obtain financing for preleased projects or for existing income properties that meet standards for underwriting.[3] Most experts doubt that the standards will swing back to the easy money of the 1980s once the current cycle changes.

Thus, private lenders for new downtown projects will be varied in the future. The demise of S&Ls will probably impose a hardship on small borrowers. More of the $2 million to $5 million projects will have to be financed by larger institutions, which traditionally have been concerned about the liabilities and underwriting costs involved in smaller transactions. At the other extreme, U.S. commercial banks will often team with foreign partners on large financing offerings.

Commercial Banks and Thrift Institutions

Commercial banks, which were able to race far ahead of thrifts and life insurance companies in providing mortgage commitments during the 1980s, benefited from the wholesale deregulation of financial institutions by the Garn–St. Germaine Depository Institutions Act of 1982. Banks' real estate lending increased dramatically throughout the 1980s, all the way through the third quarter of 1990, when total real estate loans by banks increased 10 percent over 1989, to $820 billion.[4] By that date, real estate loans made up 40 percent of banks' total loans, up from 29 percent in 1980, an unprecedented shift, given the inherent illiquidity of real estate.

The well-publicized woes of the lending industry beginning in the late 1980s, however, began to be reflected in banks' construction loan totals that same quarter. A slight decrease (2.3 percent) in construction and land development loans, to $133 billion, was exacerbated by the forced shutoff of credit by S&Ls to the same borrowers. Legislation passed in 1989 to bail out the S&L industry put a 15 percent cap on the amount of money a thrift could lend to one customer. Overnight, thrifts around the nation, which typically finance a majority of the nation's construction and land development loans, had to reduce their outstanding loan balances by billions of dollars to comply with the new regulations.

By the third quarter of 1990, the thrift industry had lost $600 million in that quarter alone, twice the loss of the second quarter of 1990 but not a big surprise, given the number of institutions still in trouble. According to Thomas P. Horton, deputy director of marketing for the Resolution Trust Corporation (RTC), between 700 and 1,000 S&Ls are either in conservatorship or teetering on the brink.

For existing borrowers from savings institutions, the message is clear: restructure the deal now before the Feds take over. Working with the RTC is and will be much more difficult than dealing with a local lender as a result of the broad range of powers granted to the RTC by Congress in the Financial Institutions Reform, Recovery, and Enforcement Act of 1989. "It's like the difference between a wrestling match and an ax fight in the dark," says Joseph E. Robert, Jr., whose company has won major asset management contracts from the RTC.

While every industry goes through cycles, the changes in the banking industry will have pronounced effects for many years. Projects developed in downtown areas, which often are not considered high-growth areas relative to many emerging suburban centers, face the prospects of increased difficulty for financing from financial institutions. New rules about risk-based capital will govern lending practices by financial institutions in the years ahead.

---

[2] ULI–the Urban Land Institute, "Recommendations of the Real Estate Credit Task Force," Draft (Washington, D.C.: Author, December 21, 1990).

[3] According to a ULI survey conducted in December 1990 through January 1991.

[4] FDIC *Quarterly Banking Profile*, 3d quarter 1990.

Banks, in addition to providing market-rate construction loans and miniperm financing (interim financing before the permanent loan is available) for downtown projects, are also a major source of funds for low-interest loan pools, a popular tool for downtown revitalization, particularly during periods when interest rates are high. Loan pools have been amazingly diverse, ranging in size from $30,000 (Eagle Pass, Texas) to over $2 million (Salisbury, North Carolina). Some provide capital only for improvements to facades, while others provide working capital for expansion and relocation of businesses. Pools have been capitalized by a variety of sources, including local lending institutions, foundation grants, and public funds, such as CDBG allocations. Loan pool funds typically are leveraged two to four times their value in conventional financing.

In some loan pools, all participating lending institutions contribute equally to a lump sum fund and loan repayments are evenly distributed to all lenders; in others, contributions and repayments are proportionate to the participating banks' assets. In some programs, borrowers receive loans from a common pool; in others, loans are made by borrowers' own banks, which can sometimes borrow funds from other participating banks if their own share of the pool is depleted more quickly. Some pools expire upon depletion and must be reseeded to continue; others are revolving, with loan repayments automatically replenishing the fund. And some loan funds have been created with the help of state enabling legislation; others exist through the coordination of banks and the downtown organization.

Texas "Main Street" towns (downtowns that are part of the National Historic Trust's Main Street program) have used loan pools extensively. As early as 1975 in Jefferson (population 2,643), First National Bank began offering loans for rehabilitation of facades at 2 percent, with a cap on the loan of $10,000. Since then, over 40 Main Street towns have established loan pools, with rates ranging from 5 to 8 percent. Approximately $200 million has been reinvested in downtowns as a result of the programs during the nine-year period ending in 1989. Though not attributable only to the loan pools, net new businesses in the downtowns totaled 1,300, net new jobs 4,100.

With the stabilization of interest rates during the late 1980s, many loan pools became inactive. With the economic decline and tighter credit of the early 1990s, however, loan pools are becoming popular once again.

Source: National Main Street Center, National Trust for Historic Preservation.

Bank Community Development Corporations

As early as 1968, banks began organizing for for-profit and nonprofit community development corporations (CDCs). Reversing the traditional lending philosophy of avoiding risk, CDCs owned by banks and bank holding companies are characterized by a high degree of flexibility that enables the parent organization to tailor the corporation's mission to meet a particular need. Under the CDC program, which is authorized and regulated by the Office of the Comptroller of the Currency (for national banks) and the Federal Reserve Board (for bank holding companies), banks can make direct equity investments in CDCs, business ventures, or community projects serving predominantly civic, community, or public purposes. Thus, national banks may establish wholly owned bank subsidiary CDCs, help form and capitalize multibank CDCs, invest in existing CDCs, or invest in qualifying community development ventures or projects.

For example, three banks, the city of Fort Collins, Colorado, the local development corporation, and the Downtown Development Authority all participate in a nonprofit CDC organized in 1990 to stimulate private reinvestment in downtown Fort Collins through the redevelopment and adaptive use of commercial and industrial buildings in the CBD. A secondary purpose of the new CDC is to create a long-term public/private partnership between the local banks, small businesses, the city government, and Colorado State University to facilitate economic development.

As a first project, the CDC provided financing for the purchase of a 23,000-square-foot historic building in the heart of downtown. One West Contemporary Arts Center acquired the former U.S. Post Office building, built in 1911 and vacated in the 1970s, for $475,000. The CDC provided $250,000 of the purchase price, with each bank contributing to the pur-

The North Carolina National Bank's (NCNB's) CDC was the earliest community development corporation to focus on urban redevelopment. A subsidiary of NCNB formed in 1978, this nonprofit corporation initiated and participated in the revitalization of Charlotte's Fourth Ward, which, at the turn of the

4-4   Charlotte's Fourth Ward in the foreground, redeveloped through funding by the NCNB CDC.

4-3   The Poplar, a $2.8 million condominium conversion in Charlotte's Fourth Ward.

century, was one of the city's most fashionable neighborhoods. To revitalize the neighborhood, existing properties were renovated, new units built, and below-market mortgages provided. The original $700,000 loan fund grew to more than $25 million, and the tax-assesed value of the area increased by $14 million between 1974 and 1981. By 1981, more than 1,400 new residents were living in the Fourth Ward.

Since then, the NCNB CDC completed several affordable housing projects, entering into commercial ventures as a strategy for subsidizing affordable housing. Gateway Center, located at the entrance to downtown, for example, includes office and retail space. A companion project, an eight-story hotel was built as well. The CDC also manages the historic City Market, a downtown farmers' market that had fallen into disrepair. City Market is now home to 55,000 square feet of retail and restaurant space and 17,000 square feet of office space.

chase based on a prorated share of its deposit base in Fort Collins. The former owner of the building made a tax-deductible gift of $225,000 to fund the balance of the purchase price.

The building now houses Colorado State University's continuing education offices, a CSU gallery, the Fort Collins Symphony Orchestra, Open-Stage Theater Company, the Junior League, Illustrated Light Photo Gallery, a ticket sales store, and a visitors information center. A cafe, art studios, and an art school are planned.

Insurance Companies

Overall, insurance companies do not have the exposure to real estate that banks and S&Ls do. They provided only about 6 percent of the long-term real estate mortgage loans and less than 1 percent of construction loans as of the end of 1990. With more than one-quarter of the life insurance companies' assets tied up in real estate loans and investments, however, life insurance companies are being careful. Still, they offer an opportunity for downtown financing in this decade. Like other financial institutions, insurance companies will be tightening underwriting standards in the wake of increasing delinquency rates on mortgage loans.

Pension Funds

Pension funds, although relatively new as major players in the real estate capital markets, are maturing and growing quickly, but at a pace that still leaves their total equity commitments well short of the dollars that these funds have allocated for real estate. Since 1982, the percentage of total real estate capital provided by pension funds grew from 0.9 percent of total real estate holdings to approximately 4 percent by 1990.

Pension funds, more diverse and less regulated than other financial institutions, usually invest in real estate that has started to produce income and has a proven history of performance. In the 1980s, major pension funds representing unions and municipal employees provided substantial equity funds and mortgage loans in many downtown development projects around the country.

Because pension funds are less regulated and more flexible in how they approach new opportunities for investment, they should be considered a good source of capital available to developers, even though it is likely that real estate will continue to be added at a slower rate of growth than in the past. According to Joseph O'Connor, president of Copley Real Estate Advisors, Inc., at ULI's fall 1990 meeting, "Pension funds invested in real estate because they thought returns were less volatile. They were less volatile, but they were also less." As a result, says O'Connor, underwriting standards in the 1990s are likely to be more like those in the 1960s: more cash, more personal liability for borrowers, and underwriting not only deals, but also developers. With those standards in mind, the move by pension funds away from office buildings and primary cities will continue in the 1990s as funds discover that secondary property types (industrial and residential, for example) and secondary regions can offer attractive opportunities for investment.

Real Estate Securities

Real estate securities, including real estate limited partnerships (RELPs) and real estate investment trusts (REITs), have grown to be an important force in the real estate capital market. The securities sector has been flexible enough to respond to changes in taxation and securities laws, which resulted in new programs focusing on safer, income-oriented invest-

ments rather than on deals built primarily upon tax advantages, a category of product that no longer exists. Since these regulatory changes, most public offerings of equity interest have been cash deals or leveraged offerings based on low loan-to-value ratios. A return to both public and private real estate syndications is expected as vacancies lessen and rental income increases.

Foreign Capital

Foreign sources of money are growing but are not nearly as important as their high visibility would suggest. A 50 percent decline in Nikkei stocks coupled with a rise of 300 basis points in interest rates through the first 10 months of 1990 wreaked havoc on Japan's financial system, according to Masao Konomi, president of Konomi, Inc., which specializes in connecting American and Japanese investors. Thus, bad experience with existing U.S. real estate loans and increased currency risk have resulted in Japanese banks', insurance companies', and construction

4-5 North American Taisei Corporation entered a joint venture for the development of the 650,000-square-foot 225 Wacker Drive in Chicago.

companies' retreating from the market. Yutaka Hashimoto, a director of Nippon Life Insurance Company, the largest life insurance company in Japan, however, offered this hope at ULI's fall 1990 meeting: "Sooner or later the time will come when we will increase our U.S. investment volume again."

Other foreign investors, including European investors and Pacific Rim investors from Korea, Taiwan, Hong Kong, and Singapore, have also been accumulating portfolios of U.S. real estate. For European investors, however, the prospect of a more integrated European Community in 1992 combined with broadened investment interests, including suburban office buildings and industrial and retail properties in other than CBDs, suggests increased difficulty in securing financing for downtown projects from these sources.

Corporations

Corporations, much more important in real estate investments than is generally recognized, annually invest billions of dollars in U.S. real estate. It is likely that they will represent a declining source of real estate capital in the next decade, however. The turbulent corporate financial scene, manifested in leveraged buyouts (LBOs), suggests that increasing significance will be placed on the consequences of corporate real estate decisions. Many LBOs, which use corporate real estate to secure the capital to fund takeovers or to pay off acquisition debt, have been motivated by the perception that corporations control substantial real estate assets whose values inadequately reflect prices of shares. In this event, corporate real estate enters the investment market.

The changes in the private real estate financing market will result in more conservative lending policies, diversification of investments into products other than office buildings located in other than primary market areas, and increased demands for feasibility and acquisition and management skills to help investors in their financial decisions.

Financing Vehicles

Financing vehicles will also change in the coming years, with the most popular ones likely to be:

- Straight construction loans from commercial banks, which could include open-ended or "bullet" loans and short-term loans not secured by takeout financing, usually given only to developers with outstanding reputations and very high credit ratings.
- Combined construction/takeout loans from insurance companies and other institutional lenders.

- Forward loan commitments with participation from insurance companies and credit corporations, including standby loan commitments in connection with new construction through which the lenders are paid a fee to protect a borrower against a sharp rise in rates when takeout financing is used.
- Presales of properties to pension funds directly or through their advisers and insurance companies.
- Participating and convertible mortgages structured by many financial players, which include alternatives that shield developers and lenders from sharp fluctuations in interest rates, provide lenders with increased cash flow over the life of a project (often called "kickers"), and increase yields to lenders as they might also participate in the proceeds of sales and/or refinancing.
- Mortgage bond financing as an alternative to conventional higher-interest-rate loans, which is used as alternative financing for health care facilities, hotel properties, and apartment developments. Bonds issued by surety companies in combination with letters of credit provided by banks are the most common methods of "enhancing" a transaction for the rating of bonds to be resold to the public.

Public Sources of Capital: City Deal Makers

The evolution during the 1980s of public/private development techniques has led to a more entrepreneurial approach by public entities. City officials are now more aggressive in offering incentives to attract developers who are considering competing cities and suburban growth centers for their investments. They have adopted a less adversarial style and have replaced passive, nonparticipatory involvement with a more energetic, competitive, deal-making attitude. Fine-tuning public development and financing skills has enabled city officials to become increasingly professional and competent. The public sector uses the process described in the following paragraph to determine whether significant assistance in public development and financing will be required in a downtown project.

First, it is necessary to determine total costs by project component. Next, the level of privately supportable financing is determined by estimating the achievable loan amount either by capitalizing projected stabilized net operating income to arrive at a project value and then applying current loan-to-value ratios *or* by backing into a loan amount based on the current required debt service coverage ratios. After a supportable loan amount is determined, supportable equity is calculated based on the requirements of known potential sources. Finally, total private funding capacity is determined, which produces the gap between that capacity and total project costs.

When deciding the number and amount of incentives to offer developers to help close financing gaps, public entities need to consider public risk and reward and to examine several factors:

- How competitive must the city be to entice private reinvestment in the downtown area?
- If nonfinancial measures will not suffice, does the city have the financial tools required to give rise to a successful public/private venture? At what price to the city? At what risk?
- Could the city place itself in a conflict of interest and a breach of fiduciary duty to its citizens by discouraging competitive projects or withholding support from them, thus increasing performance thresholds on favored projects?
- Should a city sell or lease its public assets to create a public/private venture?
- Can a community spur private reinvestment downtown by adopting the philosophy that it will share rewards but not risks?
- What is the negative side of a failed project?

An example of a city's adopting an activist attitude toward attracting new private investment is Cleveland, Ohio, and its rebuilding a competitive position in the hotel market and convention industry. Though the city undertook extensive renovation of the Cleveland Civic Center to make it competitive within the industry, the downtown lacked a sufficient number of hotel rooms to support a convention center. By the mid-1980s, downtown Cleveland had approximately 3,000 fewer hotel rooms than it had in 1960, and its ability to attract regional and national events had deteriorated.

As part of Cleveland's Civic Vision 2000 downtown plan, a downtown hotel overlay zone was created that encouraged convention hotel development near the Civic Center but discouraged it in other locations. In addition to concentrating development in a defined district, a package of development incentives was also created, which included commitments of public and private funds to attract developers and operators. The package included offers of permanent financing, cost sharing, development of support facilities, and tax abatement. Enhancements to public spaces, including landscaping, lighting, and climate-controlled pedestrian connections, were developed to induce new Marriott, Hyatt, and Ritz-Carlton hotels and an addition to the existing Stouffer's hotel in downtown Cleveland. These projects will add the targeted 1,400 to 2,800 new hotel rooms to the downtown area by 2000.

Once a community determines that it needs and wants to participate in a real estate project, it can use the financing tools discussed in the next section.

Public Financing Techniques

Public financing techniques for downtown development projects can take the form of indirect and direct measures to assist public/private ventures. Indirect, or nonmonetary, measures, while not financially involving local government in a real estate project, can have an equal or greater impact on project financing than direct public financial participation. Motivated by a desire to avoid direct financial participation or by a lack of financial resources, these measures can effectively close financing gaps for a project.

Indirect Measures

Zoning and Density Bonuses

By using its land use ordinance, a city can create value for a site by upgrading the land use or density allowed as well as by creating disincentives for developing in competing areas. It is important to note, however, that increased density might not translate into increased value if the market cannot support the size of the project. (The section on zoning in Chapter 2 discusses bonuses and other zoning-oriented techniques in more detail.)

Government Commitments to Rent Space

A public commitment to lease space in a new development makes it considerably easier for a developer to obtain financing. Even if government commits itself to leasing only a minor portion of a proposed project, its favorable credit rating as a lessee makes it easier for the developer to obtain other lease commitments. By carefully structuring the terms of rent escalation and renewal options, a municipality can minimize the cost of space at the same time it encourages private development.

Transfer of Development Rights

Transferring development rights from one site to another not only encourages development within a given location, but also relieves development pressures on other sites, notably where historic structures are lo-

4-6   TDRs—the unused development rights for midrise, often historic, properties deemed worthy of saving—can be sold to another developer.

cated. The transferred development rights can be used to increase a building's total floor area and to increase its lot coverage beyond what the zoning ordinance would normally allow.

Transfer of Air Rights

Air rights over public land can be leased or transferred to another property to provide opportunities for development. The city, however, retains ownership and control of the land. Typical financial arrangements include the city's offering attractive lease payments and property taxes to the developer while retaining a share of the profits for itself. Applications of this technique include building skywalks over streets or developing space on top of public garages.

Regulatory Relief from Zoning and Building Codes

Flexible regulations and zoning measures can create market opportunities in depressed areas. Trading permitted maximum floor area for the provision of improved pedestrian circulation, greater public open space, better shopping, and coordinated development has been used in cities nationwide.

Facilitating Project Approvals

Cities can take steps to facilitate permitting, reduce processing time, and champion public approvals in projects they politically support. Reduced approval times can result in lower interest and overhead costs to a developer and place the income-producing property on the local tax rolls faster. Organizing a one-stop office to receive city approvals, where a developer can coordinate all approvals through one person, has been

particularly effective. It can also be used to remedy problems caused by changes in zoning ordinances or planning policies before a project's completion.

Quick Take by Eminent Domain

Taking by eminent domain, a mechanism that allows immediate public possession of private property for public use, has been a major redevelopment tool for downtowns. It facilitates the assembly of parcels of land for development and reduces the time and cost required to ready a site. Several states have now enacted laws that allow localities to grant this power to private developers who build properties in accordance with locally approved plans; the Missouri 353 corporations are an example. Some states can use eminent domain in areas that are not blighted or are only somewhat blighted.

Encouragement of Financing by an Ancillary Party

The public sector can influence the availability of financing for private development projects by facilitating civic funds, patient capital, or soft equity money to be placed in a project. It can also orchestrate the placement of foundation funds or can direct the

4-7   Skywalks are a typical use of the transfer of air rights.

56

4-8 The city of Phoenix used its power of eminent domain to purchase a portion of the land for Arizona Center. *Source:* ELS/El-basani & Logan Architects.

placement of equity through local nonprofit organizations to facilitate tax deductions and contributions for investors.

Local banks might be persuaded to make concessions in return for deposits of government funds in their institutions. While the monies might or might not be lent to the project, their presence can have a positive effect by creating a supply of loan funds that otherwise would not have existed.

Design Coordination in Public/ Private Projects

When public and private uses are linked in the same project, two or more design teams can be involved, one for the public components and one for the private components. Though not always the case, this situation can create problems because of the lack of coordination. Selecting one design team to be coordinator can be a safeguard.

The same point applies to project construction. In some cases, a single construction manager overseeing the initiation and administration of contracts, bidding, and negotiations, supervision of contractors and subcontractors, scheduling of activities, and monitoring of work in progress can be a more effective approach. Coordinating design and construction results in lower costs for a project.

An example of coordinated design is the award-winning Old Town Square project in Fort Collins, Colorado. In a public/private partnership, a mixed-use office and retail project within a downtown historic district was completed in 1985 that includes a large pedestrian plaza bisecting the development and a publicly built parking ramp located across the street. Both the private project elements (office and retail space) and the amenities were designed by the same architect, which ensured a cohesive design between the two elements. Outdoor seating for the restaurants and second- and third-story terraces all face toward and overlook the plaza's staging area, where performances have attracted crowds of over 10,000 people.

Preservation Easements

Building owners might agree that a building's exterior physical features will not be changed to preserve its historical or architectural importance. Cities might convey buildings to developers under an agreement that the developer donate the exterior to the community while renovating the interior for income-producing uses. The effect is a reduction in front-end costs through the tax savings generated by the charitable contribution. Cities also covenant with developers to make no changes to any part of a building, interior or exterior, with this loss in value representing a charitable contribution that can qualify as a tax deduction for the acquiring developer.

Local Tax Incentives

Cities can legislate local historic districts or establish enterprise and foreign trade zones covering parts of the downtown area. These mechanisms permit developers and/or their tenants to generate additional tax savings.

When the city of Athens, Georgia, wanted to develop a mixed-use project linking the downtown and the University of Georgia, it engaged a multidisciplinary team to formulate a strategy for development and implementation. The identified project included a civic center, retail space, parking, hotel, and a condominium development. The project was funded in part by $20 million from local-option sales tax revenues.

4-9   Audubon Court in New Haven, Connecticut, is a downtown residential and office/retail complex developed in partnership with a nonprofit arts council. The city contributed streetscaping and relief from property taxes.

The tax was approved by a vast majority of area residents based upon the documentation of a significant portion of sales tax receipts generated by university students and the surrounding rural counties. Additional funding was provided by federal grants, local matching funds, and private debt and equity. The civic center is now undergoing final design and development.

Other Indirect Measures

Other measures can save costs in public/private ventures, including the public sector's assuming some or all of the responsibility for preparing environmental impact statements or reports; arbitrating or otherwise settling disputes involving equal opportunity, minority contracting, and affirmative action; instituting a crime prevention program in a declining area targeted for downtown revitalization; providing cheaper energy by integrating community energy systems into its

downtown renewal plan; acting as a liaison and information source for local neighborhood groups, surrounding property owners, merchants' associations, and others who have opinions regarding aspects of the proposed project; and selling downtown through a regular and carefully directed public affairs program. Many of these items should already be part of the downtown plan.

Direct Measures

Direct financial involvement in public/private ventures can come from many sources and can take many forms. Sources include federal and local funds, described below.

Federal Sources

Though federal funding for downtown redevelopment has been cut and though it still comes with complicated wage requirements, federal monies do still exist. The cortisone of dilapidated downtowns, HUD's Urban Development Action Grant, has been eliminated, but repayments of UDAGs can be used. Community Development Block Grants as well as money from the Economic Development Administration (EDA), the Farmers Home Administration (FHmA), and the Small Business Administration (SBA) are still available, in some instances wide open, for feasible projects.[5]

EDA Grants and Loan Guarantees. Most EDA grants are used in conjunction with other local, state, or federal monies for rehabilitating or constructing infrastructure and public works facilities as part of industrial or commercial development. EDA's two categories of grants include *public works grants* (for example, water, sewer, and road improvements), which typically cover 50 percent of a project's costs, and *economic adjustment grants* for areas experiencing long-term or sudden, severe loss of jobs. Economic adjustment grants can cover up to 75 percent of a project's costs and can be used to fund, for example, incubator facilities or low-income housing projects. EDA funding is targeted to "highly distressed" locations and, in about 65 to 75 percent of the cases, to rural areas.

Reuse of UDAG Loan Repayments. Communities fortunate enough to have received the now terminated UDAGs are using the repayments from the earlier investments. Discounting or capitalizing the income stream from development loans financed with UDAGs is an excellent way to generate current cash, which may be reinvested in a second wave of redevelopment in downtowns.

Philadelphia, for example, has created a mini-UDAG program with paybacks. Los Angeles has used $5 million in repayments as security to leverage a $40 million revolving loan fund for small businesses. According to a 1990 HUD study of UDAG projects, $443 million in repayments are projected through 1995, with over $2 billion total in repayments due.[6]

Community Development Block Grants. CDBG funds can be used for direct or secondary loans to developers; to fund loan guarantees, collateral, insurance costs on notes and bonds, and loan fees; and for planning and administrative costs related to a city's development program. The objectives that must be met to receive CDBGs have become increasingly difficult to meet, however. CDBG-funded activities must meet one or more of three objectives: 1) benefit low- and moderateincome people (60 percent of the people benefiting from the funded activities must be low or moderate income); 2) eliminate slums and blight; and

3) fill urgent community needs. Furthermore, union wage requirements imposed by federal legislation discourage use of the funds.

Nevertheless, CDBG funds, administered by HUD, are still being used successfully in many downtown projects. In the Buffalo Theatre District redevelopment project, for example, CDBG funds were used to purchase two deteriorated office buildings, to renovate theaters, and to acquire property for new construction. Another $29 million in CDBGs was used as a short-term loan, allowing the developers to receive no-interest loans during construction and to issue taxable revenue bonds.

Section 108 Guaranteed Loans. Section 108 of the Housing and Community Development Act allows communities entitled to CDBG monies to borrow against future grants to finance major projects. Communities can borrow up to three times their annual CDBG and repay the loan over a period of up to six years by pledging the future CDBG funds as security. Section 108 loans, administered by HUD, can be used for almost any CDBG-eligible rehabilitation or economic development project, and because of the collateral, loan rates are low. The application process is short as well—six to eight weeks. Section 108 loans are not affected by the caps on volume and other restrictions of the Tax Reform Act of 1986, nor are they limited by any local debt ceilings.

FHmA Business/Industrial Development Program. Targeted to communities with fewer than 25,000 population (though loans have been made in communities with populations up to 50,000), the Business/Industrial Development (BID) program is administered by the Department of Agriculture and is designed to stimulate job growth and to bring new technology to rural areas. Grants, direct loans, and guaranteed loans can be used to buy land or property and/or to rehabilitate buildings.

SBA Section 504 Loans. The SBA 504 program provides financing for acquisition of fixed assets and real property to individual businesses, usually through a local SBA-certified development corporation. Typically, the development corporations, through a private intermediary, sell SBA-guaranteed (up to 40 percent) debentures. A 10 percent injection of equity is required, but other public financing can be used to satisfy that requirement.

---

[5] National Council for Urban Economic Development, "Emerging Trends in Real Estate Financing" (Washington, D.C.: Author, 1989), pp. 23–28.

[6] David Rymph and Jack Underhill, *An Analysis of the Income Cities Earn from UDAG Projects* (Washington, D.C.: U.S. Dept. of Housing and Urban Development, 1990), pp. i–iii.

4-10, 4-11   Adler Block in Asheville, North Carolina, before and after restoration. The city's loan guarantee made the 13-building project financeable.

Local Sources

To be acceptable to private investors, the public's share of the return in most cases comes after private investors have earned a return sufficient to attract their investment in the first place. This objective for profit sharing has led to a shift from outright grants to private developers to loans with the repayment schedules and interest rates depending on the project's performance, similar to those used by conventional mortgage lenders. Thus, direct public financial assistance is now focused on the particular problems frustrating private investment and development, reflecting the more business-like and sensitive approach public entities are taking to spur greater interest from private investors and developers.

Subsidized Loan Interest. This subsidy is normally implemented through loan pools established with local or federal funds matched to other than public assistance (see Figure 4-1 for more information).

Loan Guarantees. Local government can shift some of the lender's risks by guaranteeing a loan, a portion of a loan, or a portion of the debt service payments made to retire loans, thus increasing the likelihood that developers can obtain private funds. Similarly, if the local government agrees to lease or purchase the project at a percentage of projected market value in the event the projected return does not materialize, the project becomes more attractive to equity and mortgage investors.

In Asheville, North Carolina, the city agreed to guarantee partial repayment of the private financing for Park Plaza, a downtown project consisting of 11 adjacent historic buildings dating from the late 19th century, a new office/commercial building, and a new 320-car parking structure. City financing was necessary to justify restoration of these structures and to interconnect the three blocks of buildings so that marketable floor plates and efficient elevator cores could be offered.

In the event the project did not generate net operating income sufficient to cover the first mortgage payment to a consortium of local private lenders during the first five years of the project, the city pledged that it would make available a $200,000 line of credit to the developer. If $200,000 were not needed in any one year to cover the payment, the funds paid by the city would be only the amount necessary to cover the mortgage payment. The partnership agreement called for any funds paid by the city to the developer under the line of credit to be repaid by the developer with interest upon sale or refinancing of the project or no later than 10 years after initial project occupancy.

Public Grants. Grants of surplus or unused public monies to fund the public portion of a public/private venture can be made. Typical sources of local revenues include surplus water and sewer funds and leftover urban renewal funds.

Direct Loans. In a highly competitive capital market, direct loans from the public sector at below-market interest rates can fill a gap created when no private funds or insufficient funds are available for a particular portion of a project's financing. In addition to the benefit of encouraging new development, local governments also get the benefit of exercising a level of control that it would not have otherwise. If its interests are at stake, the city might wish to offer a below-market direct loan, even if a project does not require it financially. Many states have resolved the prohibitions against the use of public funds for direct loans by passing enabling legislation allowing the creation of economic development corporations or other special vehicles that serve as a conduit for city grants, loans, and contracts to private entities.

Jacksonville Landing in Jacksonville, Florida, is one example of a city's taking direct financial interest in a project. In recognizing the potential for public benefit from development of a major festival marketplace in its core downtown, the city of Jacksonville solicited interest from the Rouse Company of Columbia, Maryland, to develop the facility. The resulting $43.5 million project, which includes 187,000 square feet of specialty retail and entertainment space and four integrated pavilions around a central court, was financed in large part with city funds—over $36 million lent to the developer to generate the project's development. The public funding involved an innovative tapestry of sources, including revenue bonds, the subordinated loan of CDBG funds, CDBG float

loans to offset the need for some private construction financing, and tax increment financing. The developer contributed approximately $7 million in conventional debt and equity for the project, which opened in 1987.

Public Funding of Predevelopment. Involving a private developer early in the project could hinge on the public sector's willingness to underwrite some or all of the front-end expenses. This technique has successfully attracted developers to assess the potential for a project by removing one of the major obstacles to urban development, the difficulty of convincing developers to invest time and money in an assessment of a project's feasibility in weak or uncertain markets. Most developers view the probability of a reward from front-end investments under these conditions as very low and therefore choose not to make the effort. The willingness of the local government to undertake some such development costs creates an atmosphere conducive to further negotiations and possible involvement.

4-12   Jacksonville Landing was financed through the city's direct financial interest.

In New Bern, North Carolina, for example, the city, through a nonprofit development corporation, funded studies by consultants for market, financial, and design feasibility assessments in an effort to attract developers to dormant, unused urban renewal property along the waterfront adjacent to the downtown area. The property, located at the confluence of two rivers, had been cleared 14 years earlier but had remained unproductive. The city's underwriting initial expenses attracted a developer to the project, and construction of the $22 million development, which includes a 100-room hotel, a 400-seat meeting center, 10,000 square feet of retail space, a 100-slip marina, and 40 residential condominiums, began in 1985.

Support of Other Public Objectives. Cities desiring high-quality amenities that the market might not be able to support, public art, for example, can offer to pay for the increment of cost necessary to create the amenity.

Tax Increment Financing. Tax increment financing (TIF) is a mechanism that allows city redevelopment agencies to fund downtown revitalization by capturing the increased property taxes that result from revitalization. This annual increment of revenues, which otherwise would be split with local taxing entities, is then used to pay for the public improvements directly or to secure the repayment of bonds used to finance public improvements. Bond issues based on tax increment revenue are not direct obligations of the city; therefore, they do not require voters' approval once approved by the city council.

A city implements TIF by designating a district to be redeveloped that is blighted or declining in value. The tax base for the area is then established and frozen for a specific period of time. A redevelopment plan must be approved and followed; future taxes over the amount of the frozen assessment are then used to implement the plan. In most states, the standards for establishing blighted areas are liberal, powers over the use of monies are broad, and the administration of the process is relatively easy—so much so that TIF is sometimes considered a downtown redevelopment director's dream.

Controversy over TIF, however, centers around a concern that the development being financed could occur without public financing and that, as a result, local taxing entities like school districts and counties are unnecessarily deprived of revenues. Thus, to ensure passage of enabling legislation for TIF, any proposal must persuasively set forth the long-term economic return to the community from the funded activities.

For example, tax increment financing was used in the renovation of Old Town Square in downtown Fort Collins, Colorado. After Sears and J.C. Penney moved out of downtown to a regional shopping center, the city created a downtown development authority that, under state enabling legislation, had the power to use tax increment financing. Prompted by this public action, a local developer retained consultants to investigate market conditions and to suggest a public/private project to revitalize the Old Town portion of downtown. Based on the consultant's findings, the developer assembled properties located on both sides of a street running through a national historic district.

Under a public/private partnership agreement, the local developer has completed a $23 million project containing 110,000 square feet of well-blended historic restoration and infill construction. A community focal point for shopping and entertainment, the project includes a mix of office, retail, and restaurant space, including a brewpub that makes its own beer on the premises. Approximately $5 million in TIF was used to convert a street into a pedestrian plaza and to build a parking ramp to serve the project. The pedestrian plaza features a water fountain designed around large boulders, a staging area for live theater and musical performances, and extensive landscaping. The project consistently ranks as the primary attraction for visitors to Fort Collins and, at this writing, enjoys nearly full occupancy.

4-13   The Fort Collins Downtown Development Authority used tax increment financing at Old Town Square.

Improvement or Business Development Districts.
An improvement district combines the financing vehicle of assessment districts, in which all properties in a defined area are levied against for all or part of the cost of certain improvements, with additional administrative powers, such as planning, maintenance, and promotion of improvements or downtown activities.

Typically, the city levies a charge on the property in a specified single- or multipurpose district (a downtown area, a commercial strip, or a historic preservation area), and the funds collected are used to retire bonds issued by the city (or the district itself) to pay for the improvements and services in the district. The bonds are repaid directly from the tax revenues collected or from the city's general fund, which is later reimbursed by the special tax revenues.

General Obligation Bonds. Backed by the city's full faith and credit, these bonds are used to finance general public improvements. Ad valorem tax revenues are used to retire the bond debt. The city's current financial status must be evaluated to identify its capacity to issue general obligation bonds, and the interest rates the bondholders charge the city reflect the municipality's bond rating. General referenda could be required to issue general obligation bonds, and sufficient debt capacity must remain for the city to enter the bond market.

Revenue Bonds. Revenue bonds are retired directly with the revenues generated from a specific facility. Parking fees from garages, hotel or bed taxes, and sales taxes, for example, have been used to pay debt tied to parking facilities, visitor facilities, group meeting space, and other similar ventures.

Industrial Development Bonds. Issued by a public agency or authority, IDBs are revenue bonds for private projects with a public purpose. The Tax Reform Act of 1986 limits the amount of the bonds to $50 per capita or $150 million per state, whichever is higher, and their use to multifamily housing, mass transit, airports, docks, wharves, utilities (electricity or gas), hazardous waste disposal, and sewage and water facilities. The following types of projects cannot be financed with IDBs: sports, hydroelectric, air/water pollution, and parking facilities, convention/trade show complexes, and commercial activities.[7]

Tax Concessions. Through tax concessions, a city encourages privately financed improvements in specified areas by not collecting the real estate taxes on those improvements for a number of years or by freezing the assessment at the predevelopment level.

In Phoenix, Arizona, for example, the city abated taxes for eight years for the 1 million-square-foot mixed-use Arizona Center. The abatement was part of

4-14   In Phoenix, the city abated taxes for eight years for the 1 million-square-foot mixed-use Arizona Center. The abatement was part of a comprehensive public financing package. *Source:* ELS/Elbasani & Logan Architects.

a comprehensive public financing package, including vacated public right-of-way in exchange for equity in the project, access to tax-exempt municipal bonds, and ownership of public space.

In Trenton, New Jersey, the developer of Trenton Commons pays 15 percent of rents received annually in lieu of property taxes for 15 years, an effective abatement of 50 percent. Other variations of tax concessions have included exempting the increased value of redeveloped property from property taxes and gradually decreasing abatements.

Site Assembly. In a downtown where most of the land has already been subdivided and developed, the acquisition of a suitable site can be a major problem. Because most of the land has been divided into relatively small parcels owned by separate parties, the problem of acquisition increases with the size of the site required.

---

[7] National Council for Urban Economic Development, "Emerging Techniques in Real Estate Financing," p. 31.

The public sector can alleviate these problems by purchasing property, removing clouded titles from privately purchased property, and/or by instituting land banking. Land banking allows a city agency or local development corporation to acquire and assemble land suitable for development and to hold the land until a suitable user is identified.

Land Writedowns and Deferred Land Payments. Traditional urban renewal projects used land writedowns to attract developers to renewal sites, and the incentive is still popular. After an analysis of the residual value of the land (calculated by capitalizing the net income to arrive at the value of a project and matching it with the capital cost of producing or replacing it), the writedown, or reduction of price to a level the proposed development can support, can be established.

Alternatively, rather than a one-time payment for the land, the public entity holding the land could agree to receive installment payments from the developer. This practice reduces the requirement for front-end cash and allows the developer to stage the payments to better match cash flow from the project.

Relocation Assistance. Even though a public agency might not directly aid site acquisition, it can help a private developer assemble a site by helping to relocate space users in property slated for development. Relocation assistance can take the form of loans and grants to pay moving expenses or aid in finding or developing a new site for those who must move. Both parties can benefit. The relocated activity has a chance to leave obsolete facilities and an inadequate location, and the community gains economic benefits from new businesses.

Insuring Condemnation or Acquisition Costs. The unusual but effective practice of securing an insurance policy to cover local government's risk of excessive court-negotiated acquisition costs during eminent domain proceedings can mean the difference in whether a project is feasible or not. Local government units can pay for or share in the costs of a one-time premium payment made to an insurance company that assumes the risk that total acquisition costs will not exceed an agreed-upon level. This practice makes it possible to avert stalemates in negotiations that occur when cities are reluctant to use eminent domain unless they are certain of the maximum acquisition cost. Similarly, developers who agree to pay for city-assembled land avoid surprises or excessive payments resulting from court proceedings subsequent to their negotiated transactions with public entities.

Site Clearance and Demolition. Once sites have been assembled and the existing residences and businesses relocated, government funds can be used to demolish and clear the site and prepare it for new development.

Provision of Infrastructure and Public Facilities. To attract private investment, local governments can provide a range of improvements adjacent to or on the project site, including major capital improvements (transit systems, highway and street alignment, transit stops, storm and sanitary sewers, utilities), major public facilities (schools, parking, a civic center, government office buildings, hospitals, neighborhood centers), or public amenities (outdoor recreational plazas, open spaces, landscaping, or pedestrian bridges). A city's investment in public facilities can generate demand for specific kinds of private investment tied directly to those facilities, such as hotels, office buildings, or residential projects.

Sharing Space. Shared use of space allows the developer of a mixed-use project to avoid duplicating facilities and to minimize the requirements for open space that cannot be amortized by privately incurred debt. An impressive foyer, lobby, entry, or parking garage can be shared by city and private users to amortize or set aside those aspects of the public/private development that cannot be amortized. Kitchen and registration areas can be shared in hotels and convention centers, for example.

Shared Expenses for Maintenance. In a large, complex project combining public and private space, agreements are usually fashioned to define responsibilities for public and private sectors' maintenance and management of those facilities. The general trend is to consolidate most management and maintenance under one entity, with other participants paying for their share of services.

Off-Budget Debt Financing. Agencies have entered into securitized lease/purchase and other installment capital deals in which the use of tax-exempt financing (often through certificates of participation or COPs) results in lower-than-normal annual costs for public buildings. Voters' approval is usually not required, as the "requirement to pay" ends at the end of each year when certificates are used. Nonappropriation carries significant penalties, however, and can result in a strong negative mark on a city's credit rating.

Defaults rarely occur with this type of financial transaction, as tax-exempt lease/purchase arrangements are usually made for unpopular but essential facilities. COPs are an expanding and widely used alternative to general obligation bonds and have been used to build schools, jails, public administration buildings, and other projects. Typically, COPs are slightly more expensive than issuing general obligation bonds, but investors' confidence has grown and

Certificates of participation are tax-exempt financing vehicles used by local and state governments and their related authorities to build public facilities. Used with increasing frequency since the mid-1980s, COPs are a relatively new method of public financing originated successfully in California after Proposition 13 severely impaired the ability of governmental units to finance capital construction through the traditional route of general obligation bonds. Initially used by governments to finance essential but unpopular projects like prisons, public power plants, and government office buildings, COPs have gained more widespread acceptance as a vehicle to finance portions of downtown projects, including civic and convention centers, parking and other transportation facilities, theaters, and parks.

Basically, a COP represents a proportionate interest in a "conditional purchase agreement" under which a tax-exempt entity (state, city, county, public authority, hospital, or college) finances the acquisition and/or construction of assets, conditioned upon the obligation of the entity to make continuing installment payments toward the full purchase price or construction cost. COPs are usually sold at a higher interest rate than general obligation debt and are prepaid out of annual appropriations. While tax reform legislation made tax-exempt investments like COPs less attractive for commercial banks to own, investment banking firms have aggressively marketed COPs in the public market because of several of their attractive features.

Unlike a bond issue, the sale of a COP does not require voters' approval. The tax-exempt entity can thus reach the market quickly and without the bureaucratic red tape associated with a bond issue. Likewise, the installment payments are generally considered to be a current operating expense—subject to an annual appropriation by the governing body—and do not constitute a direct debt of the tax-exempt entity. Neither the full faith and credit nor the taxing power of the tax-exempt entity is pledged to the payment of principal or interest on the COPs.

Even though traditional pledges by taxing authorities are not offered, investors' confidence in these issues has been strong. Credit is sometimes enhanced through bond insurance to support investment decisions, depending on perceptions of risk. Defaults on COPs have been rare, however, because the bonds typically are used for essential government facilities and because nonappropriation by

4-16 CERTIFICATES OF PARTICIPATION BY UNIT OF GOVERNMENT, JANUARY 1985 TO MAY 1990

TYPE OF MORTGAGE ISSUER	AMOUNT ($ MILLIONS)	PERCENT OF TOTAL	NUMBER OF ISSUES
City, Town, or Village	$5,245.7	24.0%	431
District (School, Utility, Etc.)	4,642.9	21.3	420
Local Authority	3,771.2	17.3	139
County/Parish	3,711.3	17.0	185
State	2,333.6	10.7	55
State Authority	1,838.7	8.4	78
College or University	305.0	1.4	33
Total	$21,848.4	100.0%	1,341

Sources: Securities Data Company, Newark, New Jersey; and Basile Baumann Prost & Associates, Inc., Annapolis, Maryland.

the taxing authority carries significant penalties, including a strong negative mark on its credit rating.

Another attractive feature of COPs is that they allow the public entity and a developer/contractor to avoid government procurement processes, facilitating negotiations for fast-track, turnkey construction services, materials, and equipment for public facilities. If, for example, the City University of New York had used its usual financing/construction agent, the New York State Dormitory Authority, when it developed a new facility for the John Jay College of Criminal Justice in New York, the project could have cost $43.6 million more, partly because of the state's procurement and construction processes and policies.[1]

As shown in Figure 4-16, over 1,300 COPs were issued during roughly the last half of the 1980s in the United States, predominantly by such mortgage issuers as cities, districts, local authorities, and counties. The issues amounted to nearly $22 billion in debt financing, with the average issue about $16 million. During the first half of the 1980s, in contrast, approximately $3.3 billion in 139 COPs was issued, about one-sixth of the activity in the last half of the 1980s.

▶

4-17 CERTIFICATES OF PARTICIPATION
BY SPECIFIC USE OF PROCEEDS,
JANUARY 1985 TO MAY 1990

USE	AMOUNT ($ MILLIONS)	PERCENT OF TOTAL	NUMBER OF ISSUES
General Purpose/Public Improvements	$ 7,506	34.4%	448
Primary/ Secondary Education	3,913	17.9	345
Water/Sewer Facilities	1,822	8.3	119
Civic and Convention Centers	1,299	5.9	32
Correctional Facilities	1,145	5.2	47
Higher Education	941	4.3	73
Hospitals	786	3.6	35
Electricity/ Public Power	722	3.3	16
Government Buildings	593	2.7	31
Parking Facilities	577	2.6	29
Other*	2,544	11.6	166
Total	$21,848	100.0%	1,341

*Includes solid waste facilities, multifamily housing, lifecare/retirement facilities, flood control equipment, fire stations and equipment, economic development, libraries and museums, recreation, telephone, sanitation, and mass transportation facilities, and a variety of other uses.
Sources: Securities Data Company, Newark, New Jersey; and Basile Baumann Prost & Associates, Inc., Annapolis, Maryland.

COPs have been used for a wide variety of developments (Figure 4-17), including downtown civic and convention centers, hospitals, government buildings, and parking facilities. While many of these facilities were built and financed by units of government in California, public officials in most states now have experience with using COPs. Civic and convention centers were financed and built using COPs in Idaho, Minnesota, and Kansas. Parking facilities were financed and built in Missouri, North Carolina, Iowa, and Colorado during the last half of the 1980s.

While nearly seven of 10 COPs were issued in western states, the use of the technique has spread rapidly eastward. Government units in large urbanized states, such as New York, New Jersey, and Florida, have used the technique extensively. In fact, during the last half of the 1980s, COPs were issued in 45 states and Puerto Rico; only the District of Columbia, North Dakota, Wyoming, Hawaii, Vermont, and New Hampshire have not seen a COP issued there.

The widespread use of these "off-budget" or "off-balance sheet" types of financing will probably continue to increase, and innovative financing for other downtown projects should be expected. But with the increasing use of this technique could come challenges, for some see COPs as a way to circumvent the will of the general citizenry. Some legislators and courts have reviewed challenges where plaintiffs allege that installment payments constitute long-term public debt and, as such, must comply with all of the restrictions on the issuance of general obligation debt. Regardless, experts feel that COPs will continue to be a significant financing technique throughout the 1990s to create downtown (and other) development projects.

[1]Dympna Bowles, "The John Jay College Project," Urban Land, October 1989, pp. 20–23.

their yield is now within a narrow range of general obligation debt.

As installment purchase contracts for a capital project, COPs allow developers to build public facilities for a fee. The public entity agrees to lease the facility for a stated time period. At the end of the lease, the public entity purchases the building for a nominal fee (usually $1). Such arrangements also lower total costs, as the public and the developer can avoid government procurement processes and can negotiate fast-track, turnkey construction services, materials, and equipment for the public facilities.

Ground Leases. While ground leases are not new, local governments have not employed them to a large degree outside of several western states, including California. Public entities, using vacant public lands,

Throughout the country, cash-strapped local governments with big goals for downtown have gone into the development business, with participation leases the tools they use to secure long-term revenues and to finance—and thereby gain some control over—development.

Participation ground leases can benefit both the landowner and the developer. For the development company, the ground lease is beneficial because the developer does not have to come up with the capital required to purchase land, particularly important in large downtown developments. If the lease is subordinated, the ability to obtain financing is enhanced, because financing for land acquisition is not required. The local government, on the other hand, retains title to the property, gains some control over development of the site, and acquires a long-term source of revenue. At the end of the lease period, improvements on the property can revert to the city.

Why should the city agree to subordinate its fee interest in the property and risk the chance of losing the property if the developer defaults under the mortgage? First, the deal might not be financeable unless the lease is subordinated. Second, through subordination, the city can negotiate a higher percentage of participation in the profits to compensate for the greater risk it takes.

Successful negotiation of ground leases must be based on an analysis of the real estate and an analysis of the deal. If the goal is to negotiate a land lease that approximates market value, the discounted value of the ground lease (the deal) should be within 5 to 10 percent of the value of the land in fee (the real estate).

Valuing the land is done through the normal appraisal process. To determine the value of the ground lease, each income stream related to the lease must be quantified and discounted to a present value. Two or three streams of income are typical: a fixed amount of rent not related to the project's performance, a percentage of gross income, and/or a percentage of net cash flow. The first option is clearly the least risky, while a percentage of cash flow entails the most risk. Net cash flow is determined after operating expenses as well as after debt service. Clearly, in the latter case, each item of revenue and expense must be explicitly identified in the lease documents.

To arrive at a present value, each income stream must be projected through the life of the lease—which means developing a cash flow projection for the project—and discounted at rates appropriate to the risk of each. The higher the risk, the greater the discount factor required. Returns on alternative financial instruments, such as Treasury bills, corporate bonds, and lesser-quality financial instruments, are generally the starting point for assigning discount rates.

If the discounted value of the lease is less than the fee value of the land, the lessor should consider whether the income stream has been discounted too much. If not, the transaction substantially favors the lessee, and the lessor might wish to rethink the provisions of the lease or consider a sale instead. If the discounted value exceeds the fee value, the income stream(s) might not have been sufficiently discounted. Or the landowner might have negotiated an excellent deal and should sign the lease immediately.

Source: Robert Wetmore, "Lessor Beware: A Land Lease Is Usually a Partnership," *Urban Land*, October 1988, pp. 20–23.

enter into long-term, unsubordinated, participating ground leases with developers to create additional cash flow to supplement tax revenues. In some instances, the public sector negotiates lower lease payments in exchange for developers' providing limited building space.

Long-term leases are increasingly used in publicly assisted development because they are so flexible. The lease can provide for a minimum base payment plus a percentage of income generated by the project or by some other graduated arrangement. Thus, if the project does well, the city shares in the income and can recover some or all of its costs. Ground leases, moreover, can be subordinated if necessary; that is, the city can execute a mortgage of its land as security for the development loan made to the lessee.

For the developer, such long-term leases can greatly improve the net return on investment through improved financing terms, reductions in the equity required, and tax advantages. With a subordination clause in the lease, the advantages are even greater. The disadvantage is that cash flows to the pub-

4-19 The 17,000-square-foot site of the historic National Theatre in Washington, D.C., is leased for 99 years from the Pennsylvania Avenue Development Corporation. The theater is part of a mixed-use project that also includes a hotel, and office and retail space.

lic entity are reduced when the land is leased rather than purchased.

In San Diego, the city's redevelopment agency leased land for a new apartment building in the downtown's marina redevelopment project adjacent to the south end of Horton Plaza. In return for leasing the land at a nominal rate, the San Diego Redevelopment Agency participates in substantial cash flow after a preferred return on the developer's equity. The agency was also able to win agreement from the developer that 20 percent of all units would be set aside for low- and moderate-income households.

Privatization. Local governments can enter into contracts where the private sector acquires, owns, and operates facilities traditionally built by government. In some instances, public entities lease the facilities. Many types of public facilities have been built under this arrangement, among them parking garages and jails. Privatization usually works best when market conditions allow private developers to generate sufficient yields from other components of the project to justify building public facilities with private monies.

Transfer of Assets. Land and/or building swaps can be used to accomplish a variety of goals. Land swaps, for example, are used when the city and/or developer holds only pieces of the land it needs. The land is appraised, and parcels of equal value are traded to assemble usable sites for both parties. This technique was successfully used when a private landowner held several key parcels needed for the development of the Dallas Arts District. The landowner participated in a three-way exchange of property involving the city and the nonprofit Central Dallas Association to obtain land in another area more suitable for his business.

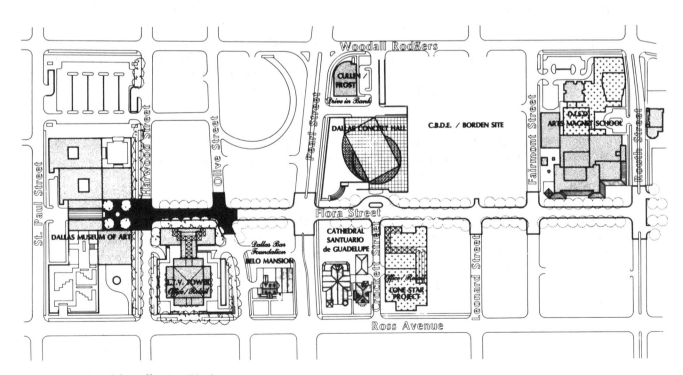

4-20 Site plan of the Dallas Arts District.

BIG DEAL IN THE LITTLE APPLE: DOWNTOWN RETAIL CENTER USES A VARIETY OF FINANCING TOOLS

Manhattan, Kansas, known locally as "the Little Apple," has made a big commitment to its downtown. After staving off repeated attempts by developers to build a regional mall in the suburbs—which would likely have proved fatal to Manhattan's struggling retail core—the city formed a joint venture with Forest City Rental Properties of Cleveland, Ohio, and JCP Realty, Inc., of New York City to build a regional mall downtown. The $59 million, 382,000-square-foot, single-level mall—the Manhattan Town Center—stands as a testament to the city's dogged determination to keep commercial activity downtown.

In 1968, the city adopted a land use plan stating that the downtown should remain the primary retail area. Many of its residents, however, frequently traveled to Topeka and even to Kansas City to shop. Manhattan, whose population totaled about 33,000, lost a large share of sales tax dollars from residents to other cities.

Ten years later, the city began a nationwide search for a qualified developer to build a retail center that would pump new life into Manhattan's retail core. After choosing Forest City, the city's main task was to assemble and prepare the 36-acre site for development, which involved acquiring and demolishing over 60 buildings and relocating over 27 residences and 70 businesses. Large firms, such as a concrete batch plant, a farmers' cooperative, and a moving company, and small firms, such as a barbershop and a shoe repair store, were moved. Few were eager to move, and none moved into the mall. The city spent $11 million to acquire over 70 parcels of private land, about $4 million over budget. Site preparation was no picnic either. Besides relocating a railroad track and a storage yard, the city removed a number of underground storage tanks.

To finance the town center, Manhattan pulled out all the stops. The extremely complicated financing package included a UDAG, federal highway funds, general obligation bonds, industrial revenue bonds, and the creation of a tax increment financing district as well as a benefit district. Public investment totaled over $27 million; private investment topped $29 million.

Under the joint venture agreement between the city and the developers, Forest City holds a 99-year lease on the 36-acre site, manages the property, and owns all the improvements. The developer's lease payments total $169,000 per year plus a percentage of the mall's gross receipts. The city owns both the parking lot and the outdoor plaza, although the developer pays taxes on both.

The city also expanded Fort Riley Boulevard to provide greater access to and from the town center.

▶

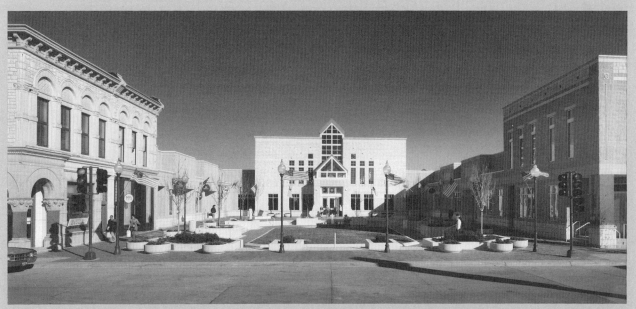

4-22   A variety of public and private financing tools were used to finance Manhattan Town Center.

To do so, it first had to spend several years in court with a railroad company to regain possession of the land needed for expansion of the highway. After asserting its rightful ownership of the property, the city received $3 million in federal highway funds from the Kansas Department of Transportation.

After being open three years, the center had met the city's two main objectives: restoring the focus of retailing downtown and recapturing a portion of the sales tax dollars that were leaking out of the city. With the contribution of over $500,000 in sales taxes per year, Manhattan Town Center is now one of the biggest taxpayers in Manhattan. In addition, the mall created over 400 new jobs and has hosted a number of community events, including the high school prom and the county health fair. Temporarily vacant spaces are made available free of charge to community groups for events like art shows and a children's museum. And the mall is open early every morning for senior citizens to walk laps.

In developing its town center, Manhattan has learned that a long-term commitment from the community is critical to the success of a large public/private project. Manhattan Town Center took about 10 years to plan and build. Changes are still being made. The exterior stores that border an outdoor plaza facing the town's main street and the stores remaining in the adjacent retail strip have proven difficult to lease. City officials hope the more than $1 million spent to give the main street a face-lift, including new benches, Victorian streetlights, new trees, and a brick sidewalk, will spur activity in the area.

Source: Project Reference File: "Manhattan Town Center," vol. 20, no. 8 (Washington, D.C.: ULI–the Urban Land Institute, April–June 1990).

Local governments can also swap properties in their inventories for private construction of much-needed public space or facilities. If the market is sufficiently strong and land values high, cities often can directly swap land for space that might be difficult to finance or be approved by voters. Usually employed when a city is legally barred from offering any direct incentives to the private sector and when a city does not have traditional urban renewal powers, exchanges or swaps can also provide a city with increased control over the project's design and construction.

5.
Design

Principles of Urban Design For Downtown

"Create a spectacular environment, not spectacular architecture," said architect Stan Eckstut at a 1990 ULI seminar on creating a great city center. This view, now held by many developers and public officials, is something of a departure from prevailing views in the 1970s and 1980s. After the building boom of the early 1980s, many downtowns, with their skylines of dramatic lighting, interesting rooftops, and varieties of color, looked better from a distance than they functioned at close range. The focus seemed to be on a project's architecture rather than urban design.

Architecture concerns itself with individual buildings, while urban design looks to the entire environment. The goal of urban design is to develop an area, whether a downtown or an entire city, as a system of spaces, structures, and inhabitants rather than as a series of unrelated buildings and streets.[1] In other words, urban design can be thought of as "designing cities without designing buildings,"[2] with a key concern the "peopling of downtown."[3] The following general principles can thus be applied to the design of a successful downtown.[4]

Develop According to an Organized Pattern

A clear pattern of development within the downtown provides a framework that helps residents and visitors understand how to get around and identify uses and activities downtown. For example, reduced spaces between buildings and increased heights should give a visual clue to the physical location of the downtown office core. Major public spaces should mark crossroads at the heart of downtown. Retail shops should be clustered in one area, very close to the office core, and other districts should be located according to their function. Though each will likely have its own character, it should relate functionally and physically to its neighboring district to promote cohesiveness downtown.

Seattle boasts a good example of an easy-to-read downtown. The retail core, where development is less dense and public spaces more prevalent, is located adjacent to the office core. Residential development is located in a less dense area closer to the waterfront and in a peripheral area called the Denny Regrade. A straightforward grid for the street system reinforces this functional organization. In Seattle, it is easy for a pedestrian, local or not, to figure out how to get around.

---

[1] Marilyn Sgigel Schultz and Vivian Loeb Kasen, *Encyclopedia of Community Planning and Environmental Management* (New York: Facts on File Publications, 1984), pp. 412–13.

[2] Hamid Shirvani, *The Urban Design Process* (New York: Van Nostrand Reinhold Co., 1985), p. 6.

[3] William H. Whyte, *City: Rediscovering the Center* (New York: Doubleday, 1988), p. 2.

[4] Cyril B. Paumier et al., *Designing the Successful Downtown* (Washington, D.C.: ULI–the Urban Land Institute, 1988), pp. 53–65.

5-1   Retail, office, and residential buildings in downtown Seattle are linked by a straightforward street grid that enables locals and visitors alike to easily figure out their way around.

Accentuate the Downtown's Distinctive Identities

In the last several decades, U.S. citizens have become accustomed to shopping malls and shopping centers—artificial environments where designs are closely controlled, from parking lots to window displays to shopping bags. Yet a community's own design characteristics—the elements that reflect its past and explain the ways it developed—are found downtown, not in the suburbs. It is this originality and distinctiveness that should be highlighted in a downtown. Stan Eckstut reminds us that "authentic places" attract people. "Don't do attractions," he says. "Make an authentic place that attracts the locals. If they come, tourists will follow."

A downtown's existing and natural features are often what make it distinctive—a location along a body of water or richly detailed historic buildings, for example. "Preservation and recycling of old buildings has been one of the big ideas and big successes in most American downtowns over the past 20 years," says Washington, D.C., chief planner John Fondersmith.[5] Hillsboro, Texas, population 8,500, for example, en-

hanced its downtown by renovating over 100 buildings between 1980 and 1986. Portland, Oregon, ripped out a freeway that separated the CBD from the Willamette River and replaced it with a riverside park.

---

[5] Madis Pihlak, *The City of the 21st Century* (Tempe: Arizona State Univ., 1988), pp. 107–12.

5-2   Downtown's distinctive identity should be accentuated.

5-3   Downtown Orlando is known for its many small lakes. Lake Eola, for example, was redeveloped in the late 1980s and now attracts both downtown workers and city residents.

Alexandria, Virginia, encouraged the renovation of its 18th and 19th century buildings, including the redevelopment of a World War II torpedo factory along the Potomac River into studios and shops for artists. Other landmarks that are not necessarily historic, clocks or fountains, streetscapes, public art, and public spaces, for example, also serve to differentiate downtowns from other parts of the city.

Foster Variety

Diversity is, at least historically, a hallmark of downtown. A mix of uses—offices, different types of shops, such as storefront shops, urban specialty centers, farmers' markets, and street vendors, cultural attractions like museums and performing arts centers, entertainment and restaurants, and houses—should be encouraged downtown when the market exists for them. Building design and materials and special events can also foster variety.

Keep It Tight

The best downtowns are compact. Workers, visitors, and residents in Boston, for example, can walk or ride

transit easily from district to district. A compact downtown facilitates access and maximizes convenience for users and, as a result, creates opportunities for economic interaction among uses.

In many cities, downtowns expanded rather than filled in during the 1980s as developers leapfrogged over undeveloped or underused land to cheaper sites

5-4   A mix of uses, such as the retail shops, residences, and offices shown here, is a hallmark of a successful downtown.

73

5-5 Special events like this festival in St. Louis draw people downtown.

on the periphery. The result: huge gaps in downtown development as growth that was expected to connect development stalled. Buildings and uses that needed to be adjacent to each other to work most effectively remained separated. In Austin, Texas, for example, the view of Town Lake lured developers to leap five blocks from the traditional office core. Despite great views (including the notorious flush of bats that wing their way at dusk from underneath the bridge spanning the lake), office leasing lagged behind projections and ground-level retail shops suffered.

With the concern over costs, locating a stadium or arena is particularly susceptible to leapfrogging. But as St. Louis and Pittsburgh would attest, a stadium that is in or close to downtown reinforces the life of the city center. Milwaukee recognized this fact when it located its new arena downtown, as did Baltimore, which built a new baseball stadium for the Orioles near the Inner Harbor downtown.

Create "People Places" by Enhancing Street-Level Activity

Experience from the 1970s and 1980s suggests that inward-focused projects and mechanisms for getting people off the street—skywalks and tunnels, for example—have tended to deaden rather than enliven downtowns. Lafayette Place, the hotel/department store complex in Boston, is one example.

> Any important building should offer its energies and its trust to the street. Instead, Lafayette Place turns a gray shoulder to the street, looking more like a prison than a row of storefronts. Its blank walls and locked doors are an insult to the city and its people. . . . Lafayette Place is

a suburban mall dropped into the middle of a city, an inward-looking building with all its life hidden inside and nothing but blank walls facing toward the world around it.[6]

Projects with this sort of inward focus tend to trap visitors inside rather than encourage them to visit other buildings downtown or to shop in the surrounding neighborhood. The gray shoulder to the street tends to repel pedestrians, leaving the project for those with cars. Projects like this one result in a peopleless downtown and in insecure visitors.

The negative response to projects with inward-oriented atria, blank walls facing the street, and underground shopping has led to the comeback of storefront retailing. Many cities now require 50 to 100 percent of the street-level frontage of new developments to contain outward-looking retail shops. Pedestrian skyways and underground tunnels are being reconsidered as planners apply the concept of critical mass to pedestrians. Rather than spreading pedestrians out over three levels—sky, ground, and underground—development should encourage them to stay at one level, the street. A people place needs a sufficient number of pedestrians to make it successful.

Encourage Visual Continuity

Improvements downtown should be unified, with improvements in one area planned in conjunction with and reinforcing improvements in other areas. Visual continuity is particularly significant to individual merchants whose success depends at least partly on

---

[6] Robert Campbell, "The Very Complex Lafayette Place," *Boston Globe*, September 3, 1986.

5-6 New use for old plazas: playgrounds for daycare centers.

5-7 Building materials, fenestration, and street-/river-level design contribute to a building that fits into a downtown setting.

the ease with which potential patrons can locate and identify their businesses. But downtown design affects a number of elements besides the buildings—public infrastructure, marketing materials, and parking areas, for example. Revitalization's design improvement program should address all components that communicate a visual message to consumers about the downtown.

Architecture

Continuity at the ground level, where impact on pedestrians is greatest, should be an important priority for improvements in architectural design. Similarities in building materials and in the massing of building forms, spaces between buildings, positive relationships in the location and proportions of facade openings, and the organization of facades into clearly defined base and upper stories should be encouraged (see "Architectural Guidelines for Downtown" later in this chapter for more information).

It is important to note, however, that while architectural compatibility should be encouraged, so should

variation in design. The basic strategy is to identify characteristic approaches to the use of design elements in creating an architectural composition and to repeat selected elements from one building to another. It is also important to realize that the closer together buildings are clustered and the smaller the downtown, the more important continuity becomes. Smaller downtowns exhibit less tolerance for dramatic contrasts in form, materials, massing, and height.

Streetscapes

Just as they can be a major factor in creating a sense of identity for downtown, well-designed streetscapes can also function as a unifying visual element. The repeated use of selected street furnishings (light standards, paving, benches, trees, news vending machines, public phones, bus shelters) creates a visual overlay that reinforces downtown's organizing structure of streets and development blocks.

Street trees can be one of the best investments in downtown urban design. Especially when upper-story architecture is uninspiring or lacks continuity, a canopy of trees can provide a unifying visual element

5-8 Shade and seating contribute to successful public spaces.

75

5-9　Seasonal plants enhance the environment for pedestrians.

5-10　A coordinated program for informational signs reduces clutter.

while preserving the visibility of storefronts from the sidewalk and the street. To reinforce the linear character of urban streets, street trees should be regularly planted a uniform distance from the curb. The Pennsylvania Avenue Development Corporation has used this technique along the Avenue in Washington, D.C., and it is particularly effective as a shield for the street-level view of the FBI Building, which, for security reasons, is a fortress at ground level. (Even FBI director J. Edgar Hoover, for whom the building was named, called it the ugliest building he had ever seen!) In downtown Atlanta, over 300 trees were planted in the last three years, all funded through private donations.

Signs

Signs play an influential role in determining the degree of visual continuity downtown. Guidelines are

necessary to promote consistency in the size, design, and placement of business signs. A simplified and coordinated program for the use and design of public directional and informational signs is also needed to reduce visual clutter. Signs can be improved at relatively low cost and within a relatively short period to yield highly dramatic results. And seasonal or event-related banners, displays, and lighting should be provided to add visual stimulation to the streetscape. This sort of constantly changing and updated addition will reinforce the downtown as a place to visit again and again.

Parking

Downtown parking areas include on-street spaces, public and private lots, and parking garages. Certainly one of the most misunderstood of the downtown's design elements, parking is often blamed for many economic problems when it actually serves only a secondary function (see Chapter 6).

Graphics

Logos, posters, advertisements, and other broadcast or print marketing materials that convey a visual message about the downtown are also important components of design. Graphics should be high quality, reflecting the downtown's distinctive characteristics.

Stress Quality

Simplicity in design, quality materials, and a high level of maintenance provide a tangible expression of concern for the quality of pedestrians' experiences and extend an invitation to use public spaces.

The highest-quality street furniture and streetscape materials affordable should be used. The fundamental elements of a public environment—paving, trees, lighting, and seating—should receive top priority. Adequate maintenance should also be funded as part of the capital expense for design improvements. Downtown San Antonians realized the importance of maintenance when newly completed improvements in the streetscape failed to achieve the expected impact because of inadequate maintenance.

Architectural Guidelines For Downtown

"People don't come downtown because of good architecture," says developer Henry Faison. "But they do stay away from bad architecture." Exactly what is good and what is bad architecture for downtown properties changed somewhat in the 1980s. Fitting in

rather than standing out became important. Or, put another way, the goal should be a spectacular environment, not spectacular architecture.

Historic Preservation and Infill Development

The Role of Historic Preservation

Historic preservation, one way to assist in creating a spectacular environment, seeks to use a building's distinctive architectural characteristics for economic benefit. People enjoy working and shopping in unusual environments that offer value, quality, and a high level of personal service. Traditional buildings in a downtown make it absolutely distinctive. At the same time, historic preservation seeks to manage change in the built environment. Because communities constantly evolve, their building styles evolve, too. When well-designed new buildings blend with existing architecture, a rich pattern of visual clues that reflect social and cultural values throughout time is created.[7]

Preservation is not antichange; it does not advocate rebuilding demolished historic buildings, applying historic themes to new buildings, or saving all old buildings just for the sake of it. Instead, historic preservation recognizes good design from the past and places where exceptional events from the past occurred. It also maintains the built environment's special characteristics and encourages good new design—whether in the construction of new buildings or in the

[7] Kennedy Smith et al., "The Elements of Downtown Design," in *Revitalizing Downtown* (Washington, D.C.: National Trust for Historic Preservation, National Main Street Center, 1988).

5-11　To encourage those attending a downtown event to eat there too, Saint Paul's downtown council funded inserts for theater programs, newspapers, and magazines, and placed billboards at strategic freeway locations.

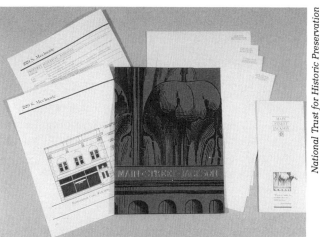

National Trust for Historic Preservation

5-12　Marketing materials reinforce visual continuity downtown.

5-13 Historic preservation is one strategy for creating a spectacular environment.

of a building might have been damaged and need to be repaired. The downtown is likely to include a variety of historical styles, which is its architectural strength, and no attempts should be made to make building facades conform to a particular style. New infill projects can reflect a 20th century appearance while enhancing existing structures through compatible scale, massing, architectural rhythm, and materials.

Building Entrances and Windows. The major building facade and entrance should be oriented to front the pedestrian spine, primary connectors, or arterials providing visibility for the project and an indication of its image. The location and articulation of entrances should replicate those of existing buildings, and the proportions of window openings should

[8] Smith et al., "Storefront Design," in *Revitalizing Downtown.*
[9] Ibid.

modification of existing ones—that is compatible with the old.

Design of Infill Projects

By its very name, infill development, which repairs and strengthens the urban fabric by eliminating gaps created by vacant lots and surface parking, must be compatible with existing development. Although each block and street has its own design characteristics, some guidelines are necessary for the design of infill projects.

Authenticity. The difference between a good reconstruction of an original building and an unsuccessful one lies in its degree of authenticity. The availability of pseudocolonial doorways, plastic, Spanish-like tiles, artificial "Swiss chalet" half-timbers, and wild West, rough-hewn cedar saloon fronts, for example, has led to the cheapening of many fine late 19th or early 20th century buildings. Authenticity is apt to be more cost-effective, for it is likely to survive longer than the passing fads of phony themes.[8]

In another unauthentic move, many downtown groups have encouraged property owners to cover their buildings with metal slipcovers, hoping that, by making a whole downtown block appear to be one building, the downtown itself would look like a shopping mall. Unfortunately, making downtown look like a shopping mall will not bring back business. In many instances, however, the aluminum or light-gauge steel panels used to cover downtown facades were usually installed quickly and inexpensively—and can be removed just as easily.[9] In other cases, authentic parts

5-14 The rebuilt South Station becomes an integral part of the pattern of Boston streets and public spaces.

reflect the pattern of upper-story windows along the block.

Front Setbacks. New development should replicate the setbacks of existing buildings to create a consistently developed edge, to reinforce downtown's pattern of development, and to enhance pedestrians' orientation. In the downtown core, existing setbacks usually coincide with the right-of-way line, making it possible for active ground-level uses to open into the pedestrian zone.[10]

Space between Buildings. Sideyard setbacks should echo the rhythm of spacing between existing buildings. In the more intensively developed urban core, sideyard setbacks are usually eliminated except where through-block pedestrian walkways are provided.

Building Height and Massing. Height and massing should be compatible with existing development. Existing low-rise development should change easily to taller new structures. The building mass should be broken into increments that correspond to the scale and massing of existing buildings through the use of setbacks and variable roof heights.

Organization of the Overall Facade. Street facades of new infill development should be organized into two major components, the ground-level storefront and the upper architecture, with strong horizontal elements separating the two. Especially on pedestrian streets where a sense of human scale and amenities is essential, ground-level storefronts should provide substantial window areas to share the building's interior activities with the street.

Separating the ground floor from the upper facade has been a common problem in the reconstruction of historic buildings. Brightly lit, oversized signs intended to attract the attention of passing motorists were plastered across the fronts of downtown buildings in the 1950s and 1960s, and many still remain. Like slipcovers, these signs are fairly easy to remove.

Building Color and Materials. While color choices in downtown buildings differ considerably depending on the materials used and the climate where the structures are built, color throughout each district should be compatible. Red brick, for example, is favored in Boston because of the use of that color in existing buildings. Further, it is best not to use the same color of paint for both the building's facade and the architectural trim, as details around windows, doors, and cornices will be difficult to see. The exception might be the use of a monochromatic scheme if such a color scheme is historically accurate.

Like unsuitable colors, inappropriate materials used to construct or alter a building can make the building stand out too much. While they need not replicate old

5-15 Liberty Place in Washington, D.C., demonstrates a sensitive transition between the existing and new buildings. Because of the setback, pedestrians can enjoy the historic building without sensing a looming presence of the new office tower.

ones, new materials should be compatible in texture, scale, and color already found in the downtown area.

In Corning, New York, for example, the nonprofit Market Street Restoration Agency, city departments, the local urban renewal agency, and merchants have restored and rehabilitated Market Street's historic structures using these principles. Dozens of too-large signs were removed and replaced with ones more in keeping with the scale of buildings and pedestrians. Efforts were made to rehabilitate the buildings authentically, even if individual buildings or ones right next to each other followed different architectural styles. The result: storefronts from the 1880s that fit comfortably next to ones from the 1930s. The Shoemaker Real Estate Building, for example, illustrates two periods of architecture: the upper, original facade, circa 1880, and the storefront, which was renovated in 1924. The

---

[10] This paragraph and the next four are based on Paumier et al., *Designing the Successful Downtown,* p. 105.

renovated Harold's Army and Navy, the only Art Deco storefront in town, features geometric and floral designs typical of the 1930s. The Eckerd Drug Store, once completely covered over (including the windows) with "modern" panels, has been restored to its original appearance.

On a larger scale, Gerald D. Hines Interests and architects Philip Johnson and John Burgee incorporated components of the existing historic 343 Sansome Building in downtown San Francisco to achieve a more economically viable building that was still sensitive to the building's history and the surrounding area. The original building was constructed in 1908 as an eight-story building in the neoclassical revival style. A 1929 renovation completely transformed and significantly modified the original structure into the current 13-story building. To achieve large, desirable floor plates, Hines added a compatible, connecting structure to the original building.

The new project's design is sensitive in scale and proportion to the existing building, using materials and details that have precedent in surrounding buildings. For example, light-colored granite cladding is used in response to the adjacent Bank of California

5-16   343 Sansome, San Francisco.

building, and terra-cotta detailing at the base of the project reflects the rich terra-cotta work in the existing 343 Sansome Building. At street level, the project features stone paving and an elegant new lobby and sculpture gallery. Traditional San Francisco bay windows are featured in the third through 14th floors, and the 14th floor houses a landscaped sun terrace. On the 15th floor, a formal loggia caps the building, lighted to achieve a striking identity for the project. The project was completed in spring 1990.

Major New Developments

The principal challenge in designing major downtown development projects is the successful incorporation of large-scale and/or high-rise structures into the existing context of smaller-scale buildings. On a street or in a district where a positive and consistent architectural character exists, the appropriate degree of compatibility is greater than that required when the existing architecture is mediocre or worse. Certainly, when the existing standard of design is poor, the repetition of negative design elements and characteristics just to fit in should be avoided![11]

When downtown's existing architecture creates a desirable identity and a human scale on the pedestrian spine and primary connector streets, it might be best to add higher-density high-rise buildings midblock or at locations bordering the traditional core. New higher-density buildings should be located within an easy walking distance of traditional retail concentrations (less than nine minutes),[12] however, if they are to reinforce downtown's economic vitality rather than create competing activity centers.

To create a sense of human scale at street level and to relate a high-rise building more positively to pedestrians, a number of design features can be used. First, to interrupt the upward thrust of a high-rise facade, a strong horizontal element that establishes a ceiling for the street can be created. The location of this lintel or setback, which defines the effective height of the facade as perceived at street level, should be coordinated with the height of cornice lines or lintels of existing buildings. The use of materials and forms that provide a scale of reference and a sense of three-dimensional articulation at ground level is also recommended. The use of reflective glass at ground level, for example, should be avoided.

[11] This paragraph and the next two are based on ibid., pp. 106–7.
[12] Lawrence O. Houstoun, Jr., "Nine Minutes to Retail: The Workplace-Marketplace Connection Downtown," *Urban Land*, December 1989, p. 28.

Kohn Pedersen Fox Associates, Jack Pottle/ESTO

5-17   712 Fifth Avenue, New York.

5-18   Bank One Center (tallest building in photograph), Dallas.

The 712 Fifth Avenue Building in New York, completed in 1990, for example, illustrates the principles of blending new buildings in with existing buildings and with pedestrians. This 52-story office/retail building, designed by Kohn Pederson Fox and Schuman Lichtenstein Claman and Efron, sits on a 17,500-square-foot site and totals 457,281 square feet of office space. The floor design, with the building core to the rear inside corner, not only provides for the maximum number of windowed offices and flexible interior space, but also relieves the street level of a looming office tower. The five-story base incorporates a public atrium and retail arcade into two landmark structures—the Rizzoli and Coty Buildings—while respecting the scale of the neighboring buildings on Fifth Avenue and on West 56th Street's special historic preservation district. At the street, the retail levels for Henri Bendel dominate the streetscape. Bendel's is housed behind the facades of several historic townhouses that constitute the base of the building along Fifth Avenue. The combination of the historic facades and original Lalique glass windows

creates a spectacular image for the retailer that was crucial to its decision to locate there.

Finally, sculpting the tops of towers can reduce the effect of a row of flat-topped high rises on the skyline. In downtown Dallas, for example, the 60-story glass prism that is First Interstate Bank Tower, Bank One Center, which features a copper roof, and Trammell Crow Center with its pyramidal top certainly add interest to the skyline. Lighting at night dramatically accentuates the top of high-rise buildings as well as the facades of historic structures. For the daytime, controls designed to preserve solar access to streets and public spaces and, for both daytime and nighttime, measures that help minimize the wind-tunnel effect and down drafts could also be considered.

Megastructures

Developments that take up a full block or span several blocks require particular care as far as their integration into the downtown environment. Megastructures must be designed to maintain pedestrian connections and view corridors along traditional street rights-of-way. It is critical that they be designed to share their internal activity with the street. Fortress-like architecture turns its back to the city, presents blank walls to the streets, and internalizes all its activity. Several steps can minimize these negative impacts:

- Breaking the horizontal expanse of long facades into increments that relate to the human scale by using fenestration, architectural details, and varying setbacks and rooflines to define a sequence of bays;
- Articulating the building mass to create an aggregation of smaller forms as a means of reducing the perception of overwhelming bulk;
- Providing a sequence of public spaces and walkways that are linked to the street grid;
- Using setbacks that reinforce the definition of the streetwall and bring interior activities to the edge of the pedestrian zone;
- Orienting major facades and entrances to the streets that serve as important pedestrian corridors;
- Using transparent ground-story facades and retail activity to integrate the structure functionally with other uses that edge the street; and
- Designing transitions in height and massing.[13]

Worldwide Plaza in New York, completed in fall 1989 by the Zeckendorf Company and Skidmore, Owings & Merrill, is a mixed-use project situated on the full block bounded by Eighth and Ninth Avenues between West 49th and 50th Streets. The site is approximately four acres, and the project includes 1.8 million square feet of office space in a 40-story skyscraper, 600 residential units in six- and seven-story buildings and another tower, 57,000 square feet of retail space in a two-story arcade, and a six-screen movie theater—definitely a megastructure but one that relates with its surroundings.

The office building, for example, steps down to lower-rise housing on the Ninth Avenue portion of the site. The rectangular residential structure reflects the prevailing neighborhood scale of six-story buildings along the side streets; the portion on Ninth Avenue, for example, is seven stories and contains ground-floor neighborhood shops. A slim 39-story residential tower sits within the interior of the block. The buildings surround an interior court and garden built on the roof of the parking garage. Six townhouse residences with stoops and private entrances sit along each side street. Access to all other apartments is from lobby entrances on 49th and 50th Streets. The indented masonry facade of the low-rise perimeter housing reflects the residential character of the surrounding area.

5-19   Worldwide Plaza, New York.

A 37,000-square-foot multilevel plaza separates the residential and commercial portions of Worldwide Plaza. The plaza contains about 50 trees, a large central fountain, two pavilions for selling food, and 1,074 linear feet of seating. The theater and 10,000 square feet of retail space are located under the plaza.

A new, enlarged 50th Street Station of the Eighth Avenue transit line and new entrances within the office building at 49th and 50th Streets will be created. Improvements to the transit line feature new escalators, an elevator for disabled individuals, and improved security. Niches carved at the two corners of the building will allow natural light to penetrate to both platform levels.

Parking

The major objectives in designing parking for downtown are to reduce its impact on the quality of downtown's visual environment and to minimize the

---

[13] Paumier et al., *Designing the Successful Downtown*, p. 107

82

extent to which it disrupts pedestrians' movement among retail uses and between the core and other activity centers.[14]

On-street Parking

It is generally desirable to maintain on-street parking for short-term convenience and to give the downtown a lived-in look. Either parallel or angled parking can work. Some prefer the urban look of parallel parking; others have found that the greater number of spaces associated with and the convenience of angled parking are worth the more suburban appearance.

Surface Lots

Surface parking lots create gaps in the downtown streetscape, interrupting the activities that make the street a vital and interesting place for people. Expanses of pavement and parked cars create a visually harsh environment that adversely affects downtown's image.

Consequently, surface parking lots must be located to minimize their visibility from major arterials and pedestrian-oriented streets. Their visual impact can be softened and screened with a perimeter landscape buffer of shade trees. A three- to four-foot-high screen wall or hedge might also be required to reduce the visibility of parked cars from the street. For security, however, a clear zone of four to eight feet should be

5-21   Some cities require retail or display windows at the ground level of garages.

maintained to ensure that the interior of the parking lot is visible from the street. Landscaped berms might not be an appropriate screening technique for the downtown area because of the space they require and the suburban image they convey.

Standards for the design of surface parking lots should also require interior landscaping, including islands defined by curbs and planted with shade trees to delineate each bay. Standards for illumination, criteria for the size and placement of signs, and booths for attendants in commercial lots are recommended.

Parking Structures

While parking structures require less land (for the number of cars accommodated) and can be screened more effectively than surface parking, their design and placement must be carefully considered. A location fronting on downtown's retail spine is not recommended. When parking structures are located on streets serving as primary pedestrian connectors, some cities are requiring 50 percent or more of the ground-level frontage to consist of retail space, a feature that can be effective if the garage is located within a large enough number of existing stores and if the demand

5-20   Landscape buffers should screen surface parking.

[14] This section on parking is summarized from ibid., pp. 85–86.

83

5-22 A landscaped setback softens the impact of a garage on pedestrians.

exists for additional ones. On streets where a parking structure's ground level will be occupied by cars, a landscaped setback should be required to soften the visual impact on the street and sidewalk.

Scale is a major factor in determining a parking structure's impact on the urban environment. The length of a parking structure's exposure on any given street should be held to a maximum of 250 to 300 feet. A maximum dimension of 180 feet, or the width of three bays of parking, is a preferred standard.

The architecture of the parking structure should incorporate exterior finish materials of the same quality as those used on nearby buildings. Neutral colors and architectural forms that echo the characteristics of adjacent buildings are also recommended. The street facade of the parking structure can be designed to replicate the fenestration patterns of nearby buildings, thereby helping the structure to blend into the core. In no case should the design of a parking structure draw attention to itself through the use of exotic shapes, materials, or colors.

Because security, perhaps more in terms of perceptions than reality, can be a concern and a disincentive to the use of parking structures, the design of the structure should incorporate safety considerations. Open or glass-enclosed stairwells, glass-enclosed elevators, and even levels of illumination can enhance the psychological comfort for users. Retail shops at ground level can have the same effect. In sensitive locations (for example, adjacent to residences), careful lighting design should eliminate views of light sources in the garage.

Parking structures that are an integral part of a building can present even more difficult problems in design than freestanding parking decks. A high-rise tower rising from a base parking podium is considered the least desirable design, for it tends to weaken the building's relationship to the street and to create an inhospitable ground-level environment. Underground parking has the least visual impact on the downtown and creates only minimal impact on pedestrians; however, underground parking is also the most costly option, at approximately twice the cost of above-grade parking structures.

6.
Transportation and Parking

Misperceptions about Commuting and Congestion

Even before the automobile, congestion was part of urban living. Over time, the degree of congestion has increased to the point of striking fear in the hearts of commuters, whether they are employees or employers. But it is a myth to assume that the major challenge of urban transportation is to improve commuting to downtown jobs. In fact, businesses averse to congestion that have moved to the suburbs to avoid traffic are discovering that growing traffic problems have caught up with them.

According to the 1980 Census, twice as many suburbanites commuted to suburban jobs in metropolitan areas as to jobs in central cities, and the 1990 Census is not expected to reveal a move away from that trend. By 1983, it was estimated that, in urban areas, the commuters to the CBD probably represented less than 10 percent of all highway travelers during the heaviest rush hour.[1]

Indeed, research shows that higher-density residential and office projects typical in a downtown generate fewer driving trips and more transit use per unit than do low-density projects.[2] Density is necessary to provide the critical mass needed to support transit. Moreover, clustering uses in a mixed-use downtown and in MXDs makes possible an orientation toward pedestrians with shopping, restaurants, and recreation available within walking distance. Furthermore, *new* development downtown can have a dramatically different effect on the rate of increasing congestion than would the same development in the suburbs. A study of mobility and congestion among Houston businesses offers useful insights into the fear that congestion in the inner city makes downtown unsuitable as a business location.[3]

The study estimates that a new office building of 1 million square feet in downtown Houston would add about 4,000 employees to the downtown work force. Assuming a 13 percent rate of transit use and a 1.38 percent rate of car pooling, 2,522 more cars would drive downtown as a result of the development of such a building. At an average suburban site, the same number of employees would add 3,600 cars, because fewer would use transit or car pool. But because downtown Houston, at the time of the study, had 84 lanes of freeway and arterial access, compared to only 20 lanes for the average suburban site, the same build-

---

[1] ULI–the Urban Land Institute, *Myths and Facts about Transportation and Growth* (Washington, D.C.: Author, 1989).

[2] Institute of Transportation Engineers, *Trip Generation*, 4th ed. (Washington, D.C.: Author, 1987), pp. 887, 1151.

[3] Rice Center, "Mobility and Congestion: Office Location Issues in Houston," Research Brief 1 (Houston: Author, 1979), p. 7.

ing would increase traffic by an average of 32 cars per lane downtown versus 180 more per lane in the suburbs—a 36 percent increase on each lane of suburban street!

Still, recognizing that transportation problems are dire in the suburbs does not minimize the fact that traffic congestion is a fact of life downtown. But while suburban sprawl—low-density development dependent on the auto—continues to affect suburban areas, it could give downtowns a market edge in the 1990s.

Solutions to Downtown Transportation Problems: Getting There

Even smaller downtowns enjoy some of the full range of transportation services needed to serve a metropolitan region. In most towns and cities, downtown is still the primary focus of the city's transportation network, which might include high-speed intercity highway and rail connections, the highest concentration of regional transit services, commercial and municipal parking facilities priced for different markets, interconnected, computerized traffic signals, convenient taxi service, access to regional airports and port terminals, and sidewalks.

The best-located suburban center rarely has more than two of these services and frequently enjoys only the locational advantage of direct access to two freeways—one to downtown and one to residential markets. Downtown, on the other hand, enjoys not only this panoply of transportation services, but also advantages of its land use. The scale and density of downtown make many shops, restaurants, services, and cultural opportunities within walking distance of offices and each other, allowing commuters a high level of service without feeling stranded without a car. It also allows shoppers and commuters who choose to drive to their initial destination the chance to complete many errands without moving their cars.

But if misperceptions exist about commuting to downtown and its congestion compared to the suburbs, so too do misperceptions exist about how to improve upon existing advantages to meet recognized transportation problems. Developers, city staff, and city officials interviewed for this book, for example, most often cited new rail transit systems as the most promising solution for remedying traffic congestion. One mayor dismissed the challenge to this assumption as a "conspiracy led by the automobile manufacturers." Other misperceptions, that highways can no longer be built in urban areas and that, if they could,

they should not be because they would only fill with traffic, or that professionals will not ride buses, only hinder the discussion and development of solutions for transportation problems. This section presents the potential solutions for downtown transportation needs while debunking the myths that surround them.

In Search of the Holy Rail

A common belief is that, in high-growth areas with low levels of transit ridership, major capital investments in new rail systems will reduce driving substantially.[4] Newly emerging cities in the South and West believe they can build rail systems that will serve their downtowns and focus development in the same way that downtown New York, Boston, Chicago, and Philadelphia have done. But the facts indicate otherwise. Even in San Francisco and Washington, D.C., which seemed to be logical candidates for subways, the systems that opened in the 1970s have had mixed success. Both systems have played important roles in serving their downtowns, although less significant than their planners hoped. In both regions, however, most of the job growth has been in the suburbs, where a rail system cannot compete with the car. Therefore, neither system has been able to increase the overall percentage of commuters using public transportation, and the traffic problems in the suburbs of each city have become legendary.[5]

Where does rail transit work? An intensive study of criteria for new transit systems found that the travel volumes needed to justify fixed guideway systems are dense residential corridors, high levels of downtown employment, and low levels of car ownership.[6] Many of the newer Sunbelt cities considering rail systems fill none of these criteria. Although the study found that 10 cities had a potential for new light-rail systems, a 1988 report by the Urban Mass Transportation Administration (UMTA) identified nine other cities with systems in the planning stages that did not meet the initial criteria.[7] Thus, rail transit works best in high-density cities that already have it. It is an expensive

[4] This section is based on Robert T. Dunphy, "In Search of the Holy Rail," *Urban Land*, May 1990, pp. 36–39.
[5] This paragraph and the next one are excerpted from ULI, *Myths and Facts*.
[6] Boris Pushkarev and Jeffrey Zupan, *Urban Rail in America: An Exploration of Criteria for Fixed Guideway Transit* (Washington, D.C.: U.S. Dept. of Transportation, Urban Mass Transportation Administration, 1988).
[7] U.S. Dept. of Transportation, Urban Mass Transportation Administration, *The Status of the Nation's Local Mass Transportation: Performance and Conditions*, Report to Congress (Washington, D.C.: Author, 1988).

NEW LIGHT-RAIL SYSTEMS IN NORTH AMERICA, 1978 to 1993

	OPENING DATE	LENGTH (MILES) OPERATING	UNDER CONSTRUCTION	CONSTRUCTION COST PER OPERATING MILE (MILLIONS OF DOLLARS)	DAILY RIDERSHIP 1987	PROJECTED[1]
Edmonton	1978	6.4	1.8	$19[2]	25,000	—
Calgary	1981	17.4	–	16[2]	65,000	—
San Diego	7/81	22.2	11.5	7	24,000	28,000–30,000
Buffalo	5/85	6.4	–	83	30,000	84,000
Vancouver	1/86	13.1	1.9	51[2]	65,000	65,000
Portland, Ore.	9/86	15.5	–	21	20,000	42,500
Miami	4/86	1.9	–	76	12,000	41,000
Sacramento	11/87	18.3	–	10	10,000	30,000–35,000
San Jose	12/87	6.0	14.0	25	–	43,000
Detroit[3]	8/87	2.9	–	69	10,000–20,000	71,000
Jacksonville[3]	1988	0.8	–	47	–	10,000
Los Angeles/ Long Beach	1990	21.0	–	38	–	35,000
Los Angeles/ Century	1993	–	17.3	13	–	65,000

[1]Earliest projections of ridership from environmental impact studies, generally for 1990. In some cases, projections assume more extensive rail systems (Buffalo and Detroit) or other transportation improvements (Miami).

[2]Costs of Canadian rail systems converted to U.S. dollars at 1988 exchange rates.

[3]Downtown people-mover system.

Sources: Urban Land Institute, *Mass Transit* magazine (various issues), UMTA staff, and Canadian transit operators.

and ineffective way to reduce congestion in a city that has not developed around rail transit.

Still, in many communities, heavy rail might be dismissed but light rail remains an idea with great

Downtown Partnership of Baltimore, Inc.

6-2   With the Inner Harbor overflowing with visitors and with the downtown office district employing 100,000 people, Downtown Partnership of Baltimore, Inc., was intent on drawing some of those people up Charles Street to shop, dine, or just visit. After exhaustive analyses of trolley systems around the country, the organization spearheaded the development of a new trolley system with the city buying the cars and another entity operating and maintaining the system. Today the Baltimore trolley system can be credited with a 20 percent increase in business and a daily ridership of 12,000.

emotional appeal. The new light-rail line must still contend with traffic, however—unless it is buried in a tunnel, an expensive proposition—and it then becomes a fixed route that cannot be adjusted to shifting markets.

Other than some special situations in cities like San Diego and Portland, Oregon, a number of recent light-rail projects have been found to be more costly than planned and to serve fewer riders than projected. A new UMTA study, for example, found that for each of the four light-rail systems studied (Buffalo, Pittsburgh, Miami, and Portland), total ridership was no more than half of original forecasts while construction costs were at least twice those of the original budgets.[8] Furthermore, operating costs were higher than expected. Still, light-rail systems are tremendously appealing to local officials, perhaps because the lion's share of the cost is often borne by the federal government.

The UMTA report suggests that the technical aspects of a rail system need to be carefully studied. If communities are willing to shoulder the burden, a light-rail—or even a heavy-rail—system could be an

[8] U.S. Dept. of Transportation, Urban Mass Transportation Administration, *Urban Rail versus Transit Projects: Forecast versus Actual Ridership Costs* (Washington, D.C.: Author, October 1989).

The San Diego Trolley, opened in 1981, is one light-rail system that has received widespread praise from the national transportation community. Completed on time and under budget, the system has already exceeded the ridership forecast for 1995 (28,000) and has achieved fares covering 95 percent of operating costs. Moreover, the system was constructed and is operated without federal funds.

How did San Diego do it? Purchasing an abandoned railway right-of-way cheaply, using off-the-shelf, proven technology, and building no-frills trolley stations helped. Linking two major destinations—downtown San Diego and the international border—and operating in a favorable political climate helped as well. The big question is whether San Diego's conditions are so exceptional that the city's experiences are irrelevant elsewhere.

service as a train, especially if both must share the street with other traffic. What counts is how well the two transportation modes meet riders' needs for speed, cost, and convenience. To offer higher frequency and better visibility, bus service can be concentrated on a single street rather than scattered over many adjacent streets, and such transit malls can be closed to autos. Denver and Portland, Oregon, for example, have used this approach successfully. Outside downtown, buses can be given a dedicated lane on a freeway or arterial street to ensure high-speed travel. Most of the high-occupancy-vehicle lanes discussed later in this chapter operate this way.

Ottawa, Ontario, considered a rail system but opted for a network of exclusive busways, offering high-speed service point to point and the flexibility of a bus to pick up and drop off passengers within walking distance of their destinations. A particularly innovative solution that blends flexibility and speed is the newly opened bus tunnel in Seattle, which allows buses to operate on electric power in an exclusive facility under busy Third Avenue and then to switch to diesel power outside downtown.

appropriate choice. As a result of the UMTA study, however, at least cities now have a better idea of the costs involved.

High-Caliber Bus Service

While rail might be the answer for some downtowns, other options should certainly be investigated. For most downtowns, a bus can offer the same level of

New Roads and Improved Highways

Some say that highways can no longer be built in urban areas, believing that the problems involved in building metropolitan highways are insurmountable. In addition to the normal difficulties encountered in building highways in established areas, today's engineers must cope with resentment over past projects that were insensitive to the surrounding community,

6-4   Seattle has coordinated its transportation hub with its downtown retail hub. Westlake Center, a specialty retail center, is not only a monorail terminal but also a connection to the city's new underground bus tunnel. The bus station mezzanine (shown here) connects shoppers to Westlake Center and three department stores.

such as elevated highways that separate downtown from a waterfront. A general decline in funding nationwide, the cost of land and construction, and growing sensitivity to environmental and community impacts, some say, will continue to rule out highway improvements as a potential solution to congestion.[9]

But highways are still being built. Some cities have overcome considerable political and financial problems to build highways even in downtown or built-up locations, typically as part of the interstate system. Boston, for example, is reconstructing the Central Artery at a cost of $3.5 billion, and Los Angeles built the $1.8 billion Century Freeway. Such projects are expensive and controversial, but despite differences of opinion about whether they make sense, they demonstrate that, given sufficient political support and money, highways still can be built.

Part of the controversy surrounding new or improved highways is the myth that a new road generates increased traffic without relieving existing facilities. The weakness of this argument becomes clear if it is applied, say, to new schools (they just fill up with students) or libraries (they only fill up with books). The fact that a new highway is well traveled demonstrates its success in offering a shorter or cheaper route for users or access to new markets for industry or better jobs, housing, or shopping for travelers. Not surprisingly, a new road in a congested area attracts traffic, especially where few new roads have been constructed. Attracting traffic and relieving other facilities are exactly what it was supposed to do. The Federal Highway Administration has calculated that each dollar invested in improving the interstate highway system saves five dollars in costs to users—a substantial economic benefit.[10] Improved highways are essential to a balanced regional transportation system. They can be and are being built in urban areas, and their use is an indication of the need for them, not a sign of their failure.

In addition to the consideration of building new or improving existing roads and highways, techniques for managing existing highways leading to downtown at peak efficiency must also be considered. Three options can improve efficiency.

Clear the Road to Reduce Congestion

One recent realization is that the time wasted as a result of accidents, overturned trucks, drivers running out of gas, and so on accounts for most of the delay on urban freeways.[11] As a result, one very effective technique to reduce congestion is to detect and clear the incident as soon as possible, perhaps by having a tow truck posted at incident-prone locations.

It can also involve a more sophisticated electronic surveillance, control, and information system.

Move More People, Not More Cars

By restricting access on a major thoroughfare to only buses or vehicles carrying several people (the exact minimum to be determined locally), it is possible to increase the carrying capacity of a corridor and to encourage higher speeds. Because downtowns have the highest percentage of commuters car pooling or riding transit, such high-occupancy-vehicle (HOV) lanes present an opportunity for improving travel to downtown. A 1990 survey of HOV lanes in North America found 40 projects in 20 different metropolitan areas—virtually all of them serving downtown markets. Although most of the projects involve freeways, the concept has also been applied to arterial streets in downtowns.[12]

Improve Traffic Flow

A variety of traffic engineering techniques are available to improve traffic flow to and within downtown. Improved traffic signals have been found to provide a high payoff in higher speeds and reduced delays. Other proven techniques include reversible traffic lanes, improved intersections, and turning lanes.

Transportation Management Programs

When light-rail systems or new roads are not the solution to congestion, transportation management programs have become popular. The concept makes sense: by promoting transit, urging commuters to car pool, bicycle, or walk, convincing employers to offer flexible hours, and raising interest in telecommuting and a host of other options, transportation management takes vehicles off the road.[13] These steps, in turn,

[9] This paragraph and the next two are excerpted from ULI, *Myths and Facts.*

[10] American Association of State Highway and Transportation Officials, *Keeping America Moving: The Bottom Line* (Washington, D.C.: Author, 1989).

[11] Jeffrey A. Lindley, "Urban Freeway Congestion: Quantification of the Problem and Effectiveness of Potential Solutions," *ITE Journal*, January 1987, p. 27.

[12] Katherine F. Turnbull, "A Summary of Operating High-Occupancy Vehicles in North America," paper presented at the 1990 National HOV Facilities Conference, Washington, D.C., April 10–12, 1990.

[13] Robert T. Dunphy and Ben C. Lin, *Transportation Management through Partnerships*, Foreword (Washington, D.C.: ULI–the Urban Land Institute, 1990), p. 1.

6-5　Transit corridors might require deep waiting areas, but riders do not want the area to feel deserted even when it is not crowded.

reduce congestion, especially during the critical morning and evening peak travel hours.

Programs Offered by Developers

In some areas, developers and property owners have taken the initiative to finance transportation management or commuter assistance programs. Such programs are often useful in marketing new projects to both prospective tenants and buyers. Other programs are created through negotiations with local officials during development approval. At Citicorp Plaza in downtown Los Angeles, for example, the developer offered to match riders, subsidize van pools and transit fares, and provide preferential pool parking to the 5,000 workers in the building as part of a negotiated program with the city.

Although a few developments, mostly in California, require the active participation of tenants and buyers through covenants, conditions, and restrictions in leases and deeds, the vast majority of

6-6

SELECTED DOWNTOWN ORGANIZATIONS OPERATING COMMUTER TRANSPORTATION SERVICES

BUSINESS ORGANIZATION	RIDE SHARING AND TRANSIT PROMOTION	EMPLOYER TRANSPORTATION COORDINATORS	FARE SUBSIDES/ TRANSIT SERVICES	IN-HOUSE RIDE-SHARING MATCHING	HELPED TO ESTABLISH COMMUTER ASSISTANCE ORGANIZATION SUBSIDARY	REGIONAL RIDE-SHARING ORGANIZATION
Bellevue Downtown Association	Yes	Some	Fares only	Via TMA[1]	Bellevue TMA[1]	Seattle METRO
Central City Association of Los Angeles	Yes	Some	—	—	Downtown Los Angeles TMA[1]	Commuter Computer
Century City Chamber of Commerce	Yes	Some	—	Via TMA[1]	Century City TMA[1]	Commuter Computer
Charlotte Uptown Development Corporation	Yes	Some	Yes	Via TMA[1]	Uptown Transportation Council	City of Charlotte
Newport Center	Yes	Some	—	Via TMA[1]	Newport Center TMA[1]	OCTD Commuter Network[2]
The Denver Partnership	Yes	Some	Fares only	—	Denver Civic Ventures	Denver Regional COG

[1]Transportation management association; includes transportation management organizations.
[2]Organized network among members.
Sources: ULI survey, 1986 to 1990; and Robert T. Dunphy and Ben C. Lin, *Transportation Management through Partnerships* (Washington, D.C.: ULI–the Urban Land Institute, 1990), p. 43.

developer-sponsored commuter programs involve voluntary participation by employers and tenants. It can be difficult, however, to enlist their cooperation. When created as the result of negotiations with local officials, such privately financed commuter assistance programs are usually required for new developments only. Existing developments and employers remain unaffected, despite their substantial contribution to area traffic.

Transportation Management Associations

In addition to developer-sponsored commuter assistance programs, the 1980s saw a movement toward creating specialized nonprofit organizations to facilitate the private sector's involvement in resolving transportation problems. Narrowly focused on transportation issues, these organizations are most commonly referred to as "transportation management associations" (TMAs). Because TMAs are established primarily to mitigate traffic problems in rapidly growing areas, many involve active participation by developers as well as employers.

To help change workers' travel behavior, TMAs try to involve as many existing and new employers as possible in ride-sharing programs and the promotion of transit. Sharing a larger, common data base of applications for ride sharing throughout a downtown increases the probability that an applicant will be successfully matched. In addition, TMAs can pool resources to provide services like matching riders or shuttle and area circulator transits that individual developers and employers often find too expensive to sponsor themselves. And TMAs have become actively involved in assisting employers and developers to create and operate transportation management programs in communities with trip reduction ordinances.

While the majority of TMAs already established are located in suburban growth centers rather than downtowns, the number in downtowns is increasing as downtown developers and public officials attempt to take advantage of every tool possible to keep the CBD competitive. TMAs are either fully operational or being organized in downtown Hartford, Los Angeles, San Diego, Charlotte, North Carolina, and Sacramento.

Ordinances to Increase Ride Sharing And Using Transit

In response to rising congestion, some communities, such as Bellevue, Washington, and Fort Collins, Colorado, and some counties in Maryland have passed ordinances encouraging employers and developers to implement trip reduction measures, usually through sponsorship of voluntary commuter assistance programs.[14] Such ordinances allow development to continue so long as road conditions do not deteriorate to the point that a substantial number of community residents demand a moratorium on growth. In Fort Collins, for example, a formal system for evaluating real estate development proposals assigns "development approval points" for programs to mitigate traffic congestion. Points are also assigned for other desired outcomes of development, such as quality of design, mix of land uses, and location.

Seeking a greater impact on areawide traffic congestion, some municipalities and counties have enacted local ordinances that *require* employers and developers to sponsor or participate in traffic mitigation programs. These trip reduction ordinances might specify that employers and developers stipulate reductions in the proportion of commuters driving alone to a local work site. The reductions could be calculated for an average weekday or only for peak traffic hours. Large employers and developments usually face additional requirements, such as providing an on-site transportation coordinator and developing an approved transportation management program. Most ordinances require employers and property owners to take at least four actions:

- Regularly post and distribute information about ride sharing and transit schedules;
- Conduct an annual survey of workers' travel patterns;
- Designate a transportation coordinator; and
- Develop a plan of specified commuter programs to reduce the number of trips.

Nationwide, at least 23 communities have mandatory requirements for participation in such programs, and at least 12 other jurisdictions are considering such ordinances. Found mostly in California, trip reduction ordinances are relatively new, most having been implemented within the last five years. Because smaller cities are grappling with rising congestion as a result of rapid growth during the 1980s, however, such ordinances are increasing in popularity.

Joint Development

Joint development, real estate development that is closely linked to public transportation services and stations, is another form of transportation management. With the many new rail systems and extensions of existing systems that broke ground nationwide

---

14 This section is based on ibid., pp. 38–39.

The Gallery at Market East is one of the first contemporary shopping malls to be developed in the old downtown of a major U.S. city. Using a strategy of joint development, project developers, which included a host of public and private entities, hoped to revitalize what had been a preeminent shopping address in Philadelphia and to enhance the area as an office location as well.

Located on Market Street East between Eighth and Eleventh Streets some six blocks east of City Hall in Philadelphia, the project was built in two phases. Finished in 1977, Gallery I contains 1.35 million square feet of gross leasable area in an enclosed, midblock mall connecting two major department stores at four levels, with 2,000 parking spaces (850 of which are in a garage connected to the mall by a covered skyway). Gallery II, completed in 1983, is an adjacent four-level, 350,000-square-foot complex that includes a J.C. Penney department store and approximately 600 additional garage parking spaces. One Reading Center, a 619,000-square-foot, 32-floor office tower adjacent to The Gallery, was finished in 1984.

Market Street East had always been well served by transportation, but goals for the Gallery included joining transit lines and thus adding capacity, enhancing existing transit facilities, and integrating a mix of other uses at the transportation hub. Toward that end, Gallery I was designed so that the Eighth and Market Street subway station, with stops for all three of the region's subway lines, opened directly into one of the department stores, Strawbridge and Clothier, and into the mall's lowest retailing level. The station itself was improved by widening the concourse and installing new lighting, floors, and fixtures. Further, Gallery II connects to a new sta-

6-8   The Gallery at Market East, Philadelphia, is a transportation and retail hub.

tion for the commuter rail tunnel that links the Penn Central and Reading Commuter trains.

The project has succeeded in accomplishing a number of its goals. The transportation hub brings thousands of commuters a day into the concourses of Market Street East buildings. The retail portion is 93 percent occupied, employs 2,500 people, and, despite some slowing during the recession in 1990 and 1991, reported sales of $320 per square foot in 1990, nearly double the national average. The Market Street East office submarket, which has grown by over 2 million square feet, to a total of 7.3 million square feet, has a 5 percent vacancy rate, compared to 12.8 percent overall downtown.[1]

---

[1]Leslie Scism, "A Drive to Restore Luster to Downtown Philadelphia," *New York Times*, May 26, 1991.

during the 1980s, joint development will increase in the 1990s, particularly in downtown transit hubs. Jointly developed projects can be office towers built over a subway station using air rights or retail malls with a direct entrance to a transit terminal. Regardless of the form it takes, joint development pairs private and public resources to achieve a project that will benefit both sectors. Participating developers stand to benefit from the increased market appeal of new developments linked with transit facilities, providing a competitive advantage in a soft market with chronic traffic problems, and opportunities to avoid the costs

of land acquisition and site preparation or at least to share construction costs and risks with a public agency. At the same time, the public stands to benefit from 1) increased ridership for the transit agency and increased convenience for transit riders with the proximity of residential or commercial developments and transit facilities, 2) additional revenues to the transit agency from the sale or lease of real estate held by the agency, 3) reduced capital costs by sharing some of the costs of land acquisition and construction for new transit facilities with private developers, 4) improved connections between different modes of transportation and connections between public and private transportation systems, and 5) an enhanced environment through station amenities added by private developers.

Certain risks are involved in creating joint developments, however. First, the real estate market is often unpredictable. If a market is already weak, public involvement could be perceived as adding risk. Second, delays are a chronic source of aggravation with joint development projects. And delays can arise from many sources: public opposition, planning and impact studies required for funding or approval, legal problems, staff changes in public agencies or in elected officials, delayed grant funds from state and federal agencies, and natural disasters.

Site Access Planning

For most significant downtown projects, a site access study should be conducted. It is now a requirement in a growing number of cities, and local standards establish the guidelines. The Institute of Transportation Engineers suggests a traffic access/impact study be done for any project expected to generate at least 100 peak-hour, peak-direction trips, or if special concerns exist over traffic or impact on the neighborhood. Some key decisions must be worked out with the reviewer:

- How large an area will be affected? It is suggested that the study area extend at least to the nearest traffic signal, a fairly limited area for most downtown projects.
- What other off-site projects are assumed in protecting traffic in the area? This decision is

particularly critical, considering the inherent uncertainty of proposed projects.

- What improvements to the transportation network are committed?
- What horizon year must be evaluated? As a minimum, the completion date of the project should be studied. For large projects, significant interim stages should be examined to make sure that needed improvements are made on time.[15]

The results will be used not only to meet required access for the proposed project, but also to determine the need to improve nearby intersections and the developer's share. One primary advantage of a downtown retail location is that a built-in market—workers, shoppers, and visitors—is already there. Transportation expert Herbert S. Levinson, who has conducted many studies of downtowns, points out the "retail deduction" necessary for a new downtown store, where half the shoppers are drawn from existing office workers. This captive market is illustrated by results from a survey of mixed-use sites in downtowns compared to the suburbs. At the downtown sites, 61 percent of employees reported they patronized the same development, compared to only 28 percent of workers at mixed-use developments outside downtown.[16] This market synergy must be reflected in the projections of parking and traffic to avoid double counting.

---

[15] Institute of Transportation Engineers, *Traffic Access and Impact Studies for Site Development: A Recommended Practice* (Washington, D.C.: Author, 1991).

[16] ULI–the Urban Land Institute, *Shared Parking* (Washington, D.C.: Author, 1983), p. 39.

| 6-9 | ACCESS PLANNING IN DOWNTOWN BOSTON |

Since 1986, the city of Boston and the Boston Redevelopment Authority have required access plans as an element of design review for office projects at least 100,000 square feet and for residential projects containing at least 30 units. An impact assessment study analyzes the project's impact on traffic as well as other known projects on a cumulative basis, and presents mitigation measures the developer will take to minimize these effects. Recognizing the mutual efforts needed to make improvements, the access plan outlines steps and procedures that the city and the project sponsor can take to ensure implementation. After responsibilities are negotiated, the transportation commissioner, the director of the

redevelopment authority, and the developer sign an access plan agreement. The city benefits from the applicant's willingness to make capital investments and to implement measures that will encourage alternatives to driving—setting up ride-sharing and parking management programs subsidizing transit passes, for example. If successful, the benefits to the developer include being able to count on improvements promised by the city.

Source: Richard A. Dimino, Chi-Hsin Shao, and Andrew J. McClurg, "Development Review for Traffic Mitigation: Boston's Access Plan Experience," in *Technical Papers from ITE's 1990, 1989, and 1988 Conferences* (Washington, D.C.: Institute of Transportation Engineers, 1990), p. 404.

6-10   Providing for vehicles does not have to come at the expense of pedestrians. Note the "bus only" lane and the inviting sidewalks.

Pedestrian and Vehicular Circulation: Getting Around Downtown

Once downtown, commuters should encounter an efficient vehicular circulation system that strengthens downtown's attractiveness as a market. The grid system, a traditional circulation system in downtowns, certainly goes far toward meeting this goal. The grid could well be the best pattern for accommodating both automobiles and pedestrians, so much so that even suburban planners are turning their backs on culs-de-sac and curvilinear or discontinuous streets—now thought to cause congestion rather than prevent it—in favor of the neotraditional grid.[17]

A hierarchy of streets within a grid system, including major arterials, collectors, transitways, and local access streets, is the best way to accommodate both vehicles and pedestrians. Major arterials, which carry the heaviest traffic volumes, can accommodate parallel pedestrian movement and crossing points, but the safety and efficiency of traffic flow should remain the primary concern on these streets. In contrast, collector streets serve a more important role for pedestrians and must provide a better balance between vehicles' and pedestrians' needs. Transitways and local access streets are the most important of downtown's pedestrian network. Their design should give priority to the scale and amenities appropriate for downtown's most important people places.

Catering to Pedestrians, Not Cars

To create a downtown that will support a mix of uses, it is essential that the downtown, while providing for vehicles, also provides for pedestrians. And, while providing for pedestrians might appear to come at the expense of motorists, providing adequate space for sidewalks and special walk phases in the timing of traffic signals encourages downtowners to walk, itself a form of relief from congestion.

Downtowners are already predisposed to walking. In Houston, for example, a city not generally noted as a city of walkers, a 1986 survey found that two-thirds of all trips made within the downtown were pedestrian trips, compared to only one in five trips made by workers within the other three major activity centers—Post Oak, Greenway Plaza, and West Houston. The survey noted that downtown workers were willing to walk farther than those employed in other centers.[18]

Clearly emphasizing the development of an on-street pedestrian system downtown should be the primary element of downtown pedestrian circulation, not only to take advantage of the existing framework

---

[17] Except where noted, this paragraph and the following eight are summarized, for the most part, from Cyril B. Paumier et al., *Designing the Successful Downtown* (Washington, D.C.: ULI–the Urban Land Institute, 1988), pp. 65–73.

[18] Houston/Galveston Area Council, "Houston's Major Activity Centers and Worker Travel Behavior" (Houston: Author, 1987), p. V-29.

and to maintain the visibility of businesses and access to services, but also because the alternatives, pedestrian malls and skywalks, entail problems. The downtown's spine should be readily identifiable as the primary corridor by its concentration of retail shops and streetscape treatment and should stand out as the most richly designed component of the pedestrian system. Ideally, major anchors should be located at each end of the spine to maximize the volume of pedestrians along the spine's length. In addition, the spine is the main location for street vendors, cafes, outdoor performances, displays, and special design elements, such as paving, public art, and water features.

Primary connectors are the streets that serve as major paths of movement for pedestrians and should provide the primary physical connections between downtown's activities and amenities. Like the spine, they should be designed to attract and accommodate pedestrians. In Atlanta, for example, the Central Area Plan identifies "primary pedestrian routes," where pedestrians are expected and encouraged, truck loading and driveways are discouraged, and low vehicle speeds are encouraged.[19] Secondary connectors should provide a minimum level of amenity for pedestrians.

6-11 Sidewalks along Miami's Ocean Drive have gone from five feet—with utility poles and parking meters—to 15 feet—with palm trees—reflecting a more pedestrian orientation.

Through-block connectors in the form of open-air walkways, courtyards, covered arcades, or lobby atria are also important, as they provide shortcuts through developed blocks.

Another important consideration in pedestrian circulation is the design of the streetscape in general, including the width of sidewalks, paving, landscaping, and furniture. Streetscaping on the spine and primary connectors should help create a unified image and defined visual structure for downtown and an inviting and comfortable environment for pedestrians. Simplicity and consistency are the keys to successful streetscaping.

A minimum width of 15 feet for a sidewalk is desirable along the pedestrian spine and primary connectors. One 15-foot zone provides for both a 10-foot pedestrian zone adjacent to storefronts and a five-foot zone adjacent to the curb. A 20-foot sidewalk allows seating and public art to be incorporated without intruding on pedestrians' space. Transit streets require broader sidewalks to accommodate waiting areas at the curb.

The use of special paving on primary streets has a tremendous effect in creating a sense that pedestrians belong on the street and that streets are not just for vehicles. When used consistently, paving also provides a visible link that reinforces the pedestrian system and makes the pedestrian zone highly visible to motorists. Paving materials should provide a smooth surface that is comfortable in all weather for people in all types of footwear, including high heels, and for people in wheelchairs or pushing strollers.

Seating is best provided in the design of buildings, plazas, and parks by using ledges, steps, walls, movable tables and chairs, and more conventional benches. Seating should be provided rather than avoided because of possible use by street people. "The notion that we can't do something because it will be misused is barbaric," says Pennsylvania Avenue Development Corporation executive director M.J. Brodie, discussing the rationale for not including seating in a streetscape. People-oriented seating will attract many people, in turn tending to repel "undesirables."[20]

Many cities use an expanded cache of tools that moves beyond streetscaping to encourage pedestrians: zoning codes that prohibit surface parking lots in the downtown (which pedestrians hate to walk by and find difficult to walk through), regulations banning the blank walls of copycat suburban malls in a down-

[19] Central Area Progress, "Central Area Study II" (Atlanta: Author, 1988), p. 46.
[20] William H. Whyte, *City: Rediscovering the Center* (New York: Doubleday, 1988), p. 158.

6-12   The mile-long 16th Street Mall is a reserved right-of-way for pedestrians and slow-moving transit vehicles. It acts as a "horizontal elevator" to move pedestrians through the heart of the downtown Denver business district.

town location, and requirements to include retail uses in new office buildings and parking garages. Even plazas, the darling of designers in the 1960s and 1970s, are being redefined.[21] The cumulative result of these approaches goes far beyond such improvements for pedestrians as wider and more attractive sidewalks and street furniture to create a vibrant environment that actually draws pedestrians into wider walking horizons.

Still, studies indicate that downtowners tend not to want to walk very far. The median walking distance in Edmonton, Pittsburgh, and Dallas, according to one recent study, ranged from 400 to 500 feet, while 80 percent of the walking trips in those cities were less than 1,200 feet, or less than one-quarter of a mile. Even in Boston, where the median walking distance was about 1,000 feet, only 20 percent of pedestrians walked more than 2,000 feet.[22] In another study, data indicated that 80 percent of the potential downtown market will walk for only nine minutes to reach retail shops.[23] Efficient circulation systems, then, are needed to link offices and retail districts, to provide access to intercity rail terminals, and to serve remote parking areas.

To make getting around downtown easier, many cities offer a special shuttle service for shoppers,

[21] Terry Jill Lassar, *Carrots and Sticks: New Zoning Downtown* (Washington, D.C.: ULI–the Urban Land Institute, 1989), p. 109.

[22] Institute of Transportation Engineers, *Traffic and Transportation Engineering Handbook*, 2d ed. (Englewood Cliffs, N.J.: Prentice-Hall, 1982), p. 255.

[23] International Council of Shopping Centers, "Office Worker Retail Spending" (New York: Author, 1988).

6-13   HARTFORD'S DOWNTOWN SCOOTER

Just about anyone who wants to can get around downtown Hartford quickly, whether they are employees or shoppers. The "Scooter," a network of full-sized and midsized buses and vans, has been in operation since late 1989. It runs every 30 minutes from 6 A.M. to 6 P.M. and every 10 minutes during the morning and afternoon rush hours.

For years, individual corporations had offered private shuttle services to carry employees from one company to another. When the Rideshare Company (a local transportation management association) and the Greater Hartford Transit District proposed to consolidate the shuttles, the Scooter was born. Arthur Handman, executive director of the Transit District, noted in a recent interview that the participating companies have saved 15 percent on operating costs

for the shuttles by switching to the Scooter. Moreover, Scooter service has been made available to the general public for a one-way fare of $1.00.

Paul Ehrhardt, chair of the Transit District's board of directors, notes, "We're carefully trying not to duplicate the service offered by Connecticut Transit. We want to *supplement* that service." Plans are afoot to expand the service into the area around the capitol for state government employees who need access to downtown and for lawyers and accountants downtown who need to get to government buildings. Shuttle service between downtown and suburban employment centers is also planned.

Source: "New Shuttle 'Scoots' People around Downtown Hartford," *Commuter Register*, May 1990, p. 9.

commuters, or both. Such service can be provided through a bus or rail connection and can operate in mixed traffic or a dedicated mall. The Denver Partnership, Inc., for example, has established a fareless transit zone for its downtown bus shuttle. By providing an alternative to driving, the Denver service improves traffic circulation on the 16th Street Mall, a 13-block area downtown designated for pedestrians and transit. The mall was completed in 1980 with partial financing through a special assessment district. And Hartford has the Downtown Scooter (see Figure 6-13).

Downtown Skywalks

Another improvement to circulation—skywalks—has been around for a long time.[24] Toronto's system dates to the 1890s, Houston's to 1947, and St. Paul's to 1956. Alternative pedestrian networks have been built in more than 30 North American cities, and

cities are still building them. Many older systems, including those in Syracuse, Milwaukee, Minneapolis, St. Paul, Duluth, Toronto, and Montreal, were undertaken to provide pedestrians a means of escape from freezing weather.

Recent construction, however, has been motivated by economics rather than by weather. A number of cities with relatively mild climates—among them Charlotte, Cincinnati, Los Angeles, Dallas, and Portland, Oregon—have built off-street networks of pedestrian bridges and, in some cases, tunnels in their downtowns. A 1986 survey of North American skybridge systems conducted by the city of St. Paul reported that economic development was the main motive for building such systems in 11 of the 24 responding

---

[24] This section is summarized from Terry Jill Lassar, "The Pros and Cons of Downtown Skywalks," *Urban Land*, December 1988, pp. 2–6.

6-14   GRADE-SEPARATED PEDESTRIAN NETWORKS IN NORTH AMERICAN CITIES[1]

	NUMBER OF BLOCKS	NUMBER OF BRIDGES	NUMBER OF TUNNELS	YEAR BEGUN	OWNERSHIP
Calgary	42	41	0	1970	Public
Cedar Rapids	10	12	0	1978	Joint
Cincinnati	15	18	0	1970	Joint
Dallas	36	15	26	1965	Joint
Des Moines	21	27	0	1982	Joint
Duluth	13	17	0	1974	Public
Edmonton	24	9	16	1970	Joint
Fargo	7	7	1	—	Public
Ft. Worth	31	16	10	1968	Private
Houston	60	21	51	1947	Private
Lexington	6	6	0	—	Private
Milwaukee	13	11	0	1961	Joint
Minneapolis	32	34	2	1962	Private
Montreal	32	1	2[2]	1962	Joint
Rochester, New York	18	6	1	1972	Joint
Rome, New York	8	2	0	1977	Public
St. John, New Brunswick	3	2	0	1983	Joint
St. Paul	33	39	1	1956	Public
Sioux City	11	13	0	1975	Joint
Spokane	13	16	0	1961	Private
Syracuse	8	6	1	1966	Joint
Toronto	20	3	13	1890	Private
Waterloo, Iowa	4	3	0	1983	Public
Wichita	6	4	0	1964	Private

[1]The City of St. Paul surveyed 28 cities in June 1986; 24 responded, and four known to have grade-separated pedestrian systems—Atlanta, Buffalo, Omaha, and Rochester, Minnesota—did not.
[2]12 kilometers.
Source: St. Paul Department of Planning and Economic Development, "Survey of Downtown Grade-Separated Pedestrian Circulation Systems in North America," December 1986.

6-15   This easy-to-see and easy-to-use entrance to the skywalk at street level invites public use.

cities. Weather was the primary reason in only five. Skywalks proliferated during the last decade, often because cities funded them as elements of their overall strategies to thwart the exodus of downtown stores to suburban malls.

Some skywalks have indeed become major generators of retail activity. In addition to retail stores, however, the skywalk systems in American downtowns link a variety of other uses, including office buildings, convention centers, hotels, apartment buildings, and railway stations. As systems mature, they attract more and more retailers attempting to take advantage of heavy pedestrian traffic, and they take on the character of multiblock urban shopping malls. The 1986 survey in St. Paul reported that three-fourths of the city's downtown retail business takes place on the skywalk level, where rents exceed ground-floor retail rents by about $2.00 per square foot.

Skywalks can have unintended side effects, however. The problem is not that they do not work but that they work too well.[25] A downtown can support just so many stores and restaurants. Add another level and something has to give. Thus, at the same time business is flourishing in the skywalks, street-level retail sales often plummet. A recent study of skywalks in five midwestern U.S. cities found that the most pressing problem of skywalks is their tendency to exert a negative effect on retail sales and property values on the ground level, thereby deadening streetlife.[26]

In downtown Charlotte, North Carolina, for example, the Overstreet Mall might have helped to persuade two department stores to remain downtown, but the system still has received mixed reviews. A survey of retailers revealed that 40 percent of downtown's on-street merchants felt overhead retailing had hurt their businesses.

Physical design—the failure to provide links between the skywalk or tunnel system and city streets and transit stops—is part of the problem. Whereas skywalks are commonly connected to the peripheral parking facilities used by automobile commuters, direct entrances from the street level are scarce, and connections to public transit facilities are rarely a high priority. Often, passersby cannot easily see entrances to skywalks, particularly those embedded in buildings, and they feel uncomfortable venturing too far into private space.

The design of a skywalk can be influenced by its ownership and methods of funding. Many of the problems encountered by Minneapolis's all-private system—hours of operation that are not uniform, lack of security, uncoordinated signs, and discordant design—stem in part from its multiple ownership. The individuality of each bridge's design also robs the overall system of visual continuity. In contrast, St. Paul's all-public skywalk system shares nearly identical design features. Some say that the bridges' standardized pattern represents a "public" or civic style and complements an orderly city dominated by governmental and institutional activity. Others, though, feel that the uniform design is monotonous.

[25] Whyte, *City*, p. 199.
[26] Kent Robertson, "Pedestrian Skywalk Systems: Downtown's Great Hope or Pathways to Ruin?" *Transportation Quarterly*, July 1988, pp. 457–84.

6-16   Lords a-leaping! Unpredictable and harsh weather in Edmonton, Alberta, prompted use of a skywalk for a Christmas parade. Imagination abounds to create floats that meet the restrictions of a 2.5-foot width and seven-foot height. The parade draws 10,000 people downtown on a Saturday morning.

Although limiting and reevaluating skywalks are the trends in many downtowns, Cincinnati is one city that is encouraging the development of skywalks. Its 1987 regulations for the downtown development district offer incentives for building additional connections and bonus floor area if the connection meets specific criteria stipulated in the zoning ordinance. For instance, the connection must be designated on the Skywalk Overlay Map, requirements for continuity of retail stores and the skywalk's transparency must be met, and public access must be available except from 2 A.M. to 6 A.M.

One reason for Cincinnati's favoring skywalks is that the success of second-story retailing seems not to have been at the expense of ground-floor shopping. Pedestrian traffic on both levels has swelled in the past 10 years, and city officials regard the skywalk system as a safety valve to accommodate increased traffic congestion. The city's high-density development projects in its compact downtown core, in addition to the zoning requirement that at least 60 percent of certain building fronts must be devoted exclusively to retail uses, also intensify pedestrian activity. And Cincinnati's seasonal extremes more readily justify the use of skywalks.

Banning Cars: Streets for People and Transit

During the late 1960s, growing concerns about the environmental impacts of automobiles combined with fears about the future of downtown businesses, particularly retailers, resulted in a new strategy: banning the auto from downtown. Following the first "auto-restricted zone" in Kalamazoo in 1959, their incidence eventually accelerated, until, by 1981, over 100 cities had adopted such zones.[27] The vast majority of the malls constructed in the 1960s and 1970s were traditional pedestrian malls. During the 1980s, however, some of the pedestrian malls were converted to shared malls, and the few new malls built during the 1980s were transit malls.[28]

Studies completed within the last five years have cited mixed results for all three types of malls. A 1984 evaluation of four pedestrian malls and four shared or transit malls found that, in three of the four pedestrian malls, the number of retail and service establishments decreased after the mall was completed. The transit or shared malls performed better: in three of the four, the number of retail and service establishments increased. It is important to note, however, that in two of the cities where the number of establishments decreased and in the one city with mixed results, the

6-17   Transit malls must be carefully planned if a goal is to encourage retailing.

trends for the mall areas were similar to those in the rest of the CBD.[29] One might conclude, then, that downtown retailing did not decline because people could or could not walk in the streets downtown. It declined because consumers with the most money found shopping more convenient and more diverse at suburban centers. Similarly misguided logic should not be applied to the "demalling" of downtowns—a high-dollar revitalization tool of questionable return.[30]

In another study of three transit malls, two pedestrian malls, and one shared mall, the transit and shared malls performed significantly better, as measured by vacancy rates, than did the pedestrian malls. For the two pedestrian malls, vacancy rates ranged from 14 to 16.4 percent, while the highest vacancy rate for the transit/shared malls was only 6.8 percent. City planners in the two downtowns with pedestrian malls are considering conversion to a shared mall.[31] Indeed, city planners in an increasing number of cities are considering opening their malls to transit systems or limited automobile traffic (taxis, for example), as in Boston's Downtown Crossing. Now that the federal funds that financed many of the existing pedestrian malls are no longer available, this sort of

[27] Phillippos J. Loukissas and Stuart H. Mann, *The Implementation of Downtown Auto-Restricted Projects* (Washington, D.C.: Urban Mass Transportation Administration, Office of Management, Research, and Transit Services, 1984), p. 2.

[28] Kent A. Robertson, "The Status of the Pedestrian Mall in American Downtowns," *Urban Affairs Quarterly*, December 1990, p. 250.

[29] Glen Weisbrod and Henry O. Pollakowski, "Effects of Downtown Improvement Projects on Retail Activity," *American Planning Association Journal*, Spring 1984, pp. 152–57.

[30] Lawrence O. Houstoun, Jr., "From Street to Mall and Back Again," *Planning*, June 1990, pp. 4–10.

[31] Robertson, "Status of the Pedestrian Mall in American Downtowns," pp. 250–73.

6-18   The transit mall in Portland, Oregon. *Source:* ELS/Elbasani & Logan Architects.

change could make more sense than completely removing the mall. In any case, a change should be carefully analyzed in light of all the factors that influence the revitalization of retailing.

Downtown Parking: How Much Is Too Much? How Much Is Not Enough?

Parking in downtown is expensive, space consuming, sometimes ugly—and critical to a successful downtown. Office tenants, shoppers, and visitors must be attracted from competing locations in other parts of the city or in the suburbs, and many prefer to drive. On the other hand, if parking is widely available at inexpensive rates, downtown workers are less likely to use public transit or a car pool. Too much parking adds expensive construction costs and offers an incentive to drive rather than to commute by transit or a car pool. Too little can affect a project's economic success.

Traditionally, the public sector's interest in parking was in regulating the on-site parking supply of new developments to ensure that ample parking spaces were available to meet peak demands. Over the last decade, however, many cities have become concerned about rising traffic congestion in and around the approaches to their downtowns. Thus, some cities have legislated changes in the zoning code to reduce the supply of parking. High Point, North Carolina, for example, reduced the requirements for off-street parking in some sections of its CBD to encourage the use of transit and because of the lack of available land. Portland, Oregon, San Francisco, Orlando, and Seattle have set ceilings on the maximum allowable number of parking spaces for new developments in downtown areas and have eliminated minimum parking requirements. Boston and Portland have set limits on the total parking supply in their downtowns. In addition, the development of stand-alone parking facilities is restricted in Chicago, San Francisco, and Seattle. The resulting deficit in parking usually has led to higher parking prices, as demand has exceeded supply. Transportation professionals have argued that a reduced amount of available parking and higher parking costs encourage downtown travelers to use transit and to share rides, especially commuters working downtown.

Parking Reduction Ordinances

During the late 1970s and early 1980s, a smattering of cities nationwide tried experiments in parking regulation (sometimes called parking reduction ordinances).[32] Directed only at developers with proposed commercial projects, virtually all of these ordinances were designed to be purely voluntary. Some communities used the carrot of reduced requirements for off-street parking in exchange for developer-financed ride-sharing and transit services. Some of these ordinances also offered developers the option of contributing to a trust fund that would finance publicly managed commuter assistance programs. Reductions offered could be substantial, ranging from 15 to 60 percent of minimum parking requirements. In 1986, a limited survey of parking incentive ordinances

found 13 communities in seven states that had enacted such ordinances.[33]

A barrier to the successful use of parking ordinances as incentives for ride sharing is the fact that the parking policies of employers and property owners, which ensure abundant free or subsidized parking for commuters, are often left unchanged. Under such conditions, few developers or investors are willing to negotiate for reduced parking. While on-site parking is an expensive investment in terms of construction costs and land used, parking facilities are considered capital assets with readily quantifiable value. In contrast, financing ride-sharing programs to reduce vehicle trips in many communities is perceived as a risky investment with uncertain results. Until a community's areawide parking supply is tightened through, for example, an outright ban on or higher charges for public street parking, or by setting maximum limits on parking construction at private developments, many developers and lenders will continue to believe that providing less than code-

---

[32] This section is based on Dunphy and Lin, *Transportation Management through Partnerships*, pp. 67–70.
[33] ULI–the Urban Land Institute, unpublished survey, 1986.

6-19   PARKING INCENTIVES IN SEATTLE

In some jurisdictions, reductions in parking have been successfully used as incentives to commercial developers and property owners to provide ride sharing and transit subsidies for commuters. Since 1979, city officials in Seattle, Washington, have encouraged developers to offer incentives for employees in their buildings who use HOV lanes. In 1983, guidelines for negotiating reduced parking were put into administrative form, and in June 1985, the city council amended the land use section of the Seattle Municipal Code to require that all institutions and buildings with a commercial area of 10,000 square feet or more establish a transportation management program. Under this "trip reduction ordinance," the basic program must include a building transportation coordinator, semiannual promotion of HOV lanes by the building owner, a commuter information center, and bicycle racks. It must also provide, at a significant discount, at least 20 percent of the available parking for the exclusive use of car pools and van pools.

In combination with a transportation management program, however, credits for a reduction in

parking of up to 50 percent of the already low, off-street parking requirements specified by local zoning are provided for subsidizing parking spaces for pool vehicles. At the same time, up to 15 percent of requirements in the code can be met by providing free transit passes to all building workers. In fact, unless a developer obtains a special exception, a ceiling of one parking space per 1,000 square feet of nonresidential uses is established. All components of the program must be in place before a certificate of occupancy is approved for an affected building. The city uses quarterly reports and an annual survey of commuter travel to each building to monitor performance and compliance. Incentives for using HOV lanes in 1985 totaled $528,000. The success of this program was partly the result of a tight parking supply in downtown Seattle and, not surprisingly, of the fact that many property owners and employers charge employees for parking.

Sources: Alan Bennett, ride-sharing coordinator, Seattle Engineering Department; and Seattle Municipal Ordinance 112303.

required parking detracts from a project's appeal to potential tenants and buyers.

On-Site Parking

Determining parking requirements for a downtown project is much more complex than for a suburban project. First, the developer must decide whether to build all of the parking spaces expected to be required for the project. In some cases, either city regulations or site restrictions will preclude adding much parking. It then is necessary to estimate the demand.

The most widely quoted source for estimating demand is the "parking generation" report prepared periodically by the Institute of Transportation Engineers (ITE). The new version planned for 1992 is expected, for the first time, to report data separately for downtown and nondowntown sites. Second, almost every state department of transportation or highways has conducted a number of transportation and land use studies, summarizing trip and parking generation data by land use. Third, planners can identify an existing development comparable to the one proposed and determine characteristics of trip generation through a survey. The use of this sort of local data is always preferred, according to ITE. In addition to being more accurate than national data, a local study can help assure tenants and lenders that parking will be adequate. Finally, the developer can use information about parking demand derived from suburban studies, adjusted to reflect the higher rates of transit ridership and car pooling expected for a downtown site.

Shared Parking

A downtown is one of the best examples of a mixed-use business district where the same parking space can serve many users: daytime commuters, shoppers, and visitors, and evening diners and theater goers. A mixed-use project offers a special opportunity to combine uses with parking demands that peak at different times of the day.[34]

Parking in Historic Areas

A special problem exists in providing parking in downtown historic areas. In many cases, no on-site parking exists, as access was provided initially by public transit. Current parking requirements could be too high to be met on site without destroying some of the very structures that are being rehabilitated. As Marsha Root, a member of Pasadena's redevelopment staff says, "Parking is the soft underbelly of redevel-

6-20   This pedestrian walkway links public parking with Orlando's downtown entertainment and retail district.

opment, necessary to make historic districts work, but not a desired use."

In old Pasadena, California, for example, parking was a key issue in the historic district. Much of the early development occurred in the 1920s and 1930s, when the area was well served by the Red Cars, an extensive trolley system serving greater Los Angeles. Because no parking was available, the market moved east, and many older structures became obsolete. Later, however, the structures were rehabilitated as offices, restaurants, and upscale shops, all of which needed more parking.

To meet the demand for parking, two sites were located where new parking structures could be built. The garages were financed through certificates of participation backed by the city that will be repaid through tax increment financing, retail leases, and parking contracts. The structures have been well received by the community and cited by Pasadena Beautiful.[35]

Public Parking Downtown

A municipal parking authority is one avenue for providing public parking downtown, and a number of cities now operate such programs. What can a downtown organization do, however, when the city is reluctant to get involved? Vancouver, British Columbia, and Kansas City, Missouri, are examples of cities that found alternatives. When the city of Van-

---

[34] See ULI–the Urban Land Institute, *Shared Parking*, for a methodology to combine mixed uses with a substantial reduction in parking.

[35] For a detailed description of certificates of participation, see Chapter 4.

couver refused to create a public parking authority, the Downtown Vancouver Association created the Downtown Parking Corporation Limited as a way of acquiring key parcels for development of parking structures. The land is acquired with funds raised through the sale of debentures to downtown property owners. In Kansas City, the Downtown Council Development Corporation was formed in 1981 as a for-profit corporation to build parking structures in partnership with the city, which buys the land and leases it to the corporation. The result is parking at rates that allow new offices to be competitive with suburban projects.[36]

Free Parking Downtown

Although market-rate parking is seen as a good way to encourage rational choices of mode and parking supply for commuters in large downtowns, smaller downtowns must frequently search for ways to reduce parking costs to be competitive with suburban juris-dictions. The conventional approach is a parking validation program, in which businesses give stamps or tokens to customers, who then receive free or low-cost parking.

Another approach is an integrated system like the one in Kingsport, Tennessee, in which short-term shoppers park free on the street, all-day parkers park in long-term lots using permits, and shoppers needing more than two hours use the lots but pay for the privilege. The key is an enforcement program that ensures that the all-day parkers do not monopolize the on-street spaces. The program is funded partially through fees, with the gap picked up through assessments on properties in the parking district.[37]

---

[36] Robert T. Turk, "Downtown Council of Kansas City, Missouri, Builds Public Parking for Downtown," *Center City Report*, January/February 1988, pp. 1, 6.

[37] Laurence A. Alexander, *Better Parking Downtown: Increasing the Supply and Managing It Better* (New York: Downtown Research and Development Center, 1987), p. 8.

6-21	PARKING VALIDATION PROGRAMS

Downtown retailers who wish to reserve free or low-cost parking for shoppers have helped to create parking validation programs in downtown Duluth, Minnesota, Harrisburg, Pennsylvania, Hartford, Connecticut, Portland, Oregon, Seattle, Washington, and Tulsa, Oklahoma, among others.

The simplest and most common validation method is the use of park-and-shop coupons, usually small (two-inch by three-inch) colored pieces of paper with an overall design in the paper rendering the coupon difficult to copy. Like any store coupon, it has a value (usually $.25 or $.50) printed on its face and an area where it can be stamped with the date it was given to the customer. Typically, the only other text on the coupon indicates where it can be used. Coupons can also be sequentially numbered.

Coupon programs are often started by chambers of commerce or downtown organizations working in conjunction with the owners of parking facilities. Area businesses buy the coupons from the originating agency at full face value. They are stamped with the current date and handed to customers at checkout. Store employees follow the retailer's rules, for example, requiring a minimum purchase or not giving one unless a customer requests it. The customer uses the coupon as cash at the exit booth. The parking attendant turns coupons in to the parking office as part of the day's accounting records. Office personnel record the receipt of coupons daily by facility, banks them by fifties or hundreds, and turns them over to the bookkeeper at the end of the month. The parking facility's bookkeeping department accounts for the coupons as cash receivable.

A coupon program has several advantages:

- The originating agency usually makes money because only about 80 percent of the coupons are used;
- The parking agency, if it is not the originating agency, usually breaks even;
- The program is easy for the parker to understand; and
- Coupons are inexpensive to produce.

But it can also include disadvantages:

- The parking agency can potentially lose a small percentage of revenue if it is not the originating agency and has to pay a handling charge;
- Coupons can be easy to reproduce;
- Coupons can be illegally sold; and
- Parking attendants or store employees can easily lose coupons.

Source: Marie Witmer, "Validation Programs," *The Parking Professional*, August 1987, pp. 22–25.

More Productive Use of On-Street Parking

On-street parking represents an important share of the parking supply in smaller downtowns. Decisions about whether to meter it or not and other methods of making the streets more productive are important. Vancouver, Washington, for example, uses valuable on-street parking to meet clearly stated city goals. The retail and commercial part of downtown has primarily one- and two-hour meters. A ring around downtown a bit farther out, which has a more diversified mix of parking for customers, employees, and residents, includes 410 short-term spaces for customers, 1,010 long-term spaces for employees, and 600 spaces of permit parking. The permit parking is available on a first-come, first-served basis to workers, who pay a moderate fee, and to residents, who do not.

7.
Mixed-Use Development

One fundamental characteristic that made the traditional downtown a focus of economic and social activity was its mix of uses. Even today, a diversity of uses is one of the most important characteristics of a vital downtown—so much so that cities encourage a mix of development types through zoning and financial incentives.

Mixed-use development is becoming a preferred approach to revitalization by the public sector, primarily as it relates to incorporating housing into

employment areas, an important goal for many downtowns in the 1980s and 1990s. This issue of a balance between jobs and housing is not the only driving factor, however. As the golden age of sprawl seems to be coming to a close, concerns about transportation and the most efficient use of land and existing infrastructure mount. And a related desire to create more lively downtowns also drives the shift in public policy toward mixed-use development.

It is because of the paramount importance of mixed-use development in downtowns that the second part of this handbook begins with a brief discussion of MXDS.[1] The purposes of this section are to summarize only the essentials of mixed-use development, particularly as they relate to downtown development, and to present some of the trends in this area in the 1990s.

Public policy is not the only push for mixed-use development downtown. Some believe that the prognosis for less new development could actually encourage MXDs, because the best locations are often best suited for mixed-use development, and they are the only locations that will get developed in coming years. Further, MXDs are usually undertaken by ex-

7-1   Charleston Place, including a hotel, conference center, 30 stores, an athletic club, and a parking deck, has helped revitalize Charleston's economy while preserving its historic environment.

[1] See Dean Schwanke et al., *Mixed-Use Development Handbook* (Washington, D.C.: ULI–the Urban Land Institute, 1987) for in-depth coverage of downtown and suburban MXDs.

7-2 Warehouse Row in downtown Chattanooga, Tennessee, includes 100,000 square feet of gross leasable area housing a designer outlet center on levels one and two and 150,000 square feet of office space on levels three through five. Eight historic warehouses were restored as part of the project.

perienced and well-financed developers, the only ones who will be in the position to undertake new projects. Finally, MXDs create better urban environments, allowing them to be more competitive than freestanding projects, essential in a tough market.[2]

With the competitive edge, however, comes complexity, particularly in a downtown location where small but expensive sites add risk. One mistake that is easy to make is to assume that more economic synergy exists among uses than is actually the case. In reality, each component of a project must be analyzed on its own merits rather than on its being "carried" by the demand and synergy created by the other uses. Additionally, the higher holding costs in MXDs as a result of the longer time frame for development must not be understated.

Long lead times and high front-end costs during the planning and feasibility stages for an MXD require large amounts of equity to be put at risk if the project does not proceed. Several options are available to counteract this risk, including phasing the components of the project and, particularly in a downtown setting, seeking public involvement. Phasing different components of the project allows for some cash inflow from the finished part of the project to go toward construction of the next part. It also permits separate financing for each part of the project, which can add the flexibility needed to take advantage of interest rates, tax requirements, and future opportunities for selling the project. With the high-profile public/private MXDs developed in the last 20 years— Horton Plaza in San Diego, Copley Place in Boston, Pioneer Place in Portland, Oregon, Arizona Center in Phoenix, among them—developers and public officials alike are primed for even more MXDs in the 1990s.

[2] Dean Schwanke, ed., *Development Trends, 1991* (Washington, D.C.: ULI–the Urban Land Institute, 1991), p. 30.

7-3   KEY FEATURES OF MIXED-USE DEVELOPMENT

Although it is sometimes hard to distinguish mixed-use projects from multiuse ones, the components of a mixed-use project include three features:

1. *Three or more significant revenue-producing uses* (such as retail, office, residential, hotel/motel, entertainment/cultural/recreational uses) that are mutually supporting. This requirement usually connotes a large scale (generally 500,000 square feet or more) so that the project has enough space to integrate several uses;

2. *Significant physical and functional integration of project components,* including uninterrupted pedestrian connections. Orienting the project to pedestrians is a major aim of MXDs; thus, the project must include a pedestrian circulation network to and from its principal components, either in the same structure or close to it. In many downtown areas, projects with several uses are close to each other, but because they are not dense enough or do not have significant physical integration, they are classified as multiuse projects rather than MXDs; and

3. *Development in conformance with a coherent plan* (which frequently stipulates the type and scale of uses, permitted densities, and related items). This type of planning is quite different from the unplanned mix of uses in projects by different developers.

Source: Dean Schwanke et al., *Mixed-Use Development Handbook* (Washington, D.C.: ULI–the Urban Land Institute, 1987), p. 3.

Planning and Design

Like other aspects of MXDs, planning and design are more complex than single-use projects, because the various uses have numerous and often conflicting needs. The developer plays an expanded role as the overall coordinator for architects, engineers, planners, economic experts, and property managers, making sure that designs take into account the goal of the project as a whole.

This phase includes several requirements: configuring each use in conjunction with the others to provide maximum use and appeal in a considerably larger project space, making sure that mechanical systems and infrastructure are adequate and integrated, maximizing the flow of pedestrians, solving parking and transportation problems, carefully planning the central focus of the project, ensuring that the project's atmosphere and function blend with the surrounding community.

To guard against the often fortress-like quality of some older downtown MXDs, newer projects emphasize an orientation toward pedestrians and more interaction and integration with adjacent uses. The design team for National Place in Washington, D.C., for example, planned the MXD's retail space at street level to interact with the established retail shops in the downtown area.

Some projects, depending on the climate, feature an open-air segment to accomplish this outward orientation. Arizona Center, an 18.5-acre MXD in downtown Phoenix, is a good example of such a design. Its focus is on creating a gathering place for fun and

7-4 Contrasting themes of openness and shade are used throughout Arizona Center. The retail component is shown here. *Source:* ELS/Elbasani & Logan Architects.

7-5 Rowes Wharf, a 1.1 million-square-foot MXD in Boston, is exemplary in its contextual design and in the quality of its public spaces and waterfront promenades.

entertainment amid gardens, restaurants, and nightclubs. The Mercado, a smaller project a few blocks from Arizona Center, echoes this orientation but strives also to preserve the cultural heritage of the area in an open-air setting. Vibrant colors and tile work rim the Spanish colonial architecture that encircles the office and retail space, cultural center, and museum space.

Zoning

Zoning has become a key element in planning and designing downtown MXDs. Some downtown areas do not allow a mix of uses in one district, and a growing number are shaping the size and nature of downtown projects by their zoning requirements. Many such cities have put in place a flexible or incentive zoning system in which bonuses are granted to developers who provide certain amenities or uses that the city seeks. The specific nature of these bonuses can be negotiated with the city or reviewed during hearings before the public and the planning

7-6, 7-7 Rockefeller Center, a planned group of offices, theaters, and public spaces on a multiblock tract in midtown Manhattan, is still a model for mixed-use development.

commission or spelled out in a list of trade-offs so that the developer knows exactly what the project must provide to be awarded the bonuses.

Some cities allow mixed uses downtown if projects include a residential component. For example, Hartford, Connecticut, adopted housing overlay district zoning in 1987, requiring new projects within certain areas to devote a percentage of the floor area to housing. Portland, Oregon, adopted its Central City Plan in 1988, specifying that all commercial sectors and one industrial sector would be mixed-use zones and allowing the construction of housing within either mixed-use or single-use projects.

Other cities use special districts to shape redevelopment of infill areas, such as to preserve certain historical or cultural aspects. New York, for example, has 34 such special-purpose districts.

The Future of MXDs Downtown

MXDs now account for a very small percentage of total development; even a large increase in activity would still mean a relatively small share of the pie. But the idea of MXDs is compelling and seems to be winning over the public as an effective way to keep downtowns dynamic, for they contain several uses in efficient, high-density spaces with a unified design that encourage use by pedestrians. Continued education regarding the impact of MXDs on traffic, however, is still necessary. The misperception persists that MXDs generate traffic, when in fact they promote use by pedestrians while downplaying the car as much as possible. In Battery Park City, the enormous MXD in southern Manhattan, for example, 45 percent of the residents walk to work.

One feature that is likely to gain importance in the 1990s is the increasing emphasis on the residential component of MXDs. With the office market expected to be stagnant for the next several years, MXDs could focus on other uses, in some cases incorporating existing office structures into a new design. Entertainment facilities related to residential uses will also gain momentum. The entertainment center at Arizona Center, for example, is a key part of the project's marketing strategy. The project features three clubs and includes a 25,000-square-foot sports bar with 30 television monitors, a caged free-throw basketball court, an outdoor patio with an 18-hole miniature golf course, and a sand volleyball court. Creative developers will make good use of the flexible concept that defines mixed-use development in the next decade.

8.
Downtown Office Buildings

The downtown office market traditionally served as the engine of downtown revitalization. Particularly in the 1980s, office development allowed downtowns to participate in the historic increase in employment resulting from the baby boom. As well, office buildings housed workers who supported downtown retailing and housing. Where new office development occurred, property values increased (current declines in value as a result of overbuilding notwithstanding) and provided, through property tax revenues, a source of funds for further revitalization.

Existing downtown office development will continue to be an important part of the downtown economy. New development will be a less important factor in this decade than it has been in the past, however. For this reason, and because a handbook devoted entirely to the subject of office development already exists,[1] this chapter discusses the current state of the industry, particularly as it relates to downtowns and the role of the office market in downtown revitalization in this decade, rather than a step-by-step presentation of office development.

Factors Affecting the Downtown Office Market

Just as changes in the national economy dramatically affected the office market in the 1970s and 1980s, so

the reversal, or at least the plateauing, of those changes is dramatically affecting the 1990s. The baby boom was followed by a baby bust, and, as a consequence, the number of new entrants—defined as those between the ages of 15 and 29—to the labor force is projected to fall sharply during the 1990s. The group that will grow most rapidly—the 45- to 60-year-olds—is exiting the work force at a record rate. The overall result will be a sharp drop—to only about 1 percent per year—in the growth of the work force during the 1990s, down from 2.4 percent per year in the 1970s.[2]

Several other trends are converging in the national economy to cause a significant change in the office market. Growth in white-collar employment appears to have peaked, slowdowns continue in the banking and real estate industries, and clerical jobs are being eliminated as computer and telecommunications technology advances. The rate of growth for women entering the job market has stabilized as well, as women who deferred starting a family finally do so. At this writing, markets across the country are dramatically overbuilt, and demand is slackening as a result of business reversals and uncertainty regarding the

---

[1] Paul O'Mara, with John A. Casazza, *Office Development Handbook* (Washington, D.C.: ULI–the Urban Land Institute, 1982).

[2] David L. Birch et al., *America's Future Office Space Needs: Preparing for the Year 2000* (Arlington, Va.: National Association of Industrial and Office Parks, 1990), p. 12.

8-1   Fifth Avenue Place, Pittsburgh.

depth and duration of the regional and national economic downturn.[3]

For companies located downtown, a focus on the bottom line has exacerbated the pressure to move back-office operations or even headquarters staff to less expensive suburban locations. One-third of the downtown respondents in one study of office tenants indicated that they would consider relocating to the suburbs, while only 14 percent of the suburban respondents said they would consider moving downtown.[4] And the number of professionals working at home has negatively affected the office market. An estimated 23 percent of the U.S. labor force now works at home at least part of the time.[5] Finally, capital for new office development is severely limited. In fact, in 1991, ULI's Real Estate Credit Task Force recommended a halt to lending for speculative new commercial development.

It is no wonder, then, that a 1990 survey of ULI council members showed downtown office space as having the third lowest potential for development and

investment among all property types. In terms of real estate values, about two-thirds of the respondents indicated that downtown office values were declining. On the other hand, a 1990 study comparing the performances of downtown and suburban office investments during the two periods of economic contraction studied, 1973 and 1987, found that properties in the CBD outperformed suburban properties on the basis of adjusted risk.[6] And according to Coldwell Banker, downtown vacancy rates in September 1990 were 3.5 percentage points lower than those for suburban areas, 17 percent versus 20.5 percent. It is clear that these changes make feasibility analyses more important than ever.

[3] Dean Schwanke, ed., *Development Trends, 1991* (Washington, D.C.: ULI–the Urban Land Institute, 1991), p. 16.
[4] Alton J. Penz, *Office Tenant Moves and Changes* (Washington, D.C.: Building Owners and Managers Association International, 1988), p. 15.
[5] Donald C. Bacon, "Look Who's Working at Home," *Nation's Business*, October 1989, p. 21.
[6] Charles H. Wurtzebach and David J. Hartzell, "Comparing the Performances of City Center and Suburban Office Investments," *Real Estate Review*, Winter 1990, pp. 39–42.

8-2   GROWTH RATE OF LABOR FORCE
                    1900–2000

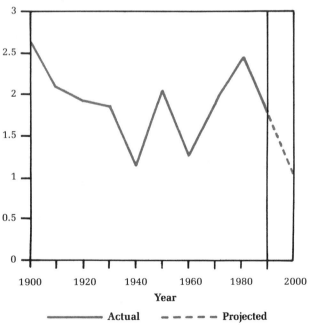

Average Annual Growth Rate (Percent)

——— Actual   – – – – Projected

Source: David L. Birch et al., *America's Future Office Space Needs: Preparing for the Year 2000* (Arlington, Va.: National Association of Industrial and Office Parks, 1990), p. 13.

112

The Future Need for Office Space

As a result of the changes, demand for new office space will surely be less in the 1990s than in the 1980s. One major study sponsored by the National Association of Industrial and Office Parks (NAIOP) projects a need for significantly less space.[7] Taking into account not only reduced demand but also the tremendous quantity of unleased space currently on the market, the study projects that the need for new construction in the entire United States will range from 6 to 35 percent of the construction levels that prevailed during the 1980s, or from 138 million to 750 million square feet of new primary office space. (The wide variation is the result of different assumptions about vacancy rates and the degree to which obsolete space will be replaced.)[8] Some believe, however, that the variation is too narrow, that demand will be considerably higher in the 1990s. A spokesman for the National Association of Realtors, for example, calls the projections "speculative at best." Even so, most concur that office construction in the 1990s will be only a fraction of what it was in the 1980s.

How much of this projected need can downtowns expect to garner? In many markets, existing supply is expected to meet demand for the entire decade. In fact, using NAIOP's most conservative assumptions, more than 50 percent of the markets studied fall into this category. As one might expect, the need for new construction will be concentrated in the South and West, where projections of population and employment growth are the highest.

In those locations, factors that have always favored downtown locations will continue to do so. An analysis of the differences between suburban and downtown firms in the evaluation of key factors influencing choice of location found that 82 out of 135 downtown firms listed proximity to clients and proximity to business contacts as the most important locational factors.[9] Only 45 of the 135 suburban firms, on the other hand, listed proximity to clients as important, and none listed proximity to business contacts as important. Conversely, nearly 25 percent of the suburban firms listed proximity to employees' residences as important, whereas only 6 percent of downtown firms rated this factor as key. Other significant factors included proximity to financial institutions, air travel service, and access within the CBD.

In addition, the prestige and visibility of a downtown location continue to affect corporate decisions about location. The increasing shortage of labor could also positively affect downtown's competitiveness.

8-3   Seattle's downtown bus tunnel.

To the extent that special amenities exist—superior transit, a plethora of cultural and entertainment events, historic architecture, or other features like a waterfront, retailing, and housing—downtowns will be able to compete for what demand exists for new office space. In downtown Seattle, for example, the move of back-office users was stemmed, at least in part, by the downtown's superior transit service: employees at a number of large insurance companies wanted to stay downtown because of the bus system. (In one major downtown building, 90 percent of the employees use the bus system to get to and from work.) Additionally, a large percentage of projected demand is expected to be for other than first-class office buildings or for buildings in which office space is not the major use (hospitals or schools, for example). To meet this demand, downtown developers might take a new look at rehabilitating older buildings and adapting buildings formerly used for nonoffice purposes, vacated department stores, for example.

---

[7] Birch et al., *America's Future Office Space Needs*, p. 70.

[8] Wurtzebach and Hartzell, "Comparing the Performances," pp. 31–33.

[9] J. Thomas Black et al., *Downtown Office Growth and the Role of Public Transit* (Washington, D.C.: ULI–the Urban Land Institute, 1982), pp. 28–29.

Estimating Supply And Demand

One result of the decreased demand for new office space will be a heightened need for market research and feasibility studies. In addition to forecasting supply and demand by market, a new emphasis on tenant surveys, focus groups, and/or polling will be necessary to assess accurately tenants' needs and desires for new development and for existing projects. *Retaining* tenants will be the paramount consideration in the 1990s, and owners must know what their tenants want and are willing to pay for.

Just as owners will need to expand market analysis to regularly include research on tenants, so the forecasting of supply and demand will need to become more precise. Any factors that differentiate downtown in the process of forecasting must be considered.

For example, the first step in any analysis of demand, setting the geographic boundaries for the proposed project's primary and secondary markets, can be different in downtown and suburban locations. The area from which prospective tenants can be expected to be drawn for a downtown building could be larger than for a suburban building. Because some tenants *must* be downtown—bank headquarters and the law firms that serve them, for example—the distance key decision makers will be willing to commute will be farther. And when a downtown is also a transit hub, the relative ease with which employees can travel to the city center tends to broaden primary and secondary markets.

Forecasting growth in employment is the next step when more precise calculations are necessary. Cognetics, Inc., the firm completing most of the research for NAIOP's study, has determined that corporate start-up, closing, movement, and growth rates depend upon 1) how large the establishment is, 2) what industry it belongs to, 3) who owns it, and 4) where it is located. The firm found that studying these four categories of employment, rather than simply total employment for an area, yields more accurate results. Forecasting employment for any market area, then, entails calculating how many firms (by type) will be added, how many will close, and how many will change from one size class to the next, and translating these figures from jobs by type of business into jobs by occupation. The concentration of financial and legal firms downtown will certainly affect the outcome of such calculations.

The next step in determining the demand for office space is converting the estimates of employment into projections for office space. Again, the type of tenant usually attracted to downtown locations affects this calculation. Cognetics, Inc., makes these estimates based on its analysis of about 17 million firms over the past 20 years:

Occupation	Average Square Feet
Managerial	419
Professional	283
Clerical	227
Sales	185[10]

Once demand for office space is determined, the actual need is finally projected by subtracting existing supply from total demand. The additional study done to analyze the feasibility of a particular office project downtown is no different from that for office projects

---

[10] Birch et al., *America's Future Office Space Needs*, p. 24.

Some say the individuality of downtown Boston renders its experience inapplicable to other downtowns. Boston *is* unique in many ways. No other downtown has the same combination of rich history, compactness, strong transit, historic architecture, and a waterfront—not to mention the much-written-about Faneuil Hall and Quincy Market. And Boston boomed in the late 1980s, while many other downtowns languished because of overbuilding.

But Boston's experience *can* benefit other downtowns. Boston's policy of "metering" or controlling office supply has had an important positive effect on the market. In freewheeling Phoenix and Denver, for example, office vacancy rates in the central city hover around 25 percent. Washington, D.C., San Francisco, Seattle, and Boston, however—cities known for their restrictive climate for downtown development—are experiencing the lowest vacancy rates in the country—from 14 to 17 percent at this writing, according to Coldwell Banker. Even developers with a history of working in "free-market" cities are recognizing the benefits of developing in

controlled markets. ULI trustee Gerald Hines, for example, said at the fall 1989 meeting of trustees that his firm was looking at markets that were "restrained by code."

In 1985, the city of Boston began a policy of metering office supply through the regulatory approval process, with a goal of maintaining vacancy rates within 8 to 12 percent. By controlling supply, the redevelopment authority believed real estate values could be protected and competitive rents to commercial tenants assured. Despite adding 10 million square feet of office space to downtown since 1984, Boston's vacancy rate for Class A downtown office space in 1990 was only slightly over 14 percent. Although vacancies could rise if the city's biomedical research industry does not experience the job growth projected, the crushing oversupply that other downtowns have experienced has been avoided.

The city regulates the supply of office space through a tripartite process that includes the Boston Redevelopment Authority, the developer, and the

8-6   In cities known for restrictive downtown development policies, vacancies have been lower.

community. As the city's redevelopment and planning agency, the redevelopment authority wields an incredible amount of power. With a $20 million budget and 300 employees, not including consultants, the agency conducts extensive research to support its metering, has the final say on approving development, and acts as the public partner on projects it wants to especially encourage. When the agency decided to dispense with its remaining land in the South End, for example, a requirement for 50 percent affordable units stifled developers' ability to obtain financing. Switching hats, the agency stepped in with bridge loans and grants.

The agency must review development plans for buildings over 50,000 square feet, which is the process used to control supply. Some projects never complete the process. Others do but, because of the length of the process, miss the market and never get built. Of the 43 office projects submitted to the agency for review in 1987, 25 have been completed or are being built, four are still under review, and 14 have been postponed or canceled.

The length of the design review proces is partly the result of the tough goals the agency has set for urban design and for the downtown's social and cultural environment. In the zoning for downtown's new Harborpark District, for example, buildings of 100,000 square feet or more are required to provide daycare facilities. As well, 50 percent of a project's lot must be open space, and 25 percent of the ground floor must be for cultural uses (for example, legitimate theater, a museum, or performance space). The

8-7   KIDS BUILDING BOSTON

In Boston, developers not only pay the $6.00 per square foot linkage fee for the "privilege" of building downtown, but many also make additional voluntary contributions. Spaulding & Slye, for example, has developed the ultimate in hands-on development education for children. A class of about 30 fifth graders from a school in East Boston has been targeted to participate in the development of 125 High Street, a 1.5 million-square-foot, $450 million office project now under construction in Boston's financial district. Over a three-year period of monthly meetings, the students will see the project from start to finish.

Through field trips and lessons, they have already learned some facts about development:

- An on-site construction class during a tour of the 55-foot-deep foundation;
- A lesson in urban planning taught by Boston Redevelopment Authority director Stephen Coyle at City Hall;
- Exposure to skyscraper engineering at John Hancock Tower, the 60-story building noted for its problems with windows' popping out as a result of wind pressure;
- A model-making workshop at Trip Tech Models and a woodworking laboratory at Wentworth Institute;
- A plumbing lesson at the Massachusetts Water Resources Authority treatment facility; and
- Lessons in stone cutting and marble hanging during trips to a granite quarry and a local stone cutter's shop.

In addition, the children have met with community leaders, including Mayor Raymond Flynn, and will continue to mix with leading executives, who demonstrate what life after school is all about. In fact, one of the goals of the program is to expose the children to new opportunities for careers. "For some of the kids," says 125 High

8-8   During a visit to a woodworking laboratory at Wentworth Institute in Boston, students from Kids Building Boston learned the correct way to drive a nail.

city's linkage fee, $6.00 per square foot for office projects over 50,000 square feet, includes $5.00 for housing and $1.00 for job training. In requirements for design, the agency requires not only contextual design but also expensive materials and detailing. And skyscrapers are almost an endangered species. Heights of buildings downtown are capped at 155 feet except in select areas where growth is encouraged. There, height is capped at 465 feet.

Input from the community is another feature of development in downtown Boston that lengthens the process. Before the redevelopment authority even considers a proposal, the developer must meet with all individuals and citizens' groups that might be affected or concerned. The mayor's office provides a list of local groups, and developers work with the agency to determine who should be contacted. By the time a project is officially submitted to the agency, a consensus plan should have been developed. The process thus polices itself. "I've seen one guy stand up in the back of the room and say, 'Nobody contacted me.' And the deal was tabled," says Muhammad Abdus-Sabur, deputy director of urban design for the agency. Developers have learned to talk to everyone.

They have also learned that input from the community is not all bad. One of the most popular features of Rowes Wharf is the monumental arch and dome in the center of the project. Original plans called for doors that blocked views in that area of the project. Bostonians and visitors alike love the redesign, with its ferry terminal, hotel, offices, and

Street project manager Dave McGarry, "it's a chance to get out of school and have a great lunch. But for others, it's, 'Wow! I never knew these opportunities existed.'"

In creating the program, Spaulding & Slye evaluated the construction process and developed a conceptual three-year curriculum, which it presented to the Boston superintendent of schools. The educator immediately embraced the program, and a class of fifth graders was selected. An education consultant then developed a detailed monthly curriculum and reviewed it with the class's teachers.

Each month, the consultant meets with the chosen Spaulding & Slye employee or other appropriate professional to prepare that person for teaching the class. One week before the monthly field trip, the consultant visits the school and teaches a preparatory class to help students understand the elementary concepts of the subject at hand. The consultant also works with teachers to help integrate the program into the school curriculum, providing vocabulary words (like "excavation," "retaining walls," and "foundation"), work sheets, and topics for essays.

Kids Building Boston has received kudos all around, from the redevelopment authority, the media, and other developers. Even Spaulding & Slye's attitude about it has changed. "Originally," admits McGarry, "it was part altruism, part mar-

8-9 Students from Kids Building Boston learn about retaining walls and tiebacks as part of their on-site construction class.

keting. The program is a marketing person's dream. Now, there is much more of a sense that these children are real people. They're not just there to help us; we can help them." In fact, with the three-year program almost completed, Spaulding & Slye is looking for ways to stay involved with the students. For those desiring to pursue an interest developed through the program, McGarry is researching scholarships, summer jobs, and internships. The sky could be the limit for these youngest of hard hats.

100 condominiums (that sold out in 100 days). "On balance," says Beacon Companies executive vice president Robert Perriello, "it's been better that the agency and the community groups have been able to have their say."

Developers of Copley Place share the same thoughts. "Ultimately, did it make a better project? I think it did to a degree," says Rudy Umscheid, executive vice president of JMB/Urban Development Co. "Building the bridges was a tremendous benefit to the project." In addition to other changes suggested by citizens, the developer added pedestrian bridges for easier access from the surrounding neighborhoods. Copley Place is a $530 million mixed-use project built over a highway interchange on 9.5 acres of air rights. It includes two major hotels, a retail mall, four office buildings, residential units, and indoor parking.

But even as developers recognize the benefits of Boston's stringent controls and lengthy review process, they also see the negative side. "We think the end result is good," says Spaulding & Slye partner Bill Whelan, "but it was very difficult to get through. In a down market, you can't afford to do it, which is why a number of projects in this city have simply gone away. They can't start because they're too expensive and have missed the market. Would these projects have been under way—would there be more jobs—if the agency had been less stringent?"

Whelan claims that between $5 million and $10 million in costs, mainly attributable to interest

8-10 Pedestrian bridges at Copley Place were added at citizens' urging.

charges on the land, were added to the cost of 125 High Street because of the lengthy approval process. And that amount does not include linkage fees or added costs of materials and labor resulting from changes made during design review. The 550,000-square-foot tower was about 33 percent leased when it opened in October 1990. How does the redevelopment authority respond to the idea that it double dips developers with linkage payments and requirements for a variety of public benefits like parks or child care? "Boston has been hit with a wave of volunteerism," deadpanned Stephen Coyle, the agency's executive director, when asked about the issue at ULI's fall 1990 meeting.

in other locations and includes a projection of achievable rents and absorption rates. Net operating income is then projected to determine whether the building can cover debt service at prevailing rates and achieve desired returns for owners.

What types of businesses will grow fastest in the 1990s, and where do they tend to locate offices? The following categories are projected to be fastest growing: 1) computer and data-processing firms, 2) outpatient facilities and health services, 3) personnel supply services, 4) health practitioners, 5) credit-reporting and business services, 6) legal services, 7) nursing and personal care facilities, 8) research, management, and consulting services, 9) residential care, and 10) miscellaneous publishing.[11] These 10 categories of businesses plus the next group of 10 employ only 14 percent of the U.S. work force today but will account for 41 percent of the job growth over the next

10 years. Companies are small—an average of 11 employees—and needs for space small—an average of 2,500 square feet. The square footage for downtown tenants averaged a much larger 8,873 in 1988, reflecting the fact that the types of tenants tending to locate downtown are the larger ones that probably grow more slowly.[12] To compete in the 1990s, downtown owners will need to tailor their buildings, amenities, and marketing strategies toward attracting the smaller, faster-growing tenants.

[11] Donovan D. Rypkema, *Downtown in the 1990s: The Economic Future of America's Center Cities* (Washington, D.C.: Hyett Palma Publications, 1990), pp. 14–15.

[12] Building Owners and Managers Association International, *1989 BOMA Experience Exchange Report* (Washington, D.C.: Author, 1989), p. 93.

Designing Downtown Office Space

It is worth stating the obvious: achievable rental rates should drive the design and finish of a building rather than the design and finish creating a new market for higher rents. Financial returns on office investments were disappointingly low in the late 1980s. At this writing, investment returns for office properties are the lowest of all property types in the United States, according to the FRC-NCREIF Index. The Liquidity Fund's National Real Estate Index shows that, for the 12 months ending June 1990, office property prices rose a dismal 0.9 percent, the lowest of the four investment properties it tracks.[13]

In addition to the widely publicized oversupply of office space, a factor contributing to low returns, particularly for downtown projects, was over-designed and overfinished space. One study found no evidence to support the assertion that well-designed buildings are more profitable, either in the short or long run.[14] "Developers have provided high-quality space with extravagant amenities without obtaining rents commensurate with the cost, not to mention a return on the risks of those projects."[15] Owners must begin asking themselves who can pay for marble and granite. The high-growth firms that will be a major source of demand for new office space in the 1990s probably cannot.

James F. Housel

8-12   Careful attention should be given to the costs and benefits of interior and exterior finish materials.

James F. Housel

8-11   Plazas at office buildings can be enhanced with landscaping and plenty of movable seating, like this example at 1111 Third Avenue in Seattle by Wright Runstad & Company.

Sometimes the design and finish of a new building can create a new market for higher rents, but a more cautious approach is certainly fitting for the 1990s. Norwest Center in Minneapolis, for example, is a building whose design was driven by market conditions. From the very start, developer Gerald D. Hines Interests was careful to respond to the existing market's requirements rather than attempt to create a new market. Market studies indicated that tenants would pay no more than $16 to $20 per square foot for downtown office space. Hines programmed a straightforward treatment of the lobbies and other public areas, featuring less of the glitz and extravagant finishings found in the interiors of office towers recently built on the East and West Coasts.

[13] Schwanke, *Development Trends, 1991*, p. 18.

[14] Kerry D. Vandell and Jonathan S. Lane, "The Economics of Architecture and Urban Design: Some Preliminary Findings," paper presented at the ASSA annual meeting, New York, 1988.

[15] Richard Kately, "Development Niches in the Nineties," *Mortgage Banking*, September 1990, pp. 51, 53–56.

Cesar Pelli, the architect for Norwest Center, designed a building that fits in with its surroundings, another important goal for downtown settings. Earlier plans by another architect and developer had featured a 950-foot building that would have topped the city's de facto symbol—Johnson and Burgee's 1972 IDS (Investors Diversified Services) Building. Pelli's Norwest Center is two feet shorter and complements rather than competes with its neighbor. Pelli also sheathed the building in a local limestone, the same used on many historic buildings downtown. The limestone, however, was used inventively: never before had it been applied as a curtain wall on such a large (almost 1.5 million gross square feet) building.

Designing buildings to be flexible will be just as important in the 1990s as designing buildings that "fit in," if not more so. As uncertain conditions continue to prevail in the banking, real estate, and, increasingly, insurance industries, tenants must not be locked into the size, design, or technological capabilities of their buildings. The rash of mergers, takeovers, and corporate restructurings of the 1980s taught tenants more than one lesson, including how difficult it can be to reconfigure headquarters space to meet new situations. And companies that designed their buildings to stand out as a personal reflection of senior management's style found some of the biggest problems. Retenanting such a building can be costly and difficult.

In building its new headquarters, SunBanks, the holding company for the largest bank in central Florida, in conjunction with developer Lincoln Property Company, was able to achieve a building that met the bank's desire for distinction—the building is downtown Orlando's tallest—as well as flexibility. The bank did not lease the entire building but has options to expand as other tenants' leases expire. Its own floors are completely suitable for other businesses, should the bank have to downsize its operations.

Marketing Downtown Office Space

With the development of new office space to slow in the 1990s, the importance of obtaining and keeping tenants for existing buildings will take on new importance. Though developers and owners are finding an increased need to sell themselves as financially secure businesses to their tenants, they are also finding that marketing needs to speak to the specific facts about a building. Rather than presenting generic information about the developer and its projects, the building's particular benefits must be clearly set forth. According to Gerald D. Hines Interests vice president Ann Kifer, Hines now uses more of a series of materials rather than one generic brochure. Developer Richard Clotfelter of Prescott Development, based in Seattle, uses loose-leaf brochures with inserts tailored to the prospect's situation.

Marketing centers are also tailored to the base of customers. The Hines organization, known for pioneering the marketing showroom, plans each center based on prevailing market conditions and the risk profile of the project. To market 222 Berkeley in downtown Boston, for example, Hines created a lavish marketing center using highly detailed models featuring displays of interiors, exteriors, maps, floor plans, and materials, each at different stations with its own audiovisual presentations. The marketing center empties out into a conference room featuring exceptional views of the city, where the marketing agent and the prospect can discuss the building in more detail. In downtown Detroit, however, such a center would have overwhelmed the market. There, where value is an important factor to tenants, a large-scale model and a six- to nine-projector slide show was considered more effective than a host of stations accompanied by a 30-projector show.

As supply has continued to increase, one factor that will continue into the 1990s is the increasing sophistication of tenants and their use of and reliance on brokers. Owners therefore are marketing more and more to brokers. How is marketing to brokers different from marketing to tenants? For one thing, their attention spans may be shorter, as they work on several relocations rather than just one. Marketing materials and events must thus be short and concise. When they do meet with tenants, developers are finding the need to explain the technological advances of their buildings, zoned heating and air conditioning or fiber-optic cabling, for example.

In some central cities, a technique used to promote downtown retailing is now being applied in the office market. Some downtown organizations hire coordinators to work closely with developers and the business community. Having a more specialized function than the local chamber of commerce or economic development office, the coordinator keeps local developers, brokers, and prospective tenants supplied with materials on the benefits of locating downtown and arranges special events with existing or potential tenants, perhaps a series of social events with the leadership of the local bar association. Hiring such a coordinator is a strategy tailor-made for the 1990s.

Another marketing trend that will continue in the 1990s is the increasing use of *amenities* to market

8-13   The same features can be viewed as amenities downtown but ho hum in the suburbs.

office buildings, and, in this area, downtown buildings can shine. Only downtown buildings can offer truly distinctive amenities—historic architecture, proximity to cultural institutions, or access to mass transit, for example—as well as amenities that might be similar to those in suburban locations. In downtown Orlando, for example, a task force of developers and brokers studied downtown and suburban markets to develop ideas for retaining downtown tenants. The study indicated that tenants viewed the downtown's features like its many lakes, restaurants, and stores as amenities, while they did not view similar features in the suburbs as amenities. The task force concluded that all downtown buildings that included amenities like food service, dry cleaners, newsstands, health clubs, car care operations, child and elderly care, conference rooms, or even chapels, needed to be more aggressively promoted.

Just as suburban buildings found some of their original ideas for amenities in downtown projects, so

downtown buildings can look to suburban projects for new ideas. One building in Tampa, Florida, for example, offers on-site training in computers, accounting, and management through two of its tenants: branches of the local community college and technical high school. Child care in office buildings, once seen only in the suburbs, has moved downtown. In downtown Chicago, the new $150 million federal office building built by Stein and Company boasts a health club, a medical services office for employees, and that city's first downtown daycare center. Developer Richard Clotfelter says he included a Montessori school in his Pacific First Centre in downtown Seattle as a marketing tool. Providing the school helped secure at least one of the building's major tenants, a large law firm whose lawyers are glad to pay the $650 per month for their children's education. Though this 44-story building did not qualify, Seattle's zoning ordinance provides a bonus for downtown buildings that include up to 10,000 square feet for daycare (see Figure 8-14).

Just when the likelihood of seeing more daycare centers in downtown office buildings as a result of linkage or bonus systems—or even altruism—seems to be declining with the decreased demand for new office space, developers are looking at daycare centers in a new light. With the emphasis in the 1990s on retaining tenants, child care is seen as an amenity that will help owners convince tenants to stay put. "The child care center may become the driving force behind our tenants' desire to remain in our building," says Steve Trainer, a senior vice president for Wright Runstad & Company in Seattle. "We thought it would help us attract new tenants," adds Robert J. DeGrilla, executive vice president of Wynne/Jackson, Inc., a developer in Dallas that opened a daycare center in Plaza of the Americas, a mixed-use project downtown. "It didn't do that as much as it helped us keep tenants."

The Demand for Daycare

Is child care the "amenity of the 1990s"? Or is it likely to become just as overbuilt as other segments of the real estate market, rendering it no longer an amenity? Demographic changes will certainly affect this segment of the market. Projections of the labor force for 1988 to 2000 indicate that the rate of increase in the population of women in their child-bearing years continues to slow.[1] The study also projects that almost all of the growth will be among women aged 20 to 44, with an actual decline projected in the number of working women between the ages of 20 and 29.

Still, by 1995, nearly two-fifths of all pre-schoolers and over three-fourths of all school-age children will have mothers in the labor force.[2] A study of the industry indicates that this latter group is increasingly cared for in centers, part of the reason the authors project rapid growth in child care services through 2000, albeit at a slower rate than that posted in the 1980s.[3]

"We like CBD locations. The demographics are a cinch," says Glenda McClure, a vice president with Discovery Learning Centers, which operates or is developing nine daycare centers in high-rise buildings in downtowns or growth centers in Houston, Dallas, Atlanta, and Detroit. McClure also notes a calmer atmosphere in downtown centers because the children know that their parents are close by. At the same time, letters and comments from both clients and nonclients indicate that the centers have a positively humanizing effect upon the workplace.

"When things get tough," says McClure, quoting a man who works on the 45th floor of a neighboring building, "I spin my chair around and watch the kids on the playground. Seeing them laugh helps me put things in perspective."

A second reason for projected growth is the increased involvement of government and employers in promoting and funding child care. Both see the provision of adequate child care as a way to increase employees' productivity as well as to attract new employees, of particular concern with tightening labor markets in the 1990s. Sixty-nine percent of employees of companies that offer child care say the program is the reason they stay with their employer.[4] Furthermore, according to a Census Bureau survey cited in the same issue, 8 percent of mothers using a babysitter lose time from work, while only 1 percent of mothers who use group care

8-15 "Even the meanest businessman can't help but smile when he sees these kids 'at work,'" says the executive vice president of one downtown project with daycare.

with 33 percent of its spaces filled, unusual in a business where parents want to see what they are getting before committing anything to it.

Selecting a Child Care Provider

Choosing the right operator is another key element for developers' consideration. First, operators should be licensed to ensure that the primary caregivers are at least 18 years old, that staff has passed medical and criminal background checks, and that the number of staff is adequate. Accreditation by the National Association for the Education of Young Children also means that staff members are trained in first aid, cardiopulmonary resuscitation, teaching, and techniques of discipline.

8-16 Daycare centers in the CBD emphasize security.

miss work. The Conference Board reports that the number of employers providing some kind of child care grew from 110 in 1978 to 3,500 in 1988.

Though national trends suggest that demand exists for additional daycare centers, the existing supply of such centers in projects close to a downtown development should be surveyed to test the need for additional daycare in a specific project. If no supply exists, a survey of employees should be conducted to determine the level of interest in daycare and the price employees would be willing to pay for such an amenity. If the survey's results are positive, building owners might consider providing space close to the location of the proposed center for operators to hold orientation and marketing sessions. At Kids at Work at Plaza of the Americas, orientation sessions resulted in the center's opening

8-17 Infant care is a major component of a downtown daycare center's business.

Second, the operator should establish hours that meet the needs of the employees in the proposed and surrounding buildings: early mornings and possibly late evenings. The building's employees should receive priority in enrollments, and the center should provide care for children of the appropriate ages, that is, the age of employees' children. Quality materials, nutritious food, well-planned schedules, and clean surroundings are musts. Operators should be able to provide scholarships or subsidies for lower-income and/or single-parent employees.

"We were very careful in our selection of Discovery Learning Centers as the caregiver for our first corporate child care facility," explains Louis Sklar, executive vice president for Hines Interests. "We checked them out thoroughly, made sure they carried adequate insurance coverage, and made sure that they were truly providing quality child care. We see it as a tremendous amenity for tenants and are looking at including daycare in several other properties around the country."

Other Monkey Bars for Developers

Once demand is proven and a qualified caregiver located, hurdles still remain before developers can include daycare operations in their buildings, particularly downtown buildings. In most cities, daycare centers are required to be on the first floor, thereby taking what could be prime retail space. The reason is safety. "Fifty percent of our children are under two years old," explains Discovery Learning Centers' McClure. "The only way to evacuate them is to put them in baby beds—four in a row—and roll them out." Imagine trying to get a dozen baby beds down flights of stairs in the targeted three minutes or fewer!

Some states, however, are revising codes to improve developers' ability to include child care in commercial buildings. The Massachusetts State Board of Building Regulations and Standards revised its state building code in 1990 to permit daycare facilities to be located above the ground level. The revised code allows preschool daycare centers on the first seven floors but restricts facilities for younger toddlers and infants to the first three floors.

Building owners must first comply, however, with stricter fire regulations. Centers are allowed only in buildings with a full complement of sprin-

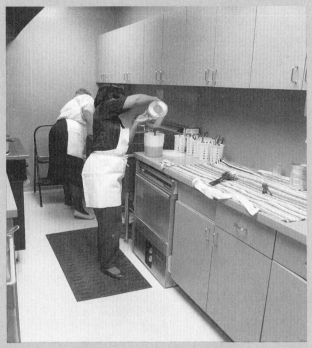

8-18 Code requirements, including mandatory commercial-type kitchens, make it difficult for downtown daycare operators to pay market rent.

klers and must be separated from all other uses on the same level by walls carrying a two-hour fire rating. A one-hour fire rating for floors and ceilings is also required.

The cost to comply with fire, building, health, and other safety codes is high and usually falls to the developer, exacerbating the disparity in rents between a retail or office tenant who pays the market rate and a daycare tenant. Typical requirements mandate approximately 50 square feet per child inside and 100 square feet per child outside. Costs to demolish existing space and build new space can range from $30 to $40 per square foot.

Other costs that add to the operator's expense and make paying market rents difficult include requirements for commercial kitchens. Well-planned playgrounds—difficult to achieve in tight downtown locations—cost from $10,000 to $20,000, plus the cost of climbing equipment. At Kids at Work in Dallas, building owners do not break even on the lease until midway through its term. Rental rates started at 65 percent of what other retail tenants were paying, and finishing costs were doubled. Rent-free deals are common.

The liability of providing child care is another concern for developers. To limit liability, they can choose qualified daycare operators rather than operating a center themselves. Provisions in the lease can include limited use of common and parking areas as well as strict adherence to regulations and insurance terms. Indemnification should be well defined. And if the center is incorporated as a separate business entity, particularly as a tax-exempt membership corporation, the developer can retain some control over the center as a member of the board.

Daycare Grows Up

As the child care industry matures, three variations on the theme are likely to be popular in the 1990s: emergency child care, care for sick children, and care for elderly parents. Emergency child care is for days when normal daycare arrangements fall through or are not available because of short notice, on Saturdays, for example. In Washington, D.C., the Oliver Carr Co. offers its tenants this amenity at Metropolitan Square. Lipton Corporate Child Care Centers leases approximately 2,000 square feet for its center, and tenants are encouraged to purchase individual spaces on an annual basis for use by their employees. Most employers purchase an average of two spaces for every 100 employees.

"On-site emergency child care saves a tremendous amount of money for a company in terms of lower rates of absenteeism. There is a profound increase in productivity when employees come to work without worrying that hastily made baby-sitting arrangements may fail."[5] A major law firm in Washington, D.C., reported recently that after one year of offering emergency child care to its employees, it saved 2,700 billable lawyer hours, which, at an average of $150 per hour, translated into $405,000.

Indeed, the fact that some law firms are opening centers of their own suggests a demand for such services. In Washington, D.C., the 270-lawyer office of Hogan & Hartson opened its "occasional use" child care center in August 1989. Fees range from $10 to $20 per day, depending on whether the parent is a lawyer or a staff person. Parents are encouraged to use the center not only when normal arrangements fall through, but also on snow days or days when the child has a doctor's appointment downtown. Hours range from 8:30 A.M. to 6 P.M. on weekdays and 9 A.M. to 4 P.M. on Saturdays and holidays.

Two other options offered by corporations could signal an opportunity for developers. Stride Rite Corp., the Massachusetts-based shoemaker, opened a center in 1991 that accommodates not only 60 children, but also 30 elderly parents. The kids and grandparents will share activities like games and cooking. In Houston, Hines Interests is a corporate sponsor of St. Joseph's Hospital's Kids on the Mend child care center for sick children. Hines employees pay $20 per day rather than the $35 per day the general public is charged for use of the center, which offers individualized care like administering medication, providing special dietary needs, and on-site visits by physicians.

8-19 Finding space for playgrounds in a CBD is tough. This one is tucked under the ramp of a parking garage.

[1]Howard N. Fullerton, Jr., "New Labor Force Projections Spanning 1988 to 2000," *Monthly Labor Review*, November 1989, pp. 3–12.
[2]Sandra L. Hofferth, "What Is the Demand for and Supply of Childcare in the United States?" *Young Children*, July 1989, pp. 28–33.
[3]Darrel P. Wawh, "Child Care Service," *Monthly Labor Review*, December 1990, p. 17.
[4]Rustom A. Cowasjee, "Maximizing the Benefits of On-site Child Care," *Development*, November/December 1990, p. 13.
[5]"Tenant Amenities—Emergency Child Care: A Trend for the New Decade?" *Business Facilities*, May 1990, p. 22.

Managing Downtown Office Space

Keeping tenants happy must be the theme for the 1990s, especially downtown where the growth tenants tend not to locate. In other words, if downtown owners cannot count on high-growth companies to fill vacated space, they must make an even greater effort to keep existing tenants. With the large inventory of high-quality Class A space in many downtowns, management can be what differentiates one building from another.

Surveys of tenants should be used to show managers where they excel and where they need to improve. Training budgets and the number of personnel might need to be expanded to provide the extensive training needed for high levels of service. According to one speaker at ULI's fall 1990 meeting, "Developers could learn a lot from Hyatt and Marriott. Those who can keep fussy tenants happy are the new heroes."

9.
Downtown Retailing

Over the last 30 years, retailers in U.S. downtowns, small and large, have struggled to react to large-scale shifts in the location and buying habits of their markets, an aging and increasingly obsolescent building stock, and changing patterns of urban mobility. They have also faced the rise of competitive suburban developments that have eroded their market share, leading, in response, to a broad range of innovations by the private sector and efforts by the public sector to revitalize downtown shopping.

Within efforts at revitalization runs a single common thread: how to reconcile the diversity and decentralization inherent in a true downtown with the proven benefits to retailers—and appeal to consumers—of centralized, coordinated project development, leasing, and management. In some cases, doing so has meant new physical models, including downtown regional malls that adapted, with few changes, the pattern of their successful suburban predecessors. During the 1980s, city advocates hit upon new models of development—among them festival marketplaces—that aimed to combine the attractive spontaneity and diversity of city markets and streets with a highly controlled tenant mix, careful planning and design, and those fundamental characteristics of the traditional shopping center: centralized maintenance, promotions, and management.

New planning and management tools also appeared during the 1980s, as downtown management organi-

zations proved to be an effective vehicle to establish a more coordinated approach among traditionally diverse downtown retail interests. Both the public and private sectors recognized the utility of viewing downtown retail enterprises as a system whose interests transcend the boundaries of individual businesses to encompass areawide issues of planning and design, business recruitment and assistance, marketing, and management. In the past, a key reason for the decline of retailing in many downtowns has been the slowness with which unorganized downtown retailers were able to react to suburban competition. New downtown management organizations—along with a series of tools, including centralized leasing and management functions—are an effective means of providing such an organized response. Progress is being made. In metropolitan cities, super regional/regional and neighborhood shopping centers in downtown/intown areas outperform suburban centers in all major categories: sales, total operating receipts, total rent, total expenses, and net operating balances. Performance of community centers is about the same in both locations.[1]

_____

[1] ULI–the Urban Land Institute, *Dollars & Cents of Downtown/Intown Shopping Centers: 1990* (Washington, D.C.: Author, 1991).

OPERATING CHARACTERISTICS OF DOWNTOWN/
INTOWN SHOPPING CENTERS: 1990
(PER SQUARE FOOT)

	SUPER REGIONAL AND REGIONAL CENTERS		COMMUNITY CENTERS		NEIGHBORHOOD CENTERS	
	MEAN	MEDIAN	MEAN	MEDIAN	MEAN	MEDIAN
Sales						
Downtown	$221.83	$209.85	$160.13	$147.18	$205.20	$193.70
Suburban	216.20	203.63	173.92	163.81	197.79	179.29
Total Operating Receipts						
Downtown	23.09	20.04	9.04	5.81	10.38	9.12
Suburban	19.80	18.66	7.62	6.74	8.44	8.05
Total Rent						
Downtown	15.28	13.38	7.13	5.21	8.10	7.41
Suburban	12.94	11.82	6.18	5.38	6.99	6.64
Total Expenses						
Downtown	10.17	8.59	2.92	1.90	5.11	2.63
Suburban	7.55	6.19	2.57	2.36	2.81	2.43
Net Operating Balance						
Downtown	12.92	11.94	6.12	3.91	5.27	5.52
Suburban	12.25	10.68	5.05	4.35	5.63	5.43

Note: Super regional and regional centers typically range from 450,000 to 1.5 million square feet and contain at least one full-line department store, community centers are typically 150,000 square feet, and neighborhood centers are typically 30,000 to 100,000 square feet. *Source:* ULI–the Urban Land Institute, *Dollars & Cents of Downtown/Intown Shopping Centers: 1990* (Washington, D.C.: Author, 1991).

Still, the challenges for downtown retail development can be formidable. Successful projects and management initiatives must overcome three basic issues: a shifting market, a problematic physical pattern, and a decentralized management structure.

Challenges to Downtown Retailing

A Migrating Market

Perhaps the most fundamental—and well-documented—shift in metropolitan economies has been the changing geographic distribution of population and income, a general spiraling outward of buying power that reflects the overarching pattern of suburbanization over the past 50 years. New investment in infrastructure, changing models of land use and real estate investment, and the growth of employment centers outside downtown have combined to erode downtown's share of retail expenditures. As earlier ULI publications made clear, newer retail centers, principally strategically located regional and super regional shopping centers, have captured an increasing share of the nation's retail expenditures. Because shopping center space was built faster than total retail sales rose, the net effect was to drain sales from one area to another. To the extent that new shopping centers were built outside of CBDs, as are the vast majority, downtowns have come up short in this zero-sum equation. Although this erosion has in some cases slowed—or even reversed—in some individual CBDs, the basic pattern continues, particularly in nonmetropolitan cities. From 1986 to 1987, for example, total retail sales nationally rose 5.1 percent; during the same period, however, sales at the nation's 30,000 shopping centers rose 8.2 percent.

The effect of this shift has been most obvious in the retail category commonly called shoppers' goods, which includes most items for which consumers comparison shop and which is dominated by full-line department stores. The most visible symbol of the erosion of downtown retailing in the 1980s is the dark downtown department store. In Baltimore, Pittsburgh, Dallas, Richmond, and, indeed, throughout the country, downtown department stores have been shuttered as downtown markets stratified, as the retail industry has shifted generally toward specialty shops, and as

9-2　Strategically located suburban regional centers have captured an increasing share of the nation's retail expenditures.

patterns of department store ownership shifted from local companies to chains.

In Baltimore, for example, the downtown market has, in the view of area officials, segmented into two distinct groups. The first, following in the wake of the departures of two department stores, is oriented toward moderately priced goods and discount retailers in the traditional shopping area. The second group is drawn to the upscale specialty retail shops centered in Harborplace, the Rouse Company's festival marketplace on the city's showpiece Inner Harbor. In effect, the market for a full-line department store has left for the suburbs. Along with it has followed a range of merchants of shoppers' goods who, in the classic manner of a suburban shopping center, thrive on the strong consumer draw of the anchor stores.

Cities have responded to this shift in various ways. Some, like Washington, D.C., have used various public incentives to attract and strengthen downtown department stores. Their goal, complicated in 1990 by the bankruptcy of a long-time downtown department store, was to use the three existing anchors along with a hoped-for fourth department store to create a diverse downtown shopping district that uses a full range of merchandise and price ranges to attract customers

from the broadest possible markets. Other cities, especially those in smaller markets that might not be able to support multiple retail centers or those with less potential to tap large office populations or visitors, have chosen to acknowledge the decline in the strength of middle-market shoppers' goods and to

9-3　Downtown Orlando's Church Street Market, a public/private partnership between the Downtown Development Board and Lincoln Property Co., is a specialty center targeting downtown workers and visitors to Church Street Station, an entertainment complex.

129

target downtown retail stores more carefully. This approach can mean more focused districts for specialty retail shops, visitor-oriented festival marketplaces, districts with restaurants and services geared toward office workers, or such niche markets as diamond districts or antique markets.

Downtown's Physical Setting

Because patterns of physical development in various parts of a city always reflect the requirements of the people who live, work, or shop there, it follows that changing downtown retail markets will require new, more appropriate buildings and public spaces. The downtown department store is once again a good example. As the market in comparison goods declined, department stores found themselves with surplus merchandise and floor space. These retailing powerhouses have continually been made smaller, even in suburban locations, over the past two decades. Indeed, the average department store 25 years ago contained 250,000 square feet, compared to today's more typical size of 120,000 to 125,000 square feet. In Columbus, Ohio, the flagship Lazarus store on downtown's main shopping street at its peak contained over 600,000 square feet—in itself the equivalent of a modestly sized regional mall.

Department stores are not the only buildings that find themselves with too much—or badly configured—space. One of the most important changes in the way urban retailers do business relates to requirements for inventory. Over the past 20 years, innovations in ordering and delivery systems have significantly reduced the amount of space required for inventory, leading in turn to a reduction in average store size. The relative proportions of storage to merchandise and display space have also shifted. Cathy Coleman of the Downtown Norfolk Council points out that as old-line downtown retailers close or move, re-leasing the obsolescent tenant space can prove difficult without sometimes dramatic reconfiguring. And often the modest expected rents are insufficient to justify the new investment.

This phenomenon of downsizing can also be apparent in terms of the overall downtown district. As downtown's overall market share has slipped, most downtowns have a surfeit of retail space. As retailers close, a once-compact shopping district can lose its mass and continuity. Such spread-out shopping areas are common in midsize U.S. cities. They make shopping difficult for pedestrians and increase reliance on automobiles and the pressure for parking.

Parking is clearly one of the most challenging aspects of downtown retail development. In recent years, city construction of parking facilities has been one of the most commonly used public incentives to help spur large-scale retail development. Even in cities where studies have shown an adequate inventory of parking spaces and where downtown management groups publicize—and often subsidize—parking for shoppers, surveys show that a lack of parking downtown is one of the most commonly perceived negatives about downtown retailing.

Decentralized Management

The economic power of today's shopping center lies not only in an efficient layout, plentiful parking, and locations convenient to markets, but also in its management structure. The degree of control inherent in centralized management has created a series of operational characteristics that, while taken for granted in shopping centers, remain the exception for downtown (see "Centralized Retail Management" later in this chapter).

Techniques include, for example, mandated hours of store operation, which facilitates comparison shopping and convenience for customers. (A recent look at Cincinnati's downtown retail operations noted 53 different patterns of opening and closing.) On-site security and maintenance personnel increase customers' sense of safety and comfort. Advertising and promotion can be carefully coordinated. Shopping center leases typically contain standard clauses governing the type of merchandise sold, the nature of displays and presentation of merchandise, and standards for in-store maintenance.

All of these efforts are linked to the basic concept of a center intended to best fit the market. The merchandise mix, price levels, and specific tenants represented at a well-conceived shopping center all reflect a sound overall concept and plan. Although a fundamental shift is gradually occurring in the way cities manage their downtown retail space, such centralization and control are absent in most downtowns.

Shopping center developers and leasing agents also have well-established mechanisms for identifying and recruiting retail tenants. Major national conventions where ongoing business relationships can develop serve as deal-making forums for both developers and tenants. Cities and their downtown representatives must compete on different terms and in different arenas for tenants.

Other Hurdles for Development

If one implication is that downtowns can overcome these challenges by becoming more like a shopping center, other hurdles can arise. One of the most daunt-

THE GRAND AVENUE

The Grand Avenue, developed through a public/private partnership, is a large-scale commercial/retail project that successfully reversed the trend of economic decline in downtown Milwaukee. The project's goal was to reserve the downtown's two traditional department stores as well as four multi-

9-6

9-5

story buildings fronting the city's main shopping street. The concept's strength came from the decision to renovate the first two levels of the six existing buildings and add a modest amount of new construction. The Grand Avenue now attracts suburban shoppers as well as downtown workers, and the local public/private partnership continues to develop downtown projects.

Project Data

Location: Milwaukee, Wisconsin
Developer: Milwaukee Redevelopment Corporation, the city of Milwaukee, and the Rouse Company
Architect: ELS/Elbasani & Logan Architects
Project Size: 245,000 square feet general retail space; 600,000 square feet renovated department stores; 400,000 square feet renovated office space; 100,000 square feet public arcade
Parking Spaces: 1,250
Year Completed: 1982

ing is the high cost of land and the extraordinary difficulty in assembling suitable sites for large projects. In many cases, cities provide a boost to larger projects by using redevelopment powers to assist in site assembly. In some cases, the developer gets a break on the land cost to help make the project feasible. Without such assistance, the prospects for many urban regional malls or specialty retail projects can be dim.

Development approvals in downtown settings can also be more complex and time-consuming than in suburban jurisdictions. Downtowns are traditionally politically complex, serving a broad range of constituencies that could have fundamentally different views of the role of downtown. The result, besides delay, can be additional exactions or linkage payments that raise the cost of development.

Construction costs can be significantly higher downtown because of more stringent requirements for zoning and building codes, particularly for utilities and servicing, or simply because of the higher costs of vertical construction warranted by the need to conserve land or because of construction unions downtown. The most dramatic difference is often in the cost of structured versus surface parking.

Opportunities for Downtown Retailing

While these shifts can mean challenges for traditional downtown retailing, they also mean opportunities for project development geared to new or emerging markets with innovative design and planning or with management structures that centralize essential functions while capitalizing on downtown's diversity and vigor.

A Changing Work Force

To varying degrees, as the population and average income of close-in urban areas have declined, the population of downtown office workers has boomed. The 30 largest U.S. downtowns added as much office space between 1960 and 1984, the most dramatic years of suburbanization, as they had developed in all previous years.[2] Some downtowns, particularly those in the South and West, literally remade themselves into office-intensive employment centers. Even in older cities, the shift was dramatic. In Cleveland, for example, the proportion of those working in manufacturing dropped a third from 1970 to 1980. Through the 1980s, downtown Cleveland saw the construction of 3.5 million square feet of office space, enough to house some 15,000 workers.

The characteristics of this daytime downtown population were themselves changing, with ever-greater participation by women in the work force. In 1975, about 45 percent of married women with chil-

9-7　A market with an international theme linked to the transit system at Citicorp Center in New York targets office workers.

9-8　Marketing to office workers usually requires an emphasis on food.

dren under 18 worked outside the home. By 1988, their participation rate in the labor force jumped to 65.2 percent. While not all these women, of course, worked downtown, survey data commonly show that women constitute a strong presence—often a majority—among downtown employees. A survey of downtown Louisville workers, for example, showed women as a slim majority, 52 percent.[3] Their importance to downtown retailers was proportionately even greater, however. Based on a series of responses about characteristics of downtown, women accounted for six out of 10 of those workers most likely to shop downtown.

But while this burgeoning office-based population seems a ready market for retailers, it requires careful targeting. The myth is that these new office workers are all highly paid, highly skilled managers and professionals. The truth is that clerical and lower-level

[2] Bernard J. Frieden, "American Business Still Wants to Go Downtown," *Wall Street Journal*, January 16, 1990.

[3] Southern Research Corporation, "Downtown Louisville: A Survey of Attitudes and Activities" (Louisville: Author, 1988), pp. 2, 4.

positions dominate:[4] during New York City's boom in finance and business services in the late 1970s and early 1980s, lower-level positions accounted for two-thirds of the new jobs; only one-third were the coveted professionals, technicians, and managers. Retailers clearly need to target a more moderate-income market.

Attractions for Visitors

Concurrent with these shifts in employment, cities have worked hard to attract new visitors downtown. The construction of new convention centers, the expansion and refurbishing of existing ones, and the concomitant construction of thousands of hotel rooms across the country have created opportunities for targeted specialty retail, restaurant, and entertainment districts downtown. In Atlanta, a city with a traditionally strong convention and conference business (the city boasts the third largest convention center in the country and some 10,000 hotel rooms), the area underneath the overpasses at the end of Peachtree Avenue was until 1981 a patchwork of bars and nightclubs serving mainly locals. In 1989, after eight years in darkness, Underground Atlanta reopened as a $142 million, 12-acre festival marketplace popular with both tourists and residents, largely because of the efforts of the city's public/private approach to the project's financing.

Public/Private Cooperation

Partnerships between the public and private sectors for project financing and development are some of the most important mechanisms to take advantage of emerging market opportunities. Motivated in many

9-9   Relocation of a warehouse invites redevelopment, like this one in Dallas's West End, now an entertainment and restaurant district targeted to downtown workers and visitors.

9-10   Especially interesting is Underground Atlanta's ratio of locals to visitors: 65/35.

cases by a business and political leadership concerned about loss of market share, cities have used public incentives to help foster the development of projects that account for key sources of retail and restaurant demand, from performing arts centers and office towers to convention centers, hotels, and museums. And, like the case of Underground Atlanta, the public sector can be the driving force in creating new retail space to serve these markets.

To a large extent, the federal UDAG program was the basic model for these public/private partnerships. Under the program, small and large cities made $2.9 billion in loans to developers. The repayments from those loans continue to be a major source of funding for economic and community development. The program was largely responsible for the broad acceptance of creative financing in urban development projects. Now, a broad variety of state, local, and—to a greatly limited degree—federal financing sources are used to structure these deals.

New Organizational Resources

This increasingly active management of downtown development has led to the creation of new organiza-

_____

[4] Frieden, "American Business Still Wants to Go Downtown."

133

tional and managerial models to identify market opportunities, solicit interest from developers, and structure development partnerships. In addition to this role in development, these organizations, which can be an agency of city government or a nonprofit private group, have taken on a longer-term management role, coordinating retail management downtown in new and creative ways. With committed retailers, this combination of development resources and management strength can vastly improve the prospects for downtown retailing.

Downtown Is Different

Finally, a major opportunity exists in the recognition that downtowns offer a diversity and vitality that simply cannot be duplicated in a fully centralized retail environment. The attractiveness of successful festival marketplaces lies in their astute combination of diverse merchandising and design with careful management systems. The result is a retail setting that attempts to maximize sales while fostering a lively—albeit controlled—pattern of activities and events. This model, downtown regional malls, and the refurbishment of traditional, street-related retail districts all have their place in U.S. downtowns. The strongest downtowns offer a balanced set of retail options, each in proportion to particular market segments and responsive to downtown's physical patterns and opportunities. Any downtown retail development strategy must recognize the systematic nature of downtown development, where quality retailing can be both a consequence of strong growth and an inducement to it.

Defining the Downtown Retail Market

From the standpoint of market demand, development feasibility depends primarily on three factors. The first includes the location and composition of the populations most likely to shop for various goods downtown. Based on past trends and anticipated future events, one can estimate the size of the market segments as well as their composition in terms of age, income, and other factors that can help to indicate what they buy, how often they shop, and how much they spend.

Second is the nature of competing retail centers, including both suburban shopping centers and unconsolidated regional shopping destinations and specialized retail districts—restaurant and entertainment districts, for example. The third factor requires, in light of both demand and supply, an evaluation of

downtown's relative ability to capture expenditures from the target markets. Such an evaluation, which focuses attention on downtown's overall competitiveness, must recognize patterns of access and circulation, the range and quality of downtown's cultural facilities and other attractions, the quality of downtown's physical environment, and the nature of existing downtown retailing.

Market Segments

Who shops downtown? The first step in defining the potential for retail development is estimating sources of market support under current conditions. Although the composition of markets in individual cities varies widely—which is the main reason that some concepts of retail development are not easily transferred—four main groups account for downtown retail demand: those who live downtown, those who live outside downtown but within the metropolitan area, downtown workers, and transient visitors. (Residents and downtown employees, of course, might overlap, and care should be taken to avoid double-counting estimated expenditures from those groups.)

Downtown Residents

Traditionally, retail submarkets derive the bulk of their market support from households living nearby. Because of the stabilization or steady decline nationwide in center-city residential populations, the relative importance of this source of support has faded. Census data show, for example, losses in downtown residential population in the nation's 20 largest cities from 5.1 percent to nearly 30 percent from 1970 to 1980. Just three of the largest cities showed gains in population. With few exceptions, the median family income of those living downtown in these cities also failed to keep pace, and, in most cases, income declined by a greater percentage than did population. The result is a loss in purchasing power from what once was a major market segment.

At this writing, downtown residential population according to the 1990 Census is just becoming available. An informal ULI survey of 20 metropolitan cities, however, indicates that downtown population might have stabilized. In several of the surveyed cities, population increased. It is difficult to draw conclusions, however, because some of the totals include for the first time homeless people and prisoners.

The experience of individual cities and of specific submarkets within downtowns, however, sometimes belies general trends. Chicago, for example, enjoys a stronger-than-average downtown retail market partly because of extremely strong development of down-

9-11 Conventional retailing is especially dependent on a strong nearby residential base.

Metropolitan Residents

As population in central cities has stabilized or declined, metropolitan areas have continued to grow. The resulting substantial and ongoing increase in suburban populations is one of the most important aspects of how downtown retailing is changing. Even in regions that grew slowly or lost population in the 1980s, metropolitan areas showed strong growth from 1980 to 1987, with just four of the nation's top 20 metropolitan areas showing declining population. And the amount of retail space in suburban shopping centers has boomed in response to this growth in population.

The extent to which downtowns can capture retail expenditures from metropolitan-area residents who neither live nor work downtown depends on many of the same factors that can potentially attract visitors. A strong series of cultural attractions like museums and theaters and special events can draw residents, which can be especially important for restaurants. In many cases, support from this suburban market requires a concentration and diversity of retail stores or a specialized retail district unavailable outside downtown. Longtime, high-quality specialty merchants, such as well-known jewelers or camera stores, for example, can remain a regional draw even in a declining downtown. In Cleveland, the developer of The

town housing during the 1980s. Some 17,000 new housing units were built between 1980 and 1990, and downtown's population increased 30 percent, according to the ULI survey. These new households lend strong support to the traditional full-line department stores and the related retail shops in the Loop as well as to high-end fashion department stores and specialty retailers on North Michigan Avenue. Coupled with strong support from downtown employees and visitors, the result is one of the best-balanced downtown retail markets in the country.

Conventional retailing, focused on department stores and related shoppers' goods, depends especially on a strong nearby residential base. Stamford Town Center in Stamford, Connecticut, for example, is a three-anchor, 900,000-square-foot regional center. The project, which opened in 1982 and is now being considered for a major expansion, was chiefly responsible for the spectacular growth in retail sales in Stamford's CBD in the early 1980s. The Town Center capitalized on corresponding growth in office and retail development to produce one of the nation's top retail markets.

9-12 Chicago's North Michigan Avenue is capable of drawing suburban residents to downtown.

135

Avenue, a 110-store downtown center, was able to attract upscale specialty retailers after extensive surveying revealed that Clevelanders shopped regularly by catalog or in other cities because the city lacked the upscale stores they wanted.

A waterfront or historic district with an attractive physical configuration, particularly if unlike anything else in the metropolitan area, can also be important. When all these characteristics are present, the combination is powerful. For these reasons, Union Square in San Francisco, Fifth Avenue in New York, Pike Place Market in Seattle, and North Michigan Avenue in Chicago all are capable of drawing large numbers of suburban residents downtown.

Accessibility is also a factor in encouraging suburban residents to shop downtown. While it is unlikely that the proliferation of urban transit systems will produce major gains in downtown retail expenditures in and of themselves, they can be an important piece of the puzzle. In Portland, Oregon, early patterns of ridership on the city's suburbs-to-downtown light-rail line, which opened in 1986, showed peaks on Saturday, as residents headed downtown to shop. In

Washington, D.C., the two major downtown department stores have benefited from direct, below-ground entrances from the city's subway system.

Downtown Workers

Downtown workers, especially office workers, have become an increasingly important source of market support as a result of the decline of the close-in residential market in many cities and the downtown office boom of the 1980s. Estimates in various cities of the proportion of retail expenditures made by downtown workers vary from 15 percent to as high as 50 percent.

As office workers supplant demand from residents, the requirements for downtown retailing shift. Downtown employees, on average, could be quite different in age and income from other markets. Some workday requirements of office workers, regardless of their specific jobs, are consistent. They generally have less time to shop, often restricted to lunch hours and some limited time after work. In most cases, they travel on foot and are therefore less mobile than other market segments. The combination of limited time and shorter travel distances (which is even more pronounced in harsher climates) means, unsurprisingly, that the most successful retailing oriented toward office workers is close to office buildings.

How close is close enough depends in part on the nature of the shopping destination. Workers will walk several blocks to a large department store or to a particular specialty store. For most kinds of convenience retail shops—drugstores, card shops, or newsstands—and for most food service and personal services, the distance shrinks considerably. One of the best sources of information on the retail spending patterns of office workers, a 1988 survey by the International Council of Shopping Centers (ICSC), notes that three out of four workers reach their lunchtime destination within 10 minutes—at an average walking speed, a distance of about 1,000 feet.[5] According to consultant Lawrence Houstoun, the ideal downtown, from the standpoint of shopping, would concentrate all office employees within a 1,000-foot radius of the retail core.

Traditionally, downtown retail cores grew up around department stores, which were located in relation to the regional residential population or at major transit hubs. Before the era of widespread automobile ownership, such major transit hubs often meant a key

9-13   Do suburban shoppers with strollers shop in *your* downtown?

[5] Lawrence O. Houstoun, Jr., "Nine Minutes to Retail: The Workplace-Marketplace Connection Downtown," *Urban Land*, December 1989, p. 28.

streetcar line or junction. In the intervening years, the resident population has started shopping in the suburbs, and office districts have grown up in other areas of downtown, far enough away from the traditional core to be inconvenient for the new market of office workers. In Baltimore, for example, the city reopened the downtown Hutzler's department store to great fanfare in 1985. Unchanged, however, was the store's traditional location, which proved too distant for office workers occupying new buildings closer to the city's Inner Harbor. Hutzler's closed again in 1989, reopening a year later as a discount clothing store, with only the main floor occupied. In Washington, D.C., the cycle is coming full circle, as the latest wave of office development boomerangs back to the traditional core in the downtown's East End.

Spending patterns among downtown workers, as indicated by the ICSC data, show clearly that the amount that average workers spend and the frequency with which they shop is related to the amount and quality of retail space downtown. Of the eight cities surveyed, four are generally associated with having an ample supply of downtown retail stores, the other four with more limited shopping opportunities. With ample opportunity to shop, 45 percent of downtown workers did so, compared to only 35 percent of those with limited facilities nearby. Additionally, average annual retail expenditures per worker are nearly one-third higher in the well-stocked downtowns.

Visitors

The extent to which downtown retailing benefits from expenditures from visitors can vary greatly and depends on both the health of other markets—office employment, for example, generates business visitors—and on a city's cultural and recreational qualities, its climate, and other factors that help to make it a destination for tourists. Few cities in the United States support a significant retail concentration on the strength of the visitor market alone, but visitors can be an important segment of demand in a well-balanced downtown. In Manhattan, for example, a strong retail setting is an important draw for tourists, attracting visitors from well beyond the immediate metropolitan setting. The visitor market is comprised of several distinct segments: business visitors, convention and meeting attendees, and tourists and other transient visitors. Each group has its own implications for retailing.

The number of business visitors is directly related to the occupancy of office space in a downtown, as well as to the presence or absence of such generators as universities, medical centers, or institutional com-

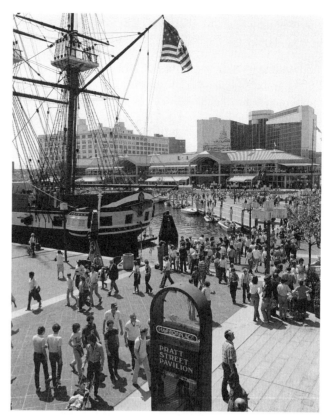

9-14 Harborplace, Baltimore, Maryland.

plexes. Business visitors tend to have limited time for shopping but can be an important source of support for restaurants, particularly for dinner, and for specialty shops located close to major downtown hotels. Mixed-use projects in particular can benefit from this relationship. The Shops at National Place in Washington, D.C., for example, is one of the most frequently cited shopping destinations for guests of the adjacent J.W. Marriott Hotel. In cities with both strong office markets and good air service, however, most business visitors are there for the day, and average retail expenditures per visit are limited.

Visitors attending meetings and conventions can be extremely important for certain kinds of retailing. Convention delegates tend to stay longer, on average, than business visitors or tourists, and could have more time to shop. On the other hand, many convention attendees face carefully programmed schedules, with meals often provided at the meeting. Although the opportunity for shopping can play a role in a meeting planner's decision to locate a convention in a particular city, such opportunities are not likely to be a major factor. Specialty restaurant and entertainment districts, however, can develop hand in hand with a strong market for meetings, with New Orleans's Vieux Carré and Cleveland's Flats notable examples.

137

Street vending can make a downtown more animated, for both downtown workers and visitors tend to buy goods from them. A study of downtown street vending drew the following conclusions:

1. *Licensing is more effective than permitting.* While permits were found to be the more common method of regulating street vendors, they were also found to be less satisfactory. Requirements for permits tended to be less stringent, and, in many communities, the automatic process for renewal that is typical for a permitting system resulted in long-term vending operations without regulation.

2. *Regulating the number and location of vendors is key.* Downtowns with the most successful operations specified distances from intersections, public transportation entrances or stops, and other vendors, as well as established the maximum number of vendors to be permitted in the downtown.

3. *Standards must be promulgated for the design of pushcarts.* Among the methods for controlling design and appearance are ordinances that:
   - Spell out dimensions and design criteria;
   - Require a picture or drawing of applicants' carts or require inspection; and

9-16   Regulating the number, location, and design of pushcarts is key.

   - Require the rental of a specifically approved cart to vendors.

4. *The street vendor program should be coordinated through a centralized management program, preferably privatization.*

Source: Downtown Idea Exchange, November 15, 1989.

These districts, like the successful festival marketplaces in Boston and New York, also draw tourists. Baltimore's waterfront festival market, Harborplace, benefits from reasonable proximity to Washington, D.C., but its setting in the Inner Harbor has helped to make the city a tourist destination in its own right. Similarly, Indianapolis has targeted tourism related to major sports events as a centerpiece of its effort to revitalize downtown. In most cases, however, cities will have already established a strong market for tourists as a result of climate, geography, history, or other traditional reasons, before creating retail uses to take advantage of the visitor market. San Francisco is one of the nation's best examples: the city's largest new retail project, San Francisco Shopping Centre, reportedly derives 70 percent of its business from tourists.

Competing Retail Centers

Another factor affecting market demand is the extent to which competing retail centers are located nearby. One way to understand the nature of the competition is to categorize it. Shopping centers fall into three major categories.[6] Neighborhood centers provide for the sale of convenience goods and personal services, and, in the case of suburban centers, have supermarkets as anchors. Neighborhood centers usually serve a trade area of 3,000 to 40,000 people within a five- to 10-minute drive.

In small towns, a neighborhood center could be the downtown as a whole. In larger towns and cities, neighborhood centers outside the downtown would not compete directly with downtown stores. Instead, the office-oriented retailing found downtown could be viewed as a neighborhood retail center, with an office building or buildings serving as anchor(s) and downtown employees serving as the population of the trade area.

Many downtowns today might be described as community centers; they have a junior but not a

---

[6] John A. Casazza and Frank H. Spink, Jr., *Shopping Center Development Handbook*, 2d ed. (Washington, D.C.: ULI–the Urban Land Institute, 1985), pp. 4–7.

full-line department store. Because community centers need a market area larger than the neighborhood of downtown to prosper, however, it is difficult for the downtown to compete as a community center. A junior department store might not be enough of a draw to attract city residents, but downtown workers might not be interested in shopping there either.

Regional shopping centers offer as their main attraction a full-line department store, with super regional centers having three or more such anchors. The regional center needs a population over 150,000 people who will often travel more than 25 to 30 minutes to shop there. It attracts customers by offering a full range of shopping facilities and goods. For most downtowns, it is the regional center that, beginning in the late 1950s and 1960s, sapped downtowns of their viability for retailing.

The specialty center, difficult to define but often done so by citing the absence of a traditional anchor tenant, is a variation of these three major types of centers. Often another descriptor like "festival center" or "outlet" is used to describe a specialty center more accurately. Because of an existing or potential distinctive character, downtowns often use specialty centers as a strategy, but the very nature of specialty retailing—often oriented toward a destination—means that specialty centers located outside downtown will certainly compete with downtown.

The nature of the competition among downtown retailers as well as the competition between downtown and suburban centers have become even more complex in recent years. The pace of development of suburban malls, although slowed, has continued to outpace growth in retail sales. In addition, suburban developers have begun to recognize that, while the traditional model of a shopping center is a powerful one for capturing retail sales, some of the attractive elements of downtown—diversity, spontaneity, and distinctive tenants, for example—can also prove attractive in the suburbs. Mall developers are adding entertainment and recreational elements to larger centers.

Forest Fair Mall near Cincinnati, for example, is primarily an entertainment center—100,000 square feet of sporting event attractions ranging from miniature golf to batting cages, along with the more familiar multiscreen cinema and video games—but also includes two larger stores, one a discounter and the other a full-line store. Suburban developers are also approaching the layout and design of malls in a much more sophisticated way, paying close attention to storefronts, public spaces, and merchandise mix. The objective, particularly in smaller specialty centers, is to combine the best of the traditional "downtown" street-related retail model with the advantages of the suburban prototype (ironic in light of some downtowns' pinning their hopes for recovery on becoming more like malls).

In another wrinkle, as suburban employment centers continue to thrive, retailing geared to office workers follows. A more balanced suburban activity center can prove even more attractive to office tenants, further eroding downtown's market share. Mature suburban employment centers, which resemble traditional downtowns in size and economic strength if not in form, are seeing an unprecedented growth in upscale specialty retail shops as well, a consequence of their ability to tap residents, workers, and, in some cases, visitors.

The advantages of suburban centers lie in their locations near resident populations, their relatively easy access, and their abundant, free parking. Additionally, most larger suburban centers across the country are a relatively predictable product, with a more or less conventional balance of anchors, a familiar circulation pattern, and protection from the elements. In the pursuit of expenditures, these advantages are formidable.

Downtown's Drawing Power

Downtowns can compete with such alternatives with the right combination of attractions and a high-quality physical environment. Their ability to capture various kinds of regional retail expenditures depends first on the geographic distribution of population and income, on daytime populations downtown, and on patterns of visitor trips. Within the context of these basic parameters, however, a series of variables determines how well downtown competes with alternative retail centers.

Given the fact that in most cities the largest single retail market segment—residents—will drive to downtown, accessibility and parking are preeminent issues. In the wide range of public incentives available to help produce downtown retail projects, the provision of public parking facilities is perhaps the most frequently used, particularly in smaller cities, where relatively low retail and office rents might not support the cost of structured parking. Cities also often provide coordinated programs to advertise the availability of public parking, often at a nominal cost or with a portion of the time free. Even when an adequate supply of parking exists, however, consumers used to free parking at suburban malls might perceive a shortage of parking or think the cost is prohibitive. Much of the effort devoted to downtown retail management revolves around changing such perceptions. In some cases, the availability of transit can help, but unless a retail destination is particularly attractive and/or congestion or parking costs severe, relatively few resident consumers will ride transit downtown to shop.

The most successful downtowns are not comprised simply of office buildings, hotels, stores, and residences. Downtowns by definition contain facilities and attractions designed to serve a whole community or to attract visitors to a city. Centers of government, universities, stadia and arenas, museums, concert halls, and parks are all such elements. None by themselves are capable of supporting a diverse supply of downtown retail shops, but a well-conceived combination of attractions can help a downtown retain a well-balanced retail market that captures a healthy share of regional expenditures. The effect of such attractions is to increase the effective trade area for downtown retailing.

Just like in a successful mall, a clear, easily negotiated physical environment is conducive to successful retailing. Strong downtowns have recognizable shopping districts, often with specialized subdistricts geared to a particular price level or type of merchandise. Anchor stores serve as major destinations, with smaller retailers, less likely to afford the major promotions and advertising of the anchors, gaining from their proximity. Walking distances are reasonable to allow for comparison shopping and to decrease dependence on the automobile. Active storefronts are reasonably continuous along major shopping streets.

In addition, shoppers are dissuaded by an unpleasant or threatening pedestrian environment. Although many of the downtown pedestrian malls of the 1960s and 1970s might have been misguided, their goal—to reduce conflicts between those in vehicles and those on foot—was sound. In addition to safety for pedestrians, comfort is a key concern, with careful attention required to directional and promotional signs,

9-18   Downtowns by definition offer attractions designed to serve a whole community.

landscaping, and the design and management of public spaces.

The quality of existing retail stores is one of the most telling characteristics of a downtown's ability to support additional expenditures. Major indicators include the quality of merchandising and displays, signs, storefront design, and area maintenance. The unfortunate cyclical pattern commonly seen in smaller downtowns is one of steadily declining sales, often following the loss of an anchor store, which in turn puts pressure on funds available for maintenance and upkeep, maintaining a current inventory, and rent. Building owners, lacking sufficient returns to justify the investment, forgo physical improvements, and the declining physical environment depresses sales further. Assuming a healthy market, attractive and sound structures, especially with an existing concentration of retailers logically clustered by price level or type of merchandise, can be a strong basis for additional efforts.

Market and Development Feasibility

The feasibility of downtown retailing is not always a question of market support. One issue lies in the relationship between downtown's higher costs for land and development, on the one hand, and the potential revenue from retailing supported by the market, on the other. When development markets are strong and costs high, the developer will face substantial pressure to forgo retailing in favor of street-level uses that pay higher rents.

On the other hand, many developers see retailing as a way to make a project more distinctive or as a way to provide an additional amenity for office tenants,

9-17   Parking is a preeminent issue for downtown retailers.

140

both of which can help support higher office rents. The problem arises when the popularity of this idea results in a proliferation of upscale retail stores, often in the face of a market that might be more inclined toward moderately priced goods. Without these benefits of marketing, however, retailing often lacks the economic appeal of other uses, such as banks, airline ticket offices, and other service businesses that can pay rents similar to offices. When such an economic equation is pervasive, the result can be deadening at street level. The basic elements of downtown retailing—visibility, continuity, and concentration—begin to erode. Many cities, in turn, have created requirements based on zoning for ground-floor retail uses in key downtown districts.

A related issue in strong markets is that productive retail uses that can pay high rents, such as bars and tourist-oriented specialty shops, can squeeze out neighborhood retail shops and local merchants. Such has been the case in the Georgetown area of Washington, D.C., where an influx of tourists and weekend crowds has created a fundamentally different mix and character from those that existed a decade ago. T-shirt shops, high-volume jewelry stores, and representatives of national retail chains have replaced drugstores and used-book shops. To date, Georgetown has attempted to manage the changes through initiatives by the private sector, mainly the peer pressure of a merchants' organization. In Berkeley, however, the zoning ordinance actually limits the number of boutiques, restaurants, gift shops, and galleries in an attempt to maintain neighborhood retail and local services.

Estimating Market Support for a Downtown Retail Project

One of the most important steps in evaluating the feasibility of a downtown retail project is estimating expected sales. An estimate of sales can be the key to evaluating a project's retail concept, its size and merchandise mix, and the feasibility of achieving target rents. This kind of analysis must take into account the project's overall concept and target market, patterns of retail expenditures in the area, trends in growth and development, the characteristics of the competitive supply of retail space, the accessibility and image of the project and its location, and numerous other factors that can affect the project's market appeal.

The specific process used to estimate retail sales varies depending on the purpose of the analysis, the type of project, the availability of data, and the resources available to the analyst. Sources of information include census data on population, income, and retail sales; studies prepared for the downtown, for the subject property, or for other projects, including intercept surveys, mail surveys, interviews of merchants, and focus groups; statistics from convention bureaus; and studies prepared by research institutions, for example, ICSC's *Office Worker Retail Spending* or ULI's *Dollars & Cents of Shopping Centers*. In its fundamental elements, however, the process is relatively straightforward. Often, the objective is not only to reach a basic decision about proceeding, but also to estimate the optimum size of the project's various components or to define more closely a marketing strategy. This kind of demand analysis can also provide useful information for project architects and designers regarding themes and identity, parking and access, the character of public spaces, and other physical characteristics. For the development team, estimates of expected sales in specific retail categories can help to formulate a sound merchandise mix and leasing plan.

A typical downtown retail market analysis contains several basic components:

- *Based on the initial concept for the project, identify likely target markets.* These market segments could include office employees, downtown residents, residents of surrounding areas, and, depending on the project's location, nearby hotel guests or convention visitors, students, or visitors to area cultural attractions.
- *Determine trade areas for each target market segment.* This step requires the analyst to define specific physical boundaries that contain the populations most likely to visit and shop at the project. Most projects have a primary and secondary trade area that reflects the relative propensity of people within the trade area to shop at the project. For some projects, it is useful to account for potential expenditures that originate from beyond the boundaries of the trade area.
- *Determine target market populations within the trade areas, and estimate growth and change over time.* This step is key when downtown retail market analyses differ from those in locations outside downtown, particularly the suburbs. Downtown office workers and hotel guests are important target markets for a downtown retail project. Nondowntown residents, the primary target market for many suburban centers, could be a less important market. The analyst also needs to forecast changes in these populations. New office development, for example, could increase the population of nearby workers. Anticipated construction of roads or mass

transit could expand a project's trade area and attract more residents.

- *Identify the amount spent on various kinds of retail goods by each of the target market segments.* Using the categories of neighborhood, community, regional, super regional, and specialty centers might be helpful. These estimates are sometimes based on a broad range of secondary sources, such as national surveys of office workers' expenditures. More accurate estimates can be generated by surveying the actual target market or by using documented spending patterns from, for example, the Census of Retail Trade.[7] Although expenditure patterns can be expressed on a daily basis—for convention visitors, for example—or on a weekly or annual basis, most analysts project expenditures annually to evaluate a project's market support. By multiplying the population of the market segment in the various trade areas by the expected per capita annual expenditures on various categories of retail goods, one can estimate overall market expenditures or buying power available.

- *Identify the competitive characteristics of the proposed project in relation to all other existing retail concentrations in the trade area as well as to proposed competitive projects, and estimate the proposed project's proportional share of total area expenditures.* This step is the most critical one. Assuming that the proposed project will indeed be competitive with other concentrations of retail space, a key step in projecting demand is evaluating the proportion of total available expenditures that the project will capture. Capture rates, often expressed as a percentage of total available expenditures, can be estimated for each specific market segment and each trade area. They are based on a range of factors, including the project's location and accessibility, visibility, image, strength of anchor tenants, merchandise mix, and management, and can be estimated based on analyses of existing or new studies.

An Example of Estimating Demand

Figure 9-19 illustrates a typical demand analysis for the retail portion of a proposed mixed-use project in the CBD of a major U.S. city, presenting a simplified version of the process described in the previous section. For each of the three major target markets, the process of estimating expenditures can be described as follows:

Office Employees

The trade area is based on walking distance to the project, which can be field tested. Within this trade area, the total square footage of occupied office space is estimated, which in turn is the basis for an estimate of area office employees by allocating average office square footage per employee, in this case 250 square feet.

Survey research in the sample city shows average annual expenditures per downtown office worker of $1,100 for food and beverages and $858 for retail goods. Based on past trends, these expenditure levels are expected to grow at 2.5 percent per year after inflation. Multiplying the estimated area population by the average annual expenditure shows total potential sales generated by this market segment of $27.5 million for food service and $21.5 million for retail goods. Although the proposed project's capture rate will vary depending on the location of these employees, analysis of survey data results in estimates of an overall average capture rate of 9 percent for food service and 12 percent for retail goods, in turn yielding expected project expenditures of about $2.5 million for restaurants and bars and $2.6 million for retail goods.

Hotel Guests

Estimates of expected hotel guests within the trade area are used to project demand from overnight business visitors, tourists, and convention delegates. Trade area boundaries are again based on walking distances to the project and on the location of other nearby concentrations of retail stores and restaurants. Within the primary trade area in this example are an estimated 625 hotel rooms, with an additional 1,246 rooms in the secondary area. A new 290-room hotel is planned to open in the secondary trade area in two years. Based on an estimated annual occupancy rate developed from a survey of area hotels and on an expected number of persons per room, the analysis estimates annual room-nights in both market areas to total 485,000. In this case, research by the local convention and visitors bureau shows daily expenditures per visitor made outside the hotel of $35 for food and beverages and $10 for retail goods. (This analysis could be better fine-tuned by estimating separate levels of expenditures for business visitors and convention delegates, and so on.)

---

[7] The most recent edition of this document, published every five years by the U.S. Bureau of the Census, is 1987.

ANALYSIS OF RETAIL DEMAND
(CONSTANT FIRST-YEAR DOLLARS)

OFFICE EMPLOYEES

Office Space in Occupied Trade Area (square feet)		6,250,000
Estimated Number of Employees (250 square feet per employee)		25,000

Annual Potential Retail Expenditures	YEAR 1	YEAR 2	YEAR 3
Per Employee	$858	$879	$901
Total Potential Expenditures (000)	$21,450	$21,975	$22,525
Average Capture Rate (%)	12	12	12
On-Site Expenditures (000)	$2,574	$2,637	$2,703

Annual Potential Restaurant/Bar Expenditures	YEAR 1	YEAR 2	YEAR 3
Per Employee	$1,100	$1,128	$1,156
Total Potential Expenditures (000)	$27,500	$28,200	$28,900
Average Capture Rate (%)	9	9	9
On-Site Expenditures (000)	$2,475	$2,538	$2,601

HOTEL GUESTS	EXISTING	PROPOSED (YEAR 3)
Primary Trade Area		
Number of Hotel Rooms	625	(Included in
Estimated Annual Occupancy (%)	64.6	Secondary Area)
Estimated Annual Room-Nights (1.1 persons per room)	162,106	
Secondary Trade Area		
Number of Hotel Rooms	1,246	290
Estimated Annual Occupancy (%)	64.6	71.0
Estimated Annual Room-Nights (1.1 persons per room)	323,174	82,669

Annual Potential Retail Expenditures (primary area only)	YEAR 1	YEAR 2	YEAR 3
Per Guest per Day	$10.00	$10.25	$10.51
Annual Total Potential Expenditures (000)	$1,621	$1,662	$1,703
Average Capture Rate (%)	22	22	22
On-Site Retail Expenditures (000)	$357	$366	$375

Annual Potential Restaurant/Bar Expenditures (primary and secondary areas)	YEAR 1	YEAR 2	YEAR 3
Per Guest per Day	$35.00	$35.88	$36.77
Annual Potential Expenditures (000)			
Primary Area	$5,674	$5,816	$5,961
Secondary Area	$11,311	$11,594	$14,924
Capture Rate (%)			
Primary Area	20	20	20
Secondary Area	10	10	10
On-Site Retail Expenditures (000)	$2,266	$2,322	$2,685

TRADE AREA RESIDENTS	YEAR 1	YEAR 2	YEAR 3
Total Households	1,939	2,114	2,214
Average Annual Household Income*	$34,650	$34,650	$34,650
Total Household Income (000)	$67,186	$73,250	$76,715

Annual Potential Retail Expenditures (000)	YEAR 1	YEAR 2	YEAR 3
Apparel and Accessories (2.6 percent of household income)	$1,747	$1,905	$1,995
Home Furnishings (1.5 percent of household income)	$1,008	$1,099	$1,151

Annual Potential Restaurant/Bar Expenditures (000)	YEAR 1	YEAR 2	YEAR 3
Trade Area Total (3.9 percent of household income)	$2,620	$2,857	$2,992

Estimated Capture Rates (%) and Total Projected Expenditures (000)	CAPTURE RATE	YEAR 1	YEAR 2	YEAR 3
Apparel and Accessories	7	$122	$133	$140
Home Furnishings	10	$101	$110	$115
Restaurant/Bar	5	$131	$143	$150
Total Expenditures by Residents		$354	$386	$405

SUMMARY OF SUPPORTABLE SPACE	TOTAL PROJECTED EXPENDITURES (YEAR 1)	ESTIMATED REQUIRED:		SUPPORTABLE SQUARE FEET		
		RENT PER SQ. FT.	GROSS SALES PER SQ. FT.	YEAR 1	YEAR 2	YEAR 3
Retail Goods	$3,153,691	$26	$325	9,704	9,987	10,253
Restaurants/Bars	$4,871,861	$35	$438	11,136	11,436	12,423
Total	$8,025,552			20,840	21,423	22,676

*Projected to remain flat.

Because of the competitive offerings, analysis suggests that the project could capture 20 percent of the average expenditures of visitors for food and services in the primary trade area. Because the project is slated to include a well-known area restaurant, it is expected to draw hotel guests from both a primary and secondary trade area and should therefore also capture about 10 percent of expenditures in the secondary trade area. Existing competitive retail shops are sufficiently strong to restrict the proposed project's attractiveness for retail purchases by hotel guests in the primary trade area, however. Thus, to estimate demand, hotel guests' retail expenditures in the secondary trade area are excluded. This process yields expected on-site expenditures of $2.3 million for restaurants and bars and $357,000 for retail shops from area hotel guests.

Metropolitan Residents

The proposed project is located within a well-established downtown shopping district, capable of drawing nearby residents as well as downtown workers and visitors. Figure 9-19 shows a simplified analysis for a single trade area. Separate trade areas could also be delineated to account for the shopping preferences of downtown residents, residents close to downtown, and those living in the metropolitan area and beyond.

Overall buying power is based on total available household income, which is derived by multiplying total area households by average household income for the trade area. Area households are expected to increase with the addition of new housing units currently under construction and in the planning stages.

Annual retail expenditures as a proportion of total household income are then estimated for two specific categories of retail goods anticipated for the project: apparel and accessories, and home furnishings and household equipment. Spending levels by the average household in the trade area for these categories of retail goods are estimated using Census of Retail Trade data. Expenditures in the metropolitan area in restaurants and bars have also been estimated using Census data. Capture rates are determined, again, by evaluating the project's likely competitive profile and ability to draw residents from throughout the trade area. In this case, because of the broad range of places available in the trade area to shop, capture rates are relatively modest. Residents' expenditures are shown by each specific category; they total approximately $354,000 for the first year of the analysis. (To avoid double-counting, this total would typically be adjusted by subtracting the amount spent by nearby residents who also work in downtown offices and thus are already accounted for. For the sake of simplicity, this step is omitted.)

The final step is to estimate the amount of supportable square footage for the project in each category and to identify the expected relationship between rents and productivity, or sales per square foot. As shown, the project is expected to support a total of $8 million in sales per year. A review of recent lease terms for comparable projects in the area shows an acceptable rent range of $25 to $35 per square foot. In addition, the project's preliminary pro forma shows that net retail rents of $18 and restaurant rents of $27 will be required to support the investment in the project. Other occupancy costs to be charged to retail tenants, for common area maintenance, security, marketing, and taxes, for example, will raise gross rents to $26 and $35 per square foot per year. If the subject project were to greatly increase supply, however, achievable rent levels could fall. In this example, as will be seen, the proposed square footage would probably not be high enough for it to occur.

The amount that typical retailers can pay in rent and related costs depends on the characteristics of individual businesses and on overall gross receipts. In most cases, the average retail tenant can expect to pay from 7 to 10 percent of annual sales as rent and related occupancy costs. (In some projects, such as festival marketplaces, these costs can run as high as 11 to 14 percent.) The requirement for gross rents of $26 to $35 per square foot implies required sales per square foot of $325 to $438. Dividing this required level of productivity into overall projected expenditures yields the amount of supportable square footage in each specific retail category and for the project as

a whole. An alternative approach to this relationship is to estimate supportable square feet by dividing an expected average sales per square foot into the total projected expenditures. Data on sales per square foot for various retail categories are presented in *Dollars & Cents of Shopping Centers.*[8]

In this example, between 20,000 and 23,000 square feet can be justified in terms of market demand in the subject location. Including any more than this amount would require a subsidy—by the developer, the public partner, or both—to be feasible. It is important to emphasize again that the subject property is adjacent to additional retail stores. When the subject property is combined with surrounding retail facilities, a critical mass is formed. Given the small amount of projected demand, it is critical that the subject retail space not be the only retail space in the primary trade area. Finally, it is also important to emphasize that this analysis assumes that workers from surrounding office projects will patronize the subject property. As part of a mixed-use project, it would be important that the retail space not have an interior focus. The property must have an outward orientation to attract targeted customers.

This process of analysis has been simplified for the illustration. This basic structure can be refined in a great many ways to more accurately define or project target markets, trade areas, patterns of expenditures, and likely capture rates. The fundamental logic of this analysis remains the same, however. Equally important, this kind of demand analysis is but one component of a more comprehensive market analysis that should include a detailed examination of underlying economic conditions and trends in growth, patterns of capital investment, characteristics of the infrastructure, the experience of competitive projects, and other factors that will depend on the proposed project's specific characteristics and the developer's objectives.

Strategies for Downtown Retailing

Any successful downtown retail strategy is likely to be a bundle of initiatives designed to create an environment conducive to sales. Such a strategy combines aspects of districtwide planning and urban design, storefront design and merchandising, downtown retail management, and marketing and promotion. In

---

[8] The most recent edition of this triennial publication is ULI–the Urban Land Institute, *Dollars & Cents of Shopping Centers: 1990* (Washington, D.C.: Author, 1990).

9-20   The latest addition to downtown Portland, Oregon, Pioneer Place, includes a new Saks Fifth Avenue, which forms a two-story base for the 13 floors of offices above and, on the adjacent block, a retail pavilion of specialty shops. *Source:* ELS/Elbasani & Logan Architects.

addition, strong downtowns invest their efforts in various specific types of projects, from renovations and facade improvements to more intensive development of new regional centers or festival marketplaces. This section first outlines some of the basic principles of physical planning and design for retail districts and shopping streets, and then treats in detail types of retail redevelopment projects, retail marketing, and management.

Basics of Retail Design

Retailing is a rather basic and ancient practice whose fundamental rules have changed little over the centuries. Stores must be visible, attractive, and accessible.

They should be logically clustered to encourage comparison shopping. These clusters should in turn have a clear identity relative to competitive areas. These kinds of basic principles all argue for a retail core that is concentrated in its physical area and where sufficient retail stores encourage the kind of spontaneous purchases that are the foundation of the regional mall: first attract consumers with a specific destination, say a department store, then provide additional stores and services in sufficient quantity and variety, attractively presented and conveniently located, to make additional purchases easy. The design can greatly influence the success of this strategy. Key issues exist for both the area and for individual stores and shopping streets.

Districtwide Issues

The image of a commercial district is derived from a complex series of perceptions. At the street level, the most important elements of a shopping district relate to the quality and character of storefronts and signs, the heights and setbacks of buildings, the quality of sidewalks and streets, and key landmarks or places that orient visitors. Certainly, all of these building blocks of urban design contribute to a memorable retail area.

Equally important, though, are a range of more complex perceptions about a place, such as the familiarity of the setting and its relationship to a local or regional context. Similarly, attitudes of property owners and merchants are reflected in the condition of buildings and displays. This condition, along with the number of people and variety of uses and activities present, can create a feeling of security and safety or one of isolation and fear. And the perception of a retail area reflects its purpose: for example, a bustling lunch-hour corner or an eclectic, evening- and weekend-oriented district of cafes and galleries.

Both research on expenditures by office workers and the experience of regional malls show the value of compactness. As a general rule, the maximum walking distance between anchor stores in a regional mall should fall between 800 and 1,000 feet, the equivalent of three to four city blocks, or a five- to 10-minute walk. Just like in a regional mall, this overall distance can be extended with a particularly strong retail destination or with a well-modulated sequence of shopping or high-quality public spaces along the way.

Continuity, even within short overall distances, is also key. Gaps between retail stores or concentrations of retail space frustrate the kind of comparison and

9-21   Continuity on a retail street is key, as gaps frustrate comparison shopping.

9-22   Stores with ample window areas and attractively displayed merchandise are one component of a good shopping street. This window promotes men's clothing as well as a downtown art festival.

convenience shopping and impulse expenditures that successful downtowns require. In many downtowns, surface parking lots are the greatest challenge to such street-level continuity. Equally disruptive, in many cases, are nonretail service businesses and offices at the ground floor, such as bank lobbies and airline ticket agencies.

Storefronts

The basic unit of a good shopping street or a strong specialty center or a regional mall is the individual storefront. Despite centuries of development in building materials and technology, the visual characteristics of the retail storefront have changed very little. Whether the specific offering is shoes, food, apparel, or electronics, good storefronts all possess a common set of characteristics:

- Ample window area for displaying merchandise;
- A clear place to enter the business;
- A logically placed, visible sign that identifies the business;
- Compatibility with the rest of the building but a clear distinction for the retail area;
- An identity distinct from neighboring businesses.

These characteristics transcend architectural styles or geography. Storefronts on Madison Avenue and Fifth Avenue in New York are dimensionally similar to those on Regent Street in London or, for that matter, those in South Coast Plaza, a regional shopping mall in Orange County, California: 20 to 30 feet wide and from 12 to no more than 18 feet tall. Even large department stores break their longer frontage into repeating, storefront-sized bays with display windows.

This rhythm of repeating storefronts allows a retail street to function in a predictable way that shoppers instinctively understand. For this reason, retail development programs that recess storefronts in arcades or around interior spaces do not produce the kind of street-level animation that many cities desire. On the other hand, these internally focused projects are more easily centralized in terms of management and controlled in terms of design and can provide a higher level of security. If the goal is to animate streets with people, however, pedestrians' movement should be encouraged along the street wall, not shifted inside buildings or along arcades.

Pedestrians' activity and animation are often related to the rhythm of storefront openings per block. A good standard for the maximum distance between operable doors in storefronts is 30 to 40 feet. Larger stores can use display windows or multiple entrances to reinforce this rhythm. Some cities have reinforced this scale by limiting the floor area for retail businesses in certain districts. On Worth Avenue in Palm Beach, Florida, for example, businesses are limited to 2,000 square feet, thereby limiting the dimensions of the storefront.

Effective merchandise displays require transparent storefronts. Ideally, at least 60 percent of the total storefront should be transparent. Reflective or heavily tinted glass can greatly reduce a street's shopping appeal. In addition, a coherent street requires that storefronts have a common vocabulary of design elements that all reinforce the notion of a framed merchandise display area. Individual displays should be separated by vertical piers that differentiate one storefront from another, and by upper and lower bulkheads. The upper area is often where business signs and other identifying elements like awnings are attached. The storefront should be designed as an inte-

9-24, 9-25   Effective merchandise displays require transparent storefronts.

gral part of the larger building's composition. In many downtowns, storefronts do not relate well to the building's upper floors, often because of intrusive ground-floor remodeling, inappropriate facades, or oversized signs.

Canopies and awnings have historically been integral parts of individual storefronts and an important element in establishing a business district's retail character. Besides their functional attributes of shelter and shade, canopies and awnings can be an appropriate location for signs and can add color and variety to the street. While the increased height of new buildings has reduced the practical need for such elements, canopies and awnings remain important symbolically. They are often an important part of good shopping streets.

In recent years, flags and banners have played a similar role. These devices, along with special districtwide signage or graphic identifiers, can help promote the notion of a special downtown retail district and can provide a dynamic element if they are updated regularly to reflect seasonal changes or special events.

9-23   The rhythm of repeating storefronts allows a retail street to function predictably, that is, so shoppers instinctively understand them.

Signs

Besides all these indirect cues to potential customers, businesses use signs to announce their presence. But signs can be one of the most problematic aspects of downtown retail management. Most frequently, the problem is one of inappropriate size, with signs so out of scale with the storefront or the building that they obscure important details and break the desired connection between the storefront and the upper floors. This problem is particularly noticeable on older or historic buildings that have been remodeled to accommodate new tenants.

New office buildings that contain retail space sometimes minimize its presence at street level or recess stores inside an arcade. In larger buildings, the design of the building might not be compatible with a retail zone oriented toward pedestrians. As a result, the logical area for a retail sign is too small for the sign to work as a design element. In such cases, a clearly visible zone for retail signs should be encouraged.

Besides scale, the most common problem with signs is that they are confusing, with too much information presented. Signs with too many words, too many colors, complex or multiple typefaces, or moving elements can be difficult to comprehend and, from the retailer's standpoint, are counterproductive.

Ordinances covering signs are ubiquitous in today's zoning and development regulations. Often, however, these regulations do not go far enough toward ensuring a coherent retail streetscape, and additional design guidelines or overlay districts for downtown shopping areas are needed. The general principles are clear. In most districts, the number of signs should be limited to a pedestrian-oriented painted window or awning sign and a store sign incorporated into the storefront. Size should relate to the sign's purpose, with pedestrian-oriented signs the smallest and architecturally integrated signs identifying a business in scale with the entire structure. The number of colors should be limited, generally to three. Illuminated signs should be treated very carefully in response to the district's desired character. In recent years, for example, flashing signs have fallen out of favor, but stylish neon signs are everywhere. At the same time, guidelines should allow substantial flexibility to develop the wide range of graphic styles, materials, placement, and location that characterize a good shopping street.

Strategies for Specific Types of Projects

Successful downtowns employ a range of strategies and specific types of projects to achieve a retail sector that performs better. Although some overlaps and hybrids exist, in most cases their efforts fit into one of six basic categories: restructuring and renovating existing concentrations of retail space, developing pedestrian malls, developing festival retail centers, creating new regional shopping centers downtown, integrating retail space into mixed-use projects, and requiring ground-level retailing in new and rehabilitated buildings.

Restructuring and Renovating Existing Space

This series of revitalization tactics aims to work primarily within an established downtown framework to alter fundamentally the perception of, and hence market support for, retail operations. An overarching principle of restructuring is to apply the successful lessons of centralized shopping center management to the decentralized structure of a downtown. This approach generally has four aspects: organizational strategies, promotions and special events, an integrated approach to design, and a longer-term program of economic restructuring.

Timothy Hursley

9-26 Signs should be clear and appropriately sized and placed.

149

This four-point program was initially articulated by the National Main Street Center, a special program of the National Trust for Historic Preservation; most big-city downtown management organizations subsequently adopted it to varying degrees. The founders of the influential Main Street program were initially intrigued by the success of efforts in the 1970s in Corning, New York, and elsewhere. In Corning, program founder Norman Mintz used substantial corporate support—the town is the headquarters for Corning Glass—to change the image of downtown, chiefly through excellent rehabilitations of storefronts and strong promotion of downtown.

Many saw these efforts, while laudable, as inherently limited in scope, focusing only on design and physical renovation, for example. The Main Street program, which started as a three-city demonstration program in 1977, instead sought to change the structure of downtown through a close examination of local institutions and attitudes. Only by changing the image of downtown, they reasoned, could people be lured back. Time has proven the wisdom of the approach, with Main Street programs in place in 42 states and efforts under way in over 600 communities. Tom Moriarity, one of the program's founders, notes, "The relatively low expenditures have leveraged substantial private investment, a ratio of public to private dollars on the order of eleven to one. And the four-point approach is still intact. If anything, Main Street's experience is that an integrated approach is critical to success."

In larger downtowns, where downtown and interregional politics are more complicated and markets more complex, such a lesson is still relevant. In many cases, however, the existing retail base is substantial,

and the need for restructuring goes substantially beyond renovating facades and changing the streetscape. One of the most effective tactics larger cities have used is to create new retail components that make the most of the existing context. Such efforts can seek to reinforce nascent retail districts with a special character or particular design appeal. Examples include Denver's Larimer Square area, in which historic preservation played a strong role in creating a distinct identity. Often, areas with particular physical charm are especially suitable for clusters of restaurants and entertainment spots or for specialty retail shops. Such efforts can be geared to the creation of a concentrated shopping area that follows the model of a regional mall, with key anchor department stores, supporting retail shops, and the layout of a traditional mall.

Philadelphia, for example, successfully restructured the eastern portion of center city's retail core along Market Street by relocating one department store, renovating another, adding over 100 stores and restaurants, and providing convenient links to parking and to the city's mass transit system, all in the setting of an enclosed mall. The resulting project, the Gallery at Market East, was one of the major downtown success stories of the 1970s and remains highly successful even today. For the 1990s, however, the challenge for center city Philadelphia is to link disparate concentrations of retailing into a coherent whole in light of the tremendous surge in office construction on the west side of downtown. This development boom has concentrated major new office populations well away from the more popularly priced retail concentrations on the east side but has opened new opportunities on the west side. In addition, the city is taking a more comprehensive, integrated approach to downtown retailing that goes beyond physical development. For example, a proposed special assessment district will fund ongoing management, maintenance, and security services in the retail core.

Developing Pedestrian Malls

A key characteristic of the shopping center is its separation of pedestrians from auto traffic. In the spirit of eliminating conflicts between shoppers and cars and of encouraging the kind of environment for pedestrians from which shopping centers derive income, cities across the country have created pedestrian malls or transit malls where cars are restricted in parts of their downtowns. One of the first pedestrian malls was built in Kalamazoo, Michigan, in 1959. Today the mall faces relatively high vacancy rates, even with its two department stores intact. In Denver, a 13-block-long transit mall is an effective

New West Photography

9-27 Areas with physical charm are especially suitable for restaurant and entertainment clusters or for specialty retail shops. Oktoberfest is celebrated at Denver's historic Larimer Square.

9-28   Church Street Marketplace, Burlington, Vermont.

The exception appears to be in locations with markets strongly predisposed to walk. College towns like Boulder, Colorado, and Burlington, Vermont, are good examples. In Burlington, Church Street Marketplace, with three blocks fully devoted to pedestrians and parking restricted on a fourth block, serves both students and downtown workers despite an employee population of fewer than 10,000. Importantly, the mall has a full-time executive director and receives the attention of a five-member city commission whose annual operating budget is about $350,000, funded, as are most such efforts, through a special assessment district. This kind of attention to retailers' needs is evident, notes former director Penrose Jackson, in the fact that during the mall's construction a full-time construction coordinator was hired to mitigate the conflicts between shoppers and contractors. As a result, no business was forced to close during the two construction seasons of the mall's development.

Developing Festival Marketplaces

Perhaps no development prototype in the last 50 years has sparked the imagination of the downtown development community—and many of the nation's mayors—in the way that festival marketplaces have. Partly as a result, many of the concepts contained in the first, most successful, festival centers have been incorporated into other kinds of specialty centers and have become far more familiar to consumers. The concept has also been inappropriately applied in enough markets to render the basic concept suspect. Still, the appeal of the formula when it does work is powerful enough to make festival marketplaces an

way to connect the state capitol building with Union Station, in the process helping to add structure to a diverse retail district. Tabor Center, a mixed-use project near the mall's center, contains 117,000 square feet of specialty retail space in a single-loaded corridor parallel to the street, an unusual design strategy for a shopping center that helps to reinforce the street-related retail core.

The history of pedestrian malls and transit malls is decidedly mixed, however, and many of the smaller communities that installed them have begun to re-open streets to auto traffic. As the experiences with Denver's 16th Street Mall and Boston's Downtown Crossing show, some big-city pedestrian malls can work if the concentration of downtown employees is high enough, but in many cases downtown malls are built as a way to reinforce a traditional shopping street, even though the major office concentration might have shifted a few blocks away. In addition, the loss of traffic and related visibility and the disruption caused during construction can severely affect street-level retailers.

9-29   Distinctiveness is the appeal of festival centers. Underground Atlanta features the existing and re-created elements of the 19th century storefronts that originally lined the district.

9-30 The core of the festival marketplace is the notion that shopping is recreation.

important component of a downtown retail strategy in selected markets.

A festival marketplace is a subspecies of a specialty center. (In fact, most of the newer centers being developed downtown that might have been called festival marketplaces in the 1980s are now called urban specialty centers.) The most telling characteristic of a specialty center is the lack of a conventional anchor tenant. In addition, festival centers play heavily on a specific theme, emphasize restaurants and food service, and are often located in areas with particular historic, architectural, or natural appeal, such as a waterfront. At its core, however, is the original concept developed by the Rouse Company in its formulation of Boston's Faneuil Hall Marketplace—that shopping is a recreational experience and that the shopping center should be a fun place, capable of drawing a diverse market from across the community. According to developer Roy Williams who worked on Faneuil Hall, "Customers at Faneuil Hall don't go to shop or to eat. Proximity to one's office isn't the issue either. But people do shop and eat there, to the tune of $100 million a year. Distinctiveness is the appeal."

Accordingly, design and merchandising take on heightened importance for a festival marketplace. A sense of place must exist. Entertainment is also key, so promotions and special events provide nearly constant activity. The merchandise mix emphasizes the unusual, impulse purchase, and kiosks and other temporary tenants provide a changing set of attractions.

The market experience of the most successful festival marketplaces—those in Boston, Baltimore, and New York—shows the somewhat limited applicability of the concept in its traditional form. In Boston, visitors reportedly account for 60 percent of the market. In its early years, New York's South Street Sea-

port, with lower Manhattan not yet a frequent tourist destination, struggled to achieve the performance of its predecessors. It eventually improved when tourist traffic picked up and when the retail mix was tuned to attract more of the area's abundant population of office workers.

Further, because expenditures per visitor tend to be lower than in conventional shopping centers, where the purpose of the visit is more closely focused on shopping, festival centers require very large numbers of people. At the same time, overall sales must be quite high to achieve the rents necessary to cover the substantially higher than average costs of construction and operation. These centers cost more to build because of the heightened importance of design and cost more to run because of the added attention to management required and the high ratio of common area to gross leasable area. A review of the operating economics of several of these centers showed extra charges, including common area maintenance, insurance, taxes, and marketing, running at up to 130 percent of base rents, compared to a more typical average of 30 to 50 percent.[9] Still, the early experience

[9] Halcyon Ltd., unpublished review, 1986.

9-31 A festival marketplace is a subspecies of a specialty center: no anchor but lots of specialty stores.

CITYFAIR
CHARLOTTE, NORTH CAROLINA

Let it be said loud and clear: festival marketplaces are not panaceas for downtown retailing. Some festival marketplaces have done spectacularly well, but many have not. Still, the allure of a festival marketplace was, for a time, so strong that even relatively healthy downtowns fell prey to a common problem: misanalysis of the market.

While Charlotte, North Carolina, did not pin all its hopes on a festival marketplace, it certainly thought one would enhance its downtown. This city of 450,000 supported some 50,000 downtown workers, and office development was strong as a result of healthy growth in the city's trade and banking industries. Two of the 15 largest banks in the country, NCNB Corporation and First Union Corporation, were headquartered in Charlotte. As office development grew, so did ground-level retailing when the city's 50 percent rule (that is, 50 percent of the ground floor of new projects had to be reserved for retail uses) took effect in the mid-1980s. In total, downtown was home to approximately 700,000 square feet of retail space, including three department stores, when the marketplace was being considered.

Cityfair was conceived as a collaborative effort of the city of Charlotte and private industry to provide new retail space downtown that would appeal to local residents and the local work force as well as to business travelers and visitors. The land for the project was assembled by a private developer in the mid-1980s, purchased by the city in 1985, and leased back to the developer under a long-term ground lease. Totaling 2.9 acres, the site was well located on the majority of the city block bounded by Tryon, East Fifth, North College, and East Sixth Streets, just north of the Belk's department store, adjacent to Ivey's, the other leading department store, and in the same block as Montaldo's, a third, junior department store. Just beyond the site was the public library, a hands-on science museum, an arts center, a new apparel mart, and a new hotel. A key feature of the design of the new project was linking it with a skyway to Belk's department store, considered an anchor for the center.

After the project was designed and out of the ground, however, Belk's announced that it was closing its store. Upon opening in October 1988, Cityfair, totaling 58,625 net leasable square feet, was truly unanchored. Furthermore, the entire design of the project was compromised because of Belk's

9-33 Cityfair's entrance on Tryon Street, Charlotte's main street downtown, is easy to miss.

closing. Because the plan was for most customers to enter the project through the second-level Belk's skyway, the food court was placed at ground level. Without the skyway, customers entered at the ground level into the food court; many never made it farther up than that, a problem that was exacerbated by an awkward stairway and elevator system. Belk's closing also made it possible for NCNB and the developers to assemble an entire city block for a headquarters facility, performing arts center, and hotel. The massive hole in the ground for that project acted as a barrier to pedestrians trying to reach Cityfair.

Other site and architectural features hampered the project's success. Though the building did not front on Tryon Street, downtown Charlotte's main street, a circuitous passageway from the project through another building did culminate in a small entry on Tryon. Difficult to see, the entrance was rarely used. Most customers entered at the nondescript Fifth Street door. (Directly above this entrance would have been the Belk's skyway.) The main entrance to the project was located at the back of the project at the rarely used corner of College and Sixth Streets.

The entrance to and exit from the city-owned eight-level parking garage was problematic as well. The one-way entrance made it difficult to get to, and traversing the entrance ramp was akin to going up a steep roller coaster—scary. Lighting and connections to the building were scary, too, so much so that customers not from downtown avoided the project after initial encounters. ▶

But perhaps the most important lesson learned on the project related to the merchandising plan. A reevaluation of the project 15 months after it was completed but based on 1988 data indicated a demand for only 20,000 square feet of new comparison goods and 60,000 square feet of new food and beverage establishments in the entire downtown. The reviewers noted that the 50 percent rule for new developments would have supplied all of this demand for comparison goods and much of the demand for restaurants and bars. Furthermore, demand was projected to increase only slightly by 1995.

The actual performance of Cityfair confirmed these figures. The first floor of the project, including a Fat Tuesdays bar and restaurant and the food court, leased quickly and experienced strong sales.

Fifteen months after opening, the remaining two floors were less than half leased. Concern about the center's lack of critical mass was really a moot point. Demand for the type of space being merchandised, that is, for comparison goods, was limited and apt to be supplied elsewhere in the near future.

By November 1989, the city had taken possession of the property from the first leasehold mortgagee, who had acquired title to the developer's leasehold interest through a negotiated settlement. In June 1990, the city sold the land and building (but not the garage) to a development subsidiary of an Oklahoma-based insurance company. The new leasing strategy is targeted toward food and beverage establishments on both the first and second floors. Plans include a $100,000 renovation of the garage, to be paid for by the city.

---

of Underground Atlanta suggests that opportunities still exist for the successful application of the concept. It should be noted, however, that the food and entertainment components of Underground Atlanta make up an even higher percentage of total space than in other similar projects.

9-34   ESCONDIDO FARMERS' MARKET

Downtown organizations across the country have tried farmers' markets as a way to bring people downtown on a regular basis, but many have found them more difficult to implement than expected. Downtown Escondido, California, however, has found a formula that works.

The Escondido Certified Farmers' Market Festival differs from others in that only products that are grown, raised, or made by the participants can be sold at the market. Adding family-oriented entertainment and special events like "Soapbox Night" for politicians and "Bring a Parent, Get a Prize Night" for children has helped lure people, too. The project is funded by fees from the 25 farmers, 14 craftsmen, and seven food vendors as well as by redevelopment funds from the city's Community Development Commission.

After only eight months in operation, the market has been attracting more than 1,000 residents to the Grand Avenue location each Tuesday between 4 and 8 P.M. Even with major construction a block away, merchants in the area report that sales are up 200 to 1,000 percent during those four hours over any

9-35   Farmers' markets bring people downtown.

eight-hour period during the week. In fact, the project has been so successful that only two-thirds of the city's designated funds will be actually needed to complete the market's first year of operation. The market is expected to be self-supporting by the third year.

The second generation of festival marketplaces has been less successful. Smaller cities, captivated by the atmosphere and excitement of the prototypes, found that attracting developers required substantial public investment in the form of low-cost financing, direct equity investment, free or discounted land costs, and other subsidies. (In fact, these incentives were present from the start, with major public assistance in site assembly and clearance in Baltimore and substantial public investment in Boston.) In smaller markets like Toledo, Norfolk, and Flint, Michigan, these incentives represented a relatively larger portion of local economic development resources. In many cases, cities held substantial equity positions in the projects. And their hopes were correspondingly higher.

In some cases, second-generation festival marketplaces are generally considered successful from the standpoint of urban redevelopment if not from a strictly financial one. Norfolk's 120,000-square-foot Waterside, built in 1984 and soon to be expanded by 40,000 square feet, is located about six blocks from the traditional retail core. Cathy Coleman of the city's Downtown Council says the project has drawn customers—and spin-off development—to the waterfront, but at the expense of the traditional core. And although the project sustains rents that are up to three times those of retail stores in the downtown core, it has not yet seen a positive cash flow. Nor is it likely to, acknowledges developer James Rouse, until the mid-1990s, when it is 10 or more years old.

Waterside also benefited from a robust Norfolk-area economy in the 1980s. In Toledo, Ohio, and Flint, Michigan, economic downturns and plant closings combined with what might have been optimistic market assumptions to undercut the support of similar projects. In Flint, operating costs of $25 per square foot tower over gross rents of $3.00. The city took over the center, sustained heavy losses, and closed its doors in 1990. The most recent plans call for a conversion to more productive office space for the local branch of a state university. Other projects require more minor adjustments. In Richmond, Virginia, the tenant mix at the 6th Street Marketplace has been changed to create a more traditional retail destination, one less dependent on large crowds of tourists.

This less-than-positive experience seems to be concentrated in those midsized industrial cities that, bypassed by other redevelopment and facing transitional economies, latched onto festival marketplaces as something of a panacea. With the right concept and the right developer, they believed they could remake their downtown retail markets. Other cities of various sizes have long included elements of the festival retail concept, though in a less self-conscious, more broadly

9-36   To overcome difficulties of developing retail space downtown, public/private partnerships are often necessary, as was the case with San Diego's Horton Plaza.

appealing way. Seattle's Pike Place Market is one of the best examples of an indigenous institution—the farmers' market—that has gradually evolved into a retail destination that attracts well-balanced support from employees, residents, and visitors alike. Pike Place is now the centerpiece of a specialty retail and downtown residential district, attracting significant spin-off development and complementing other nearby retail districts downtown.

Creating New Downtown Regional Centers

For sheer economic power, the most impressive of the basic strategies for revitalizing downtowns is the new generation of downtown regional and super regional shopping centers. These projects often use a range of public incentives to overcome the difficulties of site assembly and high land costs, insufficient parking, and deficient infrastructure. In most respects, however, these projects follow the formula for a conventional regional center, with a roughly equal balance between space for major anchor stores and specialty shops, abundant and usually free parking, and a retail mix designed to offer merchandise and stores not found elsewhere in town and maximize spin-off buying and impulse purchases. The developers of Cleveland's $105 million The Avenue, for example, proceeded with the project when studies indicated that Clevelanders shopped regularly by catalog or in other cities because the city lacked the upscale stores they wanted.

When such centers represent the major concentration of regional retail space, they can be extremely successful. The Stamford, Connecticut, Town Center is a good example of a dominant regional center that happens to be located downtown. But while the 900,000-square-foot project has produced dramatic sales and economic benefits for the city, the downtown's remaining street-level retailing has declined. Many cities, however, faced with the choice of further eroding street-related retailing on the one hand and losing these substantial benefits to a suburban location on the other, opt for the regional mall.

In Syracuse, for example, the city's strategy in the mid-1980s focused on The Galleries, a retail and office center anchored by the county's public library and located near two existing department stores. Despite this new investment, however, the larger department store closed shortly after the project's opening, and the project has struggled with low occupancy rates and sluggish sales ever since. Now, comparison goods in downtown Syracuse face further competition from a 1.4 million-square-foot super regional center a mile north of downtown. For the city, faced with the dilemma of undermining its earlier efforts or reaping the benefits of the new mall, the choice was difficult. In the end, the city supported the new project but linked its development to the provision of a number of public redevelopment projects. In the final

analysis, however, the most effective strategy for downtown Syracuse could be to reorient retailing toward the still-dominant population of office workers and new specialty retail and restaurant business from a planned convention center.

Denver's downtown was hit particularly hard by the energy slump of the 1980s. In 1990, the city saw not only the opening of a dramatically renovated and expanded mall in the close-in Cherry Creek area, but also a proposal, linked to a $16 million public subsidy, for a second large retail project, farther out but just inside the city limits. While the city clearly saw the taxable sales—much of which would be generated from suburbanites—as a major benefit, some downtown boosters bristled at what they saw as the city's willingness to undercut retail revitalization downtown through the subsidy of outlying retailing.

In larger markets, downtown malls seem to better coexist with other kinds of retailing. In Philadelphia, for example, a regional center like the Gallery at Market East can fill one set of retail needs, but sufficient support exists for street-related upscale retailing as well, such as that along Walnut Street on the downtown's west side. Such segmentation can also work within individual projects. San Antonio's new

9-37   Stamford Town Center, Connecticut.

Retailing in downtown San Antonio has awakened from a long siesta. The city had long been known for its Riverwalk, first proposed in 1929 and hailed for its blend of tranquil parks with busy commercial and cultural centers along the San Antonio River. But while tourists and conventioneers discovered the city and its Riverwalk, locals abandoned the CBD, at least for shopping. By Christmas 1987, no department stores were left downtown.

Work that began almost 10 years earlier, however, came to fruition in 1988 with the opening of a $400 million regional mall and hotel complex. Located at the terminus of an extension to the San Antonio River is Rivercenter's focus—a turning basin for water taxis and pedestrian traffic from Riverwalk. On the north, east, and west, the basin is surrounded by a three-level glass-enclosed arcade. A terrace at the river level with tables, chairs, and benches encourages public use of this urban space. An extension of the terrace forms an island in the basin that serves as a performance space or another spot from which one can enjoy the view. A two-level pedestrian bridge connects the east and west sides of the mall with the hotel. The city owns and maintains the river extension and turning basin as well as the adjacent walkways and landscaped areas.

The retail area totals approximately 1 million square feet and contains 110 specialty shops and restaurants. Anchoring the mall are Foley's and Dillard's, the latter of which is located in the former Joske's complex, a landmark building downtown built in the 1890s. A food court with seating for 550 is located inside the mall at river level. The largest convention-class hotel in the city, a 1,000-room Marriott Hotel, is located in the southwest corner of the complex, while the existing 333-room Menger Hotel, where Teddy Roosevelt rounded up a number of his Rough Riders, is at the northeast corner. A 426-seat IMAX theater is located inside the mall's north entrance on Crockett Street. The project also includes a multiscreen theater. Retail parking totaling 1,660 spaces is available in two garages; an additional 752 spaces for the hotels are located in an underground structure.

Planning and Development

Work on the project began in 1979, when a group of downtown businesses commissioned a market study for a 28-acre site where Rivercenter is now located. The study indicated a demand for a major

9-39   Early planning at Rivercenter recognized the importance of establishing a strong relationship between the project and the river and Riverwalk.

retail/hotel and office project at that location. Based on the study, the city forged a strong working relationship with the Edward J. DeBartolo Corporation, which joined in partnership with Allied Stores Corporation, then owner of the Joske's building and its adjacent land.

In 1981, the city received a $15.75 million UDAG for the project. With UDAG funds and city commitments in place, the idea for the project moved from feasibility to reality in 1982, when DeBartolo and the former Williams Realty Corporation formed a joint venture to develop an 11-acre portion of the targeted area. Williams coordinated the project's master plan and provided expertise on the office and hotel components, while DeBartolo handled UDAG negotiations, land acquisition, overall leasing and management, and recruitment of additional department store anchors. Meanwhile, the city handled land acquisition and clearance, and relocation of tenants for the construction of the river and Riverwalk extensions. It also coordinated improvements in traffic circulation, including the construction of new ramps from a nearby limited-access highway, completed in conjunction with the Texas Department of Highways and the Federal Highway Administration. Overall, the project involved 23 city agencies and a number of special citizens' advisory boards.

Though the original program for the project called for a 760,000-square-foot retail mall with four department stores, a 500-room hotel, two office buildings, and three parking facilities, further market analysis suggested the elimination of the office components and the addition of another hotel pad.

▶

9-40   Rivercenter's Commerce Street facade extends from the historic Joske's complex to the 42-story Marriott Hotel.

It also became clear that the retail mall would be the major activity center in the project and that the mall should be integrated with the river extension. Urban Design Group joined the project team in 1985, preparing a series of schematic design concepts incorporating the latest program elements. To emphasize the project's location on the river, an alternative to traditional double-loaded corridors was explored. The team recognized that a single-loaded corridor would provide panoramic views of the river from inside the project. This single-loaded configuration has helped to establish a sense of place for Rivercenter, bringing sunlight into the project and improving pedestrians' orientation.

Early market research also indicated that the project would attract both tourists and residents from the metropolitan area. (The ratio of locals to tourists is currently averaging 50/50.) To cater to these two very different market groups, the development team decided to cluster tourist-oriented shops and services on the river level—in keeping with the nature of Riverwalk—and to reserve the street and fashion levels for traditional retailers and boutiques.

The development program continued to be refined during the planning process to ensure optimal results. When Dillard Department Stores acquired the Joske's chain, planners had an opportunity to revise the master development plan to provide additional features for the project. Because the Joske's building was underused, the team worked with Dillard's to reduce the department store's selling space from 500,000 square feet to 132,000 square feet. The mall was extended into the structure, and space was provided for an additional department store pad, the multiscreen theater, offices, and retailing. After the project was already opened, another department store buyout changed the merchandising mix of the center again. The May Company, the new owners of Lord & Taylor, decided to convert the store to the more midline Foley's, thought to be a stronger store in the San Antonio market.

The retail shops in the Joske's building were developed on the exterior of the department store building to open onto Blum Street, formerly used for loading and exiting capacity by both Joske's and the Menger Hotel. The city has redeveloped the street into a pedestrian walkway as part of an improvement program to Alamo Plaza, the pedestrian-oriented retail area located in front of the Alamo. Though the walkway links Alamo Plaza with the project, it has not materialized into a major entrance to or exit from Rivercenter. In fact, most visitors enter the project by car.

At the northwest entrance from Crockett Street adjacent to the Alamo, a 30,000-square-foot pad was used for an IMAX theater. Featuring an original film depicting the battle of the Alamo—produced especially for IMAX—the theater is an additional attraction for the tourist and convention market.

UDAG funds were used to purchase the land required for the river extension and turning basin. Site clearance involved demolishing several structures and moving the masonry shell of the historic Fairmount Hotel to a new location several blocks away. Construction actually began in 1985.

City-provided improvements, managed by Day & Zimmermann, were completed ahead of schedule and approximately $2 million under budget. Improvements to streets and relocations of utilities were completed in March 1986, the Commerce Street bridge for the river extension was completed in December 1986, and the river extension, turning basin, and improvements to Riverwalk were completed by January 1988. In terms of permanent infrastructure for the city of San Antonio, this new extension is the most modern and easily maintained portion of the river and Riverwalk. The channel is constructed of concrete with an aeration system that controls the color and quality of the water.

The major retail portion of the project opened in February 1988, and the Marriott Hotel opened in October 1988. Less than eight months after opening, the center was 93 percent leased. Tenants have reported excellent sales, with nearly every store showing sales figures greater than projections.

According to project manager Robert Dunlop, the food court is the second-best-producing food court in the entire DeBartolo organization. Dillard's management is pleased with its store's performance as well, according to Rudy Million, a regional manager with DeBartolo.

Management

The design and the customer base of Rivercenter make it management and maintenance intensive.

Because of a desire to maximize river views and to cater to the many tourists in the area, the project demands more of just about everything. The 66,000 square feet of glass that facilitate great views of the river require an army of window washers. Custom-designed lighting fixtures and the center's 10 restrooms require intensive labor to clean. More signs are required, because, for example, tourists tend to forget in which of the two garages they have parked. More directories and information booths are available as well, with booths providing information on

---

9-41   PROJECT DATA

Land Use Information:

Site Area:

	Acres
River Extension	0.56
New Construction	9.21
Menger Hotel Site	0.25
Joske's Site	2.49
Future Hotel Site	0.71
Total	13.22

Gross Building Area:

	Square Feet
Retail (3 levels)	386,120
Anchors	318,335
IMAX Theater	25,215
Former Joske's Building (for future development)	195,800
Marriott Hotel (1,000 rooms)	844,285
Menger Hotel (333 rooms)	244,335
Parking Garages	945,950
Truck Docks/Ramp	57,740
Total	3,017,780

Total Retail Space: 1,068,000 square feet
Floor/Area Ratio: 3.50[1]

Parking:

	Spaces
Commerce Street Garage	729
Crockett Street Garage	931
Marriott Hotel (subterranean)	752
Total	2,412

Economic Information:

Site Acquisition Cost: $13,700,000[2]
Publicly Funded Improvements: $16,942,000

Construction Costs:

New Retail Construction/ Joske's Renovation	$48,097,000
IMAX	3,560,000
Marriott Hotel	95,000,000
Menger Hotel	7,630,000
Commerce Street/Crockett Street Garages	11,286,000

Construction Cost per Square Foot:
New Retail Construction: $63.97
Rehabilitation of Joske's: $39.32

Retail Tenant Information:

Classification:	Percent of Total Tenants	Percent of Space
Apparel	37.2	19.2
Shoes	7.7	2.6
Jewelry	6.4	1.3
Cards, Books, and Gifts	5.1	2.2
Food	19.2	6.9
Service/Professional	2.6	0.5
Specialty Stores	17.9	4.3
Theater/Variety Store	1.3	5.4
Department Stores	2.6	57.6
Total	100.0	100.0

Lease Information (Retail Leases):

Rent per Square Foot: $30 to $60[3]
Length of Leases: 5 to 7 years

---

[1]FAR equals gross building area (less parking and truck docks and ramps) divided by total site area.
[2]Includes Joske's building but does not include existing Menger Hotel.
[3]Plus overage rent.

a variety of topics, including how to get to the historic missions across town or the downtown events scheduled for that day.

Marketing is extremely complex as well. One challenge has been studying the tourists who are customers. "It's difficult to really target and study your customer in a tourist center," says Dunlop. "They all look alike wearing shorts and Reeboks." Regular promotions like Foley's Red Apple Day on Wednesdays are not effective either with the tourists.

The primary marketing challenge for attracting local shoppers has been competing against suburban malls by promoting the project's special character while addressing concerns about safety and convenience. Advertising campaigns employ a tag line, "just add water," to underscore what makes Rivercenter distinctive. Two hours of free parking are offered with validation, no purchase necessary, and security personnel in sheriff-style uniforms are visibly present.

Experience Gained

1. Development in an urban setting must relate a new project to the city's history and character, because successful projects are carefully interwoven into the city's cultural fabric.
2. As in many downtowns, a midline department store, in this case Foley's rather than Lord & Taylor, was a better choice, given the market.
3. It has been difficult to attract people to the out-of-the-way Blum Street walkway.
4. Signs are important in such a large project, particularly one with two public garages. The high volume of traffic (as a result of the tourists) combined with the custom-designed interior and exterior appointments require more than the average staff to maintain.
5. This complicated urban development could not have been undertaken without a strong public/private effort and local as well as federal subsidies. The commitment of public funds established an essential foundation for the public/private cooperation.

Sources: Project Reference File, "Rivercenter," vol. 18, no. 20 (Washington, D.C.: ULI–the Urban Land Institute, October–December 1988); and interviews with project manager Robert Dunlop and regional manager Rudy Million.

9-42 Sited on North Michigan Avenue in Chicago, Water Tower Place was one of the nation's first large-scale mixed-use developments.

Rivercenter mall orients the stores at the river level to tourists and those at the street level and above to downtown workers and area residents.

One of the key ways downtown retail projects differ from their suburban counterparts is the high cost of land downtown. Multilevel retail configurations thus are common in downtown malls. Like any vertical configuration, the quality of retail space can vary highly with location, and creative merchandising strategies are required to overcome the difficulties of getting shoppers to climb several levels. Perhaps the most extreme examples of vertical retail development are Chicago's Water Tower Place, an eight-level mall where the retail space starts three levels above the street, and San Francisco Shopping Centre, where Nordstrom anchors floors four through seven of a 1 million-square-foot center.

Integrating Retail Space into Mixed-Use Development

Adding stores and restaurants to hotels, office buildings, and other major downtown buildings represents a simple principle of retailing: follow the customers.

High land costs or limited street frontage often leads to downtown retail schemes that incorporate retailing on several levels. In unconsolidated streetfront retail districts, this scheme is usually limited to second floors and basements. Even in healthy markets, these spaces can be difficult to lease and usually achieve lower rents. Often, space above or below the ground floor is most suitable for service tenants or, in some cases, restaurants and bars. Strong destination retailers can also work well in upper-story space, but they usually require a strong street-level identity and entrance. An exclusive boutique in Washington, D.C., for example, moved from street level to the second floor but used a dramatic curved stairway on one of downtown's most important corners to announce its presence.

Downtown malls generally incorporate several levels, much like suburban regional centers where land values are relatively high. In most of these projects, floorplates are relatively large, and shopping is usually limited to no more than five floors.

Recently, however, in high-density, high-value locations, developers have been willing to defy convention with retail centers of up to nine levels. Many such centers have been built as part of mixed-use projects, including Water Tower Place in Chicago (614,000 square feet on eight levels) and Trump Tower in Manhattan (a four-level atrium with 115,000 square feet). In these projects, high-end retail stores and restaurants provide an important market identity and prestige.

Other vertical projects have focused more squarely on retailing, and, unsurprisingly, several have been developed in Manhattan, well-known for its density, strong retail market, high land values, and skyscrapers. One of the first of the vertical malls,

9-44   SAN FRANCISCO SHOPPING CENTRE: RETAILING MOVES TO NEW HEIGHTS

The site was located in a dying area on the wrong side of Market Street in downtown San Francisco. Known for its tourist shops and fast-food restaurants, critics believed sophisticated San Franciscans would be loathe to shop there, especially at an interior mall that would require as many as seven flights of escalators.

But San Franciscans do patronize this eight-level mall on a very small site—1.7 acres. The challenge of attracting shoppers inside has been addressed through the design of an elliptical eight-story skylighted atrium featuring three pairs of Mitsubishi-built spiral escalators, their first use in this country. The atrium is linked to the adjacent Emporium department store at four levels, and to Fifth Street, Market Street, and the Hallidie Plaza through the Bay Area Rapid Transit and the Muni Metro Rail systems, the main transit links to the entire city and the Bay Area. Because of the access to transit, parking is provided through the 10,000 existing spaces within a five-minute walk of the project.

The center's 220,000 square feet of retail space is on the first four levels of the building. The ground floor incorporates a mezzanine for dramatic inside displays and features 21-foot-high outside show windows on the Market and Fifth Street sides. Nordstrom's 333,000-square-foot

9-45   San Francisco Shopping Centre.

store, the largest in the chain, is located on the fifth through eighth levels. While the spiral escalators, attractions in themselves, allow a sweeping view of storefronts and draw visitors upward toward the retractable skylight, the lure of Nordstrom's reputation cannot be underestimated. Were Nordstrom at ground level, many would not bother going any farther up, spectacular escalators or not.   ▶

9-43 (continued)

Herald Center, included 130,000 square feet on nine levels at a traditional retail location opposite the flagship Macy's. An upscale merchandise mix in a middle-market location, inconsistent marketing, and design troubles doomed the project, in the view of many New York retail brokers.

Undaunted, Melvin Simon and Associates opened A&S Plaza a block south of the troubled Herald Center on the former site of Gimbel's. The new project is much larger, 600,000 square feet on nine levels, and is anchored by a 330,000-square-foot Abraham & Strauss. Besides a leasing plan more in keeping with the enormously bustling but moderately priced neighborhood, the developers have used

an "edge atrium" design that effectively allows street-level shoppers a glimpse of the storefronts and activity inside on the upper levels. Another tactic to bring shoppers upstairs is a top-level food court, which even in troubled Herald Center is a popular lunchtime destination for area office workers.

Location, market-based merchandising, and design, the foundations of retail feasibility, remain the most important determinants of the success of these vertical ventures. Longtime observers, however, note the difficulty of overcoming gravity, pointing out that even strong multilevel department stores see sales per square foot drop on upper floors and in lower-level space.

9-44 (continued)

The center is further enhanced with high-quality finishes. Approximately 50,000 square feet of Porta Santa marble was imported from Italy, nearly 15,000 square feet of green fountain granite from Brazil, and 3,000 square feet of Breccia Pernice stone from northern Italy. Approximately $125,000 worth of Australian bronze was used in constructing the center's escalator banisters and atrium railings.

In a city known for its highly regulated development environment, San Francisco Shopping Centre, completed in late 1988, has been greeted warmly. Surrounded by historical buildings, the project seems to fit in. Originally planned to include office and retail space, the building was scaled back and changed to all retail space in response to public concern. And even this smaller version of the project looks smaller than it really

is—670,000 square feet—because of the stepbacks designed in the roof. This design also allows light on the popular Hallidie Plaza year round.

Some retailers believe that vertical retailing is really the same as the old-fashioned multistory department store with a twist. But vertical retailing à la San Francisco Shopping Centre is more complex: the existence of a number of tenants rather than just one is the key difference. While department store managers might have little concern over trying to get every customer to every floor, managers at a vertical center have to get as many customers as possible to as many levels as possible. With its strong anchor department store on the top luring customers on spectacular escalators toward the dramatically lit skylight, San Francisco Shopping Centre does a good job with a tough assignment.

Mixed-use projects offer the opportunity for retail stores to benefit from the proximity of potential shoppers. The overall project can benefit from the retail space as well, however, helping to create a more memorable project and perhaps providing an important amenity for office tenants, hotel guests, or residents.

The basic concept of mixed-use development is to create a synergistic relationship among various market segments. Hotel guests, office workers, and residents, if housing is included, provide a captive market for a well-conceived retail mix. The concept is not new, for Rockefeller Center, among others, was a

leading early prototype. In many cases, however, these efforts did not go beyond providing basic services and convenience retail and food tenants in office buildings. More recently, mixed-use retailing has grown increasingly sophisticated in design and merchandising, with examples ranging from anchored regional centers, such as Water Tower Place in Chicago and Broadway Plaza in Los Angeles to sophisticated specialty centers like Tabor Center in Denver.

Perhaps as important, in many MXDs retailing is the single most important component contributing to the development's image. Retail space is often a col-

9-46   At Arizona Center in Phoenix, the shops and a three-acre garden park are the most important components creating an image for the MXD. *Source:* ELS/Elbasani & Logan Architects.

orful and festive part of the design of a mixed-use project and the use most associated with street-level or interior public spaces. Citicorp Center in Manhattan is distinctive not only for its sharply sloping roof, but also for its three-level retail and restaurant complex. In 1978, The Market at Citicorp Center proved a highly innovative and influential retail concept. The retail section, which is linked to the Lexington Avenue subway line and is organized around international food and household products and furniture, has been key to transforming what might have been merely a distinctive corporate office building into one of midtown Manhattan's landmark destinations.

When stores accommodating comparison shopping or specialty goods are included, the retail component is usually heavily promoted and advertised as a retail destination. As a result, the retail component drives the project's image. It is a good bet, for example, that most Chicagoans identify Water Tower Place as a retail mall, even though the multilevel shopping center is only one component of a mixed-use project. In Philadelphia, the rehabilitation of the former Bellevue Stratford Hotel offers 70,000 square feet of retail space, which will no doubt become the project's sig-

nature in the minds of most city residents. Manhattan's Trump Tower, even with a moderate amount of retail space, is another good example, primarily because of its orientation toward extremely high-end specialty merchandise, consistent with the project's overall approach.

The formula for adding retail space to mixed-use projects is a delicate one and requires a careful assess-

9-47   The market at Citicorp Center in Manhattan.

9-48   Lower profile for high fashion? Developers of high-end office space or MXDs might want the prestige of high-end specialty retail shops, while customers prefer moderately priced convenience items.

ment of the specific sources and magnitude of likely demand, competing retail centers, and the project's ability to compete for retail expenditures. Although the power to create the image of a successful retail element can be extensive, the pitfall is that the retail tail can sometimes wag the mixed-use dog. An excessively large or ill-conceived retail project can undermine the market credibility of the other uses in the project. For example, few projects can support significant amounts of retail space solely with the on-site population. They instead depend on their ability to draw shoppers from nearby concentrations of development and downtown attractions. To the extent that the retail preferences of this off-site support are consistent with those of the on-site population, the amount of overall retail support increases. If, however, the project is poorly located in relation to other downtown populations or if the market preferences of those other populations are inconsistent with the mixed-use project, the retail component can suffer. A study of downtown Washington, D.C., for example, concluded that while the Washington region had a large number of high-income households, the demographics of downtown office workers, trade area residents, and visitors suggested a mix of retailers providing a wide range of popularly and moderately priced soft goods.[10] Still, many developers of high-end office projects gambled on the prestige of high-end specialty retail goods or fine restaurants.

Physical design also needs special attention to take best advantage of the on-site market and to mitigate conflicts between retailing and other uses. Among the key physical issues are making the most efficient use of the base building to maximize the size and quality of the leasable area, providing clear orientation and

circulation for shoppers, ensuring the visibility of storefronts, establishing appropriate controls over tenant designs, and ensuring adequate tenant services. The best mixed-use retail centers are those where retailing is a primary element in the architectural program from the earliest stages of design.

Clearly, merchandising strategies should reflect the project's overall concept, with the proportion of retail space by type linked to careful estimates of market segmentation. Given the right market, for example, a project can support services and convenience food geared to office workers as well as specialty retail or comparison goods oriented toward visitors. Such a strategy, however, requires leasing plans and tenant layouts that respond to the circulation patterns, the size and expected levels of expenditures, and the shopping patterns (rushed or leisurely, for example) of each market segment.

An interesting emerging area for downtowns is the development of retail facilities as part of transportation hubs, convention centers, and other major public structures. In the late 1980s, train stations dominated this area of redevelopment. Union Station in Washington, D.C., is a highly successful transformation of this city landmark into a vibrant transportation hub (train, subway, bus, and tourmobile), a retail destination for residents and tourists, and a catalyst for a development boom in surrounding parcels. A nonprofit corporation undertook the project, working with a private development team that was responsible

---

[10] Hammer, Siler, George Associates, "Downtown Potentials: Analysis of Existing Conditions and Opportunities, Downtown Washington Retail Core" (Washington, D.C.: Author, February 1989), p. 98.

9-49   Union Station in Washington, D.C., is a hub for Amtrak and the city's subway system as well as a shopping center.

9-50   Union Station, Hartford, Connecticut.

for the shopping, entertainment, and food service facilities. The $160 million venture meticulously restored the building and in the process added some 175,000 square feet of retail space and restaurants that attract nearby residents of and employees on Capitol Hill, tourists and travelers, and residents from throughout the area, many of whom arrive by subway. The developers of the commercial space at the station report strong sales, including an extraordinary $1,200 per square foot in the food court. Surprisingly, they estimate that Amtrak travelers are responsible for 25 percent of the project's gross sales.

Union Station, like many transportation facilities, is located outside the traditional downtown core, but these kinds of retail projects can have the practical effect of extending the boundaries of traditional business districts. Such was the case in Pittsburgh, where the Station Square mixed-use development used 150,000 square feet of retail space to lure downtown workers across the Monongahela River from the downtown core. Even in smaller markets, these facilities can present an attractive opportunity. In Hartford, a complex financing structure involving UMTA funds, a local government contribution, and a creative, low-interest loan package provided the impetus for the successful renovation of that city's Union Station. The project's development team added 20,000 square feet of destination restaurants, food service, and convenience retail stores to the historic structure, in addition to reconfiguring its active transportation functions. The project has provided additional momentum for an emerging restaurant and entertainment district in the immediate vicinity of the station.

Requiring Retail Space Downtown

Another strategy used in many downtowns is to require ground-level retailing in all new or rehabilitated projects to energize the downtown streetscape. Many code requirements specifically exclude banks, travel agents, or airline ticket offices, as they are not oriented toward pedestrians. As well, the requirements are usually limited to a designated area within the downtown.

Developers as a rule balk at such requirements for a number of reasons. The need for the retail facilities to be massed together in sufficient quantity rather than spread out is most often cited. Though most ordinances require such retailing in only a limited area, in many cities that area is still too large. In downtown Charlotte, North Carolina, for example, any new development in a nine-block by two-block area must devote 50 percent of its net first-floor area to retail activities. The office and retail core stretches along only five blocks on only one main street. Orlando's requirement stretches for 10 blocks. As new office buildings have developed in these extended areas, so have dabs of retail space—15,000 square feet here and 20,000 square feet there—without the critical mass to be successful. And much of the new space is vacant.

In a related problem, developers note that specialty retailing must occupy center stage to perform its role successfully. "Specialty retailing buried in an office building doesn't work," according to Union Station developer Roy Williams in Washington, D.C.

Analyzing the market before any such requirements are made is one way to fine-tune this zoning tool for effectiveness. Before any retail requirements are considered, a study of demand for additional retail space over a specified period should be completed. As a component of that study, the types of retail stores in demand should also be determined. An estimate of the amount of space that would be added under any requirement should be compared with actual demand and any proposed requirement adjusted to reflect that demand.

Bolstering retail requirements with design standards can also be effective. Standards might include specifications for frequent entryways directly to the sidewalk, encouragement of windows with clear glass or display space on the first floor, and limits on inward-facing arcades and atria. All of these features are meant to make retail uses more visible and accessible.

Portland, Oregon, is one city where retail requirements have been effective, perhaps because they have been used in conjunction with a comprehensive retail strategy. Since the early 1970s, retail space has been required in at least 50 percent of new ground-level space in a designated area downtown. The city's policy of severely limiting new connections to the skywalk has also channeled pedestrian traffic back to

9-51   Some of the details, implemented during several years, that paved the way for Portland's Pioneer Place include light rail, a transit mall, streetscaping, and uninterrupted ground-level retailing around the project. *Source:* ELS/Elbasani & Logan Architects.

street level. As well, the city's limit on parking spaces downtown has encouraged the use of public transit, including buses and a light-rail line. Since then, retail sales have increased dramatically along the transit mall and light-rail route. The Rouse Company's Pioneer Place, completed in August 1990 and including a 60,000-square-foot Saks Fifth Avenue, 145,000 square feet of specialty retailing, and a 284,000-square-foot Class A office building, is the latest evidence of downtown Portland's healthy retail market.

Centralized Retail Management

Advocates for downtown made great strides in the 1980s in the creation of new organizational forms and management tools to help revitalize downtown retailing. Cities have gradually come to realize that downtowns present a special set of opportunities and problems requiring special services that public agencies are often ill-equipped to provide. Older models created by the private sector abound. Merchants' associations and chambers of commerce, for example, have long been active in most downtowns. These organizations, however, are often limited by their scope of activity or concern, which is either too broad or too narrow to effectively manage downtown retailing. Few have the necessary amount and continuity of funding. Merchants' organizations can sometimes be parochial and defensive about competition and independence. Various government agencies have often stepped in, using public powers to accomplish major development projects. These entities, usually the creations of state enabling legislation and local statute, have had substantial muscle to create change but often lacked the ongoing resources and expertise to manage complex retail issues day to day.

Using the lessons derived from shopping centers as their initial inspiration, business and political leaders in many cities sought a new model—called centralized retail management (CRM)—to help develop the consensus and steady funding necessary to integrate issues of market definition and retail mix, marketing and promotions, physical maintenance, and planning and design.

CRM is no new concept to managers of suburban shopping centers.[11] When a center is initially leased and then re-leased, the managers pursue a particular tenant mix, coordinate marketing promotions, and offer opportunities for training. That process is part of what any shopping center owner expects from its manager.

A downtown, however, does not have just one owner, and many of the several owners might not be based locally. It has been only recently that they, along with merchants, have begun to coordinate store hours, pursue targeted tenants—even when that meant turning down opportunities to lease long-vacant spaces—and develop programs to keep businesses. CRM programs change frequently, but some techniques have worked and the results have been encouraging. Not surprisingly, the same overall techniques that work for revitalizing a downtown also work for CRM—developing widespread support and a plan, and then systematically implementing the plan.

The Market Analysis and Merchandising Plan

One of the most important undertakings in improving downtown retailing is an analysis of the market, not just for one project, but for the entire downtown. Usually involving an experienced professional consultant, the market study identifies current and potential customers for downtown business and permits the development of a targeted tenant mix or merchan-

---

[11] This section draws heavily on James A. Cloar et al., *Centralized Retail Management* (Washington, D.C.: ULI–the Urban Land Institute, 1990).

9-54 A merchandising plan identifies classes of businesses to be discouraged or excluded, such as this "adult" bookstore.

dising plan. The merchandising plan informs all involved of the objectives of the downtown retail revitalization program. It also helps establish priorities for recruiting retail businesses. It can be somewhat general, identifying businesses by type, such as women's apparel, shoes, or pharmacies, and it might indicate classes of businesses specifically to be discouraged or excluded. It can also be quite specific, including objectives about quantity (total square footage or number of establishments) and location (by block or even by parcel).

In a downtown setting, however, decision making on compatible uses is problematic. The high retail vacancy rate that might have prompted implementation of CRM means that a community must summon up its courage and patience if it is to be selective when filling an empty storefront. At its first opportunity to do so, for example, Neenah, Wisconsin, did not veto a nonconforming tenant but gained important concessions from the tenant. In a later instance, the Downtown Neenah Action Committee prevented the inclusion of an incompatible tenant but was able to obtain a desirable substitute. In Oak Park, Illinois, bonuses for brokers apply only to leases for qualifying types of

businesses. And in Tulsa, Oklahoma, the rental abatement and low-interest loan programs are available only to businesses included on the target list.

Some communities have concluded that they are unlikely to command the authority to directly control tenant mix. Instead, they seek to exert influence over the selection of tenants by requiring or requesting owners to provide notification of expiring leases and expected vacancies. The organization then works with the owner to identify desirable tenants and to assist in recruiting them.

Master Lease Controls

In addition to implementing a merchandising plan, ensuring an overall high standard of retail operation and appearance is central to improving the attraction of downtown as a shopping destination. A major asset that shopping centers enjoy is their ability to control at least a minimal level of quality. Typically master lease covenants detail the needed controls. Cooperating property owners incorporate them into new or renewed retail leases and pledge to make the best effort possible to incorporate them into existing leases as well. The covenants are similar to those used in shopping centers, controlling such items as cleanliness of display windows, obstructions to sidewalks or entryways, external noise or light, handmade signs, chronic sales (going-out-of-business or fire sales), maintenance of exterior frontages, and approval for remodeling programs.

9-55 Master leases control such items as display windows and the maintenance of exterior frontages.

One more controversial aspect of lease covenants deals with establishing common or uniform hours. A complaint potential downtown customers frequently voice is the lack of predictable, uniform, and convenient business hours. Before Neenah instituted its CRM program, some stores closed at midafternoon during the hunting season. In Scottsdale, Arizona, merchants have complained that neighboring stores operated by retirees opened or closed on the owner's whim.

Generally, the notion of common or minimum hours suggests extended evening and weekend operations. "Evening shopping has become a major force in retailing. The practice has shifted the peak hours of trade in the traditional shopping schedules to such a point that most centers now stay open six nights a week. Evening sales now typically account for 30 to 40 percent of a center's trade."[12]

The extent to which extended hours can succeed in a downtown setting, however, is complicated. Many smaller merchants employ a limited sales force, and extended hours can represent a hardship. Furthermore, in most cities, the downtown work force constitutes a large part of the customer base not present during extended hours.

Traditional CRM agreements emphasize a minimum set of hours, including late closing on one weekday evening. A task force of merchants, seeking to balance the need for enough activity against undue hardships on individual operations, usually establishes or recommends the precise hours.

Services Offered

To help effect the merchandising plan, CRM also builds on traditional planning and promotional activities and complements them with directed initiatives to increase the level of convenience for parking, security, maintenance, and other areas of concern. The committee in downtown Neenah, for example, ensures that the most convenient parking spaces are reserved for shoppers. All-day parking for downtown workers is available (and enforced) a block or two farther away. Seattle's Easy Streets program discounts parking rates and transit fares in conjunction with purchases made at participating stores. Promotions make potential customers aware of the benefit.

Common Area Maintenance. Common area maintenance is another longtime program found in shopping centers that has been applied in downtown settings, though not necessarily with a retail orientation. Urban design controls and other planning tools produced, over the last 20 years, a plethora of civic squares, plazas, and greens that were often unused or,

9-56   The downtown equivalent of a mall's "common area" is a park or plaza that must be managed and maintained.

with city maintenance budgets stretched thin, neglected. Without active management, they became refuges for what author William Whyte called "the undesirables," which led the mainstream downtown population to avoid them further. Such spaces must not only be properly designed, but also actively managed and maintained.

In Orlando, the Downtown Development Board undertakes more cleanup and maintenance for such spaces than the city ordinarily provides. Like security, common area maintenance for retail spaces should reflect downtown shopping hours and the importance of making a favorable impression on downtown visitors. Proper disposal of refuse is an element of the lease provisions generally incorporated as part of CRM.

Planning and Design. Relatively few city planning or economic development agencies have strong in-house staffs capable of managing in detail the physical design of downtown retailing. Typical urban design divisions, to the extent they exist at all, are

---

[12] Casazza and Spink, *Shopping Center Development Handbook*, p. 185.

stretched thin between the needs of downtowns and other neighborhoods and must necessarily focus on a broad range of issues besides retailing. As a result, downtown management organizations are often the logical location for centralized planning or design review, guided by clear policy directives, such as a downtown plan or guidelines for retailing and storefront designs. Guidelines should clearly be derived from the overall market concept and marketing strategy for downtown retailing and should respond to the needs of retailers.

Traffic, Transit, and Parking Management. Because of the importance of access, mobility, and parking to successful retail operations, management groups often create specific programs to make getting around easier for potential consumers. These efforts can be substantial and capital-intensive, like the development of parking garages, or primarily informational, designed to change the perception of congestion or difficult parking, for example.

Links to existing transit systems are one mechanism, and planning for transit routes can accommodate retail uses by design or as an afterthought. Transit malls typically involve a downtown management group and a transit agency working closely to manage routes and timing, the design of stops and shelters, and even operations and characteristics of vehicles. Rubber-tired trolleys and other special vehicles, for example, are popular ways to distinguish downtown transit whose aim is to move shoppers.

The Downtown Seattle Association's Easy Streets program offers shoppers at participating businesses a token good for either a transit trip or free parking at 300 available garages and parking lots. Other cities provide zones in downtown retail districts offering free use of the transit system, discounts from merchants for transit riders, and discounted fares for retail employees. These kinds of programs are popular and effective ways to help overcome potential resistance to shopping downtown, but they require constant and creative promotion to reinforce the message. In addition, they should be viewed as a way to *support*, not create, a strong downtown retail mix. A good parking program or transit link cannot, for example, overcome a poor merchandise mix or an inappropriate physical layout.

Security. An enhanced security program must consider some factors for centralized management. First, it should consider the hours of store operations, which should include evening and weekend shopping hours. Second, it should recognize that downtown shoppers are less familiar with their surroundings than workers and might therefore need special assistance or courtesies to orient themselves to the shopping area. These

9-57   Highly visible patrol officers put police in close contact with shoppers and visitors.

same shoppers might also have unfounded concerns about their personal safety; thus, visibility of patrol officers takes on special importance.

Marketing, Promotions, and Special Events. Budgets for advertising and promotions in super regional shopping centers can run up to 5 percent of total receipts in any given year.[13] For a larger center, that amount could add up to $1 million or more. In contrast, few downtowns, even those with strong programs, market themselves as aggressively, although downtown Seattle currently budgets about $600,000 for these activities. Coupled with uncoordinated advertising by individual businesses, such a program can have a substantial impact.

Indirect promotional efforts include downtown maps and guides intended for areawide distribution or coordinated logos and slogans that reinforce a particular theme. A strong graphic identity has myriad applications, from shopping bags to banners, for creating a distinctive image of a downtown shopping district.

One of the more traditional retail-oriented downtown programs is joint or cooperative advertising, and cities where CRM is common have ratcheted up its level of sophistication by relying on market studies and the experience of professionals. CRM advertising programs have become more strategic in terms of targeting appropriate newspapers or broadcast media, developing an overall theme or image, and specifying effective schedules or timing to achieve the greatest overall impact for the dollar spent.

Festivals, parades, outdoor concerts, and other special events have long been popular techniques to create a greater public awareness of downtown. Re-

---

[13] ULI–the Urban Land Institute, *Dollars & Cents of Shopping Centers*, p. 19.

tailers, however, are not always pleased with the results of such events. Particularly when held during the popular weekday lunch hour, such events compete with stores for the attention of downtown workers, cutting into one of the few remaining stable market sources. To counteract retailers' opposition, Burlington, Vermont, for example, takes care to include retailers in planning the events. It might also be appropriate to limit the frequency and/or duration of special events. Activities, for instance, could be limited to 20 minutes to leave time for shopping. At the same time, organizers should keep all retailers informed of plans for such events and advise or even assist them in developing strategies to take advantage of the activities.

Business Development and Retention. Because a downtown location can suffer from difficult or unusual constraints on starting and operating businesses, direct incentives must sometimes be available to support retail marketing. In Tulsa, the combination of a potential six months of free rent and a low-interest loan program was successful in generating a renewed focus on downtown as a business location. Oak Park, Illinois, offers a special bonus program as an incentive to real estate brokers to draw desired businesses

to the downtown. Reduced credit card fees and lower insurance premiums made available by the Downtown Neenah Action Committee have provided savings to several merchants sufficient to offset their annual membership dues.

Equally important but often overlooked is a formalized program to *keep* businesses once they locate downtown. The closing or relocation of a quality downtown business should not catch a city off guard. Ongoing communication, including frequent face-to-face contact, visits to merchants in their stores, advice to retailers about activities that will affect them, and an ear for merchants' complaints should keep the management team informed and better able to help retailers. Newsletters and other informational pieces are important supplements. News that a proprietor is considering a move out of town, however, should trigger a set of strategies, including financial incentives, to retain local businesses.

Evaluating CRM

Various types of surveys are important tools in evaluating the orientation and effectiveness of retail management and support programs. Two used in Seattle

9-58   Outdoor concerts and other special events have long been a popular technique for enlivening downtowns. An event's organizers, however, should work with retailers to make sure the events enhance, not detract from, shopping.

9-59 The Downtown Partnership of Baltimore, Inc., provides retailers with professional, in-store consultation in management, marketing, and operations as part of its centralized retail management program.

are worthy of mention. One is used to determine awareness of and reaction to the Downtown Seattle Association's various marketing and promotional campaigns, permitting the organization to determine whether its efforts have had the desired results. The second survey, the association's survey of retail sales volume, has generated a great deal of interest in other cities. Relying on a respected outside accounting firm, Seattle has promised confidentiality to respondents and, as a result, enjoys the undisputed capability to measure and thereby demonstrate progress toward meeting the program's objectives. In the absence of such data, information about the overall state of retailing would be more likely to be anecdotal, possibly negative, or give the impression that conditions are better than they are in fact.

Conclusion

Centralized retail management is a strategy for competitive times. It focuses on the essentials: cooperation, integrated action, an understanding of the market, and the bottom line. It is an important complement to downtown development and business recruitment, promising to improve returns on investment. CRM is the capstone to successful downtown management and promotes an essential ingredient of a downtown's vitality and the center city's renewal—a healthy retail market.

10.
Downtown Housing

Socioeconomic Changes Affecting Downtown Housing

The 18-hour city was a big idea in the 1980s. People living downtown would serve a variety of purposes, including providing a ready market for retailers, a work force more predisposed to working downtown, and an increase in the perceived level of safety and security. The demographics of the 1980s certainly supported the idea. According to one major study, the United States gained nearly 5 million office jobs during the decade, many of which were the kind likely to be downtown.[1] The average age of the U.S. population continued to rise, as did the number of non-child-oriented households.

In fact, downtown population and housing did appear to stabilize, if not increase, in the 1980s, at least in metropolitan areas. In an informal ULI survey of 20 metropolitan downtowns completed in March 1991, downtown population increased by about 15 percent from 1980 to 1990, though the extent to which growth in the homeless population contributed to these increases was not clear. (The fact that the number of residential units built over the same period grew by roughly the same percent could minimize this concern.)

In the early 1990s, however, some of the compelling forces for downtown housing are abating as others surface. According to the same study mentioned in the first paragraph, employment growth is expected to drop to 1.1 percent per year in the 1990s. With the oversupply of office space as this handbook goes to press, the net demand for new office space in the 1990s will be sharply less than that of the 1980s. Furthermore, the sharp rise in the female labor force is expected to level off as women who have deferred having a family leave the work force to do so.[2] Perhaps this situation will change as downtowns become more child-friendly, but, at this time, child-oriented households are not key prospects for downtown housing.

On the other hand, the aging segment of the population continues to grow. Those aged 45 to 60 will be the fastest-growing segment of the population in the 1990s, and they are retiring at unprecedentedly early ages.[3] As this segment of the population swells, so could the demand for downtown housing.

The same factors that affect what should be a decline in new office construction in the 1990s could also bode well for downtown housing; that is, with

---

[1] David L. Birch et al., *America's Future Office Space Needs: Preparing for the Year 2000* (Arlington, Va.: National Association of Industrial and Office Parks, 1990), p. 1.

[2] Ibid., p. 14.

[3] Ibid., p. 12.

10-1   Balconies, windows that open, and a location in Seattle's Denny Regrade neighborhood on the perimeter of downtown all helped Arbor Place, a 159-unit apartment complex, achieve 100 percent occupancy soon after opening in 1989.

development opportunities for downtown office space waning, the development of housing, if its feasibility can be proven, should increase. The Pennsylvania Avenue Development Corporation predicted this phenomenon when it created its original plan in the late 1970s. Assuming that the demand for office space would slacken, the plan calls for residential development as a strategy for revitalization. In 1991, with no office buildings under construction in the plan area, residential units being built or recently completed total 745.

Another factor related to office development will affect the development of downtown housing in the 1990s—zoning. At the very least, zoning incentives will encourage housing. Cities such as Bellevue, Washington, Cincinnati, Portland, Oregon, Hartford, and Seattle have incentive programs that include housing among their bonus options. Others, including Hartford and Portland, have made housing mandatory in certain areas through the use of housing overlay districts. In Orlando and other cities, an area adjacent to

downtown has been downzoned to encourage residential building there and to limit office development to the CBD.

Difficulties in Developing Housing Downtown

Despite the forces that might be suggesting the time is right for downtown housing, feasibility in many cities is still uncertain, mainly because of development costs and unavailable financing. Downtown land is typically the most expensive land available for housing. Furthermore, construction costs increase when high-rise construction is planned, typically the case when high density is required to offset high land prices. For example, buildings over six floors are usually constructed of steel frame or reinforced concrete, and buildings over three floors typically require sprinkler systems to comply with state and local codes. The requirements of unions and building codes, a prohibition against the use of plastic pipe, for example, can result in what some believe are unnecessary costs. And the new emphasis on sculptured skylines affects construction costs as varied roof shapes, more articulated building forms, and a variety of building materials are used.

With higher land and construction costs come greater risks. In most U.S. cities, the market for downtown housing must be created; that is, most downtowns have little market-rate housing to speak of. When markets have to be created, risk is higher. Further, this created market is apt to be a shallower, narrower market than that for other kinds of housing (see "Mar-

10-2   Restored and reconfigured historic buildings as well as newly constructed townhouses and apartment units provide a diverse 25-block neighborhood known as Quality Hill in Kansas City, Missouri.

ket and Feasibility Analysis" later in this chapter). Adding to this risk is the fact that sites usually have to be assembled, which takes more time and leaves the possibility of having to deal with outparcels that can disrupt master planning. Development approvals are usually more difficult and time-consuming to obtain, and the existence of or potential for rent controls all add risk. Many developers adept at downtown construction are skilled in commercial, not residential, development. Finally, the risk of developing market-rate housing downtown is certainly exacerbated if the downtown is not livable enough to attract targeted residents.

What Creates a Livable Downtown?

Livable downtowns generally have many of the same characteristics as neighborhoods:

1. *Diversity* is evidenced by a mix of housing, including some wood frame and some brick, some low rise and some high rise, some old and some new, some for sale and some for rent. Downtown Vancouver's residential neighborhood is an example, with its mix of single-family detached houses more than 50 years old and five-year-old high-rise towers. In Milwaukee, those interested in living downtown can choose from buildings like the historic Cudahy, a white glazed brick and terra-cotta project built in 1908, or the more modern Yankee Hill, completed in 1987. In Kansas City's Quality Hill, an urban revitalization project that is part of a 25-block neighborhood by the same name, mixed-income housing is provided through restoration of old structures and construction of new ones.

   Even—or especially—if a downtown neighborhood is being created from scratch, as was Battery Park City's Rector Place in Manhattan, it can be diverse. Rector Place is comprised of 10 buildings of varied heights, colors, and textures, all inspired by the city's domestic architecture. Some are for sale, others for rent.

2. *Services* include, for example, grocery stores or markets, hardware stores, drugstores, daycare centers, restaurants, and entertainment. Just a block or two from Milwaukee's Yankee Hill (and the other residential projects in the area) is a grocery store. To encourage such uses downtown, Bellevue, Washington, offers a bonus for grocery stores and exempts hardware and drug stores from calculations of floor/area ratio.

3. *Street-level amenities*, such as active uses at the ground level, streetscaping, well-designed plazas, plenty of movable seating, water features, outdoor sculpture, and landscaping, all enhance a pedestrian's experience downtown.

10-3, 10-4, 10-5   A mix of downtown housing makes for a more interesting urban neighborhood.

10-6 Whitney Grove in New Haven provides active ground-level retailing with townhouses, offices, and parking.

Downtown residents who also work downtown are the most apt to be on foot and to appreciate such street-level amenities.

4. *Public spaces* like waterfront parks and esplanades have gone a long way toward creating a neighborhood for strolling, jogging, or playing football in Portland, Vancouver, Orlando, and Battery Park City, to mention a few downtowns. In fact, 30 percent of the land in Battery Park City is used for public open space. In Bellevue, a new 17-acre park was built downtown, and in Boston, the Boston Redevelopment Authority is proposing to create a park from a substantial portion of the 27 acres that will become available when one of the city's major thoroughfares is placed underground.

5. *A geographically compact area with efficient public transit* helps create a sense of place. Perhaps Portland, Oregon, is the best example of a geographically compact downtown resulting from its 200-foot blocks and efforts to encourage infill development rather than development at the edge of downtown. The city's light-rail system enhances the ease of getting around downtown on foot.

6. *A concentration of cultural and entertainment facilities* and other special places—historically significant buildings or waterfronts, for example—encourages residential development. Though a significant amount of downtown housing has not yet been built in Dallas, the city is developing the kind of cultural and entertainment districts that will encourage housing. The 60-acre Arts District includes the Dallas Museum of Art, the Morton H. Myerson Symphony Center, the Dallas Theatre Center, and two facilities used for traveling art or cultural exhibits and performance space. The downtown's West End Historic District includes 150 boutiques, restaurants, and clubs. The grand state capitol and Town Lake in Austin, Texas, provide beautiful views for many of the residents of downtown's half-dozen or so residential projects.

7. *Enough existing units or enough land* creates a neighborhood. Cincinnati's half-dozen downtown residential projects are scattered throughout the downtown. As a result, residents are aware only of individual buildings, not a residential neighborhood. Along the same lines, downtown housing tends to perform better when located on the periphery of downtown rather than in the heart of the CBD. In Dallas's State Thomas area, an 80-acre historic neighborhood sandwiched between downtown and a close-in restaurant/entertainment district, the first new downtown market-rate housing project opened in mid-May and was entirely leased a month later. Residents like not only the access to downtown and the McKinney Avenue shops and restaurants, connected to downtown by trolley, but also the period street lamps, widened sidewalks and streets, decorative brick paving, iron fencing around newly planted trees, and stone gateways.

8. *The size of a city and its work force* affect housing. Workers with commutes of 20 minutes or less are less inclined to live downtown than those with longer commutes; hence, larger

10-7 Public parks and open spaces are key amenities for downtown neighborhoods.

10-8   Located in the State Thomas area with room to grow a neighborhood, the 132-unit Meridian is Dallas's first downtown housing to be developed in decades.

cities are able to attract residents to downtown easier than smaller ones. Cities with large white-collar and professional work forces, that is, work forces apt to work downtown, are more logical candidates for downtown housing.

9.   *Security* helps to create an environment that attracts downtown housing. Downtown must be perceived to be at least as safe a place to live as other neighborhoods from which prospective residents are likely to come. While a project's amenities can and should include security features, other factors contributing to a livable downtown improve the security of downtown as well, like the existence of restaurants, for example. In the East End of Washington, D.C., the area of downtown where the Pennsylvania Avenue Development Corporation is encouraging housing, the sense of security in the area increased substantially when three new restaurants were added in 1990 and 1991 as part of mixed-use projects. Restaurant patrons and valet car parkers enlivened the streets, making the area feel more safe. The walk in front of the FBI Building, which has no active ground-level uses, is the only portion of the area along the Avenue that the PADC is revitalizing that still seems insecure.

Downtown Housing Plan

Downtowns with many or all of these features probably already have housing. Those without them should consider developing a plan for obtaining them, either in the form of a downtown plan or a more narrowly focused downtown housing plan. Specific problems should be cited in the plan and specific solutions developed to overcome the problems. The

plan should also include the entity or person responsible for implementing the solution as well as a timetable for completion. The case study in Figure 10-11 includes more information on developing such a plan (see also "The Downtown Plan" in Chapter 2).

Market and Feasibility Analysis

Three essential questions must be answered in any market and feasibility analysis for downtown housing:[4]

1.   *What is the site's potential for development?* That is, how well will the subject site compete

---

[4] Portions of this section are from Julian Fore and Ginger Gelb, "What Makes It Work: Feasibility and the Ingredients for Success," Draft (Washington, D.C.: GA/Partners, 1987).

10-9   Towers are edged by two-story townhouses, creating a residential scale at street level, at Yankee Hill in Milwaukee.

10-10   Bice, a fashionable restaurant in Washington's emerging Pennsylvania Avenue Corridor, is open into the evening. Patrons and valet car parkers enliven the street.

The city of Portland, Oregon, has developed and is implementing a comprehensive strategy for creating residential units downtown. Toward that end, it has used a combination of planning, zoning, public incentives, and public improvements to increase its downtown housing stock. For the 12 years from 1978 to 1990, total downtown housing stock increased by a net of approximately 400 units, an accomplishment many downtowns cannot claim because of major losses in single-room-occupancy (SRO) units. In Portland, SRO units are estimated to have decreased by about 1,100 to 2,380, while other low- or moderate-income units are estimated to have increased by about 365 to 2,400. Middle- or upper-income units increased by 1,156 to 2,600.

The city's comprehensive approach as it has evolved began with planning initiatives. Five major initiatives on downtown housing policy were adopted during the 1970s and 1980s:

1972 The Downtown Plan was created, which supported downtown housing by laying out specific objectives.

1975 A limited (10-year) property tax abatement ordinance was adopted, to be used as a financial incentive for housing.

1977 AX/RX zoning (an area of downtown rezoned from commercial to residential) was created, making downtown housing more feasible. In the rezoned area, a minimum of 60 percent of a building's area must be used for residential purposes, while non-residential uses are limited to 40 percent in most areas.

1979 The Downtown Housing Policy was adopted to support a broad range of housing types.

1988 The Downtown Plan was updated and renamed the Central City Plan. It established a goal of 5,000 new housing units by 2005 and plans for implementing the goal.

The policy initiatives of the 1970s, combined with the zoning and financing initiatives set forth in the 1988 Central City Plan have yielded significant results.

Zoning

Zoning changes as a result of the 1988 Central City Plan incorporated many progressive techniques, specifically a housing overlay zone, bonuses for hous-

ing, and the transfer of development rights. The plan calls for residential development in those sections of the city most conducive to and attractive for housing, including sites along the Willamette River (for example, the RiverPlace development described later), close to major public open spaces (the South Park Blocks described later), or near both light-rail transit and major retail centers. A residential exaction, affecting some 100 acres of commercially zoned land in the CBD, requires at least 15 dwelling units to be developed as part of a project for each acre of land on the site.

Portland has offered bonuses for housing since 1979. The current bonus, applied to all commercial and light industrial areas, uses a ratio of three to one (an additional FAR of 3:1). The city also offers height bonuses that, in the case of housing, could amount to as much as a 75-foot increment beyond prevailing height limits. To encourage use of the bonus (starting in 1988), the ratio is more generous for those projects with residential components built within the first 10 years of the plan.

The Central City Plan also offers TDRs to encourage the preservation and maintenance of SRO housing. Qualifying developments may transfer their potential surplus floor area to other sites in the central city. The property owner executes covenants with the city that are recorded with the deeds of both the site transferring and the site receiving the transfer of floor area.

Financial Incentives and Public Improvements

In 1985, the city moved toward realizing its objectives for housing by making new financial tools available to developers. The city council approved the South Park Urban Renewal Area (SPURA) plan for a 134-acre area in southwest downtown. SPURA's primary goal was to create 1,600 new middle-income rental housing units, with "middle-income housing" defined as units renting for $500 to $1,350 per month (1989 dollars). SPURA was to be implemented by the Portland Development Commission (PDC), the city's urban renewal and economic development agency.

Designating the South Park Blocks as an urban renewal area allowed the city to use tax increment financing to fund development and to offer incentives to builders. Specifically, low-interest loans, limited property tax abatements for 10 years, reve-

10-12 University Park Apartments.

nue bonds for multifamily housing, and land write-downs were the primary tools used. More than $31.2 million in public funds, plus some private financing, has been invested in housing in this area. As a result, since 1985, 370 units of middle-income housing have opened in four new apartment buildings along the park blocks. Low- and moderate-income housing has increased by a net of 378 units as a result of new construction and rehabilitation.

Concurrent with the new housing developed, the city completed $2.2 million in park and public improvements to the area. Improvements included the renovation of a linear park extending along six blocks that are part of the original platting of the city of Portland. The renovation of the park in 1987 consisted of new landscaping, new pedestrian areas, wider sidewalks, new lighting, and renovated public sculptures in the park.

Profiles of tenants in the two largest projects indicate that downtown housing serves residents in a variety of career fields—from retail clerks to teachers and accountants. Approximately 75 percent of the tenants work in the downtown area, and 65 percent are single-person households. Thirty-three percent are under age 30; 46 percent are between the ages of 30 and 60. Twenty-one percent are over 61, and 15 percent are retired.

RiverPlace, also developed with the aid of public incentives, is a 10-acre multiuse development on the west bank of the Willamette River. It was initiated by the PDC in accordance with Portland's Downtown Plan. The project includes a 74-room hotel with 90 percent occupancies and $117 average daily rates, 190 condominium residences, all of which

have sold, 108 rental units completed in 1990 and another 212 under construction, a 200-slip marina with a floating restaurant, an athletic club, 41,600 square feet of office space that is entirely leased at effective rates of $14 per square foot, 35,000 square feet of retail space, most of which borders the waterfront esplanade, and over 750 structured parking spaces. The goal for both the city and the developer has been to create a residential neighborhood with enough mass to attract city residents to the south waterfront area all year.

In Phase 1 (all but the rental units and about half of the parking), the PDC offered substantial financial incentives. Public improvements totaling over $12 million included a five-acre park adjacent to the hotel, the riverside esplanade and park furnishings, the floating breakwater and marina basin, improvements to roads and utilities, and land acquisition and resale at a discount. To encourage the building of middle-income units priced between $50,000 and $120,000 (1982 dollars), however, the city stipulated a surcharge on the residential land equal to 10 percent of the difference between the selling price of the unit and $120,000. As unit prices increased above $120,000, the commission's subsidy

10-13 South Park Square.

179

10-14   CHARACTERISTICS OF PORTLAND'S DOWNTOWN/
CLOSE-IN MIDDLE-INCOME HOUSING

UNIT TYPE	NUMBER OF UNITS	PERCENT OF UNITS	MONTHLY RENT PER SQUARE FOOT	WEIGHTED AVERAGE SIZE (SQUARE FEET)
Studio Units	220	7.0	$.50–1.13	429
1 Bedroom/1 Bathroom	1,639	52.1	.42–1.19	677
1 Bedroom/2+ Bathrooms	32	1.0	.83–1.06	811
Loft Units	218	6.9	.75–1.13	1,025
2 Bedrooms/1 Bathroom	358	11.4	.60–1.15	918
2 Bedrooms/2+ Bathrooms	607	19.3	.58–1.65	1,075
3 Bedrooms/1 or 2 Bathrooms	69	2.2	.47–1.45	1,152
3 Bedrooms/3 Bathrooms	1	–	.60	1,300
4 Bedrooms/2+ Bathrooms	3	.1	.65– .71	2,344
	3,147	100.0	.79	794*

*Excluding lofts.
Source: Portland Development Commission.

decreased. Market conditions precluded building $50,000 units, and unit prices ranged from about $85,000 to $340,000. A softer-than-expected market for sales caused the developer to change to leasing. When the project had proven itself, however, a number of lessees purchased their units.

In Phase 2 (the rental units), the PDC included not only a writedown for land sales but also a tax abatement on the housing (but not the retail) component. The units will be priced from $500 to $1,000, with two-thirds (72 units) priced from $500 to $650. The 300-space garage includes retail shops at the ground level, in keeping with Portland's requirement for "no blank walls."

Like many downtowns, the rental market proved to be stronger, initially, than the sales market. Because the project has proved its success and the waterfront overcame its perception as frontier territory, however, resales are now strong, occurring at about $120 per square foot in 1990.

The mix of commercial and residential uses achieved the desired activity on the waterfront, but the noise generated by nighttime uses (restaurants, a lounge, and the hotel) disturbed some residents.

10-15, 10-16   Public improvements for Phase 1 totaled over $12 million and included this riverside esplanade, the floating breakwater, and the marina basin.

10-17　Residential buildings feature a midrise design of wood frame construction, pitched roofs, and extensive landscaping.

That problem was partially alleviated by converting the three residential units above a restaurant/lounge to office space. In addition, the hotel is now leasing a building of 10 condominium units equipped with kitchens and laundry facilities to expand its guest accommodations and meet the demand for long-term stays.

Another challenge related to the mix of uses was to balance activities generated by the public spaces with the desired security for the residential units. The solution was to sandwich the residential units between commercial and retail uses and to place the hotel and athletic club on the periphery, closest to the public spaces and streets. This strategy also helped to buffer the housing from vehicular noise. Entrances to the residential units themselves and to their courtyards and parking are thus secured.

Visually differentiating the mix of uses in the project proved important. Residential buildings feature Northwest-style, wood frame construction, and commercial buildings feature brick and stone. Each of the seven residential buildings has a separate identity with different muted colors. Split-face concrete blocks on the residences and brick on the hotel sharply define those uses at street level.

RiverPlace has achieved its goal of creating a year-round destination "urban resort" along the Willamette River. The city's financial incentives, including extensive public improvements and rigorous (but speedily approved) design controls (Phase 1 was approved in six weeks) have contributed significantly to the project's success.

Other Public Improvements and Facilities

Contributing to the success of the South Park Blocks and RiverPlace projects has been a systematically implemented program of public improvements to enhance the livability of downtown. One of the city's greatest resources is the Willamette River, and, to make the most of it, the PDC replaced an expressway in the mid-1970s with a mile-long park. Improvements, including a new public plaza with a fountain, river view, and restaurant in a restored historic building, ornamental lighting, benches, and landscaping, continue to be added, and the final section of the park is about to be completed. When it is, the park will run from one end of downtown to the other.

Portland's light-rail system also runs from one end of downtown to the other; it is free for passengers who travel within the downtown core. The system has been designed to run at street level rather than above or below grade, so that it is visible and easily accessible. It is clean, quiet, not overbearing, and Portlanders love it, all 20,000 per day who ride it during the week and 15,000 per day on weekends.

Two short blocks from a light-rail stop is the Center for the Performing Arts, which consists of a renovated 20th century Italian Renaissance–style concert hall and new theater buildings. PDC tax increment financing as well as general obligation bonds financed the projects.

▶

Timothy Hursley

10-18　Portland Center for the Performing Arts. The street separating the new and renovated theaters is open for traffic only during the day; at sunset it becomes a pedestrian plaza for entertainment. *Source:* ELS/Elbasani & Logan Architects.

Adding to Portland's already healthy downtown retailing is Pioneer Place. The PDC was instrumental in all stages of the project, from the purchase of the property to the ground breaking. Developed by the Rouse Company and completed in 1990, the project includes the Pacific Northwest's first Saks Fifth Avenue, a four-level retail pavilion with 80 specialty shops (opening with 80 percent occupancy), a 17-story office tower, and a city parking garage for shoppers.

In the heart of the retail core and along the light-rail line is Portland's main public plaza, Pioneer Courthouse Square. Completed in 1984, the project features an all-brick, two-level urban plaza, 12 monumental columns running along the south side, two amphitheaters opening onto the plaza, a fountain, a restaurant, and retail space. The center plaza is used for open-air cultural and recreational events year round. The PDC developed the square using tax increment financing, UMTA funds, and other public and private monies.

PDC financing has also helped rehabilitate and preserve dozens of historic buildings in the Skidmore/Old Town, Yamhill, and Chinatown districts. Architecturally, the late 19th and early 20th century buildings are distinguished for their cast iron construction and glazed terra-cotta facades. In Chinatown, an elaborate gateway has been added to the entrance of the district and street lamps have been added throughout. The original city street lights were specially refurbished in red with gold detailing.

Low-Income Housing

Portland has developed three programs to encourage the development of low-income housing downtown: a housing preservation program focused on acquiring and rehabilitating SRO units, a rehabilitation loan program for investors, and a requirement to set aside 20 percent of the units developed as part of the initiative for middle-income residents as low-income housing.

The city's Downtown Housing Preservation Program is designed to preserve and increase the supply of low-income housing in downtown Portland in conformance with its downtown housing policy. The PDC operates primarily through a partnership with the Housing Authority of Portland, Central City Concern (a nonprofit manager), and the chamber of commerce. Under the agreement, PDC directly develops the projects, the housing authority

10-19   The 145,000-square-foot Pioneer Place is four stories high, far below the allowable density, to relate it to the historic Pioneer Courthouse across the street. *Source:* ELS/Elbasani & Logan Architects.

provides federal rent subsidies to operate the buildings, Central City Concern owns and manages most buildings, and the chamber helps identify funds for social services to tenants. Since the start of the program in 1988, 322 units have been completed and 157 are in design. Additionally, a new goal of 800 units over the next three years has been set.

Through the Investor Rehabilitation Loan Program, financial and technical assistance is provided to low- and moderate-income families rehabilitating residential property. Since the beginning of that program in 1978, 1,356 units have been rehabilitated.

Conclusion

Included in Portland's comprehensive strategy for creating a livable downtown are action plans for creating a lively, secure environment, providing retail stores, fostering neighborhoods, and developing both market-rate and affordable units. The increase in the number of residential units and residents, the success of Portland's downtown retailing, and the overall livability of the central city indicate that the strategy is working.

Sources: Portland Development Commission, "1988 Central City Plan: South Park Blocks Urban Renewal Area," 1989; PDC, "Housing and Public Investment in the South Park Blocks Urban Renewal Area," 1990; PDC, "Survey of Middle-Income Rental Housing in Downtown Areas," 1990; interviews with PDC staff; and *Project Reference File*, "RiverPlace," vol. 18, no. 3 (Washington, D.C.: ULI–the Urban Land Institute, January–March 1988).

in the market, and what are the implications for the product, price, pace of development, and profile?

2. *What is the market potential?* That is, in the competitive market area, what is the projected demand for the residential product? Given the projected supply, what opportunity for development exists?

3. *Is the project economically (financially) supportable?* That is, do the potential rents or sale prices support the expected costs of development, and will income from the project sufficiently cover debt service?

Clearly, this type of analysis is not mechanical, especially when housing is being considered in a market with little or no existing supply. In fact, much of the process is given to qualitative evaluations of the preference of key market segments, the site's overall quality and appeal, and the extent to which the property can be competitive with other properties in the market, that is, its capture rate.

Site Potential and Evaluation

Site evaluation includes considerations of accessibility, visibility, and the surrounding neighborhood, each of which affects a proposed project's performance. The relative importance of each factor, however, must be judged case by case, for each site is distinctive.

Accessibility can be viewed in three ways: immediate, local, and regional. Immediate access to a downtown site depends on the site's location within the downtown network of streets. Local access, or access within the downtown, is very important, because downtown residents usually live downtown in part because of the ease of getting to work or entertain-

10-20 Views from and of a project establish its presence in the neighborhood.

ment. The site's proximity to pedestrian as well as transportation networks will determine how accessible it is to downtown employment centers and amenities. Regional access, including access to airports, is also important and depends on driving time to the site from major arterials and interstate highways.

Visibility to and from a site is related to the height and density of surrounding development. Good views *from* a project provide a marketing advantage. Good views *of* a project enable it to establish a presence in the neighborhood.

The type and quality of the development surrounding a site affect how a project on that site actually looks and influence how the project is generally perceived. High-quality design and maintenance of nearby buildings have a positive effect on a location. Noise levels generated by surrounding development have a negative impact. Older households place more importance on the safety of the neighborhood, although it is important to all potential buyers and renters. Mature but well-kept neighborhoods are perceived as less risky in relation to the investment value of for-sale units.

Market Potential

Market Area

Once the site has been analyzed, the larger area where it is located should be studied. In an analysis of market potential for downtown housing, one of the steps typically used to analyze other real estate products is turned on its head. For example, in an analysis of the potential for retailing, determining the perimeters of the primary and secondary markets is crucial, because shoppers will travel only so far for certain kinds of goods. For downtown housing, *where prospects work* and *who they are* are more important than where they currently live. Downtown workers, wherever they live, are prospects for downtown housing, and childless downtown workers who fall into certain age and income categories are primary prospects. Gathering information about downtown workers, then, is a key source of information in the market analysis. Still, some will choose to commute in the opposite direction and/or live downtown for other than work-related reasons. For this reason, city or even regional boundaries can be used as market perimeters delineating the areas where potential residents might come from.

Demand

In a city with little or no existing supply of market-rate downtown housing, demographic information about downtown workers should be the primary source for developing estimates of demand. This approach is a conservative one and does not include retirees. In an untested market, however, as is the case in most U.S. downtowns, a conservative approach is warranted. Supplemental information on the entire downtown work force should result from surveys of downtown workers regarding their interest in and ability to live downtown.

A study by the Real Estate Research Corporation of downtown office workers in Grand Rapids, Des Moines, Milwaukee, and Cincinnati indicates that households of three or more people with at least one downtown worker aged 30 to 45, younger singles, or two-person, childless professional households appear to be the primary market for downtown housing.[5] The study indicates that younger professional workers are particularly susceptible to the excitement of living in a downtown with a nearby concentration of entertainment and recreational facilities and the convenience of walking to work. Couples aged 45 to 60—the fastest-growing segment of the population in the 1990s—also appear to be a large and growing segment of the market for downtown housing.

Supply

The market area for a proposed downtown project could be one of several downtown submarkets. In Milwaukee, for example, the downtown consists of at least five potential residential submarkets: the lower East Side, the Brewery District, the old Third Ward, west of the river, and Westown. To determine supply for downtown Milwaukee, then, one would need to include existing and planned residential units in each submarket.

The projected capture rate used in the analysis of demand is the reconciling factor for how the subject site or project will compare to projects in these other submarkets. In Milwaukee, the capture rate for projects in the lower East Side, where the greatest number of attractive units already exist, is higher than west of the river, which has a less residential presence and character. Further, the downtown could compete with other locations outside downtown (other close-in neighborhoods, for example), in which case units in those areas should be considered in the study of supply.

If existing downtown housing is of a substantially different quality from that contemplated for new development, property outside downtown that is competitive in terms of proximity to downtown, quality of units, and so on could be studied. For example, properties located along major commuter roadways or mass transit corridors beside the area or properties located close to but not in the downtown might be studied.

Once the areas are determined for which data about supply will be gathered, the following information should be collected for both existing and planned projects; it can be used in analyzing market potential as well as in developing a project design and marketing program tailored to the market.

1. Location
2. Number of units for sale or for rent
3. Size and mix of units
4. Average rent or sale prices
5. Vacancy
6. Absorption rates
7. Amenities
8. Type and age of structure (high rise, midrise, townhouse or low rise, loft)
9. Condition of the project
10. Renter/buyer profiles

Using this information for supply and demand, one can project market potential, in this case for a rental or for-sale project.

To check the reality of the calculations, the figure of 217 units per year shown in Figure 10-21 should then be calculated as a percent of the total annual projected demand in the entire city and possibly in the region. Also note that retirees and those who said they would "consider" living downtown have been excluded from the calculations. The small percentage of people living in the subject downtown justifies such a conservative approach. On the other hand, in established markets with unusually low vacancy rates, pent-up demand could possibly justify more new supply or faster absorption than could otherwise be justified.

Proposed Development Program

A development program can then be fashioned from this quantitative and qualitative review, addressing four "P's":

- *Product:* Type, number, mix, and size of units, features, and project amenities;
- *Price:* Rents, sale prices adjusted for unit premiums (for example, views);
- *Pace:* Pace of preleasing and leasing; pace of presales and sales based on product, price, and

---

[5] M. Leanne Lachman and Robert E. Miller, "Downtown Housing: Where the Action Is," *Journal of Real Estate Development*, Summer 1985, p. 21.

Number of people working downtown	73,000
Number of households (based on number of spouses working downtown)	67,500
Number responding "yes" to "Would you live downtown?" (12.4 percent)	8,370
Number indicating plans to move in one to three years (44.7 percent)	3,740*
Number earning minimum of $24,000 per year** (50 percent)	1,870*
Minus: Number of existing competitive units (supply)	125
Estimated demand based on projected capture rate (25 percent)	435
Estimated demand on a yearly basis	217

*Thus, the figures shown are for a two-year period.
**Assuming that rents or mortgage payments for new downtown housing would be at least $600 per month and that households could afford to spend 30 percent of their income on housing, a household would have to earn at least $24,000 per year to qualify for a new unit downtown.

the current economic environment (mortgage rates and so on); and

- *Profile:* Characteristics of target market segments, including age, family, occupation, income, and workplace.

Project Feasibility

If the project's site and market are promising, the third and remaining question can be addressed: is the project economically feasible? In this case, the analysis is like that of any other real estate product in that projections of costs and revenues are compared to requirements for debt service coverage and return. Where an analysis for downtown housing differs, however, is in the difficulty of achieving targeted requirements for debt service and return because of high land, construction, and parking costs, particularly in a market with little existing supply and skittish prospects unwilling to pay premiums for living downtown, at least until the market is proven. Land costs for market-rate high-rise residential development can typically be as high as $10,000 to $20,000 per unit. For smaller, less dense projects, land costs per unit can run even higher. Above- or below-grade parking is expensive as well and can total up to $10,000 per space. As a result, in most downtown housing projects, some form of public assistance will be required.

Downtown Housing Strategies

Financial Incentives

Because housing is at once desirable but difficult to achieve in downtowns, cities and developers have

worked together to create solutions. Federal and local governments, for example, have provided a number of financial incentives. Tools that have been particularly effective for downtown housing include city-offered eminent domain, tax abatement, city-funded feasibility studies, below-market mortgages through loan pools, land writedowns, funding of infrastructure or parking, loans, and tax-exempt financing.

To illustrate the dynamic effect of writing down the cost of land or parking and the use of tax-exempt financing for downtown housing, assume, for example, that revenues allowing for debt service to be covered and a reasonable return to be generated consist of either $1.26 per square foot for a rental project or $130 per square foot for the sale price, in either case high figures for almost any downtown market in the United States.

Rents and sale prices can be significantly lowered by altering assumptions about cost. Reducing the cost of land or parking to zero results in a reduction of 10.3 percent in the necessary rent or sale price. Reducing costs of hard construction by $10 per square foot results in a reduction of 12.7 percent in rent or sale price.

Perhaps the greatest reduction can be achieved by reducing financing cost. Though tax-exempt IDBs for multifamily projects have been affected by the Tax Reform Act of 1986, they remain a viable source of financing. Assuming a variable-rate 10-year bond priced at a coupon rate of 4.75 percent results in a reduction of 22 percent in rent, to about $1.00 per square foot.

In combination, all of these reductions could reduce the required rent to $.65 per square foot or the required purchase price to $88 per square foot. While it is unlikely that all of these reductions would be possible, they do illustrate the dynamic relationship between cost and revenue.

10-22   The Paperworks, Memphis, Tennessee.

10-24   Some cities have downzoned close-in residential neighborhoods to prevent their commercialization.

For example, Memphis's downtown organization, the Center City Commission (CCC), has used financial incentives effectively to encourage housing downtown. In addition to promoting the kind of development that supports an 18-hour downtown (restaurants, entertainment, people movers, places oriented toward pedestrians, to name a few), the CCC presents a straightforward menu of financial incentives available to developers interested in downtown housing. The incentives include loans for face-lifts and small properties, tax-free revenue bonds, property tax abatement, dedications of historic facades (see Chapter 12), reduced fees, and the funding of public improvements and parking. The CCC also provides other services: coordinating building inspections and compliance with codes, expediting public review and approvals, assisting in the design of public projects, marketing, and recruiting tenants. CCC materials clearly set forth the criteria for obtaining each incentive.

Memphis's financial incentives have worked. The downtown residential market increased from fewer than 250 units in 1977 to 1,613 units at the beginning of 1990. The 1,400 apartments rent for $300 to $1,900 per month, and the 213 condominium/cooperative residences range from $48,000 to $270,000. Residential developments under construction or planned at the beginning of 1990 totaled over 2,100 units.

Zoning Incentives

Downtown housing is a paradox. In those downtowns awash in economic prosperity, the commercial development boom of the 1980s has apparently propelled land values beyond the prices private-sector housing developers can pay. On the other hand, in less prosperous cities, investors are skittish about committing to residential development [that] is seen as high in risk . . . . Because of these inherent economic disincentives, many cities have had to regulate downtown housing through subsidies and exactions and fashion a raft of zoning tools to speed this kind of development.[6]

Zoning incentives, voluntary or mandatory, include bonus systems, lowered requirements for parking, accelerated reviews, exemption from height and density restrictions, exemption of services that support residential development (for example, supermarkets or hardware stores) from restrictions on height and density, required housing in certain areas, downzoning, inclusionary programs (affordable or low-income units within market-rate projects), exactions or linkage fees, and housing preservation ordinances, generally designed to protect SRO units and other existing low-income housing, though many of them have been repealed in light of recent court decisions.[7]

10-23   Riverset, Memphis, Tennessee.

---

[6] Terry Jill Lassar, *Carrots and Sticks: New Zoning Downtown* (Washington, D.C.: ULI–the Urban Land Institute, 1989), p. 174.

[7] See ibid., Chapter 1, for a more detailed look at each of these zoning tools.

The push for downtown housing in Columbus started in 1983, when Wallick Development Company acquired an option to purchase three downtown parcels for a residential project. The next year, while the developer was conducting extensive telephone surveys of income- and location-qualified prospects, the city commissioned a downtown housing study, which projected a demand per year of 230 units. By 1986, construction had started on a 96-unit condominium project, and the push was on.

Buoyed by the market study and Wallick's high percentage of reserved units—80 percent—at ground breaking, the city and the major downtown organization, Downtown Columbus, Inc. (DCI), began a two-pronged approach to encourage more development. Both groups saw themselves as brokers of information and of financial incentives. On the information front, they completed an extensive survey of the existing housing stock and a survey of all other parcels downtown. The housing survey included information on the style of units, rents, utilities, and amenities as well as any special information that might be pertinent to an individual site. The survey of parcels included owners' names and addresses, current uses, value and type of any improvements, lot sizes, taxes and other assessments, and the dates and amount of the last transfer. Information from both surveys was transferred to DCI's computer, and procedures were developed to update the information regularly and provide it to inquiring developers in an easily understood format.

Based on the survey of parcels, approximately 350 specific parcels of land and/or sites were identified as potential properties for housing development. Owners were mailed a survey to ascertain their willingness to sell or participate in the development of their property. The results of that survey were then added to the data base.

To assist developers in analyzing the feasibility of specific projects and to assist in curtailing their

10-26   The Waterford, Columbus, Ohio.

out-of-pocket costs during predevelopment, a computer program generates financial projections for potential projects. Developers need only complete a form requesting information about assumptions, and DCI runs as many iterations of its 10-year model as requested. Using cost and market data from its own files, DCI can also develop the assumptions. At DCI headquarters, personal computers and personnel are set aside for this purpose so DCI can be responsive to developers' needs and time schedules.

The city has developed "one-stop shopping" for approvals for downtown housing, and inspectors' hours have been extended to become more responsive to developers' timetables. The city has not yet incorporated, however, any of the progressive zoning techniques that encourage residential development.

In 1990, the city and DCI added a new tool to promote downtown housing: a downtown housing conference. The conference was marketed to national and local developers, mortgage lenders, architects, builders, realtors, and other organizations that might be interested in multifamily housing in downtown Columbus; 150 attended. Updated market data were provided to attendees, computers were available to run pro formas, and tours of existing properties and potential sites were conducted. Sessions were held on adaptive use, design and construction techniques for new housing, financing and marketing strategies, mixed-use development, and moderate-income housing.

Before the development of the data base on downtown housing and the housing conference, DCI and the city reported that meetings with developers interested in downtown housing occurred about

10-28 Condominiums on Wall Street in Columbus's Brewery District won a Grand Award in the annual design and planning contest sponsored by *Builders*.

once or twice a month. Since then, meetings have increased to once or twice per *week*, including many with developers considering the Columbus market for the first time. The continual updating of the housing data base, follow-up with the seminar's participants, and publicity like articles in a newsletter, "Multi-Housing News," published by the city are expected to generate further interest.

Though Columbus's approach has centered around providing information for developers, it has also provided financial incentives to developers of downtown housing. Each of the three projects completed in 1989, for example, was helped by a combination of loans, tax incentives, and city-funded capital improvements: loans totaling $937,500, including HUD 312, neighborhood commercial revitalization, and business development fund loans, at the 26-unit Battleship Building; a 10-year tax abatement for the entire site of the 85-unit Brewery District project; and a five-year tax deferral for the 94-unit Market Mohawk project.

Since 1987, 321 units have been completed, and plans for an additional 300 are under way. Rents range from $375 for a 450-square-foot studio at Market Mohawk to $1,700 for a 2,300-square-foot three-bedroom unit in the Brewery District. Original sale prices for the Waterford condominiums averaged $213,000. Resales have started, and appreciation totals as high as 190 percent. Though the recent credit crunch has slowed development, DCI and the city now hope that projects in the works will result in new units in the near future.

10-27 Market Mohawk, a 94-unit rental project in Columbus, Ohio.

Strategies for Low-Income Downtown Housing

One of this country's major domestic issues is the serious and increasing shortage of housing for very-low-, low-, and moderate-income families.[8] The pattern nationally—especially in downtowns and growing metropolitan areas—is that lower-cost housing has become increasingly scarce. Working and non-working poor households seeking housing today face a squeeze caused by high housing costs, increasing competition for affordable rental housing, and a diminishing supply of assisted housing.

The passage of the National Affordable Housing Act of 1990 rolled back a decade of retrenchment by the federal government, though some contend that there still is no national housing policy. In any case, the act shifts responsibility and decision making from the federal government to states and localities, provides grants to state and local governments, encourages homeownership by low-income households, continues federally assisted construction of new housing and public housing, shores up the Federal Housing Administration's insurance program, and provides for the preservation of existing assisted housing.

10-29 "I like living here: it's so convenient to downtown and public transportation," says a downtown Seattle resident in a renovated low-income building.

Federal Programs

Three separate programs related to the National Affordable Housing Act—HOME, HOPE, and LIHPRHA—apply most directly to downtown housing.[9]

1. "HOME," a program mandated by the Home Investment and Affordable Housing Partnership, is designed to increase the supply of affordable housing, particularly rental housing, for very-low- and low-income families and individuals. It does so by providing grants to states and localities to help nonprofit or for-profit developers acquire, construct, or rehabilitate affordable rental housing. Fifteen percent of the funds are set aside for community housing partnerships—housing developed, sponsored, or owned by community-based nonprofit organizations.

2. Homeownership for People Everywhere (HOPE) authorizes grants for planning, implementation, and technical assistance to help residents of public and publicly assisted housing to purchase their units. Applicants can include resident management groups, public housing agencies, nonprofit organizations, and resident councils. Various restrictions on resale apply for up to 20 years.

3. The Low-Income Housing Preservation and Resident Homeownership Act of 1991 (LIHPRHA) is designed to preserve existing assisted housing for permanent use by low-income residents. It provides incentives for current owners of assisted housing projects to retain ownership for low-income residents or to sell them to new owners who will agree to maintain the housing for low-income occupants for its remaining useful life.

As of this writing, the U.S. Department of Housing and Urban Development (HUD) is preparing regulations and determining the organizational structure that will determine how the new law will work in practice. In the meantime, other federal programs remain in effect and will buttress the new act:

• Subsidies for occupants, primarily housing vouchers, to enable the poor to pay for subsidized and/or market-rate housing;

[8] Diane R. Suchman et al., *Public/Private Housing Partnerships* (Washington, D.C.: ULI–the Urban Land Institute, 1990), p. vii.
[9] See Dean Schwanke, ed., *Development Trends, 1991* (Washington, D.C.: ULI–the Urban Land Institute, 1991), pp. 56–57.

- Tax credits, including those for low-income housing to encourage private investment in low-income housing and those for historic properties and older buildings, which can be used to produce low-income housing (see Figure 10-30);
- Supportive housing finance programs and institutions, such as the Federal National Mortgage Association (FNMA), the Federal Home Loan Mortgage Company (Freddie Mac), the Government National Mortgage Association (Ginnie Mae), secondary mortgage markets, the Federal Housing Administration (FHA) and Veterans Administration (VA) mortgage insurance programs; and
- Public housing.

State and Local Programs

During the retreat from support by the federal government in the 1980s, states, local governments, and, increasingly, the private sector assumed the burden of ensuring an adequate supply of housing. The range of responses to date demonstrates determination, creativity, and success in tapping into existing resources or creating new ones. State housing finance agencies have long been active in a variety of mortgage finance and housing programs, particularly through the issuance of tax-exempt bonds. With the Tax Reform Act of 1986 affecting tax incentives for real estate investments and tax-exempt bonds for private purposes, however, states have experimented with a variety of programs and techniques:

- Off-budget funding vehicles, such as housing trust funds for production of housing and assistance for occupants;
- Programs to rehabilitate and retain the existing housing stock;
- Programs to aid first-time homebuyers;
- Revision of building codes and housing standards to reduce costs and facilitate production;
- Incentives and regulations to encourage the private production of low- and moderate-income rental and for-sale housing.[10]

State administration of federal programs has enabled state agencies to develop a sound base of experience. In fact, many state programs are modeled after several now-unfunded federal initiatives.

Out of necessity, local governments have also experimented with various programs and financing techniques to encourage and, at times, initiate the provision of housing. Many of the programs have been at little cost to cities and have involved the local government and nonprofit organizations and the private sector as well. Downtowns across the country have applied creative solutions to the production of affordable housing that can be replicated in other communities.

Direct or Indirect Financial Incentives

Chapter 4 describes the myriad of financial incentives used in downtowns, many of which have been used for housing, and with each year, a new twist evolves. New York City's Construction Management Program, for example, is an innovative public/private partnership that has used the profits from the development of market-rate housing to subsidize the production of affordable housing. Proceeds from the program were generated from tax-free bonds, backed by surplus revenues from the highly successful Battery Park City development. A total of 8,600 units will be produced under this program.

In Chicago, a new program to provide opportunities for homeownership to moderate-income Chicagoans calls for the construction of 1,000 single-family houses over the next five years. Ranging from $45,000 to $85,000, the houses will be built and sold by private and nonprofit developers. To help keep the new houses affordable, they will be built on city and privately owned vacant lots in older areas of the city. To make the program, called New Homes for Chicago, work, the city is prepared to give developers subsidies of up to $20,000 per housing unit and to waive various fees. The Illinois Housing Development Authority's Home Buyer Program will help new buyers with mortgage loans.

Linkage

Since 1981, private commercial development has become an important source of support for downtown low-income housing. This source can be tapped in several ways, with the ones used most often being 1) individual negotiations between the city and the developer on each project, 2) density bonuses granted by the city to private developers who produce low-income housing or contribute to a low-income housing trust fund, or 3) so-called "linkage" programs. In the latter program, commercial developers are assessed fees based on the square footage of new developments, with the proceeds used to produce new housing or contribute to a low-income housing trust fund. San Francisco, Miami, Seattle, Hartford, and

---

[10] For example, the Massachusetts SHARP program writes down interest on mortgages underwritten by the state housing finance agency to 5 percent for mixed-income rental housing.

Two tax credits continue to encourage investment in low-income housing. In place of earlier tax incentives, Congress authorized a credit in the Tax Reform Act of 1986 to stimulate investment in low-income rental housing, returning part of the costs of investment in low-income housing over 10 years. To use the credits, a syndication is structured as a partnership so that tax benefits flow to the partners, who then use the full value of the credit to reduce their tax liability.

By offering corporations and individuals the opportunity to make competitive investments that also expand opportunities for housing, the low-income tax credit has created a new pool of investors for low-income housing and is credited with the production of anywhere from 100,000 to 300,000 units. As of this writing, the tax credit is scheduled to expire on June 30, 1992; however, legislation has been introduced that would provide for a permanent tax credit.

Intended to encourage rehabilitation of older properties, the federal tax credit for historic properties and older buildings, though amended by the Tax Reform Act of 1986, still can be used to produce low-income housing. The tax credit given for the

10-31   Investors in this assisted-living housing project for the elderly receive historic rehabilitation and low-income housing tax credits.

rehabilitation of historic properties is 20 percent, that for older (pre-1936) structures not certified as historic 10 percent. In the past, half of all rehabilitation tax credits used were for housing. The rehabilitation tax credit can be used with the low-income housing tax credit, but only one tax credit can be taken against the same investment.

Santa Monica are among the cities that have housing programs linked to downtown development.

San Francisco's mandatory linkage program involves contributions from downtown developers of new or substantially rehabilitated office buildings over 50,000 square feet. Developers are required to construct or rehabilitate low-income housing units, directly or in a joint venture with a housing developer, or to contribute a fee of $5.69 per square foot of office space instead. Most developers opt to make their contributions in the form of payments to housing organizations that sponsor construction. Thus far, the contributions have assisted the production of almost 5,700 housing units—4,000 newly constructed and 1,700 rehabilitated—and generated $30 million in private contributions to housing.

Boston's mandatory linkage program requires developers to pay a fee to be used for housing of $5.00 per square foot of space over 100,000 square feet in locations anywhere in the city. Downtown office, retail, and institutional projects have generated commitments to pay over $45 million for housing. Over $17 million of this amount was paid to assist the

construction or rehabilitation of 2,000 housing units in 18 affordable housing projects. Eighty percent of these units will be rented or sold for an "affordable" price; the city targets a percentage of its obligations for housing (and job training) to those downtown neighborhoods adjoining office projects.

With the slowdown in office development and a lower projected demand for new office space, new linkage payments for affordable housing will likely decrease in the 1990s. Cities with linkage programs, however, are not likely to roll them back. A ULI survey of 12 cities in late 1990 showed that most were not tampering with existing programs. In Boston, for example, where all of the new projects slated for the Midtown Cultural District are on hold for one reason or another, a change in the linkage fee is not being considered.

Proposals for new regulations covering growth management, however, are not holding up as well. In San Diego and Portland, Maine, for example, proposed new impact fees were dropped in light of slower markets. Developers "are now prepared to say 'no' to unreasonable exactions," says Boston attorney John

Griffin. "As developers and lenders look more critically at project feasibility, they are less willing to throw money into the public coffers," he says.

Inclusionary Zoning

Inclusionary zoning ordinances require or encourage residential developers to include a minimum amount of lower-cost or below-market housing in their developments. Many such programs restrict the resale price of ownership units, and some allow alternatives like in-lieu cash payments to support a special local housing program. Inclusionary ordinances often provide incentives to compensate or offset costs, such as the waiver of fees, density bonuses for market-price units, or streamlined approval processes.

In downtown Seattle, at least 10 percent of the units in new structures containing 20 units or more must be maintained as affordable housing. The requirement for affordability, however, was not enforced until early 1990, when one person in the city government was designated to track requirements for inclusionary zoning as well as housing created as a result of bonuses and the TDR program. Inclusionary zoning has resulted in 665 new affordable units (for those whose income is 15 percent or less of the median) since the start of the program in the mid-1980s. Seattle's bonus and TDR programs resulted in an additional 502 units as of the beginning of 1991.

New York City's inclusionary housing program, passed in 1987, permits up to a 20 percent increase in the allowable FAR for market-rate residential buildings in exchange for the purchase of air rights for lower-cost housing. Intended to promote economic integration and diversity in dense residential neighborhoods on the Upper West Side and Upper East Side, the bonus may be used only within defined boundaries. The market-rate housing must be built within the confines of the community district containing the low-income housing. If located in a nearby district, the market-rate units may be no farther than a half-mile away from the low-income units. New York's inclusionary incentive is expected eventually to produce 200 to 300 units of low-income housing per year.[11]

Condominium Conversion Ordinances

Some downtowns have taken advantage of conditions in their local housing market to enact ordinances with an intent similar to inclusionary zoning. The success of such a program depends on the strength of the local housing market and existing supply of rental buildings, both of which must be ripe for conversion. Lexington, Massachusetts, for example, enacted an

10-32   The Genesis, which provides 30 units of low-income housing in Los Angeles, opened in 1989 with 100 percent occupancy.

ordinance that requires owners to create up to 20 percent low- and moderate-income housing units in converted developments.

Montgomery County, Maryland, places a 4 percent tax on the conversion of apartments to condominiums or cooperatives. The proceeds, estimated thus far at $3 million, provide revenue for low-income housing. Currently, the proceeds are being used for a rent supplement program for affordable housing units.

Single-Room-Occupancy Units

An SRO unit is a private room for one person, usually in a residential hotel or boarding house. While new SRO products continue to be developed that push the upper envelope of daily room rates (one developer in San Diego is working on a new concept for an urban SRO project targeted to the affordable market—$750 per month—rather than low-income market), most are adapted for long-term occupancy and serve primarily low-income individuals. Though many cities have lost many of their single-room-occupancy hotels as a result of downtown redevelopment, demolition, or conversion, SRO units have experienced something of a renaissance in the last few years. New York, San Francisco, San Diego, Portland, Oregon, and Los Angeles, for example, are actively involved in a revival of SRO units.

Typical SRO units consist of a single room with a sink, complete furnishings and linens, and a refrigera-

---

[11] Lassar, *Carrots and Sticks*, pp. 180–82.

Andy Raubeson, a national expert on SRO units who has spearheaded programs in Portland, Oregon, and Los Angeles, recalls a discussion with a U.S. Under Secretary for Housing in 1980 in which he was told that SRO hotels would be accepted by the U.S. Department of Housing and Urban Development as standard housing "over his dead body." Since then, as public awareness of homelessness and the lack of affordable housing increased, federal funds decreased, and downtown development resulted in the destruction of thousands of SRO units, attention has finally focused on SRO units as a viable option for affordable housing. Hundreds of historic SRO hotels have now been refurbished using a variety of financing sources. Still, one problem that developers of low-income and affordable SRO units face is convincing private financiers to lend money for the projects. Unfamiliar with this "new" product, many lenders do not understand the building design, the tenant mix, and the nature of operating expenses—particularly the unusually high management costs—well enough to extend financing.

10-34   ANNUAL INCOME AND
             EXPENSES PER UNIT FOR
               SAMPLE SRO UNITS

REVENUE	$3,670
OPERATING EXPENSES	
Salaries and Wages	$1,553
Employee Benefits	484
Equipment	161
Insurance	158
Meals	93
Repairs and Maintenance	309
Telephone and Utilities	227
Reserves	112
Other	361
Total	$3,458
NET OPERATING INCOME	212
DEBT SERVICE	119
NET INCOME	$ 93
DEBT SERVICE COVERAGE	1.78 ×

Understanding the tenant base is the first step in getting comfortable with lending for SRO hotels and, in many instances, the first misconception to be overcome. "Who lives in SRO units, according to conventional wisdom, but transients, drunks, and other unmanageable people?" says First National Bank of Chicago's Kristin L. Faust, an assistant vice president in the bank's neighborhood banking division. "We were about to find out differently," she recalls upon analyzing the bank's first opportunity to lend money for an SRO building.

Faust recalls learning that 50 percent of the subject property's occupants had lived there for over five years and that most of the desirable tenants would have actually preferred an annual rather than a shorter-term lease. Indeed, many SRO buildings require long-term leases. In Los Angeles, for example, nine of the 11 SRO hotels completed by the SRO Housing Corporation require annual leases. Occupancies average 95 percent. Approximately 75 percent of the tenants are male, 25 percent female, and the average age is 48 years. A survey of 30 SRO facilities funded under the Section 8 Moderate Rehabilitation Program reflects similar characteristics.

In the study of Section 8 SRO buildings, the employment rate among tenants was 27 percent, somewhat higher than the 20 percent rate reported in a 1988 HUD survey of shelters. A profile of income sources from SRO Housing Corp. also sheds light on typical revenues for occupants: 42 percent came from general relief funds, 32 percent from social security, and 21 percent from employment. In Los Angeles, tenants' average income was 22 percent of the median income, about the same as in the Section 8 study.

SRO Housing Corp.'s revenues (for the year ended June 30, 1990) were able to cover annual expenses per unit (see Figure 10-34). A review of operators' financial statements illustrates typical performance.

Salaries and benefits, totaling approximately 55 percent of revenue, were substantially higher than those for an average apartment complex because of the greater expenses associated with serving populations with special needs. The hotels that cater to the elderly, the mentally ill, or recovering substance abusers, for example, offer appropriate programs for those groups. The Golden West Hotel in Los Angeles, for example, provides two full-time case managers to serve its mentally ill tenants. All of the hotels offer free health care screenings. Full-time desk

10-35 Serving populations with special needs results in higher operating expenses for SRO facilities.

services and security are required at many facilities. Collecting rent, and screening and selecting tenants are all time-consuming. The Section 8 study noted, however, that without such special support services, SRO hotels were likely to fail.

Housekeeping for SRO Housing Corp. properties includes cleaning public areas as well as linen service once a week for each room. Rooms are inspected at least once each quarter to ensure that they are properly maintained and adequately equipped. In one case, again illustrating the expenses necessary to house populations with special needs, the corporation spent $800 to soundproof a room for a man who had been evicted from privately owned housing because nightmares made him scream, keeping other tenants awake. In addition to the costs that tend to be applicable only to SRO projects, certain management costs are also common. Special events, for example, are routinely planned. Some properties offer nightly video movies, free coffee,

two special meals per month, and recognition of tenants' birthdays.

Debt service for SRO Housing Corp. was considerably lower than the average for SRO hotels studied in the Section 8 review, apparently because of a higher percentage of grants and/or bullet loans to SRO Housing. Even with the higher debt service, however, the Section 8 projects were able to cover debt service at a ratio of 1.01.

Though SRO Housing Corp. is developing a new SRO hotel, its 13 existing properties are all refurbished hotels. For the smaller hotels, that is, projects with 72 or fewer rooms, development costs totaled close to $32,000 per unit. For larger projects (over 200 units), costs totaled $15,700 per unit. On average, development costs totaled $23,000 per unit, the same as those for units in the Section 8 study. Development costs per unit for both SRO Housing Corp. and Section 8 projects were as follows:

	SRO HOUSING CORP.	SECTION 8
Acquisition	$ 7,337	$ 6,900
Rehabilitation	15,641	16,100
Total	$22,978	$23,000

Lenders are learning that the right building with the right management—attuned to the requirements of SRO tenants—can be a sound lending opportunity. In addition, they are experiencing the benefits of helping to solve the pressing problems of a shortage of housing for at least some single homeless individuals, as highlighted in an unsolicited letter received from 19 residents of an SRO hotel in Brooklyn:

You have no idea what it's like to wait in line just to use the bathroom, or wait your turn to cook, or sleep in your clothes in the summer to keep them from being stolen, and in the winter to keep warm. Here we have hot water 24 hours a day, plenty of heat in the winter, two bathrooms, two showers, and a large kitchen on each floor so no one has to wait for anything, including a laundry room on the premises. Everyone has his or her own keys plus our own private mail box. I know this doesn't seem like much to you, but it's the Waldorf Astoria to us.

Sources: SRO Housing Corp. Annual Report, 1989–1990, and other materials provided by the corporation; Report to Congress on SROs for the Homeless Section 8 Moderate Rehabilitation Program, March 1990; and *Directions in Affordable Housing Finance*, March 1990, pp. 2–3.

tor. The building provides common bathroom, kitchen, and laundry facilities, although some units have kitchenettes or bathrooms. In addition, the majority of such projects provide a weekly cleaning service.

Surplus Public Land

Making publicly owned land available to developers is another strategy for increasing the supply of affordable housing. The overall cost of housing, with land the single most costly aspect (particularly downtown), can be reduced when surplus public property is a component of a comprehensive program for affordable housing. By using surplus public land in this way, local governments can turn the financial burden of vacant parcels into additional revenue.

If an agency chooses to sell or grant land to a developer in fee, a variety of techniques can be used to ensure that the land continues to be used for low- and moderate-income housing. Restrictions on use and affordability can be placed in the deed conveying the property recorded against the land at the time of sale. The deed could provide that, in the event of a violation, the land would revert to the agency. Because litigating any reversion could be costly, another tactic is to structure a land sale that is a secured loan as well as a land conveyance. By taking back a promissory note and deed of trust and including restrictions on affordability as express terms of the loan, an agency has the option of calling the note and foreclosing against the property in the event of violation. Payments of principal and interest on the note can be deferred so long as the property complies with the agency's requirements.

Boston has several programs in which the city, in partnership with for-profit and nonprofit developers, has developed affordable housing on city-owned parcels and in buildings acquired through foreclosure, and in surplus public buildings. One program, the Residential Development Program, rehabilitates buildings foreclosed for nonpayment of taxes and recently completed its 100th building.

Austin, Texas, has a program of donating urban renewal lots to the nonprofit organization Habitat for Humanity to develop affordable housing. Plans were for the philanthropic group to build 10 single-family houses in 1990 on city-owned properties.

Alameda, California, donated five acres of surplus land owned by the city's housing authority for the development of apartments for the elderly. Local funds—tax increment financing, a tax-exempt bond, and housing authority reserves—were also used for the development. Two-thirds of the building's units will be affordable for low- and very-low-income residents, with the remainder renting at market rates.

Downtown Housing Zones

A number of cities, among them Hartford, Connecticut, Portland, Oregon, Boston, and Washington, D.C., have encouraged the development of affordable housing by revising land use and construction standards to allow increased density, a smaller minimum lot size, more flexible building siting, and/or simplified approval. A study by the American Planning Association found that such revisions had a positive effect in the production of affordable housing.[12]

Expedited Permitting

An expedited permitting process can ease the time required for reviewing and appealing permits, either by setting a time limit or by creating "one-stop shopping," where all affected departments consider an application for a permit at one hearing. While this mechanism, by limiting the time required and opportunities for appeal, might aid in the production of affordable housing, it can also trigger ill will if the community believes the process does not allow adequate time to express their concerns.

Los Angeles adopted a shelter ordinance in 1986 that established expedited permitting procedures for shelters for the homeless that apply for use permits in medium-density or manufacturing zones. The zoning administrator must process the application within 60 days of its filing, and a special filing fee of $340 rather than the standard $2,000 has been established.

Transfer of Development Rights

TDRs, which allow the sale and transfer of unused development rights from downtown structures providing low-income housing to other locations within downtown, also help support affordable housing. Typically, all transfers are subject to land use regulations on both the sending and receiving sites, and assurances must be provided that the sending building will provide low-income tenancy for the life of the transfer agreement. Developer Wright Runstad and Company used this tool to obtain a higher FAR for its building at 1201 Third Avenue in downtown Seattle. The transferring building, the 19-unit Adams Apartments project, gained $165,600 from the sale of the

---

[12] Welford Sanders et al., *Affordable Single-Family Housing: A Review of Development Standards*, PAS Report No. 385 (Chicago: American Planning Association, 1984).

Ironically, what was once considered the core of the worst city slums—SRO hotels—is now thought to be one of the most viable forms of low-income housing in the country. In fact, at least one member of San Diego's Regional Task Force on the Homeless says that though cities cannot solve the problem of the homeless with SRO facilities alone, they certainly cannot solve the problem without them. But like most major cities in the United States, San Diego lost much of its SRO housing stock in making way for downtown redevelopment during the 1970s and early 1980s. Between 1975 and 1985, the city lost one-third of its supply of SRO facilities to demolition and conversion, with the result an increase in the homeless population.

In addition to approving an ordinance to preserve existing SRO hotel rooms and to promote their rehabilitation, San Diego adopted a program in July 1987 to encourage private developers to construct and profitably manage new low-income affordable housing. The program made SRO buildings with rooms a minimum of 70 square feet a permitted use in any zone where hotel/motel use was allowed, established a variance to reduce or eliminate parking requirements, defined SRO hotels as commercial uses to incorporate requirements for access for the disabled, permitted the mechanical ventilation of courts, and allowed substitutes for a host of various code items, including the use of plastic pipe

10-37   The Sara Frances "Hometel," an SRO hotel in San Diego.

for cast iron in the sprinkler system. The city also provided financial incentives, such as restructuring water and sewer connections and rates to reflect more fairly use by SRO facilities and offering low-interest loans to developers to underwrite rents for very-low-income tenants.

Using $2.9 million lent by the city, private financiers had invested over $25 million in new construction as of September 1989. Over 700 new SRO units had been completed and are occupied; over 1,700 new units were under construction or had applied for a building permit.

Source: U.S. Conference of Mayors, *Partnerships for Affordable Housing* (Washington, D.C.: Author, September 1989), p. 39.

rights for its renovation by the Seattle Housing Resources Group.

Public/Private Partnerships

In addition to local incentives and requirements to develop low-income housing, public/private partnerships have had a significant impact on housing.[13] In their least structured form, partnerships are project-oriented efforts between corporate sponsors and community groups, with local government playing an indirect role. They spring up for a specific purpose, making it possible for the community-based organization to secure an option on a site or a building, to complete a feasibility study, or to collateralize a loan, and then disappear when the project is complete. Partnerships that are based on a program, on the other hand, are more formal, permanent arrangements that bring together corporate, public, philanthropic, and community groups. They attempt to establish a highly

sophisticated delivery system that is potentially capable of financing and packaging high volumes of low- and moderate-income housing.

By now, many cities have experimented with housing partnerships; only a few have well-developed programs that have been tested over a sufficiently long period of time to yield some conclusions about the usefulness of this approach, however. Among them are the Boston Housing Partnership, Inc., the Chicago Housing Partnership, the Cleveland Housing Network, Inc., the Wisconsin Partnership for Housing Development, Inc., and the San Francisco Bay Area BRIDGE Housing Corporation.[14]

It is not possible to target one example of a public/private housing partnership, for each partnership

---

[13] This section is based on Suchman et al., *Public/Private Housing Partnerships*, p. 1.

[14] See ibid. for more details.

Nancy Smith, executive director of the Seattle Housing Resources Group (SHRG or "shrug"), says that "flexible hustle" is more important than a fixed plan when developing low-income housing. Like most developers, she spends a significant amount of time trying to find financing for projects, and no two projects are alike. Formed in 1980 by the downtown business community under the leadership of the Downtown Seattle Association, SHRG had completed the construction or rehabilitation of 1,011 units in 10 downtown buildings and one southeast Seattle complex as of 1990. The projects were completed by leveraging $1.6 million in contributions from the business community.

The 79-unit John Winthrop Apartments project, completed in late 1989, is a typical SHRG project—typical, that is, in its complicated financing. Smith recruited six different sources of funding, including Security Pacific Bank, which provided a tax-exempt loan; Pacific First Federal, a tax credit investor; the Washington State Convention and Trade Center; a neighbor of the Winthrop; and two foundations, the Boeing Employees Good Neighbor Fund and the Seattle Foundation. One of the lenders, Security Pacific, is downright bullish about SHRG projects. "They are wonderful loans," says Security Pacific Mortgage Co. president Robert Filley. "You know that the moment the building opens, it's full."

The largest project completed to date is the renovation of the Oregon Hotel, built in 1902 but vacant

10-40   The Oregon now provides 83 apartments for very-low- and extremely-low-income residents.

with 250 building code violations when SHRG purchased it. Located on First Avenue in the Denny Regrade area adjacent to the CBD, the Oregon now totals 83 apartments, including 41 in a new building abutting the old hotel. The challenge of financing the project was met with a bank loan of $1.6 million from Pacific First Federal and a tax credit investment of $1.7 million from the Boeing Company, Security Pacific, and US Bancorp. The Washington State Convention and Trade Center also contributed $750,000.

A working board rather than an oversight board has proved important for SHRG. Members are not financial contributors or their representatives, and all have experience in low-income housing. Furthermore, to serve on the board requires a significant commitment of time. The development committee, for example, meets once a week.

SHRG now manages over 600 of the apartments it has developed. Private property management companies proved unreliable, and they could not make money in the business. SHRG director Smith says that lenders are more comfortable with in-house management anyway; it keeps them closer to their collateral.

Other entities are working on low-income housing in Seattle. Each has different constituencies, a healthy trend says Smith. As for SHRG, it will remain focused but flexible as it continues to meet the housing needs of low-income residents of Seattle.

10-39   The Oregon in 1988 was a vacant building awaiting renovation.

is created within a specific political, social, and economic environment that presents its own set of opportunities and limitations. The degree of success that a partnership can achieve depends on the context in which it operates, the nature of housing needed in the community, local economic conditions and the development environment, the range and type of alternative programs and mechanisms, the kinds and amounts of support the partnership can muster, and the needs and commitment of the primary players. Each city or state partnership is different.

Opposition to Affordable Downtown Housing

In addition to the challenging issues of production and financing, opposition might arise from the residential or business communities to the provision of affordable housing. The NIMBY syndrome—not in *my* backyard—can be expressed through the adoption of government policies, such as zoning ordinances that make it difficult to establish housing and services for poor and homeless members of the community, or citizens' reactive organization and advocacy that seek to block the siting of a facility in the immediate neighborhood. Regardless of its form, it threatens a community's ability to respond compassionately and effectively to the problems of poverty and homelessness.

The solution to opposition to development of affordable housing downtown lies in the creation of a consensus that housing should be available to all of a city's residents. Through zoning codes, planning processes, funding priorities, and community outreach programs, local government can help foster a community-oriented approach to addressing problems of inadequate low- and moderate-income housing downtown.

11.
Hotel, Convention, Entertainment, And Cultural Facilities

Downtowns have been a primary beneficiary of the growth in meetings, conventions, and sports/entertainment and cultural events. As the industrial base in many cities has declined and as production of services has become the dominant segment of the economy, tourism has begun to take on a new importance. Competition among cities for tourist dollars has become fierce, demonstrated by the rush during the past two decades to build hotels, convention centers, sports arenas, and other attractions for visitors.[1] Indeed, tourism now employs more than 6 million people.[2] A hotel, convention center, entertainment center, and/or cultural facility has worked for small and large cities alike.

Downtown Hotels: A Crucial Component of A Successful Strategy

The revolution in product segmentation that overwhelmed the lodging industry in the last decade largely sidestepped the downtown hotel market. Of the four hottest products at this writing—all-suite hotels, courtyard hotels, limited-service motels, and resorts—only all-suite hotels have gained a toehold in the downtown market, and then to a very limited degree. The reason? Land prices in downtown locations, typically much higher than in the suburbs, make all but high-density hotel development infeasible. When all-suite hotels have been built, preliminary evidence suggests that they do outperform nonsuite hotels—as long as they are the only all-suite hotel downtown. The existence of several all-suite hotels, rather than undermining all other nonsuite hotels, tends to place the all-suite hotels on a level playing field with other hotels.

Thus, convention, commercial, and luxury hotels have thrived in the downtown market. But they are more than just another downtown business. Hotels—and the visitors they house—are a crucial component of a successful downtown. Restaurants, shops, theaters, and museums are all beneficiaries of the dollars business guests and tourists spend while staying in downtown hotels. As well, the residential character of a downtown can be enhanced by the existence of hotels. Guests who stay downtown after dark to eat, attend cultural events, or shop enliven the streets, in turn adding to the security of the area. It is no wonder, then, that in the 1980s, cities provided substantial

---

[1] Harold R. Snedcof, *Cultural Facilities in Mixed-Use Development* (Washington, D.C.: ULI–the Urban Land Institute, 1985), p. 16.

[2] "Revival Bought with Tourist Dollars," *New York Times*, January 10, 1990.

11-1   The Mission Inn, a 320,000-square-foot hotel in the heart of Riverside, California, has been the focal point of downtown revitalization. *Source:* ELS/Elbasani & Logan Architects.

financial incentives to encourage the development of downtown hotels.

Moving into the 1990s, however, the pace of hotel development in general has slowed as overbuilding in many markets has lowered average daily rates and occupancies. Understanding the characteristics of demand for new hotels has become increasingly important. For downtown hotels, the major sources of demand are convention and weekday commercial business.

Downtown hotels have been among the biggest beneficiaries of the burgeoning growth in meetings and conventions. Over the past decade, corporate meetings increased 60 percent, while association meetings and conventions doubled. At least 20 percent of

the room-nights at full-service facilities are generated from meetings and conventions, a share that appears to be moving upward. This percentage generally increases with the size of the hotel, accounting for nearly half of the business at the largest properties. And despite the recent boom in the construction of convention centers and conference centers, hotels still host over half of all meetings and displays.

In general, downtown hotels tend to be larger full-service properties and consequently tend to house meetings or convention travelers. With the notable exception of resort-type markets like Hawaii, Las Vegas, Anaheim, and Orlando, larger convention hotels tend to be located downtown, like the large convention centers they serve. In hotels with 400 rooms

	400–599 ROOMS		600–799 ROOMS		800–999 ROOMS		1,000–1,199 ROOMS		1,200+ ROOMS		TOTAL	
	NO.	PERCENT	NO.	PERCENT	NO.	PERCENT	NO.	PERCENT	NO.	PERCENT	NO.	PERCENT
Downtown	107	37	48	47	20	53	8	31	25	53	208	41
Suburbs	59	20	5	5	1	3	2	8	3	6	70	14
Airport	32	11	16	15	3	8	2	8	2	4	55	11
Resort	92	32	34	33	14	36	14	53	17	37	171	34
Total	290	100	103	100	38	100	26	100	47	100	504	100

Source: Hospitality Counselors, Inc.

or more, 41 percent of the rooms are located downtown. This figure rises to 53 percent of the rooms for hotels with 1,200 rooms or more. Resorts are the second highest category, with 34 percent of the rooms (see Figure 11-2).

Convention Hotels

Downtown convention hotels generally contain 500 or more guest rooms and at least 30 square feet of meeting space for each guest room. Often, but not always, they are physically connected with or are close to large convention centers. They frequently emphasize food and beverage facilities with restaurants of differing styles and price ranges.

Convention hotels have unusually large public spaces to accommodate heavy registration and checkout occurring in concentrated time periods. Convention hotels tend to have a higher than average number of guest rooms with two beds to accommodate the high percentage of multiple occupancies typical of convention groups. From 5 to 10 percent of the guest rooms are suites in many convention hotels, as the parlors can be used as hospitality suites or as spaces for smaller meetings.

To reduce the impact of conventions on frequent business travelers, convention hotels usually designate certain floors as concierge or special service floors, with personalized attention given to guests staying there. They might have their own registration areas and are virtual hotels within a hotel. Examples include Hyatt's Regency Clubs, Marriott's and Radisson's Concierge Levels, and Hilton's and Sheraton's Executive Towers sections. The hotels control access to these floors and provide them such features as a concierge, separate registration, 24-hour room service, an honor-system bar, a lobby/lounge, special in-room amenities, such as extra thick towels, bathroom scales, shower massages, complimentary toiletries, or terry cloth robes, complimentary daily newspapers, and continental breakfast and hors d'oeuvres.

Brief profiles of several convention hotels exemplify the scope of available facilities:

- The *New York Marriott Marquis* contains 1,877 guest rooms, including 141 suites and 150 concierge rooms; a 1,500-seat Broadway theater, and five restaurants and lounges; a ballroom for groups of up to 2,500 seated theater style or 2,000 for a banquet; a second ballroom/exhibit hall of 22,481 square feet; and 33 smaller meeting rooms.
- The *Sheraton New Orleans* contains 1,200 guest rooms, including 54 one- and two-bedroom suites; five restaurants and lounges; and 29 meeting rooms in over 37,000 square feet of space. The top eight floors are the Executive Level, with private check-in, concierge, and lounge.
- The *Stouffer Harborplace–Baltimore* provides 622 guest rooms, including 62 suites, as part of a mixed-use complex with a retail atrium and a 26-story office tower. Meeting space includes a 14,560-square-foot ballroom, 4,000-square-foot junior ballroom, and 12 additional meeting rooms. The hotel also has an indoor swimming pool, health club with sauna, restaurant, lounge, and lobby lounge.

11-3   Stouffer Harborplace Hotel, Baltimore.

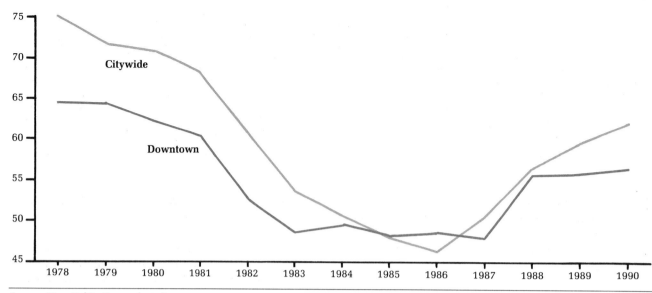

Source: Hospitality Counselors, Inc.

Commercial Hotels

The weekday commercial market is the other major source of room-nights for downtown hotels. Week-ends, however, are problematic for hotels serving this market, effectively limiting annual occupancies to 65 to 72 percent. Those cities whose downtown areas are significant tourist attractions, such as San Francisco, New Orleans, and Washington, D.C., are able to exceed the natural ceiling.

While the heavy commercial orientation of down-town hotels does tend to put a cap on occupancies, it also tends to protect occupancies during times of recession or economic dislocation. A certain level of commercial activity takes place in downtowns almost regardless of economic conditions. Houston's experience during its recent recession illustrates the point. The graph in Figure 11-4 compares occupancies in downtown Houston with citywide occupancies for the period 1978 to 1990.

Occupancies in downtown Houston never exceeded 65 percent, even when citywide occupancies were at 75 percent in 1978, thus reflecting Houston's strong commercial orientation and lack of tourist amenities downtown. When citywide occupancies plummeted to 46 percent in 1986 after the oil crash, however, downtown occupancies never fell below 48 per-cent; downtown occupancies actually exceeded city-wide occupancies in 1985 and 1986.

Downtown commercial hotels tend to be somewhat smaller than convention hotels, generally offering 300 to 500 rooms. Conventions and meetings often consti-tute an important segment served by commercial ho-tels, but the groups are smaller. Most such hotels make available a scaled-down amount of public space, with no more than two restaurants—a coffee shop and a higher-priced outlet—and limited retail space. The following examples are typical:

- The *Ramada Renaissance Hotel* in Washington, D.C., has 351 guest rooms, including 16 suites, a Mediterranean restaurant, a delicatessen, and a lobby lounge. Two small ballrooms of just over 3,300 square feet each are included in the inven-tory of 10 meeting rooms.
- The *Radisson Plaza Hotel* in Orlando has 337 guest rooms, including 33 suites, one all-purpose restaurant and bar, a 5,450-square-foot ballroom, 12 additional meeting rooms, and 12 parlors.

Luxury Hotels

Downtown luxury hotels are found primarily in larger metropolitan areas where sufficient numbers of dis-criminating potential guests have the ability and will-ingness to pay for a higher level of service. Typically, luxury hotels consist of 250 or fewer rooms, although some have as many as 400 or 500 rooms. Luxury hotels provide high-quality furnishings, a superior restaurant, and an extensive array of amenities and services for guests. The emphasis on service results in a higher ratio of employees to guest rooms than in a lower-priced, full-service hotel of comparable size. Luxury hotels could accommodate some meetings and banquets, but if they do, they emphasize small groups. The following examples are typical:

11-5　The 208-room Ritz-Carlton Cleveland is part of Tower City, which also includes a multilevel retail mall and an office tower. The project is directly served by both light- and heavy-rail transit.

- Occupying the top eight stories of a 13-story building, the *Ritz-Carlton Cleveland* offers 208 guest rooms. The Grill is an upscale restaurant; the Cafe provides breakfast, lunch, and dinner. Beverage service is provided in the club lounge and the lobby lounge. The hotel is connected to the Avenue at Tower City Center, which offers 120 specialty stores and restaurants. The largest meeting space is a 4,264-square-foot ballroom, and six more meeting rooms are available.

11-6　　　　　　MARKET MIX OF
　　　　　　　　DOWNTOWN HOTELS

	DOWNTOWN HOTELS	ALL U.S. HOTELS
Business	45%	42%
Tourist	24	33
Conference	16	11
Convention	8	8
Other	7	6
Total	100%	100%

Source: Pannell Kerr Forster.

- The *Hotel Crescent Court–Dallas* is a European-style 188-room hotel located in the Crescent, a retail/office/hotel MXD just outside downtown Dallas. Beau Nash is an American brasserie with an international menu, and the Conservatory serves breakfast and lunch next to a New Orleans–style courtyard. The hotel has two ballrooms of just over 3,000 square feet each and nine other meeting rooms.
- The *Boston Harbor Hotel* is a 230-room hotel at Rowes Wharf, a mixed-use development on the waterfront in downtown Boston. The modern hotel features a six-story grand arch and copper dome. Rowes Wharf Restaurant serves gourmet seafood and features views of the harbor. Amenities include an indoor pool, a health club, and a spa with a 60-foot lap pool. Meeting space is limited, with the largest room only 1,798 square feet and only three additional small rooms.

Public Incentives for Downtown Hotels

Many of the hotels built downtown during the past decade were part of redevelopment projects and were assisted by federal monies in the form of UDAGs or CDBGs. For the most part, this federal assistance has been discontinued, although repayments of UDAGs can be recycled into new projects. To attract hotels in support of convention and tourism strategies, local governments have had to provide incentives for hotel development. In San Jose, California, for example, the 541-room Fairmont is part of an eight-block retail, office, and hotel redevelopment. The local redevelop-

11-7　The Fairmont Hotel (at right) in San Jose is surrounded by office towers, a historic art museum, and a cathedral.

ment agency spent $28.2 million on public improvements, a garage, and a lobby and $2 million for off-site improvements, including East Market Street. The developer earns a preferred return on equity, while the agency participates in net cash flow.

In Baltimore, the 622-room Stouffer hotel that opened in 1988 and its parking structure are owned by the city. In Memphis, land for the 416-room Holiday Inn Crowne Plaza is leased for $1.00 a year; the city and county own and operate the hotel parking facilities. In Cincinnati, the city built the parking garage, sidewalks, and underground loading dock that Saks Fifth Avenue shares with the 500-room Hyatt that opened in 1984. The city assembled the land, provided a favorable lease, and facilitated a $6 million UDAG. Other cities have provided public incentives for downtown hotel development: Albuquerque (for a 403-room Hyatt Regency), Minneapolis (for an 800-room Hilton to be completed in 1992), and Nashville (for a 673-room Stouffer that is owned by the city and leased to the hotel), for example.

Public incentives to support hotel development can be reinforced by zoning that encourages a concentration of hotels in areas closest to convention facili-

11-9   HOTEL SALES PER GUEST-DAY, 1988

	DOWNTOWN HOTELS*	ALL U.S. HOTELS*
Rooms	$58.03	$43.32
Food and Beverage	30.37	28.54
Other	5.41	4.29
Total	84.80	69.32

Downtown hotels are typically more expensive to build because of land costs, but they tend to generate higher revenues than those at airports, in the suburbs, or along a highway.

*All amounts are medians and do not add to the totals shown.
Source: Hospitality Counselors, Inc.

ties and the office core as well as tourist attractions and retail concentrations, thus maximizing the economic and synergistic impact of hotel development. The relationships among land economics, room rates, and the willingness or ability of the public sector to subsidize hotel development dictate the proximity of different types of hotels to these and other downtown developments.

Convention and Entertainment Facilities

Convention and entertainment facilities, or more precisely, convention centers, stadia, and arenas, can be an important component of a downtown's strategy for revitalization or redevelopment.[3] The role of downtown has emerged in many cities as an entertainment center with restaurants and specialty shops. The entertainment elements and hotels create an attractive environment for Class A office space, which in turn reinforces support for shops and is supported by the convention center, stadium, or arena. This synergism has become important to many successful downtowns, including Cincinnati, Atlanta, Baltimore, and Albuquerque. In addition, it is not uncommon for a major new public assembly facility, as these buildings are also called, to generate new businesses or the construction of new buildings: a new hotel, a restaurant, a catering or security services business, for example.

11-8   The city of Memphis leased the land where this 416-room Holiday Inn Crowne Plaza sits for $1.00 a year.

[3] Except for the case studies in Figures 11-14, 11-19, and 11-22, this section is summarized from David C. Petersen, *Convention Centers, Stadiums, and Arenas* (Washington, D.C.: ULI–the Urban Land Institute, 1989).

Types of Public Assembly Facilities

Public assembly facilities are one-of-a-kind buildings. Few communities have more than one arena, one stadium, or one convention center. Most cities and towns have none, and only the largest have all three. Although each of the facilities shares similar functions, they are different enterprises serving unrelated industries.

Arenas

Typically, an arena has a flat floor with 8,000 to 22,000 fixed seats arranged on one or two levels. Sight lines at an arena are nearly always designed for events the size of a hockey floor: basketball games, circuses, ice shows, indoor soccer games, and arena football games, for example.

Stadia

A stadium is characterized by seating and visibility designed for a baseball or football field. Major league baseball parks contain 40,000 to 50,000 seats. The rectangular or oval football stadium can hold 65,000 to 100,000 seats. Multipurpose (baseball and football) stadia, popular in the 1960s, and domed facilities, developed in the 1970s and 1980s, have provided some additional opportunities for events and substantially changed the financial operating characteristics of the more traditional special-purpose stadia.

Convention Centers

A convention center contains exhibition space as well as a substantial number of meeting rooms. Exhibition space is usually 50,000 to 700,000 square feet of contiguous flat floors with a 25- to 30-foot ceiling. Additional space is also available for a kitchen, banquet facilities, auditorium, and other special purposes. A center can host a number of events, typically of greater variety than an arena or stadium.

Conventions are privately held meetings of professional groups and associations that commonly occur in hotels or convention centers and are attended by an association's members and/or affiliates wishing to share ideas. They often produce trade shows (exhibits) to merchandise products and services. Conventions are considered "high-impact" events, as attendees normally stay several nights in the host city, thus generating increased hotel revenues and purchases of other goods and services—food, beverages, retail merchandise, and transportation.

Trade shows are similar to conventions with exhibits, but they tend to be oriented exclusively toward exhibits and have few, if any, meetings. Compared with conventions, trade shows usually draw greater numbers of attendees whose average stay is shorter, as more attendees are from the metropolitan area.

Although merchandise marts essentially are trade shows, they differ in that buyers usually stay on the floor for only a few hours to place orders or see new products, thus generating less revenue for the local economy. The shows are open only to specific industry personnel (usually retail store buyers) to display and sell consumer product lines, such as apparel and gifts.

Consumer shows are public ticket events featuring exhibitions of consumer products for sale and/or exhibition to attendees. Boat, auto, recreational vehicle, antique, and home and garden shows are examples. They occur in convention/civic centers and, depending on the size, location, and type of merchandise sold, usually attract many local residents.

Determining Need

The need for a new or expanded sports facility or convention center most often is determined by a community's physical and locational suitability for the anchor tenant (the sports team), its ability to capture the desired market share, and the anticipated characteristics of use. The feasibility of public assembly facilities, unlike that of traditional real estate developments, is rarely measured by their return on funds invested or by operating profits.

A New Facility as a Catalyst

The most common rationale for developing a new public assembly facility is "to make something else happen." In this case, the building's secondary purpose is to host the events for which the facility is designed. The primary motive for developing the building might be to attract a large hotel or mixed-use development, to provide additional activity downtown for pedestrians or visitors, or to capture a professional sports franchise. The combined benefits obtained from all the anticipated consequences resulting from the building's development should be factored into any evaluation of its feasibility.

The publicity and big-league image that a community receives by having a football franchise illustrate this rationale to make something else happen. In a typical year, a 70,000-seat stadium might be used for only 10 professional football games, but they could be aired on hundreds of local television and radio stations across the nation and in the local region. As well, data about the team are reported in dozens of major area newspapers. The community might obligate itself to provide substantial financial subsidies to obtain the nonquantifiable or intangible benefits from becoming a big-league city. Certainly, emerging cities (like Atlanta in the 1960s, Tampa in the 1970s, and Charlotte in the 1980s) are more likely to employ this strategy to boost their standing than more established larger cities that already have acquired status and/or sports franchises.

A facility that serves conventions and trade shows has more quantifiable spin-off effects or external benefits. The average daily expenditures and length of stay are well documented for attendees and exhibitors at such events and, more recently, for those who also take a vacation in the vicinity of the meeting before or after the event. Often the taxes received by state and local governments exceed the government's expenditures required to subsidize the facilities' annual debt service and operating costs. Thus, the fiscal cost/benefit ratio is the most logical basis for determining the feasibility of such facilities.

In addition to its potential for increased expenditures from visitors, a convention center can be pursued as a component of downtown revitalization. When the Tampa Convention Center opened in fall 1990, it represented a major step by the city to transform a blighted warehouse district within three blocks of the downtown core. The center's parking garage contains retail space, the first such use in that area. In addition, the city owns land adjacent to the center that it will use as an economic development tool to entice

David Barrett Blumberg

11-10 Planners hope that the new convention center in downtown Tampa will transform a blighted warehouse district.

hotel development. In anticipation of the area's development, the city had the foresight to acquire land to allow for the facility's future expansion.

An Adequate Facility to Serve Existing Activities

Communities with facilities that serve existing activities must evaluate the size of their population and potential market in relation to the adequacy of existing facilities. Events that can attract larger audiences or more attractive rental/income opportunities, or are expanding in number of attendees or team size, could be averse to locating in a physically or functionally obsolete facility.

The demand for entertainment, as measured by number of events and size of audience, is a direct function of the size of the population within the market area. For example, a community's 8,000-seat arena might easily have met the needs of family shows and touring sports and entertainment groups in the 1960s, but if rapid population growth now demands that multiple performances be given, the same facility would be undersized and the event likely to go to another city in the same region with a 15,000-seat facility. The future attendance and number of events can be readily determined for a professional sports team that historically sells out tickets to a game, has a long waiting list for season tickets, or is using a physically deteriorated or functionally obsolete structure.

Similarly, an undersized exhibition hall will lose important old customers that outgrow their space and will have to turn away new customers because the building does not have the capacity to handle multiple bookings at one time. Therefore, the community loses a share of the market and is unable to achieve a level of performance commensurate with its convention/trade show resources. In these instances, past users, current users, and historical records can indicate the proper size and future use of a new facility. It is important to use the list of businesses turned away or lost if such records are kept by the building's management or the convention and visitors bureau.

Planning, Design, and Construction

Building, financing, and operating a public assembly facility are major long-term tasks requiring tenacious commitment. A strong and dedicated constituency of government officials, civic leaders, and the business community should be brought together to provide support for the project. The strong political support given by the city of New Orleans and the state of

11-11　Waterfront features and art can be used to create important public spaces for conference and convention centers.

Louisiana, for example, was key to the successful development of the Superdome. The governor of Louisiana backed the project's concept immediately, and his leadership enabled developers to gather the political support necessary for a project of that magnitude.

The first steps in the planning process are to identify the leadership and the organizations that will be responsible for the planning, site selection, design, financing, and operation of the facility. Ideally, the same organization will be empowered to perform all these tasks to minimize the potential for error.

One of the most important factors to consider in the entire process of bringing about a sports or convention facility is its location, which will have a major influence on attendance and occupancy: the greater the attendance and occupancy, the greater the marketability. The Washington State Convention and Trade Center has one of the most unusual locations of any convention center. It was built, through the purchase of air rights, over 12 lanes of I-5 in downtown Seattle, adjacent to an existing park also built over the freeway. Although a difficult site to develop, it was the most attractive site from the standpoint of market appeal, with a location near the heart of Seattle and the downtown hotels.

Several criteria are key in site selection:

• *Visibility.* An important civic structure should be set in a prominent, highly visible location.

The massive size of such facilities in a downtown can pose a challenge in design, but as an important marketing tool, visibility should not be surrendered.

• *Parking.* Most of the parking for an arena or stadium should be located adjacent to or near the structure, within convenient walking distance. If this requirement is not fully met by existing parking facilities, the required site area must be expanded to include new parking. A convention center, on the other hand, can be stacked and thus offers more flexibility in its

11-12　The Washington State Convention and Trade Center is built over 12 lanes of I-5 in downtown Seattle.

207

11-13 The Orlando Arena will supplement surface parking with a multipurpose garage featuring a daycare center and a restaurant.

requirements for parking on the site. The Orlando Arena, for example, will soon be served by an innovative multipurpose parking garage, now under construction. The facility will have parking spaces as well as a daycare center and a restaurant. All three will serve both daytime downtown employees and evening attendees at the arena.

- *Access.* Attendees at a public assembly facility will arrive and depart during the same brief time periods before and after an event. Therefore, high-volume access to the site is essential to disperse attendees as they enter and exit, either by foot or auto.
- *Proximity to support facilities.* Successful convention centers must be located near hotels, restaurants, stores, entertainment, and other attractions. Not only do attendees need these support facilities, but their spending at them is also essential for maximizing the economic and fiscal impact of the center—the very reason it was built.

While the cost of the site is always an issue in site selection, other issues might also be relevant if the project requires a large amount of land. For example, it could be difficult to accommodate a large site in a densely developed downtown, or the need for new parking facilities could require land assembly that results in displacing adjacent uses. Site costs can be minimized through the development and sale of air rights and through careful evaluation of on-site and off-site costs of land development and infrastructure. Many communities in recent years have asked for landowners and developers to submit proposals to

sell or grant land for a convention center. When landowners recognize the benefit to their residual holdings, the community can secure land at a more reasonable cost by avoiding the delays and inflationary effects of condemnation.

The successful development of the Hubert H. Humphrey Metrodome in Minneapolis can be credited, in large measure, to the full support and cooperation of the downtown business community. Land for the facility was donated by a group of downtown businesses in return for the right to develop the surrounding real estate that they owned. In addition, five downtown companies assisted the development process by purchasing $55 million in revenue bonds.

Downtown development of a public assembly facility, particularly a convention center, can be well suited for a mixed-use project. A mix of uses is often required for the facility's marketability (for example, the need for hotel rooms near a convention center) or for its financial feasibility (when revenues from ground leases are pledged to debt service payments for the public assembly facility). In this case, the public sponsor might want the developer of the private uses to be part of the design/build team. The owners and operators of the adjacent private use (retailing or a hotel) and the public assembly facility are then assured of continuity in the design and development of the structures and marketing of the entire complex.

Financing Development Costs

Development costs for arenas and stadia traditionally have been supported through municipal bond financing. In recent years, more innovative financing techniques have been used to minimize the burden on taxpayers for debt service. With the loss of municipal bonds' tax-exempt status, a wider range of financing mechanisms could develop. A variety of financing mechanisms have been used for downtown public facilities; it is not unusual to find several types of financing employed on a single project.

Sale/Lease of the Facility's Name

A large amount of initial capital can be raised through the sale or lease of the stadium's name to a private corporation. This financing vehicle is used in Syracuse for the Carrier Dome, for which the Carrier Corporation donated $2.7 million for use of the name; in Sacramento for the Arco Arena, for which Atlantic Richfield Co. paid $5 million for a 10-year advertising contract; and in Phoenix for the America West Arena.

America West Arena is now under construction, in the headquarters for America West Airlines. For the use of its name, the airline will contribute an annual fee toward the arena's operating costs for 25 years. The arena will be used primarily for basketball games with the Phoenix Suns, the arena's operator and prime tenant. Other, daily functions will extend its use: ticketing for America West Airlines and airport shuttle bus service, restaurants, and bars. The estimated completion date is September 1992, just before basketball season (see Figure 11-14).

Seat Preference Bonds

Seat preference bonds are sold to individuals or corporations, allowing them the right to purchase season tickets in prime viewing locations within the arena or stadium. This source of revenue is a viable alternative when the stadium project is popular and supported by the general public. A variation of this financing mechanism is planned for Seattle's new arena, which is still on the drawing boards. For a $120,000 fee, with 4 and 5 percent per year increases built in, depending on the lease term, companies and individuals will have unlimited year-round access to private luxury box suites at the arena. If the 72 suites are fully leased, the revenue would add $8.6 million to income.

Sale of Advertising Rights

Advertising within a stadium or arena is often sold or leased to derive an annual source of revenue to cover part of the debt service. Interior advertising usually consists of scoreboard messages during the event or display signs placed at various locations. Some buildings have been trading the costs associated with computer-controlled scoreboards for all or part of the advertising generated by this equipment.

Joint Development Revenues

Real estate development adjacent to a public assembly site could include hotel and office components. Income from ground leases from hotel and office developers would produce an annual income stream that could help supplement other income available for debt service. This potential relies to a great extent on the marketability (and the availability) of adjacent land for high-value uses. The Santa Clara Convention Center, for example, is part of a complex that features many uses, including the convention center and a hotel. The hotel operates under a land lease with the city and has use of the nearby city-developed tennis courts, golf course, and parking facilities. The city benefits from increased room taxes as a result of group meetings in the area and uses revenue from land leases to fund the project. The hotel benefits from increased occupancy from group meetings and

from reduced marketing costs because the convention and visitors bureau sells the convention center to groups that ultimately become hotel clients. The land lease also helped save development costs for the hotel because city-owned facilities used by the hotel were publicly funded.

General Obligation/Revenue Bonds and Tax Increment Financing

A general obligation bond can be used to finance stadia and arenas, with the annual debt service payments made from the community's general fund. Any excess revenue resulting from the facility's operations would be paid into the general fund.

Revenue bonds are secured by a defined source of revenue. The most obvious would be the annual proceeds from the operations of the facility after expenses are deducted; most revenue bonds are supplemented or backed by additional sources of revenue, such as a hotel room tax or a general sales tax. The New Orleans Convention Center, for example, was built in part using a $41.5 million local bond issue. The city's hotel/motel taxes funded the debt service on the bonding, which amounted to $13 million in revenue throughout the three years of development. Additional funds came from the state of Louisiana, a UDAG, and economic development grants.

Tax increment or tax allocation bonds are secured by a pledge of the net increases in property taxes resulting from the development of an arena or stadium within a defined redevelopment district.

The Operating Budget

The success of a public facility is measured in part by its potential economic benefits to downtown development or revitalization. In addition, its success is measured by whether it can achieve a cash flow to cover its own operating and debt service costs.

For most convention and trade show facilities, rental income represents the largest source of revenue. The basis for setting rents for exhibit space varies widely across the country. Some charge based on the gross square footage of the entire hall, while others charge only for the net square footage occupied by exhibitors. Depending upon the operating policy of the location, conventions and trade shows requiring large numbers of hotel rooms pay about 50 percent less in rental rates than consumer shows. While a separate fee schedule is available for meeting rooms, a prorated share of meeting room space is often provided free of charge to conventions and trade shows renting exhibition space.

The $84 million 19,300-seat America West Arena in Phoenix, Arizona, is scheduled to open in September 1992. It will serve as the new home for the NBA's Phoenix Suns and will host a multitude of other events. Located in the heart of downtown, the new arena is expected to revitalize the downtown area by attracting visitors to the city's business district.

Development Strategy

Both the city of Phoenix and the Phoenix Suns were motivating forces behind the development of the proposed America West Arena. The Suns, currently using the 30-year-old Arizona Veterans Memorial Coliseum, wanted to move to a newer facility downtown, where the city had been focusing efforts on revitalization and redevelopment. The city expects the proposed arena, in combination with other initiatives downtown, to increase economic activity downtown by attracting new events to the arena, especially on evenings and weekends. Preliminary estimates indicate that the facility will attract approximately 2 million people to the downtown area in its first year of operation. In January 1991, Arizona Center, an 18.5-acre mixed-use retail, restaurant, and office complex, opened its first phase just blocks from the proposed arena. A new shuttle, which transports people throughout downtown and to the state capitol, began operating in late 1990. The city has spent approximately $250 million in the form of tax abatements, public improvements, and land writedowns for downtown development. Future plans include development of a new library, two new museums, a 30-acre park, and the renovation of a historic theater.

Site and Design

The design of the arena is notable for its attempt to further a pedestrian-oriented, lively downtown. Plans include a 45,000-square-foot athletic club accessible from the street, a restaurant/sports bar that overlooks both the city and the floor of the arena, and a food court. An outdoor plaza with landscaping and water features will act as the main entrance to the ticket window, restaurant, and arena. This sidewalk plaza will contribute to a pedestrian-oriented streetscape and will avoid the monolithic face common to other public assembly facilities.

The city acquired the 11.4-acre site on which the arena sits in the south central part of downtown Phoenix for $10 million. It is contiguous to the Civic Plaza and the Symphony Hall and is close to the convention center. Within walking distance are a number of restaurants and retail and entertainment establishments.

11-15   The design of Phoenix's America West Arena is notable for its attempt to further a lively, pedestrian-oriented downtown environment.

Most arenas and stadia with major league teams break even on financial operations. Only arenas in the largest markets, with major league teams as anchor tenants, can hope to generate enough net operating revenue to pay debt service. Currently, eight to 10 cities are willing to provide new baseball stadia at rents unfavorable to themselves to bring major league franchises to their cities. Another six to eight cities are willing to do the same for a major league football team.

Public facilities rely on income from concessions as an important profit center. For many events, in fact, the facility can receive more income from sales of food, beverages, and merchandise than it receives from rent. The range of recently negotiated concession and catering agreements in arenas, stadia, and convention centers is shown in Figure 11-17. This lucrative profit center must be carefully evaluated for its impact on income.

Additional sources of revenue are box office services, rental of equipment to tenants, and, in the case of convention centers, the provision of electrical and telephone services to exhibitors at their booths.

In addition to 19,300 seats, the America West Arena will include 87 luxury suites with 12 to 14 seats approximately 30 rows from the arena floor. The average luxury suite will lease for approximately $70,000 a year and will include on-site parking passes and year-round access to all other arena events. Lease agreements will be available for five and eight years, with payment due up front.

Because the downtown area offers approximately 11,300 parking stalls within an eight-minute walk of the arena, plans for parking on the site include construction of only 1,000 parking spaces. The city, however, is constructing an additional 2,500 spaces across from the arena.

Financing

The $84 million cost for the project is being split between the city and the Phoenix Arena Development Limited Partnership, an organization formed by the Phoenix Suns franchise. The city is financing $35 million through the sale of bonds, which will be repaid through a 1 percent increase in the hotel/motel tax and a 2 percent increase in the car rental tax. In addition, the city acquired the site for $10 million. The limited partnership is financing $49 million through the sale of 30-year taxable bonds enhanced by a letter of credit provided by a consortium of banks. America West's corporate sponsorship of the arena will provide approximately $500,000 in revenues per year for 25 years.

The city will hold the title to the arena, and the Suns will become the operators, leasing the space on a 40-year, priority-fee basis. Under this agreement, the Suns will lease the arena from the city for approximately $500,000 a year at a 3 percent annual increase; they will pay the city

---

11-16   PROJECT DATA

Builder: Mardian Construction
Architect: Ellerbe-Becket, Inc.
Primary User: Phoenix Suns
Construction Began: September 1990
Scheduled Opening: September 1992

Project Information:

Site Area: 11.4 acres
Total Gross Building Area: 991,639 square feet
Total Parking: 1,000 spaces on site, 2,500 spaces across the street
Seating: 19,300 seats for basketball

Economic Information:

Site Acquisition Cost: $10 million
Construction Cost: $52.4 million
Funding Sources: The city of Phoenix and the Phoenix Arena Development Limited Partnership

---

70 percent of net revenue for the first 30 years and 60 percent of net revenue for the last 10 years.

Market Orientation

The new America West Arena is a multipurpose facility that will host not only Phoenix Suns NBA games, but also a variety of local, regional, and national events. The proposed arena is suited for concerts, hockey games, ice shows, tennis matches, and other events. In 1993, the new arena will host the U.S. Figure Skating Championships.

Source: Price Waterhouse Convention and Sports Facilities Advisory Group.

Parking is essential to a public facility and, depending on the availability of public transit and nearby competing parking facilities, can yield large profits. Facilities in a downtown often require structured parking, which is costly to maintain and operate. It is important therefore that they also be used for other purposes, such as accommodating employees and guests in nearby office buildings.

The variety of taxes used to finance the operations of public assembly facilities is as diverse as the types of taxes. Most important is a dedicated source of income or revenue stream. If the facility's net operating cost

becomes a line item in the local government's annual budget, the facility is doomed to compete for funds each year with other (more vital) community services or be heavily influenced by budgetary crises. A facility that needs funding to pay net operating expenses would be well advised to delay the development until a dedicated revenue stream or tax can be obtained.

Management

The quality of management and marketing influences the occupancy and financial operating performance

RECENT CONCESSION AGREEMENTS ILLUSTRATING
SUBSTANTIVE VARIATIONS IN LEASE TERMS

TYPE OF FACILITY/ FOOD SERVICE	RANGE IN SIZE	ANNUAL ATTENDANCE	PERCENT GROSS RECEIVED BY BUILDING
Arena Concession	10,000–20,000 Seats	500,000–2.5 million	20–40
Stadium Concession	40,000–70,000 Seats	1 million–3 million	5–50
Convention Center Concession	100,000–600,000 Square Feet of Exhibition Space	100,000–1.5 million	30–40
Convention Center Catering	1,000–3,000 Seats		10–20

Source: Laventhol & Horwath, in David C. Petersen, *Convention Centers, Stadiums, and Arenas* (Washington, D.C.: ULI–the Urban Land Institute, 1989).

of a public assembly facility more than any other factor. Professional and aggressive management can influence the number of events for the project, provide well-organized services to tenants or event producers, and give attendees an enjoyable and productive visit.

Stadia and arenas can be operated by their owners, by their primary or anchor tenants, by not-for-profit entities (with varying degrees of independence from the owner), or by private management companies. With little exception, convention centers are operated by public or quasi-public management. The advan-

tages and disadvantages of alternative forms of management are shown in Figure 11-18.

All management responsibilities need not rest on a single source. A facility can contract with separate companies for security, maintenance, mechanical equipment, and other services. This division of responsibility can provide greater expertise but is often a difficult arrangement to manage, diffusing accountability for overall performance. Regardless of the form of management, labor for specific events is contracted for each event, and services like setting up and tearing

11-18 ADVANTAGES AND DISADVANTAGES OF
ALTERNATIVE MANAGEMENT STRUCTURES

	PUBLIC MANAGEMENT	AUTHORITY OR NONPROFIT CORPORATION	PRIVATE MANAGEMENT
ADVANTAGES	Control by Owner Financial Support Coordination/Sharing of Staff	Government Representation Special-Purpose Role Increased Operating Autonomy Independent Revenues Less Constrained by Purchasing and Civil Service Requirements	Greatest Operating Autonomy Efficiency Incentives Sensitivity to Tenants Flexibility to Negotiations More Experienced Staff Greater Accountability Less Financial Risk for Government
DISADVANTAGES	Purchasing Procedures Civil Service Constraints Contract Approval Required Changing Policies Lack of Incentives Less Responsive to Tenants Limited Flexibility Lack of Dedicated Source of Funding	Subject to Political Influence Lack of Incentives Bureaucratic Inertia Board Membership Loses Status	Least Government Control Profit Motive versus Impact Motive Cost to Smaller Operations

Source: Laventhol & Horwath, in David C. Petersen, *Convention Centers, Stadiums, and Arenas* (Washington, D.C.: ULI–the Urban Land Institute, 1989).

In November 1989, the San Diego Convention Center opened its doors and hosted its first convention. Situated near the edge of San Diego Bay, this state-of-the-art facility is expected to advance the city of San Diego into one of the nation's premier convention destinations. With 254,000 square feet of exhibit space, a spacious ballroom, and several meeting rooms, the convention center will make an economic impact on the downtown area by attracting international and national delegates to the San Diego area.

Development Strategy

Since the early 1970s, city officials had regarded the development of a convention center as the most important element for success in the city's downtown redevelopment. Included as part of a comprehensive redevelopment plan, the convention center was conceived in concert with Horton Plaza, an entertainment/retail district to be located just three blocks from the center. City planners envisioned the development of a place for convention delegates to meet downtown along with a nearby entertainment area for the delegates' nightlife. Although conceived at the same time, the facilities did not open simultaneously. As a result of delays in development, the convention center opened approximately four years after the opening of Horton Plaza.

The delay in the convention center's opening did not result from construction overruns; instead, it was mostly attributable to the facility's lengthy bidding process. Besieged by controversy, the proposed San Diego Convention Center remained "proposed" until bidding was opened on the project in early 1986. City officials remained steadfast following initial bids, all of which exceeded the original estimates for the facility by more than $24 million. Their patience was rewarded when bidding was reopened, and a joint partnership of Tutor-Saliba Corp. (based in California) and Perini Corp. (from Massachusetts) submitted a low bid of $110.9 million. Delayed by more than a year, construction of the convention center finally began in 1987. By 1989, construction was complete and the first convention was held.

Hawkins Productions

11-20   San Diego Convention Center.

The center has already exceeded original estimates of attendance, attracting more than 250,000 delegates in its first year. Not surprisingly, several local retail outlets have experienced an economic renaissance. Seaport Village, an adjacent 10-year-old shopping area with several specialty retail stores, has already completed expansion plans for an entertainment area to coincide with the likely expansion of the convention center. Gaslamp Quarter, an adjacent historical shopping area featuring several restaurants and retail shops, has experienced significantly higher levels of traffic. According to city officials, many of the new restaurants within Gaslamp Quarter opened following construction of the convention center.

Other economic benefits resulting from the convention center's development include the opening of several upscale hotels within the downtown. According to the San Diego Convention and Visitors Bureau, approximately 2,700 new hotel rooms opened in 1989, the year when the convention center opened. By comparison, San Diego experienced little increase in the inventory of hotel rooms in the late 1970s and early 1980s. Most important are the two hotels adjacent to the center, a 1,355-room Marriott and an 875-room Hyatt (opening in 1992). Few destinations can match this 2,230-room on-site advantage.

Site and Design

While designing the facility, the architectural team faced two obstacles. First, while located on an 11-acre site overlooking the San Diego Bay, the chosen site offered limited space and tight dimensions. Second, the facility's exterior was subject to city policies regarding development on the waterfront. San Diego officials remain protective of the waterfront, requiring that all bayside development "enhance" the bay's beauty. Challenged with these

constraints, the architects inserted a distinctive element that is today the facility's most celebrated feature. Included in the design is an open-air special events hall located on the facility's top floor. This open-air pavilion, which is covered by a billowing, sail-like roof, adds approximately 100,000 square feet of reception/exhibition space to the facility. It also provides the facility with a nautical look, thus serving as an appropriate backdrop to the coastline. The remaining components of the design include a 254,000-square-foot exhibit hall, which can be divided into three sections, 100,000 square feet of flexible meeting and banquet space, and a 400-seat open-air bayside amphitheater.

Access and Parking

Located just four miles from the city's airport, the convention center is easily accessible by car and airport shuttle transportation. The San Diego Trolley, whose service stretches from the San Diego Depot to the Tijuana border, recently added the convention center to its destination list. This aboveground transport shuttles delegates from the convention center to many of the area's restaurants, shopping malls, and entertainment areas. Operating every 15 minutes, the trolley ride costs 50 cents. The convention center also can be reached by a water taxi that connects the facility with several waterfront hotel properties. While not adjacent to the facility, these hotels often accommodate convention center delegates during citywide conventions and trade shows.

The San Diego Convention Center features two levels of underground parking, with spaces for approximately 2,000 cars. An agreement with the adjacent Marriott Hotel requires that 700 spaces remain reserved for hotel guests. Because of the cross use of the facilities, however, guests of both facilities use many of the spaces. Additional parking facili-

down exhibits, cleaning up, ushering, taking tickets, and providing security are performed by part-time personnel.

Food and beverage concessions usually provide a net income to the building of 35 to 55 percent of gross sales. The range of profit margin is a function of the building's occupancy, the type of events, the food service company's capital investment in equipment, and the size of the building.

Marketing

A marketing plan should set forth the various activities and programs to be undertaken, assign responsibilities for each task, establish criteria for measuring the effectiveness or success of each task, and provide a detailed budget and time frame for the completion of each activity. Ideally, the successful convention center has its own effective marketing department,

ties include a recently paved surface lot adjacent to the facility. This lot, which has spaces for 1,500 cars, rests on the proposed expansion area.

Financing

Funding for the San Diego Convention Center was provided by the San Diego Unified Port District, the administrator of tideland properties surrounding San Diego Bay. By using a portion of its vast cash reserves, the Port District was able to fund the entire $160 million cost of the new facility. Because of the unusual method in which the building was funded, the San Diego Convention Center opened its doors free of debt. The San Diego Unified Port District also retained ownership of the 11-acre site, leasing the property to the city of San Diego for $1.00 a year for 20 years.

Market Orientation

The primary objectives for the San Diego Convention Center are to serve as a place for large-scale private and public meetings that produce a positive identity for the city and to generate substantial economic benefits for the entire community. To accomplish these goals, a priority booking policy, which grants favorable lead times for conventions and trade shows, has been established.

The San Diego Convention and Visitors Bureau is responsible for booking the new facility in advance of 18 months. The bureau concentrates its marketing primarily on the larger national and international conventions and trade shows. Regional "consumer events," which typically draw attendance from surrounding communities, are given second priority bookings. These events, as well as local meetings, exhibitions, and social events, are scheduled by the San Diego Convention Center Corporation. The corporation, a nonprofit organiza-

11-21	PROJECT DATA

Owner: City of San Diego
Builder: Tutor-Saliba/Perini
Architect: Joint venture of Deems, Lewis, McKinley (San Diego), Loschsky, Marquardt & Nesholm (Seattle), and Arthur Erickson Associates (Los Angeles)
Year Construction Began: 1987
Year Construction Completed: 1989

Project Information:

Total Gross Building Area: 760,000 square feet
Exhibition Space: 254,000 square feet[1]
Meeting Space: 100,000 square feet
Total Parking Spaces: 3,500

Economic Information:

Site Acquisition Cost: Leased from Port District at $1.00 per year
Total Project Cost: $160,000,000
Cost Breakdown:
  Construction Costs: $120,000,000
  Site Preparation Costs: $20,000,000
  Architecture, Engineering Fees, etc.: $20,000,000

[1]Not including the open-air pavilion.

tion created in 1985 by the San Diego City Council, is responsible for operating, maintaining, managing, and marketing the convention center. The in-house marketing department for the corporation schedules events for groups booking the facility within 18 months of the event.

Source: Price Waterhouse Convention and Sports Facilities Advisory Group.

works closely with a well-funded and well-staffed convention and visitors bureau, and enjoys an ongoing effective relationship with the marketing directors of the major convention-oriented hotels. In most cities, however, such alliances, though necessary for success, are rarely found.

For arenas and stadia, marketing is primarily the responsibility of the building's staff, event promoters, and anchor tenants. The staff negotiates discounted rates for the event promoters to obtain advertising; the event producer bears the costs of promotion.

Cultural Facilities

The fastest-growing cities in the next decade will be those that fuel the engine of economic growth—increasingly, service-oriented small businesses. One

Construction of the 70,500-seat Georgia Dome began in 1989 and is scheduled for completion by the beginning of the 1992 National Football League season. The stadium, with its soft, cable-supported dome, will play host annually to 10 Atlanta Falcons football games and several large-scale sporting and entertainment events. The 42-acre Dome's floor, adjacent to the Georgia World Congress Center (GWCC), will provide an additional 105,000 square feet of exhibit space for the Congress Center's conventions and trade shows. The Georgia World Congress Center Authority's ownership of the Dome will provide the Congress Center's management the ability to coordinate scheduling of sporting and entertainment events as a means of attracting convention groups to the GWCC and downtown Atlanta. The completion of the Dome is also expected to strengthen Atlanta's position as the Southeast's most popular destination for sporting, entertainment, and convention events.

11-23   Atlanta's Georgia Dome, superimposed onto the downtown skyline.

Development Strategy

Two primary issues led to the development of the Georgia Dome. First, the new facility was needed to accommodate the Atlanta Falcons's desire to play in a more modern stadium that offered the amenities found in the newest NFL facilities. The relocation of the Oakland Raiders, Baltimore Colts, and St. Louis Cardinals was fresh on the minds of many civic leaders familiar with other cities' attempts to lure the Falcons away from Atlanta. Second, a new indoor facility was needed to successfully attract events like the Super Bowl (which Atlanta will host in 1994), the NCAA Final Four (held previously in the Atlanta Omni), and other large-scale sporting events and concerts. Certainly, the announcement of the Dome's completion by 1992 enhanced Atlanta's successful bid for the 1996 Olympic Games.

Site and Design

The decision to build the new Georgia Dome downtown adjacent to the GWCC illustrates the forethought of the project's planners to incorporate the Dome as an integral part of the entire GWCC complex. With pedestrian walkways linking the Congress Center to the Dome, the new facility will function as a place for spectator events as well as for events requiring a flat floor. Members of the design team considered this flexibility paramount as they struggled to create a facility easily identified as a stadium but also as a spot for other functions.

The site of the Georgia Dome, which will be leased from the state for $1.00 per year for 50 years, is located near all major downtown hotels and is easily accessible by car and the Metropolitan Atlanta Rapid Transit Authority (MARTA) rail system. Two MARTA stations are within walking distance of the Dome, and no major improvements to transportation are needed to handle the expected increase in the area's traffic flow. Two thousand parking spaces will be added to the existing 10,000 that are within three blocks of the site. Hartsfield International Airport is directly accessible to the Dome area through MARTA and is a 20-minute drive from the downtown area.

The facility's design uses proven methods of construction and materials. The soft, cable-supported roof is similar in many ways to the Hoosier Dome's roof in Indianapolis. Unlike the Hoosier Dome, however, the Georgia Dome's roof will be supported by cables. The 70,500 seats include 183 executive suites and 6,304 club seats with exclusive access to the Executive Concourse, which features cocktail lounges, fine restaurants, and attended restrooms. Preconstruction leasing of these suites and club seats provided an important infusion of funds used in financing the project.

Financing

The project will be financed through a combination of private and public funds. Tax-exempt revenue bonds issued by the GWCC Authority raised $200 million in construction funds. The bonds are limited obligations of the GWCC Authority and are secured by and payable from pledged revenue consisting of 1) 39.3 percent of all hotel/motel taxes generated by the city of Atlanta and Fulton County; and 2) all operating revenue from the GWCC Authority's ownership and operation of the Georgia Dome.

By the fifth year of operation, approximately 40 percent of total revenue needed to finance the Dome's debt service and operation will be derived from the pledged share of Atlanta's and Fulton County's hotel/motel tax. The remaining 60 percent will come from the Dome's operating revenue and interest income.

The state of Georgia has no obligation to repay the revenue bonds should they go into default. The bonds are the obligation of the Georgia Stadium Corporation (a subsidiary of the GWCC Authority) and are secured by a private banking group's letter of credit.

Market Orientation

Once construction is complete, Atlanta will be able to host most of the world's largest sporting events; in fact, the 1994 Super Bowl and 1996 Summer Olympics are already scheduled. The Georgia Dome's ability to host such high-profile sporting events will undoubtedly enhance the city's image, making Atlanta even more attractive as a convention destination.

Conclusion

The Georgia Dome will have three major effects for Atlanta and the downtown area. First, the Dome will ensure that Atlanta remains the home for the Falcons, thereby retaining the economic benefits associated with being an NFL franchise city. Second, Atlanta will now be able to host most high-profile sporting events. Third, the GWCC will have a greater supply of exhibit space, often needed for many of the nation's larger conventions and trade shows. Together, these effects will translate into an increased number of visits to Atlanta, creating additional economic benefits for the city and the downtown. According to the NFL, a host city can expect an estimated $150 million economic impact and a $16 million increase in tax revenues from hosting a Super Bowl. Georgia Dome officials anticipate a $3.5 billion economic impact and an additional $175 million in tax revenues from the 1996 Summer Olympics.

11-24   PROJECT DATA

Owner: Georgia World Congress Center Authority
Builder: A joint venture of Beers, Inc., Holder Construction Company, and H.J. Russell Construction. The Barton-Malow Company's Atlanta office will also contribute.
Architect: Heery/RFI/TVS
Primary Tenant: Atlanta Falcons
Year Planning Began: 1984
Year Construction Began: 1989
Estimated Date of Completion: Mid-1992

Project Information:

Site Area: 42 acres
Stadium Seating Capacity: 70,500

Economic Information:

Site Acquisition Cost: $1.00 per year for 50 years from the state

Total Project Cost:

Land	$ 16,000,000
Construction	130,000,000
Construction, Architectural Fees	19,000,000
Financing Costs during Construction	45,000,000
Estimated Total Cost	$210,000,000

Tax-Exempt Industrial Revenue Bonds:
$196,000,000[1]

---

[1] The $14 million differential between the cost and proceeds of the bond issue is being met by hotel taxes accrued to date and a loan from GWCC's reserve account.

Source: Price Waterhouse Convention and Sports Facilities Advisory Group.

important source of fuel for these companies—the key source some say—is quality of life. Austin, Texas, for example, known for its quality of life, leapfrogged almost 20 places, from 42nd to 27th largest city, during the 1980s. Another rapidly growing city, San Antonio, has developed a comprehensive program for attracting high-technology investment to the city. At the core of its strategy: arts and education. Goals to make the San Antonio Symphony one of the 10 best in the country and to establish the city as the nation's center for Hispanic culture confirm the city's view that arts and culture are important tools for accomplishing economic development, more so perhaps than traditional investments like improved freeways.[4] Downtowns are jumping on the quality-of-life bandwagon as well, treating it as a new kind of investment in infrastructure that will create long-term value. Three strategies—developments that include cultural facilities, cultural districts, and cultural planning— have emerged as important planks in the downtown quality-of-life agenda.

Projects that Include Cultural Facilities

Projects with cultural facilities are not new. As the 1980s ushered in more mixed uses downtown, however, culture became one of those uses more often. In Roanoke, Virginia, for example, a 70,000-square-foot cultural arts facility was built to house five institutions that had been scattered throughout the area: science, art, and history museums, the arts council, and a theater. In San Diego, an art museum, theaters, and public art attract customers to downtown's Horton Plaza, a mixed-use project that also includes almost 500,000 square feet of retail space. The four department stores there had never before operated in downtown San Diego. Illinois Center in downtown Chicago features curated art exhibits in public spaces and a series of eight "culture stops" displaying information about downtown cultural institutions and events.

For each of the developers, city agencies, and cultural organizations involved in these projects, a number of goals have been accomplished. Roanoke's Center on the Square and Horton Plaza have served as catalysts for downtown development. In those cities and at Illinois Center, the cultural component adds to the project's identity, drawing visitors and customers beyond the eight-hour workday and benefiting retailing as well as the entire downtown.

At the same time, the cultural components of these or any building add to the complexity of development. The amount of time required to settle such a

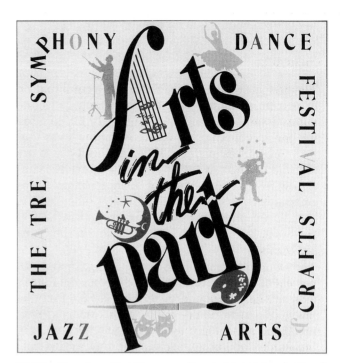

11-25 Downtown Fort Myers uses its new 10-acre riverfront park for a spring and summer series called "Arts in the Park." The series has served as a catalyst for other cultural events at the park: a dance and theater workshop, a Shakespeare festival, and concerts.

deal, for example, can increase significantly over projects without cultural components. The predevelopment stage for a typical MXD totals three to five years; for one that includes an art component, the average is more like seven to 15 years.[5] The greater number of participants in the process and the level of detail required when including cultural facilities add time to the process.

Public improvements and amenities in excess of those provided in typical real estate developments also add to the complexity and cost of projects that include the arts. Land allocated for plazas and gardens must also be accompanied by lighting, landscaping, paving, water, and street furniture. Requirements for design are usually also extensive, resulting in a need for higher-quality materials and costlier architectural and engineering fees. This extra expense and time, when combined with the typically larger size of the project and the fact that the cultural components usually do not contribute to net revenue, certainly add risk. Moreover, it is extremely difficult to quantify the value of the contribution that cultural compo-

[4] Robert H. McNulty, Dorothy R. Jacobson, and R. Leo Penne, "What Are the Arts Worth?" *Place*, January/February 1986, p. 23.
[5] Snedcof, *Cultural Facilities in Mixed-Use Development*, p. 22.

nents could make to the project. Few projects, therefore, are possible without a public/private partnership in which a public entity provides incentives to the developer for taking on added risk, even in a strong real estate market.

California Plaza in downtown Los Angeles illustrates this reality. The master plan for this 12-acre project includes two museums, a major outdoor performance plaza, a dance theater, and a reconstructed cable railway set amid six office and residential towers, a hotel, and a retail complex. The Museum of Contemporary Art and the first office tower were completed in the late 1980s, and the second office building, the hotel, part of the residential space, and the performance plaza are under construction.

With a total public and private cost estimated at $1.2 billion, California Plaza required careful financial structuring to compensate for the extraordinary financial donation ($58.6 million in October 1981) required of the developer. Most of this sum related to the cultural and open-space components of the project. One feature of the financial package, therefore, was a writedown in the cost of land. On the assumption that the developer eventually would receive some benefit from the Museum of Contemporary Art, constructed by the developer at a cost of $23 million and contributed to the city, as well as the other cultural facilities, an adjusted cost burden of $30.8 million was assigned. The full value of the land was estimated

at $89.1 million, but the city agreed to treat the developer's $30.8 million in adjusted costs as in-lieu payments, bringing the cost on which land lease payments were based to $58.3 million.

Projects that include cultural facilities can offer significant benefits for the public/private/arts coalition that creates them, the citizens of the areas where they are located, and the city as a whole. Because of their complexity, however, they will succeed only when a clear, mutually accepted vision of specific goals is established for the project at the outset and when strong, committed leadership directs the development process.[6]

Cultural Districts

Arts or cultural districts might be defined as formally designated areas with distinctive and desirable cultural characteristics for which public policies have been established to encourage the preservation or enhancement of that character. Historic districts set the precedent for this approach. Revenue-producing uses are often incorporated to make the district economically viable, while the arts attract people.[7] This balance of commercial and cultural uses has to be

---

[6] Ibid., pp. 10, 19.
[7] Ibid., p. 23.

11-26   In Fairfield, California, a downtown center for creative arts was a catalyst for revitalizing downtown. *Source:* ELS/Elbasani & Logan Architects.

219

11-27 California Plaza required careful financial structuring to compensate for the extraordinary donation required of the developer.

work well in others. A more prudent approach might be to build on existing institutions that could become the anchors of downtown cultural districts. Oklahoma City, Rochester, New York, and Trenton and Newark, New Jersey, for example, are all considering positioning their libraries as key downtown anchors. The earliest public libraries set the precedent for this now-considered-novel approach. The original Carnegie Library outside Pittsburgh had as its main attraction a boxing ring and gymnasium. Another featured a swimming pool in the central pavilion. The idea was to attract young people for recreation and then expose them to literature. Today, libraries offering daycare for children and elderly parents, restaurants, and classes for English as a second language can help reposition themselves as the anchor of a downtown cultural district.[8]

Another traditional institution, the community college or university, can become a major downtown anchor, even in the smallest of towns. Leftover land from outdated industrial uses or railroad yards, for example, often exists in a blighted condition adjacent to many downtown areas. These locations can be suitable for in-town urban campuses served by existing bus service that provide support for downtown businesses. For students, a location near the town's cultural centers (library, museums, parks, and so on), cafes, and stores, and easy access from all parts of the community can be very appealing. A strong synergistic relationship can thus be created downtown.

In Fayetteville, Arkansas, the University of Arkansas built a new continuing education campus downtown. It is used not only by local citizens, but also by two major employers—Tyson's Food and Wal-Mart—

managed carefully, however, so that commercial development does not overshadow the cultural component, as some feared would happen in the Dallas Arts District. Still, in Dallas and in other cities where office development has been an important component of a cultural district, the addition of new cultural facilities speaks for itself. The Dallas Museum of Art, the Morton H. Myerson Symphony Center, and a playhouse for the Dallas Theatre Center have certainly enlivened the city's downtown, and the cultural facilities have benefited from a built-in potential audience of over 100,000 downtown workers. In another cultural district, Cleveland's Playhouse Square, three historic downtown theaters are being rehabilitated in the largest theater restoration project in the nation. The project is an attempt to reassert cultural and allied commercial uses around a major downtown thoroughfare.

While cultural districts have appeared in many recent downtown plans, they should not be viewed as a quick fix. Furthermore, cultural facilities that have worked well in some cities will not necessarily

---

[8] Robert H. McNulty, paper presented at a ULI seminar, "Creating a Great City Center," Charleston, S.C., February 25–26, 1991.

Nathaniel Lieberman, copyright 1989

11-28 Morton H. Myerson Symphony Center, Dallas.

who train all of their employees there. The center has brought year-round activity to a formerly blighted downtown area.

In Phoenix's Mercado, which features specialty shops, ethnic restaurants, and a Hispanic cultural center, Arizona State University opened its 38,000-square-foot Downtown Center in 1990. Among its services, the Downtown Center offers upper-level undergraduate and graduate classes, computer training, interactive television courses, and community forums and workshops. Students at the Downtown Center also have access to free parking and daycare facilities.

Cultural Planning

Cultural planning is an umbrella approach to generating and coordinating artistic and cultural activities that enrich a community's quality of life. Ideally, it involves integrating the arts, cultural facilities, and events with all aspects of community and economic development. Development of MXDs with an arts component or cultural district, then, becomes a potential strategy in the overall plan.

In developing a cultural plan, cities and downtowns are encouraged to reconsider their cultural heritage. Have some aspects been forgotten or perhaps ignored out of embarrassment? In developing its cultural plan, the city of Gilroy, California, for example, thought it was embarrassed by the pervasive smell of garlic in its community and hoped to plan around it. On second thought, planners decided to incorporate this major crop as part of a strategy for economic development, and the city's Great Garlic Cookoff now attracts 275,000 visitors each year![9]

The Economics of Culture

In developing projects that include cultural elements, cultural districts, or cultural plans, the economics of a cultural strategy is an issue. The economic impact of the arts or culture on a city is measurable, usually in three categories: 1) *direct benefits* resulting from expenditures by cultural institutions in contracting for services, hiring employees, or processing goods; 2) *indirect benefits* resulting from the multiplier effect of spending by arts organizations and employees; and 3) *induced benefits* resulting from spending incidental to arts activities, for example, restaurant sales to visitors to an art museum.[10]

The city of Newark, New Jersey, for one, has used a study of the economic impact of the arts as an aid to garner more support for the arts. Using the Regional Industrial Multiplier System (RIMS) prepared by the

11-29 International districts preserve a cultural heritage and promote economic development.

Bureau of Economic Analysis of the U.S. Department of Commerce, the city determined that nonprofit arts organizations pumped $17.2 million directly into Newark's economy and attracted 412,000 people to 434 cultural events in the city in 1989. The study also determined that arts organizations generated a total of $30 million for Newark's economy, not counting induced benefits, such as money spent in restaurants or for transportation and parking. The study focused on in-depth information provided by 43 organizations, two-thirds of which were based in downtown Newark.[11] Three months after the study was published, the Prudential Insurance Co. announced a $1.5 million contribution toward the first phase of the New Jersey Performing Arts Center and a $1.3 million line of credit to help meet the need for working capital. In making the announcement, Prudential's chairman and CEO cited another economic study that projected that the new arts center would generate $12 million annually in new spending in the city, not to mention increased revenue from property taxes.[12]

Quantifying the increased return on investment achieved by integrating the arts into specific projects is more difficult than measuring the economic benefits of arts to a community. Cultural institutions and amenities *seem* to improve retail and restaurant business, increase the use of hotel rooms on weekends, stimulate employers' interest in office space, and

[9] Ibid.

[10] Kevin V. Mulcahy, "The Arts and Their Economic Impact," *Place*, March/April 1988, p. 5.

[11] Michael Redmond, "Arts Enliven Newark: Economic Study Finds Culture a 'Sizable Industry' in City," *The Star-Ledger*, February 22, 1990.

[12] Anthony F. Shannon, "Pru Backs Art Center with Gift, Credit Line, *The Star-Ledger*, May 20, 1990.

enhance a project's overall image, but the tools to estimate precisely such benefits do not exist. In fact, only when projects make financial sense apart from the inclusion of any cultural components should plans be made for including them. "The effect [of the cultural components] is marginal until all of the elements are in place," says Metropolitan Structures's Hal Jensen, describing Phase 1 of California Plaza, which includes a 1 million-square-foot office tower and the highly acclaimed Museum of Contemporary Art. "However," he adds, "[the MOCA] is an important contributor to the identity of the project and does generate traffic on the weekend." Jensen adds that the same sort of monumental project would be more difficult to accomplish now, given market rental rates.

With demand for new office space, the traditional engine of downtown revitalization, ebbing in at least the first half of this decade, other strategies will take the lead. Development that features residential, entertainment, and cultural uses is likely to fill the void as long as the public sector understands the amount of incentives necessary to accomplish such development. Including these uses, however, cannot help but result in a livelier downtown.

12.
Restoration and Reuse

The preservation and reuse of historic buildings became a significant component of downtown development during the 1980s. Specific tax incentives made more projects feasible than ever before. Often, the historic tax incentives were used in conjunction with the same economic tools—UDAGs and CDBGs—that fueled new downtown development during the decade. According to the National Park Service, over $9 billion was invested in historic preservation projects from 1981 to 1986 in cities and towns across the country. An additional $4 billion was invested from 1987 to 1990.

By the late 1980s, however, cutbacks in economic incentives for rehabilitation, growth in the number of review boards for historic districts, and the strengthening of regulatory powers relating to preserving and reusing historic buildings resulted in many downtown developers' finding the rehabilitation of existing buildings increasingly difficult. And in a number of cities, conflicts arose between the preservation community and developers wishing to maximize the use of a particular parcel.

In New York City, for example, St. Bartholomew's Church proposed to construct a large office tower on a site adjoining its historic 19th century sanctuary. The new tower would have provided rent to the church that would, in part, have been used to maintain and restore the historic building. The New York Landmark Commission, using arguments similar to

12-1 Contrast in architectural styles, typical downtown, reflects concern for the preservation of older buildings in harmony with more modern development.

223

12-2　Local historic preservation standards are still evolving. In this downtown, people disagreed about whether the Woolworth building was worthy of saving.

those it had used a decade earlier regarding Grand Central Station, denied requests by the church to construct the tower because of the visual impact it would have had on the original structure.

Still, many other projects have demonstrated the contribution that the preservation and reuse of historic structures can make to downtown development. In downtown Washington, D.C., developers and preservationists fought for over three years over the 20th century Art Deco Greyhound Bus terminal but eventually cobbled a compromise. Originally wishing to demolish the structure and replace it with an office tower, the developer agreed to preserve the terminal's facade and to incorporate the original main waiting room into a new office tower. Underground Atlanta is a multimillion dollar mix of new construction and rehabilitated older buildings designed as part of the city's overall strategy for redevelopment. Opened in 1989, the reborn Underground is a symbol of downtown Atlanta's revival.

The Orioles's new ballpark in downtown Baltimore is another example of the restoration being seen in many downtowns. The ballpark incorporates a large historic warehouse in its design as a major new sports facility in the downtown. The rehabilitated Union Station in St. Louis, intended to serve as a catalyst for future development in the surrounding area, incorporates a new hotel under the historic train shed. The reopening of Union Station in Washington, D.C., in 1989 as an urban specialty shopping center while continuing to serve as a major Amtrak and commuter rail terminal, has spurred development on abandoned train yards north of the station.

In many smaller communities, downtown development has been based on rehabilitating and preserving historic buildings. Guthrie, Oklahoma, has brought

life back to its dying downtown by rehabilitating its historic turn-of-the-century buildings, attracting tourists and conventioneers as a major new economic base. Galena, Illinois, has revived its formerly dying downtown by encouraging the rehabilitation of its historic business district over the past 20 years. Hillsboro, Texas, a town of 7,500 located 70 miles south of Dallas, has rehabilitated over 100 buildings by investing more than $5 million since 1980. In addition, four new buildings have been constructed in the downtown, the first ones built since World War II.

Federal Incentives for Rehabilitation

The bicentennial year, 1976, was a turning point for historic preservation and its role in downtown devel-

12-3　Before: The Art Deco Greyhound Bus terminal in Washington, D.C.

12-4　After: The developer and preservation community reached a compromise in 1989 to preserve the terminal's facade and main waiting room as part of a new office building near the convention center in Washington.

St. Louis experienced more historic preservation, measured by dollars invested in rehabilitation of National Register properties, than any other city in the United States from 1976 to 1988. The activity was the result of a number of incentives, including federal investment tax credits and Missouri's legislation giving development groups (the so-called "353 corporations") tax abatements and powers of eminent domain. It is also a result of the city's policy of encouraging developers to work closely with neighborhood and downtown groups when undertaking projects.

Between 1976 and 1981, approximately $68 million was invested in the rehabilitation of historic structures. The majority of this investment ($42 million) occurred in two areas, the Central West End and Laclede's Landing, and resulted in the reuse of 72 buildings. Investment in historic properties during the five years after passage of tax reform legislation in 1981 jumped to $435.6 million in 679 buildings. Of the total amount, over one-half ($223.4 million) was invested in downtown St. Louis, with the majority ($135 million) invested in Union Station.

Designed in 1891 by Theodore Link, the Romanesque Revival Union Station in St. Louis was the nation's largest rehabilitation project using investment tax credits for National Register buildings when completed. The building consists of a four-story main terminal (the head house) accented by a 230-foot clock tower and a 17-acre train shed large enough to hold the New Orleans Superdome. During its heyday, the station served 260 trains and 100,000 passengers a day. After World War II, traffic at the station declined as Americans abandoned trains for automobiles and airplanes. In 1978, Amtrak moved

12-7   Once containing 31 stub-end tracks, St. Louis's Union Station now houses a grand water feature as well as a new hotel.

its remaining operations out of the building, and the station was closed.

The station reopened in 1985 after a $135 million rehabilitation. Financing for the project totaled $35 million in equity, a $10 million UDAG with payments deferred for five years, a $65 million mortgage from two banks, a $25 million loan from Globe Investment Pension Fund, and $1 million in site improvement contributed by the city. In addition to the local incentive, financial feasibility was boosted by an IRS ruling on the use of investment tax credits. In a ruling by private letter, the IRS allowed the credits to be applied to all construction contained within the historic building, including one of the hotels and some of the retail space, both new construction located under the historic train shed.

Union Station Redevelopment Corporation, a Missouri 353 corporation, headed the station's rehabilitation. The mixed-use project contains two hotels totaling 540 rooms—480 new and 60 that have been rehabilitated—and 160,000 square feet of retail space. The specialty shops and restaurants were developed by Rouse Company of St. Louis, Inc., an affiliate of the Rouse Company of Columbia, Maryland. Hyatt operates the hotels. As of August 1990, occupancy totaled 90 percent, with sales from 1986 to 1990 averaging $450 per square foot. Parking is available for 4,000 cars.

The rehabilitated station has served as a catalyst for other development in the area. Since it opened, an 85-year-old postal facility associated with the train station has been converted into offices, a new four-story office building has been constructed on the foundations of the 1904 power plant, and a movie theater has been built under a nearby elevated highway.

12-6   The mixed-use Union Station in St. Louis includes 160,000 square feet of retail space at the junction of the old head house and the train shed.

Union Station in Washington, D.C., located immediately north of the Capitol, was completed in 1907. Designed by Daniel H. Burnham in the classical Beaux Arts style, the 760-foot by 344-foot station was the largest in the world when built. At its height, the station employed more than 5,000 people and contained, in addition to restaurants and bars, an infirmary, mortuary, bakery, police substation, swimming pool, bowling alley, and basketball court.

In 1981 following an earlier, failed attempt at redevelopment, Congress passed the Union Station Act, authorizing private commercial development in the building and providing funding for its restoration as a railroad terminal. By 1983, the Union Station Redevelopment Corporation (USRC) was established to oversee the commercial development. Modeled partially on the Pennsylvania Avenue Development Corporation, which had successfully led the development of the nation's main street, USRC selected Union Station Venture, Ltd. (USVL), in a national competition to create the new commercial spaces in the building. USVL is comprised of La Salle Partners, Ltd., Williams Jackson Ewing, Benjamin Thompson & Associates, and Kemper Financial Services. Harry Weese & Associates was selected as restoration architect.

Completed in early 1989, the reborn Union Station contains over 600,000 square feet of space with internal connections to Metrorail rapid transit, Amtrak, and commuter rail. Restaurants, upscale shops, a food court, and a nine-screen cinema are contained in the head house and main concourse. Also housed in the building are ticket and waiting areas for Amtrak and MARC commuter trains. Above the train platforms and tracks is a five-level garage for 1,300 cars and 80 buses, including the new terminal for Greyline tour buses. The District of Columbia, with funds from the U.S. Department of Transportation's Federal Highway Administration, built the garage; USRC now manages it.

Approximately $40 million was invested in the new commercial spaces, $110 million in the restoration of the historic building and construction of

the train concourse and the parking garage. The building is technically owned by the U.S. Department of Transportation; however, it has no responsibility for maintenance of the structure. USVL manages the retail spaces under a master lease from USRC, while the Amtrak and commuter rail areas are managed through leasing agreements with Terminal Realty Baltimore Co. and Terminal Realty Penn Co., an affiliate of Penn Central Corp.

Where possible, original materials were used in the restoration. For example, the red champlain marble dots used in the floor of the main hall and west hall came from the same quarry Daniel Burnham, the architect for the original construction in 1904 to 1907, used. In fact, the supply was exhausted with the order for Union Station, and Italian red marble had to be used instead in some of the vestibules.

Another distinctive feature of Union Station is the concentration of retail facilities in the historic concourse. Originally used as the boarding area for trains and open at the north end, the concourse was transformed into a three-level retail complex of dramatic new spaces, with the Amtrak ticket counter and station services surrounded by shops in the center of the main level. The lower level was created by excavating five to nine feet of previous basement service area to create the food court and the nine-screen cinema. A direct connection to the existing subway station was opened at this level. Mezzanine-level shopping was created by strengthening beams and columns and having it stand independently with no structural connection to the historic building. Instead of the original red concrete floor, the new public spaces have marble floors on all three levels.

One more distinctive feature is the construction of turnkey space and fixtures in the head house, specifically in the east, west, and main halls. USVL designed and constructed these features to meet concerns of historic preservation review agencies that retail development adhere to the quality and dignity of the existing space. Further, the movable fixtures in the east hall allow that room to be emp-

opment. Partially in response to public focus on the country's heritage caused by the year-long celebration, the federal government incorporated beneficial tax provisions for the rehabilitation and reuse of his-

toric properties on the National Register of Historic Sites and Places in the Tax Reform Act of 1976. The tax incentives encouraged the reuse of historic buildings across the country. During the next five years,

12-9   Completed in 1907, Union Station in Washington, D.C., was the largest train station in the world at the time. Still used as a transportation hub, it also includes restaurants, shops, a nine-screen theater, and a food court.

tied so that large social functions can take place; hosting functions like inaugural balls is a role that Union Station has performed throughout its history.

Perhaps the most unusual feature of the station is the successful integration of train station and major specialty retail shops. Occurring without conflict, the presence of both shoppers and passengers heightens the sense of bustle and activity within the building. Train travel has been made more convenient and enjoyable as a result of the waiting room for train passengers, which includes numerous shops, the retail mall that centers on the

Amtrak ticket counter, and the main hall, whose key structures are a cafe, an international newsstand, and a concierge desk boasting a large electronic arrival/departure board for Amtrak trains.

Initial indications are that the project will exceed projections. Based on gross sales for the first six months of the project, annual sales per square foot are expected to exceed $450.

Source: National Trust for Historic Preservation and Union Station Redevelopment Corporation, Washington, D.C.

approximately $2.1 billion was invested nationally in the reuse of National Register buildings.

To take advantage of these benefits (primarily accelerated depreciation for expenditures for rehabili-

tation), the design of the rehabilitated building had to conform to a set of design guidelines known as "the Secretary of the Interior's Standards for Rehabilitation." The standards sought to ensure that important

Located 70 miles south of Dallas, Hillsboro is the seat of Hill County. With a population that has remained fairly stable at 7,500 since World War II, downtown Hillsboro's importance as a regional trade center declined with improved highways and the construction of outlying shopping centers and office parks. In 1980, 30 percent of the downtown buildings were totally vacant, and most lacked routine maintenance. Hillsboro's distance from Dallas's suburban growth and its economy based on agriculture meant that the redevelopment of its downtown would depend primarily on recapturing a larger share of the existing retail and office uses rather than on new growth.

In 1981, Hillsboro became part of the Texas Main Street Program, an affiliate of the National Trust for Historic Preservation's National Main Street Center. The city used an incremental strategy for revitalizing downtown as the basis of its redevelopment. A key component of this strategy was the rehabilitation of Hillsboro's historic and older downtown buildings. From 1980 through 1988, the city invested over $5 million in the rehabilitation of 107 buildings and the construction of four new ones.

Investment in downtown Hillsboro was stimulated by a loan pool at 8 percent interest established by four of the city's five financial institutions. The $80,000 pool was available for the rehabilitation of downtown buildings whose design had been approved by the city's preservation board. The $120,000 restoration and adaptive use of the town's 1892 railroad depot also acted as a catalyst for further development. The funds for the depot's restoration and reuse as offices for the chamber of commerce and other tenants were raised from local foundations ($30,000) and private subscriptions ($90,000).

12-11   Downtown Hillsboro, Texas.

National Main Street Center, National Trust for Historic Preservation

Another important downtown building rehabilitated was the 1913 U.S. Post Office. Upon closing the old building, the federal government deeded it to the city, which now uses it as a public library. A referendum allowing the city to accept the building and assuming responsibility for its operation passed by a margin of 12 to 1, and the $115,000 needed to rehabilitate it was raised through private contributions.

The rehabilitation of the older and historic buildings in downtown Hillsboro has contributed significantly to a revitalization of the town. Vacancy rates have dropped from 30 percent to just over 10 percent. Jobs available have increased by 10 percent. And, despite the depressed state of the regional economy, two additional projects were planned for 1990. Further, the city has created the state's first Small Business Development satellite center.

Source: Richard Wagner and Ted Miller, *Revitalizing Downtown, 1976–1986* (Washington, D.C.: National Trust for Historic Preservation in association with the Urban Institute, 1988), pp. 87–92.

historic fabric would be maintained after the completion of rehabilitation and that any new construction associated with the building's reuse would be compatible with its original architectural character. The standards are still used today (see Figure 12-13).

In 1981, the tax incentives associated with the rehabilitation of historic buildings were changed from a deduction to a credit, stimulating even more interest in redeveloping historic downtown properties. The Economic Recovery Tax Act of 1981 included a 25 percent investment tax credit that could be applied to construction costs and to certain professional and

finance fees associated with the rehabilitation of income-producing property listed on the National Register. The act also contained credits for the rehabilitation of commercial income-producing property more than 50 years old.

Coupled with the increased use of UDAGs and CDBGs for rehabilitation projects, historic preservation projects became common development activity downtown after the 1981 act. From 1981 until the tax laws were changed again in 1986, over $9 billion was invested in the rehabilitation of projects on the National Register across the country. Some of these proj-

The Historic Sites Act of 1935 first established the National Register of Historic Sites and Places. In 1966, the scope of the National Register was expanded by the passage of the National Historic Preservation Act, which also:

- Authorized grants to states to be used in conducting comprehensive statewide historic surveys and preparing statewide historic preservations plans;
- Established the Historic Preservation Fund to provide matching funds to states to acquire and develop National Register property; and
- Established the Advisory Council on Historic Preservation to advise the federal government on preservation and to comment on National Register projects (known as a Section 106 review) involving federal funds.

Buildings, sites, districts, objects, engineering works, and landscapes can be nominated to the National Register. Typically, local historic district review boards nominate candidates, but anyone may do so. In most states, the consent of the owner of the property must be obtained before it can be placed ("listed") on the Register. To qualify for listing, the property must be significant to the nation's history, architecture, archaeology, engineering, or culture. Further, the property must meet one or more of the following criteria:

- Be associated with events that have made a significant contribution to the nation's history, or be associated with significant historical people.
- Embody distinctive characteristics of a type, style, or period of architecture or a means of construction.
- Represent the work of a master architect or craftsman.
- Possess high artistic value.
- Yield, or be likely to yield, information important to the nation's history or prehistory.

Obtaining a listing on the National Register can take three to six months or longer. First, a qualified professional must conduct a survey of the property. This survey records the history of the property and describes past alterations as well as its current state. The state review board reviews the completed survey for acceptance or rejection. If the board approves the nomination, it is forwarded to the National Park Service for final concurrence and listing. In 1990, over 750,000 buildings, objects, sites, structures, and landscapes were listed on the National Register, ranging from federal townhouses in Philadelphia to an early McDonald's hamburger stand in Illinois.

ects were substantial undertakings, such as Union Station in St. Louis or Trapper's Alley in Detroit. The vast majority, however, were smaller projects: from 1981 to 1986, rehabilitation of the average National Register project cost just under $100,000. Thus, the most common projects were small commercial or income-producing residential buildings located in small cities and towns.

Current federal tax incentives related to the rehabilitation of historic buildings listed on the National Register and commercial income-producing buildings built before 1936 are defined in the Tax Reform Act of 1986. The law provides certain tax credits for buildings individually listed on the National Register, that is, buildings listed as contributing to the character of National Register historic districts, and buildings listed as contributing to the character of state or local historic districts that have been certified as complying with or exceeding the standards of National Register historic districts. A 20 percent investment tax credit for commercial and residential

income-producing buildings on the National Register can be applied to hard costs as well as certain professional and financing fees (such as architect's fees and interest on construction loans). To obtain the credit, however, the rehabilitation must be certified by the state historic preservation office and the National Park Service as complying with the Secretary of the Interior's Standards for Rehabilitation.

Commercial income-producing buildings built before 1936 are eligible for a 10 percent investment tax credit for their rehabilitation without certification. Both tax credits must use 31.5-year straight-line depreciation for commercial income-producing projects. Credits for certified National Register projects must use 27.5-year straight-line depreciation for residential income-producing projects. Rules governing passive income associated with sheltering income in real estate development projects have also been changed, which has resulted in far less syndicated money available. The drop of 5 percentage points in credit available (25 percent to 20 percent) and the lengthen-

National Register buildings that are being rehabilitated must meet the provisions of the Secretary of the Interior's Standards for Rehabilitation to maintain their eligibility for the Register. As an incentive to meet the Standards, certain tax benefits are available for compliance. National Register rehabilitation projects that are financed totally or in part by any federal grants or loans must also follow the Secretary of the Interior's Standards.

The Standards provide broad direction in the design of rehabilitation projects. Interpretation of the Standards and how well the proposed project meets them is completed at two levels—the state historic preservation office and the Preservation Services Division of the National Park Service. In large cities and communities with local design review committees, the Standards might also be the basis for local review of National Register rehabilitation projects. The review process can take three to six months, longer for large projects. The applicant (usually the developer or architect) submits a three-part application. Part One states that the building is on the National Register. Part Two notes all changes proposed in the building's rehabilitation through plans, specifications, materials lists, and color selections. Part Three, submitted after the project is completed, demonstrates that the building was rehabilitated as approved in Part Two.

The ten standards for rehabilitation are as follows:

1. Every reasonable effort shall be made to provide a compatible use for a property that requires minimal alteration of the building, structure, or site and its environment, or to use a property for its originally intended purpose.
2. The distinguishing original qualities or character of a building, structure, or site and its environment shall not be destroyed. The removal or alteration of any historic material or distinctive architectural features should be avoided when possible.
3. All buildings, structures, and sites shall be recognized as products of their own time. Alterations that have no historical basis and that seek to create an earlier appearance shall be discouraged.
4. Changes that may have taken place in the course of time are evidence of the history and development of a building, structure, or site and its environment. These changes may have acquired significance in their own right, and this significance shall be recognized and respected.
5. Distinctive stylistic features or examples of skilled craftsmanship that characterize a building, structure, or site shall be treated with sensitivity.
6. Deteriorated architectural features shall be repaired rather than replaced wherever possible. In the event replacement is necessary, the new material should match the material being replaced in composition, design, color, texture, and other visual qualities. Repair or replacement of missing architectural features should be based on accurate duplications of features, substantiated by historic, physical, or pictorial evidence rather than on conjectural designs or the availability of different architectural elements from other buildings or structures.
7. The surface cleaning of structures shall be undertaken with the gentlest means possible. Sandblasting and other cleaning methods that will damage the historic building materials shall not be undertaken.
8. Every reasonable effort shall be made to protect and preserve archaeological resources affected by, or adjacent to, any project.
9. Contemporary design for alterations and additions to existing properties shall not be discouraged when such alterations and additions do not destroy significant historical, architectural, or cultural material, and such design is compatible with the size, scale, color, material, and character of the property, neighborhood, or environment.
10. Wherever possible, new additions or alterations to structures shall be done in such a manner that if such additions or alterations were to be removed in the future, the essential form and integrity of the structure would be unimpaired.

Source: Historic Preservation Certification Application (Washington, D.C.: U.S. Government Printing Office, 1989-0-619-549).

Since 1980, over $9 billion has been invested to rehabilitate income-producing buildings listed on the National Register. Much of this investment has been stimulated by the investment tax credits for historic buildings provided in the 1981 and 1986 tax laws. Both laws also contained provisions for tax credits for investment in older, but not historic, commercial income-producing buildings. The 1986 provisions for tax credits for historic and older buildings are summarized below.

	20% Investment Tax Credit	10% Investment Tax Credit
Eligible Properties	Commercial or residential income-producing buildings that are: • Individually listed on the National Register • Contributing structures listed in National Register historic districts • Listed individually or as contributing to state or local historic districts that meet standards established by the National Park Service	Commercial income-producing buildings constructed before 1936
Minimum Expenditures	$5,000 or amount equal to adjusted basis in a building within 24 months (or 60 months in a phased rehabilitation)	Same
Standards to Be Met	Secretary of the Interior's Standards for Rehabilitation	50 percent or more of existing external walls must be retained as external; and 75 percent or more of existing external walls must be retained as external or internal; and 75 percent or more of existing internal structure must be retained
Filing Fees	$500 to $2,500, based on cost of rehabilitation	None
Qualified Expenditures	Capital expenditures	Same
Depreciation Allowance (Straight Line)	• Commercial property: 31.5 years • Residential property: 27.5 years	Same

ing of a building's depreciable life also contributed to the decline in activity.

Because of these changes, rehabilitation has fallen substantially since 1986. In 1986, approximately $4 billion was spent to rehabilitate and reuse National Register income-producing property (out of a total of $9 billion from 1981 to 1986). In 1987, expenditures for rehabilitation were down to approximately $2.5 billion and in 1988, under $2 billion. While the decline can be partially attributed to overbuilding in

12-15 The fine architectural detailing of older structures can enhance new uses.

many downtowns, especially office buildings, the changes in tax law account for most of the drop.

The scaling back, however, has had a positive side. Review periods by state historic preservation offices and the National Park Service for compliance with the Secretary's Standards have been shortened now that the volume of projects being reviewed has dropped. Developers rely more on pretax cash flow than on tax benefits to determine a project's feasibility, and projects consequently have a better chance of succeeding financially. While many preservationists bemoan the "loss" of the tax benefits and are actively lobbying Congress to restore them, the continued benefits derived from incorporating preservation projects into downtown development strategies has been proven.

Preservation Easements

Another federal financing tool closely associated with the rehabilitation of historic buildings is the use of preservation easements. Typically, the IRS allows preservation easements for "historically important land" that substantially meets National Register criteria (for example, an archaeological site or battlefield), for National Register buildings deemed to be contributing to state or local historic districts, or for facades or important interior spaces (such as lobbies or auditoriums) that meet National Register criteria.

A preservation easement is a nonpossessory right to control the use of land, buildings, or parts of buildings owned by another. But while easements are fairly straightforward in concept, giving a developer a tax deduction based on the value of the donation of the easement, they are difficult to structure and impose both current and future costs on the donor.

Preservation easements are created by deeds executed between a donor (usually a developer) and a recipient. The recipient, according to the IRS, must be a "qualified organization," such as a government entity or a charitable organization as described in Section 501(c)(3) of the Internal Revenue Code. The donor may be an individual or a corporation, with the deduction available limited by IRS statutes.

The primary reason developers consider donating a preservation easement is the value of the deduction. That value is generally found by subtracting the value of the property after the donation from the value of the property before the donation. The value after donation is usually less because of the development restrictions placed on the property by the entity accepting the donation, thus denying the property its highest and best use.

For example, suppose a building in downtown contains 10,000 square feet of rentable space generating $3.00 per square foot of net operating income annually, or $30,000. Capitalizing the NOI at 10 percent results in a building valued at $300,000. Assum-

12-16 Preservation easements can be used for facades that meet the criteria for the National Register.

ing that zoning would allow a building of 30,000 square feet that would generate $90,000 annually at the same rate per square foot, the resulting value would be $900,000. The value of the donation thus totals $600,000.

Actual calculations of a donation's value, however, are rarely this straightforward. Restrictions placed on historic buildings through zoning or design review affect value. Restrictions placed on the donor by the entity accepting the donation—to maintain the property to a certain standard, to exactly restore damaged portions, or to create specific sinking funds for replacement of parts, for example—also affect the current and long-term value of the donation to the developer. Some accepting organizations also restrict the current and future use of the building, thereby further affecting the donation's real value.

Another factor that influences the future value of a preservation easement is the associated potential decrease in sales value. With significant restrictions placed upon the use of the building and any modification made to the structure and with the increased cost of maintenance, most buildings with preservation easements realize less value at the time of sale. In addition, because most insurance policies are based on the cost of replacement less depreciation, insurance costs for a building that must be accurately restored to its predamaged condition rather than simply returned to service typically are higher than normal.

Organizations that accept preservation easements could also be liable for unexpected future costs. Not only must they bear the expense of maintaining an inventory of donated buildings, but they must also typically bear the expense of annually inspecting the property to ensure that it is maintained at the agreed-upon level. If maintenance is required, the organization must ensure that the building's owner undertakes it or, when public safety is an issue, be liable for the cost of repair.

Currently, all but a few states have specific legislation dealing with preservation easements. One of the most comprehensive is the commonwealth of Virginia's, which authorized in 1966 the Historic Landmarks Board to accept donations of easements on registered landmarks. In Virginia, as in other states, easements have covered both buildings and land and have become important financial tools in preserving historic estates. Easements have also been used extensively in Virginia's cities, for example, as part of the 1985 adaptive use of Richmond's 130-year-old almshouse into apartments for the elderly and the 1985 restoration of the Klugel Architectural Sheet Metal Works in Emporia, which continues to be used as a metalworks factory.

Managing Historic Preservation Downtown

While federal tax laws provided incentives for private investment in the rehabilitation of historic properties in the 1980s, state programs like Missouri's 353 corporations or North Carolina's private statewide revolving loan fund for rehabilitation also encouraged preservation downtown. Hundreds of other cities and towns created low-interest loan pools to stimulate investment in historic downtown properties. For example, Williamsport, a town of 34,000 in central Pennsylvania, created a $500,000 loan pool in 1981 as part of its Main Street Program. The funds were obtained from three local financial institutions and the Williamsport Foundation, which provided a $250,000 interest-free loan to the pool. Interest rates to borrowers were 6 percent, with a maximum of $30,000 available for 10 years to rehabilitate historic structures. Within the first two years, the loan pool had leveraged $5 million in investment in rehabilitation and an additional $3 million in new construction downtown, including the renovation of the Romanesque city hall into a private office building.

During the 1980s, municipalities and county governments enacted preservation ordinances designed to encourage the retention and reuse of historic buildings. In 1965, only 50 cities had historic preservation ordinances, by 1980, the number had increased to 250 cities, and by 1990, over 2,000 cities, towns, and counties had ordinances designed to protect historic buildings and districts.

A significant factor contributing to the spread of these ordinances in the last decade was the 1978 U.S. Supreme Court decision in *Penn Central Transportation Company* v. *The City of New York*. The city's Landmark Commission had declared Grand Central Station a National Register building in the early 1970s. Under local legislation, the commission had the powers to deny the demolition of the historic building as well as any additions that would significantly alter the building's visual design.

In its suit, Penn Central argued that denial of permission to construct a new office building in the air rights above the terminal as allowed by zoning constituted an "unfair taking" of the economic potential of the property. The Court, however, declared that the restrictions imposed on the property owner were "substantially related to the promotion of the general welfare" and thus, like zoning and building codes, were reasonable. The Supreme Court also established the standard of "reasonable beneficial [economic] use" of the property by the owner rather than its highest economic use as allowed by FARs. Thus, the Court's decision helped redefine, as did federal investment tax credits, the economics of preserving historic downtown structures.

Local historic preservation ordinances are based on state enabling legislation related to municipalities' and counties' ability to enforce zoning. Typically, a local preservation ordinance creates a historic preservation commission or a design review board to review proposed changes to individual historic buildings or to buildings and landscapes located within historic districts. In most large cities, these bodies are regulatory commissions. In smaller cities and towns, historic review boards are typically advisory in nature, reporting to the zoning or planning commission. Thus, the boards' powers to regulate downtown development vary from city to city.

Manhattan, Kansas, established a review board in the late 1970s as part of its downtown redevelopment

Timothy Hursley

12-17 The five-year rehabilitation of Mission Inn in Riverside, California, met strict historic guidelines. *Source:* ELS/Elbasani & Logan Architects.

program. The board's powers are limited to review and comment on changes to buildings within the older sections of downtown. The board also obtained a memorandum of agreement allowing it to review designs for a new 350,000-square-foot mall downtown. Completed in 1988, the mall was the keystone of downtown redevelopment, which also included a low-interest loan pool for rehabilitation and new construction downtown and the use of CDBGs for improvements to public spaces.

Other cities vest substantially more power in their historic preservation review boards. Louisville, Kentucky, for example, can impose fines of up to $100 per day for violation of its historic preservation ordinance. The law in Washington, D.C., contains a provision that could require the reconstruction of a demolished landmark. Key West, Florida, recently enacted a $25,000 fine for the demolition of a historic building.

While the review process varies from community to community, most historic district review boards require the submission of plans, elevations, specifications, and material and color selections for the proposed rehabilitation. Approximately one-half of the nation's design review boards use locally established design guidelines to judge the acceptability of proposed changes to historic buildings. Many communities review proposed designs using the Secretary of the Interior's Standards, while some communities have no written guidelines or standards. (Fortunately, communities without design guidelines normally have advisory, not regulatory, review boards.)

Most design guidelines are concerned with three major issues: alterations to the exterior of the building, alterations to significant interior spaces, and additions to historic buildings. Exterior alterations, according to most design guidelines for historic buildings and districts, involve changes to significant architectural elements, such as cornices, window and door surrounds, and features such as plaques and cornerstones. Exterior materials and the treatment and placement of windows are also usually covered by design guidelines.

Significant interior spaces, such as lobbies and unusually shaped rooms like rotundas or auditoriums, in many cases are covered by specific guidelines. Additions to the front, side, or rear of buildings, as well as rooftop additions typical in cities like Boston or Washington, D.C., are covered by some design guidelines. The major issues addressed in additions to historic buildings are their size, bulk, setbacks, facade materials, and fenestration. Some design guidelines for downtown areas also address the design of public spaces as well as the

12-18 Facade-ectomy downtown.

country's first statewide historic building code, which allows alternative means of construction for the rehabilitation of historic structures. In 1979, Massachusetts adopted Article 22 of its state building code to allow each historic building to set its own minimum performance standards: after rehabilitation, the building must be at least as safe as it was before construction. Georgia in 1984 adopted a statewide building code for historic properties that allows for safe, alternative solutions to requirements for materials and egress. In the code, existing construction techniques, materials, and hall and stair dimensions are presumed to be safe unless they are clearly hazardous.

In 1987, the first national model building code specifically related to historic and older buildings was developed by the International Conference of Building Officials. The *Uniform Code for Building*

Richard Wagner, National Main Street Center, National Trust for Historic Preservation

12-19 The refurbishment of the mission at San Luis Obispo, California, instilled the community with a new design ethic, giving citizens a greater appreciation for historic buildings and compatible design.

material and character of open space associated with a building.

Most design guidelines follow the methodology established by the Secretary of the Interior's Standards; they provide standards that must be met but do not prescribe exactly how. Thus, a certain latitude is allowed in what the final product looks like, how it is constructed, and what materials can be included. Some communities, however, have established design guidelines for historic districts that restrict new construction to particular styles. In Santa Fe, New Mexico, design guidelines encourage mission-style architecture, while those in Old Town in Alexandria, Virginia, encourage brick federal-style buildings.

Another aspect affecting development of historic buildings downtown involves bringing older structures up to modern building codes. Often, bringing a historic building into compliance with the code is costly and has led to developers' decisions not to proceed with the project. Recognizing this problem, a few states have created building codes specifically for historic buildings. In 1976, California passed the

Conservation also uses the existing historic building to set minimum standards in materials, hall and stair width, volume, and so on, except where clearly unsafe conditions are apparent. While these model codes will not solve all economic and architectural issues related to the rehabilitation of historic buildings, they recognize that historic construction techniques and materials are not necessarily more life-threatening than modern techniques.

Conclusion and Trends

The Economic Recovery Tax Act of 1981 was the single most important factor in the tremendous increase in the restoration and reuse of historic buildings during the 1980s. The financial benefits provided to developers for undertaking such projects provided sufficient rewards for the risks involved. The changes to the tax laws in 1986 reduced those rewards while keeping the risks unchanged, and they significantly curtailed the use of syndicated monies available for these projects. Thus, a major reduction in the number of projects involving restoration and reuse occurred in the latter part of the decade. Developers are now far more selective in the projects they undertake, relying more on pretax cash flow to make the project

work and any local and state monies or incentives that might be available.

Another result of the restoration boom of the 1980s was the creation of a cadre of developers and design professionals who are now skilled in the restoration and reuse of historic properties. The tremendous increase in the number of design and historic review boards has also caused developers and architects to hone their skills in working with these groups and other community groups during predevelopment. As a result, developers who now undertake large historic restorations tend to specialize in such projects, searching regionally or nationally for appropriate buildings. At the same time, organizations and communities with historic properties ripe for restoration and reuse seek them out. Thus, like builders of urban specialty retail buildings or signature office buildings, a group of specialists in restoration and reuse has emerged. This trend will probably continue in the 1990s.

The present decade will offer downtown developers new challenges in restoration and reuse. The number of older buildings eligible for the National Register increases each year. At the same time, restrictions on growth for new office buildings and a decrease in demand for large, new projects could present new opportunities for historic restorations in infill locations downtown.

13.
Waterfronts

The final strategy for downtown revitalization presented in this handbook is by no means the least important. By virtue of the number of downtowns situated on waterways, waterfront revitalization must be considered a possibility for many. Until the development of the railroad, in fact, most North American cities were, and, as a consequence, many North American downtowns are located along waterways.

If developing a downtown is complex, developing a downtown waterfront is even more so. Site planning and project construction on a waterfront require spe-

cific expertise. The number of regulatory entities a developer must deal with in a waterfront location increase dramatically. And if the involvement of Icitizens is more and more characteristic of development in general, it reaches a zenith with respect to a community's waterfront. Access to this amenity is now considered a right. In San Antonio, for example, the "right of thirst" in old Spanish law has resulted in a strong tradition of public access to the San Antonio River. More recently, the movement toward rights of physical, psychological, visual, and economic ac-

13-1 Waterfront development can add vitality to downtown.

13-2 San Antonio's classic Paseo del Rio features a winding river walk, performance spaces, and river taxis.

cess is spreading. All of these factors combine to make an understanding of the nuances of waterfront development essential before embarking on a revitalization strategy centered around the waterfront.

Geographic Location

The geographic location of the site is one of the key factors contributing to the complexity of waterfront development.[1] The bodies of water where a site might be located—an ocean, river, shipping channel, bay, or inlet, for example—and their condition vary significantly. Water dimensions, configuration, flow dynamics, and quality also combine to affect the engineering, design, and construction of new projects.

In general terms, the larger the dimensions of a body of water, the greater the range of potential water-related uses. This relationship is based on common sense: a deep-water harbor on a large coastal bay is able to accommodate uses that an inland river port with a narrow channel and shallow marina cannot. Nevertheless, another side exists to this relationship: the greater the range of potential water-related uses, the greater the potential competition and conflict

13-3   Banners can add color and interest to a downtown street as well as reinforce a districtwide theme.

between and among uses—fishing versus tourism, for example.

The importance of the water's flow dynamics also cannot be overestimated. In coastal seaports, for instance, tidal fluctuations and wave action significantly affect development, because some ports experience stronger and more destructive wave action than others. Variations of flow in inland waterways are significant as well. River ports must contend with dramatic fluctuations in water level—low flows following periods of drought and flooding caused by heavy rains or melting snow. Analyzing and designing for varying water flows increase costs of development and maintenance.

Water quality is another factor affecting the character of urban waterfronts. Coastal waterfronts must endure the corrosiveness of saltwater, turbidity (the degree to which sediment is stirred up and suspended), dissolved oxygen, fluctuating temperatures, and chemical pollutants. In general, although water quality has improved over the last two decades, conditions still vary significantly.

The characteristics of the land abutting a waterway can vary as much as the water itself. The most important factors to consider are the amount of waterfront land, its configuration, its condition, and its ownership. Though in the past new waterfront land could be created by filling in water, the associated environmental degradation has led to almost complete cessation of this practice. Now, the amount of waterfront land in a given location is relatively fixed. Inland boundaries of urban waterfronts, however, vary widely, depending on the location of natural and manmade barriers like railroads or highways. More and more cities are taking steps to remove manmade boundaries. Portland, Oregon, ripped out a freeway separating its CBD from the waterfront, and Boston is planning to put its Central Artery underground.

The condition of waterfront sites is often characterized by poor load-bearing capacity and problems with erosion. It is typical for foundations from previous uses to remain and for protective bulkheads to need repair. The site of Portland's 10-acre RiverPlace development, for example, is characterized by very poor soil quality. Forty feet of sawdust from one of the site's former uses, a plywood mill, required driving pilings 70 to 90 feet deep and motivated one of the project's major design features: a concrete platform that encloses a parking garage and creates the base for the

---

[1] This section is based on Douglas M. Wrenn et al., *Urban Waterfront Development* (Washington, D.C.: ULI–the Urban Land Institute, 1983), pp. 21–27.

13-4 Retail space, residential units, and offices are water-enhanced uses, while marinas are water-dependent uses.

74-room hotel and 190 condominiums. The 100-acre Battery Park City along New York's Hudson River stands mostly on landfill, the bulk of which came from excavation of the foundations for the World Trade Center. The site on landfill, combined with its high water table, made excavation for underground parking at the Regatta, a nine-story residential project, prohibitively expensive. Residents of this luxury project must use nearby garages.

Functions of the Waterfront

The functions of a downtown's waterfront, both existing and desired, must also be analyzed in planning for development. Function is largely defined by existing land and water uses and their degree of dependency on water. For instance, some waterfronts are heavily industrialized, reflecting either current activity or past port-related functions. More common, downtown waterfronts are comprised of a mixture of industrial, commercial, residential, recreational, and transportational uses.

"Preservationists want to save the old buildings, business people want a view of the water from their office, traditionalists want to return to 1900, and yuppies want to live over the water next to their sailboats," says Pamela Plumb, a Portland, Maine, city council member and chair of the city's Waterfront Task Force, describing the mix of functions and interests affecting waterfront development. At a 1988 conference on urban waterfronts sponsored by the Waterfront Center in Washington, D.C., she stressed the importance of balancing the needs of each group.

Three classifications are typically used to sort out which functions a community wants to encourage or discourage on its waterfront: water-dependent, water-related, and water-enhanced uses. *Water-dependent uses* are those that cannot exist in any location but on the water—for example, port terminals for general commerce, ferry, and passenger services, marine construction and repair facilities, marinas, and tug and barge operations. *Water-related uses* are those that might be enhanced by the waterfront but could function away from it, including lumber mills, seafood processing plants, public resorts, aquariums, and restaurants. *Water-enhanced uses* are those that could occur anywhere (residential units, hotels, and some retail development) but attract additional patronage as a result of waterfront amenities. It is easy to see that

Statute	Description	Responsible Agency
Section 10, Rivers and Harbors Act of 1899	Regulates all activities on navigable waterways	U.S. Army Corps of Engineers, which coordinates activities with other affected federal and state agencies, including the EPA, the U.S. FWS, and the National Marine Fisheries Service (NMFS)
Section 404, Clean Water Act of 1970, 1977, and 1981, as amended by the Federal Water Pollution Control Act of 1972	Regulates dredging and filling in U.S. waters (navigable waters, tributary streams, and wetlands)	U.S. Army Corps of Engineers and the EPA (which can overrule the Corps), along with other affected federal and state agencies, including the U.S. FWS and the NMFS
National Environmental Policy Act of 1969	Regulates actions that significantly affect the quality of the environment; requires environmental impact statements in some instances	U.S. Army Corps of Engineers and other affected federal agencies, including the EPA, the U.S. FWS, and the NMFS
Fish and Wildlife Coordination Act of 1934, as amended in 1946, 1958, and 1977	Regulates adverse effects of waterway development on aquatic life	U.S. Army Corps of Engineers (final authority) in conjunction with the U.S. FWS, the NMFS, and state departments of fish and wildlife
Coastal Zone Management Act (CZMA) of 1972	Encourages states to establish planning and management systems for coastal land resources; requires Section 10 and Section 404 permits to be consistent with federally approved state CZMA programs	Office of Coastal Zone Management, the U.S. Army Corps of Engineers, and state CZMA offices

Sources: Douglas M. Wrenn et al., *Urban Waterfront Development* (Washington, D.C.: ULI–the Urban Land Institute, 1983), pp. 35–36; and J.W. Good and R.F. Goodwin, *Waterfront Revitalization for Small Cities* (Corvallis: Oregon State Univ. Extension Service, 1990), pp. 90–91.

competition from water-enhanced uses can inflate waterfront land values to the point where water-dependent uses become superfluous. State and federal agencies that must approve waterfront development, however, often place priority on water-dependent over non-water-dependent uses.

The downtown Annapolis, Maryland, waterfront appears to be winning the struggle of mixing water-dependent uses with water-enhanced ones. The fact that downtown is located along Spa Creek, an inlet off the Severn River, helps. On one side of the creek are sprawling boat repair, sales, and storage yards. Vessels lie about everywhere. Mixed in, however, are a few condominium projects, offices, and restaurants. On the other side of the creek is a narrow body of water that cuts into the waterfront and the City Dock, which is packed with recreational and harbor cruise boats and an occasional crabbing vessel. A boardwalk lines the harbor, and no railings or fences are built on the water's edge. Restaurants and shops housed in

The U.S. Army Corps of Engineers publishes a public notice of a proposed project within 15 days of receiving the completed application and distributes it to state agencies, interested parties, federal agencies, post offices, and newspapers. Work begins immediately on a preliminary environmental assessment to determine whether or not an environmental impact statement (EIS) is needed; comments on the application from interested parties must be received within 30 days. Comments from the following agencies are particularly important:

- *U.S. Fish and Wildlife Service.* The U.S. FWS may recommend modification or denial of permit. Disagreements may be resolved at higher levels in the Department of the Army.
- *National Marine Fisheries Service.* The NMFS is responsible for managing commercial marine fisheries, including anadromous fisheries. NMFS's comments relate to preserving critical habitat for these species.
- *U.S. Environmental Protection Agency.* The EPA has veto authority for Section 404 permits. Water quality is its chief concern.
- *State agencies.* Those responsible for managing fish and wildlife habitat and state coastal zone management agencies comment on the applications.

The process leading up to the Corps's decision on whether to issue a permit is called a "public interest review." Originally, the impact on navigation was the only consideration. Beginning in 1968, however, the Corps expanded its review to include additional factors reflecting the national concern for protection and use of important resources.

All public interest factors relevant to a proposal must be considered, including conservation, economics, aesthetics, general environmental concerns, wetlands, cultural values, fish and wildlife habitats, flood hazards, floodplains, land use, navigation, shore erosion and accretion, recreation, water supply, water quality and conservation, energy needs, safety, production of food and fibers, minerals, and, in general, the needs and welfare of the people.

Comments from agencies and individuals help the Corps in its public interest review. It holds public hearings if necessary, makes a final determination of the need for an EIS, and files a final environmental assessment. The Corps makes every effort to resolve any conflicts, incorporating recommendations from the agencies as much as possible.

Conflicts that cannot be resolved by the Corps district office go to a higher level for a decision. Finally, the Corps determines whether the public interest will be served by issuing the permit, develops a "finding of fact," and issues or denies the permit.

Source: J.W. Good and R.F. Goodwin, *Waterfront Revitalization for Small Cities* (Corvallis: Oregon State Univ. Extension Service, 1990), p. 93.

---

historic buildings surround the inlet, and just a few blocks away are the U.S. Naval Academy and the state capitol. The entire downtown is eminently walkable. Overall, the mix of water-dependent and -enhanced uses and the pedestrian orientation of this historic waterfront make the small city attractive.[2]

The Regulatory Process

Waterfronts generally have a jurisdictional structure that far exceeds even the typical framework of a downtown government. In addition to the usual zoning and building regulations, for example, other activities on a waterfront are regulated:

- Dredging shallow areas for moorage or for improved navigability;
- Filling water and wetland areas to create parks or other developable sites;
- Adding bulkheads to the waterfront;
- Building protective seawalls; and
- Constructing buildings on pilings over the water.

Several different federal agencies administer the different programs affecting waterfronts, among them the U.S. Army Corps of Engineers, the Environmental Protection Agency (EPA), the U.S. Fish and Wildlife Service (FWS), the Office of Coastal Zone Management, the Economic Development Administration, the National Park Service, the Department of Housing and Urban Development, and the Department of Transportation (see Figures 13-5 and 13-6).

While federal initiatives establish the framework of waterfront regulation, state agencies are directly

---

[2] Ann Breen and Dick Rigby, "Annapolis Waterfront: Winning One, Losing One," *Waterfront World*, May/June 1990, pp. 22–25.

involved in *managing* urban waterfronts. Although state coastal zone management programs differ significantly, each state participating in the federal program is required to:

- Identify permissible land and water uses;
- Determine boundaries of the coastal zone;
- Designate geographic areas of concern;
- Detail organizational arrangements; and
- Establish an implementing authority.

The greatest variation in the structure of jurisdictional responsibility for urban waterfronts, as might be expected, is found in local governments. In most cases, county and city offices administer land use regulations, ordinances concerning health, safety, and fire protection, and provisions for public services, such as roads, water and sewer systems, and utilities. Compounding the problem, many waterfronts also fall within the jurisdiction of commissions or authorities for a regional water resource, the San Francisco Bay Conservation and Development Commission, for example.

Access to the Waterfront

The issue of the public's right to access to the water and the water's edge is certainly a controversial aspect of waterfront development. The advent of cleaner water, at public expense, begs the question of who should reap the benefit. The fact that waterways are publicly owned and maintained suggests that the public should.

At the same time, waterfront land is usually privately owned. While many local governments support the public use of the waterfront, few can afford to completely finance development there. Private property owners and developers, on the other hand, maintain that public access should not overshadow their ownership rights or their right to maximize return on investment, particularly important in a venture as risky as waterfront development. If, for example, provisions for public access require buildings to be set back from the shoreline to allow for uninterrupted movement along the water's edge or limit building heights to permit visual access to the water, then the size of the development envelope for a given site can be significantly reduced, thereby affecting a project's feasibility. Or when a portion of a waterfront site is allocated to non-revenue-producing uses, the developer might compensate by building a project that can be sold or leased at a higher price or by increasing the density of development on the remainder of the site. It is ironic that government efforts to ensure public

13-7   Battery Park City's esplanade provides public access to more than a mile of waterfront.

access to urban shorelines sometimes encourage the targeting of higher-end, more exclusive markets.

The public sector's desire for unobstructed access to the shoreline and the private sector's desire to develop waterfront projects profitably, however, are not mutually exclusive. The growing trend toward mixed-use and multiuse projects goes hand in glove with the growing trend toward waterfront development, and techniques for districting and zoning sites are accelerating this trend. City development authorities' growing expertise in making deals and developing land enables them to provide valuable public improvements—breakwaters or parks, for example—as well as financial incentives to encourage developers to provide public access and other desirable features. The public promenades and improvements at RiverPlace in Portland, Oregon, Rowes Wharf in Boston, Battery Park City in New York, and the Battery in Charleston, South Carolina, are evidence that the tide is turning with respect to public/private cooperation in waterfront development.

Design

Urban waterfront sites require special consideration from design professionals. Although each setting is a special expression of a city's age, size, location, and cultural heritage, a few basic principles apply to the design of most all downtown waterfront projects.

A project's design should take full advantage of the shoreline setting and the amenities offered by the water's edge. One major consideration is to ensure that views from the city to the water are not blocked by new buildings. Additionally, existing view corridors where streets meet the water can be greatly enhanced by siting buildings to frame views of the water.

This principle of design has been effectively used to guide the development of Harbourfront in Toronto. Open plazas and walkways have been constructed where the major connecting views to the city's center—Bathurst Street, Spadina Avenue, and York Street—terminate at the waterfront. As a result, Harbourfront has successfully reunited the city's downtown with its waterfront and has become a primary destination in Toronto.[3]

Another consideration is the link between the waterfront and the land it abuts. Building at grade is one way to accomplish this goal. The fortress-like environment that results from elevating buildings on top of platforms is particularly discouraged at waterfront locations. Furthermore, designing inviting public spaces along the water's edge will serve as an important physical connection between land and water.

Particularly important in waterfront settings is to design buildings that "fit in." Architects of waterfront buildings must consider not only the functional uses of structures, but also the conditions that distinguish

13-9   The city of Milwaukee has developed a river revitalization program to expand its tourism industry. One component is the creation of design guidelines and financial incentives for the development of a river walk. Other plans include the commercial development of themed barges and water taxis.

shorelines from other urban settings. Baltimore's Harborplace is a good example of a project that relates well to its waterfront environment.

The design of Harborplace is sensitive to the configuration of the harbor and to people's desire for visual and physical access to the water. A 200-foot plaza/amphitheater separating the project's two buildings acts as a giant porthole from the downtown to the water. Glass facades and porticos spread along each building allow people to see through the structure to the water. These same features allow the lights and activity of the pavilions to shine out to the city at night. Roll-up exterior doors open the buildings to the water by day, and outdoor-but-covered porches and terraces accentuate views of the harbor. Finally, the buildings have no front or back, so the project opens up not only to the harbor, but also to the downtown.[4]

Financing

Even more so than other types of downtown development, waterfront projects usually require a tremendous front-end investment. Specialized design and engineering studies might be necessary to analyze dredge-and-fill requirements or the load-bearing capacity of existing piers. Furthermore, the regulatory requirements imposed on waterfront projects add significantly to the initial cost of development. The time required to shepherd a project through the process

13-8   By day and night, Foster's Court creates a dramatic centerpiece for Rowes Wharf.

[3] Wrenn et al., *Urban Waterfront Development,* p. 102.
[4] Ibid., p. 103.

"It's a funny little project sitting in the middle of a growing city," says architect Norton Hotson, describing Granville Island, located adjacent to downtown Vancouver, B.C. The 40-acre island, created for industrial use, was in poor repair when the Canadian government set about rejuvenating it in 1976. But rather than turning their backs on the industrial history of the site, the designers and their government client decided to redevelop the island by maintaining and building on its industrial heritage.

"The process that we used was first to analyze the context and history of the site and to look for clues for the redevelopment," says Hotson. "Second, we tried to retain and build on as many existing positive site features as possible. Third, we tried to integrate existing uses wherever possible so that there would be a continuity of activity and past events on the site." The result: an eclectic mix of uses that attracts 6.5 million people to the island a year, many of whom are repeat visitors. A cement plant operates full tilt next to a first-class restaurant, and giant cranes tower over theaters, the art school, and a brewery.

In all, 260 businesses and artist studios are housed in the island's 750,000 square feet of buildings, many of which are original to the island. The anchor is a public food market offering fresh, raw, and prepared food. Rents in the market average $100 per square foot, with some of the tenants generating sales as high as $2,500 per foot. The island also has

13-12   Granville Island is a water-taxi ride away from the heart of downtown Vancouver.

two theaters, housed in existing buildings, the arts school of over 100,000 square feet in a series of connected buildings, a dozen restaurants, a small hotel, and a community center, all fitting in with the island's industrial look. Original railroad tracks incorporated into the sidewalks and walkways as well as extensive signs featuring pipes and primary colors are deliberate attempts to retain the island's sense of place.

Another key factor driving the design of redevelopment was the waterfront setting. Visual and physical access to the waterfront has been created with walkways that surround the perimeter of the site. A maritime market brings together uses that cater to both commercial and private boaters. A privately run miniferry service shuttles passengers between the island and downtown for $1.00, and temporary moorage is available for those who come and go by boat. A floating school (offering scuba or sailing lessons) and a dozen floating residences also add to the waterfront theme.

Granville Island builds on the outstanding downtown that Vancouver already is, with its 40,000+ residents, strong retail component, and a completely accessible beachfront public park running the entire length of downtown. The city's newest urban park—Granville Island—adds another amenity to downtown.

13-11   A dozen restaurants attract tourists to Granville Island.

Source: The Waterfront Center, Washington, D.C.

results in higher interest costs on as-yet unproductive assets.

At the same time, federal, state, and local governments have realized that waterfronts represent major community assets demanding involvement of the public sector—including financial involvement. Their commitments could include the funding of planning and design studies or development itself. Coastal zone management agencies, for example, provide waterfront planning grants under Section 306 of the federal act under which they were created. Funds for land acquisition and low-cost construction might also be funded under Section 306(A), which specifically targets development enhancing public access, redevelopment of deteriorating waterfronts, preservation of historical and cultural values, and restoration of natural resources.

Most states also have an agency or interagency committee that serves as a clearinghouse for a variety of federal and state funding sources for outdoor recreation. Grants and loans to public entities (including port districts) for planning, designing, engineering, and constructing waterfront recreation facilities can be obtained from that source. In some states, funds might be available from the natural resource agency responsible for managing submerged lands. In Washington, for example, the state Department of Natural Resources administers the Aquatic Lands Enhancement Account, a fund whose monies are used, among other things, to enhance public access to beaches.

Though the level of funding from the federal government for waterfront projects has decreased—as it has for other types of revitalization—the U.S. Army Corps of Engineers continues to conduct "reconnaissance" and feasibility studies for proposed federal harbor projects when so directed by Congress. Reconnaissance studies require no local matching funds, while feasibility studies require 50 percent local participation. Projects that pass the technical feasibility and national economic benefits tests can be recom-

mended for inclusion in the federal budget through a water resource appropriation bill. The local port authority is probably the best local entity to deal with the Corps for this type of funding.

Opportunities for Waterfront Development in the 1990s

Supply for many water-enhanced uses, such as office and hotel development, continues to exceed demand in the 1990s. Given the increased complexity of waterfront development, public and private interests must not become blinded by or fall in love with the reflection in the water lest they, like Narcissus, fall in. The amenity of the water's edge will not compensate for poor judgment and bad management in developing downtown waterfront sites.

On the other hand, other national trends could signal a continuation of the move toward waterfront development. The closing of military facilities across the country in the wake of the thawing Cold War and plans to reduce the deficit could provide opportunities for development as surplus government facilities are reused. The Charlestown Navy Yard in Boston is an excellent example of such redevelopment.

Renewed interest in urban waterfronts as a provider of transportation is growing. Water taxis and passenger ferries are gaining popularity, although the financial viability of the operations remains questionable. Again in Boston, Rowes Wharf features a water taxi to nearby Logan Airport. In the same city, the Fan Pier master plan calls for the development of 18.5 acres on Boston Harbor, featuring an 83-foot-wide navigable canal lined with shops and restaurants, oriented to frame views of the historic Custom House Tower. Pedestrian and vehicular bridges spanning the canal will extend the neighboring streets and a planned park promenade into the property itself.

14.
Future Trends in Downtown Development

The 1980s were a boon for downtown development and revitalization in many cities. A historic convergence of white-collar employment growth, unprecedented numbers of women in the work force, inflation, the federal UDAG program, willing lenders, and the resulting improved physical environment yielded real estate opportunities that transformed downtowns in many cities. At the outset of the 1990s, however, most of the trends that fueled the transformation had either reversed direction or at best plateaued. What, then, can real estate professionals expect in the way of downtown development and revitalization in the 1990s?

The trends presented in these pages suggest that downtown revitalization will continue but that it will remain a challenge. While the investment climate has improved dramatically in many downtowns, livability still needs to be improved. The slackening of demand for new office, hotel, and even retail development, along with lower available public revenues from property taxes, will shift the focus of revitalization in the 1990s from super developments to management. Creating "people places" and "quality of life" will replace creating big buildings. Providing amenities and services for tenants and customers will be paramount. Culture and tourism will be important planks in economic development strategies. As downtowns become more livable, modest amounts of market-rate housing and specialty/entertainment retailing will appear. The pursuit of social goals, such as low-income and affordable housing, will move up the ladder in priority. And public/private partnerships will continue, for neither sector has the resources to accomplish these goals alone.

Planning the Work and Working the Plan

With limited resources, planning will become even more important. The results in those cities that have developed and are implementing downtown plans are encouraging. In Portland, Oregon, for example, the 1972 Downtown Plan was the title page of a remarkable success story. After 20 years, a new department store downtown is evidence of a retail comeback. Over 1,500 market-rate and affordable housing units have been added in the past 12 years, and occupancies and rental rates are healthy. The downtown is a delight for pedestrians, thanks to the attention paid to urban design. Other cities, including Cleveland, Denver, Milwaukee, San Francisco, and Seattle, have seen the benefits of careful planning.

For those cities that already have a credible downtown plan (a minority group) and have seen notable improvements, the success of the 1980s is resulting in rewriting and updating the plan. Geographic and programmatic scopes are being broadened. Portland's

14-1 Trees planted in downtowns over the past 20 years have matured enough to make a difference. Still, more are needed.

Proven Strategies

For Plan Development, An Inclusive Process

Still, the progress of the dozens of cities that concentrated on revitalizing downtown encourages others. Most cities and towns have not developed, much less implemented, a downtown plan. For them, the variety of strategies that were tried and tested in the 1980s will become fixtures of their own new plans. An inclusive planning process that gathers input and ideas from all stake holders in downtown—owners, merchants, developers, financiers, employers, workers, government, historic preservationists, residents, and citizens—will be the formula for success, because it results in greater acceptance for the plan from the beginning.

For Plan Implementation, E Pluribus Unum

Creating or using one entity (with representatives on its board of directors from key groups of stake holders) that has a full-time staff to oversee and implement the downtown plan is a proven strategy. In one city, over 25 organizations are working to promote downtown revitalization with no central coordination. Efforts are splintered and achievements hard to come by. In cities like Orlando or Boston, however, both with powerful downtown redevelopment organizations, efforts have been more successful. In those cities and others, public/ private partnerships will continue to be used as a means of accomplishing goals. With fine-tuned skills in making deals, the public sector will still be

Downtown Plan is now the Central City Plan, encompassing a larger area with broader goals, particularly ones with a social bent like providing affordable housing and quality education for central city residents. In Orlando, the boundaries of the downtown tax increment financing district have been expanded outside the traditional CBD.

Other cities are expanding the scope of revitalization because of shrinking (or at best stable) resources. Five years ago, federal funds dried up; now local funds are too as dropping building occupancies result in lower property valuations and, consequently, lower property tax revenues. Ironically, the partial success some downtowns have achieved in the past decade now hinders them from obtaining funds to complete revitalization. As priorities have changed, mayors in Phoenix and Milwaukee, for example, are on record as favoring the spreading of limited city funds to districts other than primarily downtown. In other cities—those that have not yet seriously tried to revitalize downtown—the deterioration of the last 10 years could seem almost too great to tackle or the power of downtown economic revitalization underestimated. In downtown Dallas, for example, the office boom of the last decade diverted attention away from emptying department stores, shabby streetscapes, and boarded-up buildings, not just on the periphery of downtown but on main street as well. There, public funds for infrastructure tend to head to the suburbs, not downtown, and developers are likely to follow the investment of public dollars. Though these shifts in priority may foreshadow others to come, it is hoped that the positive results of those cities with long-range plans could counterbalance the trend.

14-2 Both public and private sectors will demonstrate resourcefulness in developing low-income and affordable housing, leveraging skills developed in the 1980s.

248

needed to accomplish goals like funding market-rate and affordable housing. Developers, too, will be more adept at working with public or quasi-public entities.

Incremental versus Catalytic Approach

Downtown plans that embrace incremental strategies will prove most effective. An incremental strategy combines goals and action plans for the physical appearance of individual buildings as well as the entire downtown. An incremental strategy also addresses economic development, that is, opportunities for new businesses to be created and expanded, and social goals like affordable housing. Finally, an incremental strategy addresses how the individual relates to the downtown. Does the downtown worker, resident, or shopper see it as a secure place? A fun place? Or only as a place to work? In short, an incremental strategy puts forth a number of action plans, meant to be achieved over a period of time, to accomplish a number of goals, rather than relying on a single catalytic event or project to revitalize a downtown. An incremental strategy will take longer, but the payoff will be greater.

Downtown Baltimore, for example, did not rely only on its National Aquarium for revitalization; the aquarium was only one component of a 30-year-plus rehabilitation program begun in 1955 when James Rouse formed the Greater Baltimore Committee and joined with the Retail Merchants Association Committee on Downtown to tackle downtown and city-wide problems.[1] Granted, if ever a catalytic strategy were potentially successful, an aquarium that averages 1.3 million tourists a year putting $88 million annually into the economy might be it. But it is only as part of the Inner Harbor redevelopment and the Charles Street centralized retail management program that the aquarium has been as successful as it is.

Zoning—No New Taxes

In cities from Bellevue, Washington, to Hartford, Connecticut, zoning has been and will continue to be an effective tool for implementing downtown strategies. In exchange for granting greater floor/area ratios and transfers of development rights, for example, cities have benefited from streetscaping, public art, active ground-level uses, and affordable housing, among other amenities. At the same time, the oversupply of office buildings, the traditional engine of downtown redevelopment, has changed the equation by which new development happens. In cities where developers paid a high price for the "privilege" of developing

downtown in the 1980s, Boston and San Francisco, for example, zoning requirements will not be pursued with the same intensity in the 1990s. Linkage fees might not be reduced, but they certainly will not be increased in the near future, and amenities not required by the market will not be provided gratis as before. At the same time, cities that overhaul their zoning ordinances in the next decade will take a hard look at incentives versus requirements.

The Shift from Creating Buildings to Creating Quality of Life

Management versus Development

If developing a downtown plan has been and will continue to be a trend in revitalizing downtowns, the very heart of the plan is likely to shift in the 1990s in response to market forces. Demand for new office buildings has shrunk dramatically. Demand for new hotels and retail outlets is off as well. Lower inflation rates have dictated longer holding periods on real estate assets. As such, the next decade is likely to be one in which the new projects of the 1980s are nurtured, through a new emphasis on management. Leasing vacant space will continue to be important, but so will retaining existing tenants. Providing high levels of service, like training specifically for downtown merchants, solutions to social problems that are also amenities (child care or daycare for elderly parents, for example), other amenities like art in public spaces, and, when necessary, renovating space will take on elevated importance in the 1990s. Improvement districts will be used more and more to ensure a flow of cash from downton property owners and merchants into the downtown to fund high levels of service and infrastructure.

Creating People Places

Along with the shift from development to management will come a shift in creativity, from creating buildings to creating quality of life. This creation and re-creation will occur in individual buildings as well as in the downtown as a whole. In downtown Chicago, for example, the owners of the Sears Tower

---

[1] S. Jerome Pratter and William Conway, *Dollars from Design* (Washington, D.C.: National League of Cities, 1981), p. 17.

14-3 More than ever, attention will be focused on creating a downtown that is oriented toward people.

have created a winter garden of sorts in the building in an attempt to make it more hospitable to people. In downtown Dallas, an urban forest was created around First Interstate Tower that attracts downtown residents as well as tourists. In Phoenix, a three-acre urban park was built as a major civic gathering place.

On a districtwide basis, Milwaukee is attempting to reverse a development pattern that ignored the Milwaukee River, which bisects the downtown, by providing a package of incentives to enhance the river and the riverfront. In Bellevue, Washington, development bonuses are granted for providing grocery stores, while hardware stores and drugstores are exempt from FAR calculations. In Boston, the redevelopment authority has proposed creating a park with a substantial portion of the 27 acres of land that will become available when one of the city's major thoroughfares is submerged underground.

Cultural and entertainment facilities will continue to be concentrated downtown as part of a city's quality of life, though new facilities might be on a less grand scale than, say, Los Angeles's California Plaza. Rather, the restoration of movie palaces, the development of loft spaces for regional and experimental theater, and the introduction of art galleries and studio spaces will continue. Communities with existing facilities will nurture them as never before to keep them alive.

Management Trends in Transportation

New rail and upgraded bus and shuttle systems, new or widened thoroughfares, and repaired bridges are appearing around the country in an attempt to increase the supply of transportation options and to

shore up aging infrastructure. At least 10 cities now have some form of heavy-rail transit, and 10 new light-rail systems were completed in the last decade as well. Seattle has built a downtown bus tunnel with rails built in to accommodate future light-rail transit. Boston, San Francisco, and Hartford plan to lower or relocate freeways.

The high costs of land and construction, particularly downtown, and federal, state, and local budget constraints, however, are leading to a growing interest in management rather than development as a solution to transportation problems.

Many believe [transportation management] can obviate or delay the need for the expensive and often controversial solutions usually applied to the problem of congestion—widening roads and building new ones. Its logic is straightforward and compelling: by promoting transit use, by urging commuters to car pool, van pool, bicycle, or walk, by convincing employers to offer flexible hours, and by raising interest in telecommuting and a host of other options, transportation management takes vehicles off the road.[2]

Programs that make better, more efficient use of existing roads and facilities (by employing signalization and HOV lanes, for example) or that reduce demand (through commuter transportation programs or parking-/trip-reduction ordinances) will become more and more prevalent downtown. Already, organizations like the Bellevue Downtown Association, the Central City Association in Los Angeles, the Charlotte Uptown Development Corporation, and the Denver

[2] Robert T. Dunphy and Ben C. Lin, *Transportation Management through Partnerships* (Washington, D.C.: ULI–the Urban Land Institute, 1990), Foreword, p. iii.

14-4 This urban forest softens the impact of the adjacent 60-story building on pedestrians.

Partnership, Inc., are actively addressing area transportation needs. Each group sponsors and promotes ride sharing, the use of transit to commute, and employer transportation coordinators. Two offer subsidies of transit fares. Downtown Hartford, Connecticut, Los Angeles, and Charlotte have or are starting transportation management associations, specialized nonprofit organizations that facilitate private involvement in resolving transportation problems. And cities from Orlando to Bellevue are requiring developers to reduce the amount of parking and/or to create specific trip-reduction plans.

Outlook by Type of Product

The focus on management downtown is not to say that no new development will occur; of course it will. The following paragraphs review the outlook by type of product.

Office Buildings

Employment will continue to grow but to a lesser degree than in the 1980s. While office buildings will still be an important strategy in downtown revitalization, keeping rather than finding tenants will be the focus. Those who can keep fussy tenants happy will be the new heroes.

Office buildings that do get built are bound to be on more stable financial footing than many of those built in the 1980s. Developers with the most experience and the best sources of capital will be able to build in the 1990s. Tighter standards for underwriting projects—higher levels of preleasing to creditworthy tenants and higher levels of equity—are likely to weed out both marginal developers and marginal projects. Lower inflation rates, higher financing costs (in the form of higher fees or greater amounts of equity required), and the greater risks associated with office development in an overbuilt market will prompt developers and their architects to be more careful in cost analyses. The use of elaborate designs and materials will be scrutinized as never before. Renovation is likely to be a strategy employed in the downtown office market in the 1990s, particularly for projects completed in the late 1970s or early 1980s. Changing the skin of a building, creating a new entrance, providing on-site improvements for tenants, or reconfiguring interior space can contribute to an owner's strategy for retaining tenants.

Retail Space

Cities like Orlando, Seattle, and Portland, Oregon, provide proof that downtown retailing can be revital-

ized. In Portland, existing department stores were retained, a new one was added, and specialty retailing attracts customers. In Seattle, a spruced-up streetscape, new public spaces, enhanced transit service, and centralized retail management preceded the opening of a new specialty center in the retail core next to two department stores. In Orlando, two new specialty centers have opened downtown, which take advantage of the heavy traffic from the downtown entertainment district, Church Street Station.

But these cities have been active in downtown planning and revitalization for years, and their efforts are finally bearing fruit. For other cities that have been diligently pursuing the development of an environment conducive to retailing, results should be seen in the 1990s in the form of leased ground-level stores and, in some cases, the development of new centers, including some department stores. Those just beginning planning and revitalization should not expect speedy results. In fact, in many cities, it will take the entire decade to create the kind of environment necessary to attract major new investment. Furthermore, just as rehabilitation is expected to increase downtown, so will it also in suburban settings—which could adversely affect downtown. At the Galleria in St. Louis, for example, three anchor tenants are being added to the mall. Because of its close-in location, the expanded mall is likely to negatively affect downtown retailing.

In those cities able to attract new investment, specialty- and entertainment-oriented retailing will be the focus, with the strongest markets also adding department stores. Phoenix's Shops at Arizona Center, Dallas's West End, and Underground Atlanta all include a substantial amount of entertainment. Some cities will follow the lead of cities like Hartford to fine-tune their zoning ordinances to allow and en-

14-5 The Shops at Arizona Center reflects a trend toward food and entertainment services. *Source:* ELS/Elbasani & Logan Architects.

courage entertainment. The Hartford ordinance is being revised to allow brewpubs, for example, once considered a manufacturing use.

Other special niches might include shopping oriented toward ethnic groups, like the Mercado in Phoenix or the China Trade Center in Boston, and adaptive use. In downtown Oak Park, Illinois, a vacated department store is now in its second adaptive use. In the first round, the building was converted to an interior-focused mall. The project never leased. In round two, a more traditional ground-level scale of retailing was added by retrofitting blocked-in windows and adding others. The project is 98 percent leased to retail and office tenants.

One of the most important trends in downtown retailing has less to do with development and more to do with—not surprisingly—management. Based on the successes of a variety of different cities from Neenah, Wisconsin, to Seattle, Washington, centralized retail management will become a more widespread tool for revitalizing retail space. Master leases or "cooperation agreements," merchandising plans for entire downtowns, programs to mitigate less-than-desirable circumstances while, say, a streetscape construction program is under way, and the provision of "client" services are now proven tools. In downtown Neenah, for example, from 1983 to 1988, occupied retail space increased almost 40 percent, from 51,000 to 70,000 square feet, while the retail vacancy rate dropped 20 percentage points, to 3 percent.[3] In Seattle, retail sales stabilized rather than declined during the period when major retailing streets were turned into rubble from the construction of a bus tunnel and major new office buildings.

Hotels

Falling profit margins and rising delinquencies and foreclosures, all as a result of overbuilding in the 1980s, will continue to repel both lenders and developers from building new hotels in this decade, although some hotels in selected situations will be built. Downtown markets where no all-suite hotels exist present a potential opportunity. In cities where room rates are high, the introduction of a limited-service, economy property, perhaps as adaptive use of an existing building, will be a possibility as well. Renovation of older properties might provide opportunities in cities where the best-located historic properties were not already restored in the tax-driven early and mid-1980s. Newer "older properties," those built in the 1960s and 1970s, for example, could hold even more promise. Two Sheraton hotels in New York City, for example, are undergoing major renovations. When the Sheraton Centre's $142 million renovation is completed in 1992, it will once again be a modern convention hotel suitable for its now-fashionable neighborhood. The Sheraton Squire is being repositioned as an upscale business traveler's hotel at a cost of $47 million.

MXDs

With dim prospects for office and hotel development—historically two of the major components of downtown mixed-use properties—one has to wonder about the future of new MXDs downtown. Some believe, however, that the prognosis for less new development could actually encourage mixed-use projects. The reason: prime locations are often best suited for mixed-use projects, and they are the only locations that will get developed in the next decade. In downtown Cleveland, for example, Tower City Center was recently completed on a prime infill site. The new development adds a 380,000-square-foot multilevel retail mall, a Ritz-Carlton hotel, and a 350,000-square-foot office tower, all of which are integrated with two existing department stores and with rail and bus transit. Further, MXDs are usually undertaken by experienced and well-financed developers, the only ones who will be in a position to undertake new projects. For the same reasons, cities like having mixed-use projects downtown and could be more willing to participate to structure deals, given tight financing markets in the 1990s.

The ability of mixed-use projects to generate a synergistic effect among desirable uses—housing, entertainment, cultural attractions, and recreation—could also encourage cities and developers to consider MXDs in the 1990s. In Camden, New Jersey, a $7.5 million international trade center, a 50,000-square-foot marina, and a $5 million parking garage are under way in conjunction with Campbell Soup Company's new world headquarters and the $42 million New Jersey State Aquarium. A major component of Phoenix's new downtown MXD is entertainment in the same environment as 800,000 square feet of office space. In Washington, D.C., two recently completed mixed-use projects incorporate housing. One incorporates a major public space as well, the U.S. Navy Memorial. Housing in particular could be a more frequently used component of MXDs, given the oversupply of offices and hotels.

---

[3] James A. Cloar et al., *Centralized Retail Management* (Washington, D.C.: ULI—the Urban Land Institute, 1990), p. 27.

Carol M. Highsmith/David Patterson for
Pennsylvania Avenue Development Corporation

14-6   Market Square, Washington, D.C.

Housing

That said, will housing be the hot downtown development product of the 1990s? With opportunities to develop downtown office space waning, the development of housing, if it can be proven feasible, should increase. But many of the compelling forces for downtown housing are abating. Increases in employment growth are projected to drop to 1.1 percent in this decade, and the rise in the female work force is expected to level off as well.[4] The baby boomers who fueled employment growth and demand for office space in the 1980s are aging and are interested in buying, not renting, houses. In most cities, buying a residence downtown is still seen as a risky investment, because most downtowns still are not considered "livable."

Still, many of the projects cited in this handbook are in livable cities, and, in those cities, a modest amount of new downtown housing, particularly rental housing, will be seen. Public/private partnerships are primed for the opportunity, having honed their analytical and negotiating skills on the office, retail, and mixed-use markets of the 1980s. These same entities have advanced their skills in providing low-income and affordable housing as well, and more emphasis will be seen in those areas. The federal government's

HOME, HOPE, and Low-Income Housing Preservation programs will provide federal funds to assist state and local governments, though some still call for more in the way of a national housing policy.

---

[4] David L. Birch et al., *America's Future Office Space Needs: Preparing for the Year 2000* (Arlington, Va.: National Association of Industrial and Office Parks, 1990), pp. 1, 14.

14-7   In livable cities, a modest amount of new housing will be developed downtown.

Other Products

Opportunities could exist for the development of government or public buildings and/or cultural facilities, either to own or to develop for a fee. Chicago officials were surprised at the interest shown by qualified developers in the RFP for a new library, as the same developers had shown little interest in public projects before. In Orlando, a public/private partnership is being used to finance the new City Hall, with the developer retaining the option to build on an adjacent tract of land when the market is ready. In another push for downtown government space, the International Downtown Association will continue to keep the retention of downtown federal government offices at the top of its legislative agenda. Where possible, developers will undertake adaptive use to meet the space needs of government and cultural or other public entities. Bedford, Virginia, has a new downtown courthouse, for example, which was formerly a department store. The entirely new brick exterior is designed to blend in with the scale and look of the downtown.

As the third-largest retail service industry in the United States, tourism employs more than 6 million people. In 1989, travelers in the United States spent more than $330 billion for goods and services, according to a U.S. Department of Commerce study.[5] Clearly, tourism will remain an important part of an economic development strategy for downtown. Aquariums, often in a downtown setting, are based on a strategy incorporating tourism as well as an environmental one. Some predict such "green" attractions will continue to succeed in the 1990s. Already, Camden, New Jersey, Tampa, Chattanooga, New Orleans, Norwalk, Corpus Christi, Texas, Atlanta, Cleveland, and San Francisco are building or considering building aquariums. A note of caution, however, is warranted. A copy-cat mentality—particularly with regard to tourist attractions—can do more harm than good; market justification must exist before such projects can be built.

Tomorrow's Design

As new projects are built and old buildings reused or restored, architects, developers, and city planners will continue to be more sensitive to the fit of buildings with their downtown setting. Attention to street-level details, such as height, setbacks, materials, signs, and windows, will be particularly important, especially given the desire to create places for people. Open designs, particularly in mixed-use projects, will continue now that, in many cities, the downtown

14-8 The massing of Whitney Grove in New Haven, Connecticut, respects existing building lines and cornice heights while maintaining continuity in materials and details. Townhouses, offices, and retail space are connected to their downtown setting, a trend that will increase in the 1990s.

setting has improved enough to negate the need for fortress-like architecture. Rowes Wharf in Boston and Arizona Center in Phoenix reflect the trend toward open design and a generous amount of public space included.

The economics of design will become more important as developers and owners attempt to improve the financial performance of real estate assets. The tenants that will fuel employment growth in the 1990s—smaller, growing, start-up companies—might not be able to afford the extravagant building designs and finishes that were seen in the 1980s. For downtowns to be competitive, they must pursue these types of tenants rather than presuming they will lease space in the suburbs. Even the mainstays of the downtown office market, financial and legal institutions, will have to be more frugal. The challenge for developers and architects will be to build buildings that meet the owner's criteria for investment, urban design goals for the entire downtown, and individual tenant's needs.

Public/Private Partnerships— Still Crucial

The refrain for this entire handbook could be that, with reduced federal, state, and local monies and less demand for real estate products, public/private partnerships will be more crucial than ever to accomplish downtown revitalization. Neither the public nor the

---

5 "Revival Bought with Tourist Dollars," *New York Times*, January 10, 1990.

private sector has the funds and expertise to complete the job alone.

For those who are just beginning, not only have funds disappeared, but also a deteriorated downtown environment might at first repel private investment. For cities that have begun revitalization, both the private and public sectors are well-schooled in the subject, having perfected existing organizational and financial tools. In Massachusetts, for example, Boston redevelopment officials are seeking to stretch the use of tax increment financing, because existing state statutes currently limit its applicability. Even there, other development incentives like the issuance of taxable bonds or city-backed loans to developers are being considered—quite a change from the days when the city nonchalantly accepted contributions from developers to construct public spaces or cultural facilities as part of having development approved. In other cities, sales tax increment financing is being considered. In fact, it could be a sort of back-to-the-future approach with respect to the provision of de-

velopment incentives. Public officials and staffers, however, will not be suckers. Experience with rather complicated financing tools—leasing, certificates of participation, and UDAGs—as well as improved analytical ability will enable cities to cut better deals in the 1990s.

A continued public/private partnership will be needed for reasons other than finances as well. Downtowns still need to be managed, and public and private cooperation is required to do so. Downtown plans must be developed and implemented. The retail core must be leased, maintained, and managed just like any other shopping center. Programs to reduce automobile trips and parking spaces must be promoted and monitored. Social problems must be solved. New businesses must be cultivated, and cultural institutions must be encouraged.

Some cities are far along on this process; most are not. The authors hope that this handbook will aid participants in the development process to enhance not just their downtowns, but entire cities as well.

Selected References
and
Index

SELECTED REFERENCES

Books

Alexander, Laurence A. *Downtown Improvement Districts: Creating Money and Power for Downtown Action.* New York: Downtown Research and Development Center, 1986.

———. *How Downtowns Organize for Results: 24 Case Studies.* New York: Downtown Research and Development Center, 1987.

———, ed. *Downtown Retail Revitalization: The New Entrepreneurial Strategy.* New York: Downtown Research and Development Center, 1986.

Attoe, Wayne, and Donn Logan. *American Urban Architecture: Catalysts in the Design of Cities.* Berkeley: Univ. of California Press, 1989.

———, eds. *With Heritage So Rich.* New York: Random House, 1966.

Bacon, Edmund N. *Design of Cities.* New York: Viking Press, 1967.

Barnes, W. Anderson. *Downtown Development: Plan and Implementation.* Washington, D.C.: ULI–the Urban Land Institute, 1982.

Barnet, Jonathan. *An Introduction to Urban Design.* New York: Harper & Row, 1982.

Birch, David L. *America's Office Needs: 1985–1995.* Boston: MIT Center for Real Estate Development and Arthur Andersen & Co., 1986.

Birch, David L., Susan MacCracken Jain, William Parsons, and Zhu Xiao Di. *America's Future Office Space Needs: Preparing for the Year 2000.* Arlington, Va.: National Association of Industrial and Office Parks, 1990.

Black, J. Thomas, Libby Howland, Stuart L. Rogel, et al. *Downtown Retail Development: Conditions for Success and Project Profiles.* Washington, D.C.: ULI–the Urban Land Institute, 1983.

Black, J. Thomas, Donald O'Connell, and Michael Morina. *Downtown Office Growth and the Role of Public Transit.* Washington, D.C.: ULI–the Urban Land Institute, 1982.

Casazza, John A., and Frank H. Spink, Jr. *Shopping Center Development Handbook,* 2d ed. Washington, D.C.: ULI–the Urban Land Institute, 1985.

The Changing Office Workplace. Washington, D.C.: Building Owners and Managers Association and ULI–the Urban Land Institute, 1986.

Clay, Grady. *Right before Your Eyes: Penetrating the Urban Environment.* Chicago: APA Planners Press, 1987.

Cloar, James A., with Elizabeth Stabler and A.P. DeVito. *Centralized Retail Management.* Washington, D.C.: ULI–the Urban Land Institute, 1990.

Cowey, Ann Breen, Robert Kaye, Richard O'Connor, and Richard Righy. *Improving Your Waterfront: A Practical Guide.* Washington, D.C.: U.S. Dept. of Commerce, National Oceanic and Atmospheric Administration, 1980.

Curran, Raymond J. *Architecture and the Urban Experience.* New York: Van Nostrand Reinhold, 1983.

The Dimensions of Parking. 2d ed. Washington, D.C.: ULI–the Urban Land Institute and NPA–the National Parking Association, 1983.

Duckworth, Robert P., John M. Simmons, and Robert H. McNulty. *The Entrepreneurial American City.* Washington, D.C.: Partners for Livable Places, 1985.

Dunphy, Robert T., and Ben C. Lin. *Transportation Management through Partnerships.* Washington, D.C.: ULI–the Urban Land Institute, 1990.

Evald, William R. Jr. *Street Graphics.* Washington, D.C.: American Society of Landscape Architects, 1971.

Fleming, Ronald Lee. *Facade Stories: Changing Faces of Main Street Storefronts and How to Care for Them.* New York: Hastings House, 1982.

Frieden, Bernard J., and Lynne B. Sagalyn. *Downtown, Inc.: How America Rebuilds Cities.* Cambridge, Mass.: MIT Press, 1989.

Goldberger, Paul. *Architecture and Design in a Postmodern Age on the Rise.* London: Penguin Books, 1985.

Good, J.W., and R.F. Goodwin. *Waterfront Revitalization for Small Cities.* Corvallis: Oregon State Univ. Extension Service, 1990.

Goodwin, Robert. *Waterfront Revitalization for Smaller Communities.* Seattle: Univ. of Washington, 1988.

Gratz, Roberta Brandes. *The Living City.* New York: Simon & Schuster, 1989.

Gruen, Victor, and Larry Smith. *Centers for the Urban Environment: Survival of the Cities.* New York: Van Nostrand Reinhold, 1973.

Halpern, Kenneth. *Downtown USA: Urban Design in Nine American Cities.* New York: Watson-Guptill, 1978.

Halprin, Lawrence. *Cities.* New York: Reinhold Publishing Corp., 1963.

International Downtown Association. *Downtown Promotion Handbook.* Washington, D.C.: Author, 1980.

Jacobs, Jane. *The Death and Life of Great American Cities.* New York: Random House, 1961.

Joint Development: Making the Real Estate–Transit Connection. Washington, D.C.: ULI–the Urban Land Institute and Gladstone Associates, 1979.

Keeling, John M. *Hotel/Motel Development.* Washington, D.C.: ULI–the Urban Land Institute, 1984.

Lassar, Terry Jill. *Carrots and Sticks: New Zoning Downtown.* Washington, D.C.: ULI–the Urban Land Institute, 1989.

———. *City Deal Making.* Washington, D.C.: ULI–the Urban Land Institute, 1990.

Lennard, Suzanne H. Crowhurst, and Henry L. Lennard, *Public Life in Urban Places.* South Hampton, N.Y.: Gondolier Press, 1984.

Letchfield, Michael. *Renovation: A Complete Guide.* New York: John Wiley & Sons, 1982.

Levitt, Rachelle L., ed. *Cities Reborn*. Washington, D.C.: ULI–the Urban Land Institute, 1987.

Levitt, Rachelle L., and John J. Kirlin, eds. *Managing Development through Public/Private Negotiations*. Washington, D.C.: ULI–the Urban Land Institute and the American Bar Association, 1985.

Longstreth, Richard. *The Buildings of Main Street: A Guide to American Commercial Architecture*. Washington, D.C.: Preservation Press, 1987.

Lynch, Kevin. *The Image of the City*. Cambridge, Mass.: The Technology Press and Harvard Univ. Press, 1960.

McNulty, Robert H. *The Economics of Amenity*. Washington, D.C.: Partners for Livable Places, 1985.

McNulty, Robert H., R. Leo Penne, and Dorothy R. Jacobson. *The Return of the Livable City: Learning from America's Best*. Washington, D.C.: Acropolis Books, 1986.

Martin, Thomas J., et al. *Adaptive Use Development Economics, Process, and Profiles*. Washington, D.C.: ULI–the Urban Land Institute, 1978.

Morton, W. Brown, and Gary L. Hine. *The Secretary of the Interior's Standards for Historic Preservation Projects, with Guidelines for Applying Standards*. Washington, D.C.: U.S. Dept. of the Interior, National Park Service, Technical Preservation Services Division, 1981.

Myths and Facts about Transportation and Growth. Washington, D.C.: ULI–the Urban Land Institute, 1989.

National Council for Urban Economic Development. *Downtown Retail Revitalization: Strategies to Maximize Your Market*. Washington, D.C.: Author, 1989.

——. *Emerging Trends in Real Estate Financing*. Washington, D.C.: Author, 1989.

——. *Establishing and Operating Private Sector Development Organizations*. Washington, D.C.: Author, 1984.

National League of Cities. *Managing Design and Development Downtown*. Washington, D.C.: Author, 1981.

O'Mara, W. Paul, with John A. Casazza. *Office Development Handbook*. Washington, D.C.: ULI–the Urban Land Institute, 1982.

Paumier, Cyril B., with Constance C. Dimond, W. Scott Ditch, and Diana Rich. *Designing the Successful Downtown*. Washington, D.C.: ULI–the Urban Land Institute, 1988.

Petersen, David C. *Convention Centers, Stadiums, and Arenas*. Washington, D.C.: ULI–the Urban Land Institute, 1989.

Porter, Douglas, ed. *Downtown Linkages*. Washington, D.C.: ULI–the Urban Land Institute, 1985.

Pratter, S. Jerome, and William Conway. *Dollars from Design*. Washington, D.C.: National League of Cities, 1981.

Project for Public Spaces. *Managing Downtown Spaces*. Chicago: APA Planners Press, 1986.

Rypkema, Donovan D. *Downtown in the 1990s: The Economic Future of America's Center Cities*. Washington, D.C.: Hyett Palma Publications, 1990.

Schoettle, B. Clarkson. *Keeping Up Appearances: Storefront Guidelines*. Washington, D.C.: National Trust for Historic Preservation, National Main Street Center, 1983.

Schwanke, Dean, et al. *Mixed-Use Development Handbook*. Washington, D.C.: ULI–the Urban Land Institute, 1987.

Schwartz, Gail Garfield. *Where's Main Street, USA?* Westport, Conn.: Eno Foundation for Transportation, 1984.

Shopsin, William C. *Restoring Old Buildings for Contemporary Uses: An American Sourcebook for Architects and Preservations*. New York: Whitney Library of Design, 1986.

Smith, Kennedy, et al. *Revitalizing Downtown*. Washington, D.C.: National Trust for Historic Preservation, National Main Street Center, 1988.

Snedcof, Harold R. *Cultural Facilities in Mixed-Use Development*. Washington, D.C.: ULI–the Urban Land Institute, 1985.

Stegman, Michael A., and J. David Holden. *Nonfederal Housing Programs: How States and Localities Are Responding to Federal Cutbacks in Low-Income Housing*. Washington, D.C.: ULI–the Urban Land Institute, 1987.

Stout, Gary E., and Joseph E. Vitt. *Public Incentives and Financing Techniques for Codevelopment*. Washington, D.C.: ULI–the Urban Land Institute, 1982.

Suchman, Diane R., with D. Scott Middleton and Susan L. Giles. *Public/Private Housing Partnerships*. Washington, D.C.: ULI–the Urban Land Institute, 1990.

Torre, L. Azeo. *Waterfront Development*. New York: Van Nostrand Reinhold, 1989.

ULI–the Urban Land Institute. *Dollars & Cents of Downtown/Intown Shopping Centers: 1990*. Washington, D.C.: Author, 1991.

——. *Dollars & Cents of Shopping Centers: 1990*. Washington, D.C.: Author, 1990.

——. *Shared Parking*. Washington, D.C.: Author, 1983.

U.S. Dept. of Housing and Urban Development. *Revitalizing Downtown Retailing: Trends and Opportunities*. Washington, D.C.: Author, 1983.

Wagner, Richard, and Ted Miller. *Revitalizing Downtown, 1976–1986*. Washington, D.C.: National Trust for Historic Preservation/National Main Street Center and The Urban Institute, 1988.

Whyte, William H. *City: Rediscovering the Center*. New York: Doubleday, 1988.

——. *The Social Life of Small Urban Spaces*. Washington, D.C.: Conservation Foundation, 1980.

Witherspoon, Robert. *Codevelopment: City Rebuilding by Business and Government*. Washington, D.C.: ULI–the Urban Land Institute, 1982.

Wrenn, Douglas M., with John A. Casazza and J. Eric Smart. *Urban Waterfront Development*. Washington, D.C.: ULI–the Urban Land Institute, 1983.

Periodicals and Newsletters

American Demographics. P.O. Box 68, Ithaca, New York 14851.

Architectural Record. McGraw-Hill, 1221 Avenue of the Americas, New York, New York 10020.

Architecture. 1130 Connecticut Avenue, N.W., Suite 625, Washington, D.C. 20036.

Building Design and Construction. Cahners Plaza, 1350 E. Touhy Avenue, Des Plaines, Illinois 60018.

Buildings. Stamats Communications, 427 6th Avenue, S.E., Cedar Rapids, Iowa 52401.

Center City Report. International Downtown Association, 915 15th Street, N.W., Suite 900, Washington, D.C. 20005.

Commercial Investment Real Estate Journal. Commercial Investment Real Estate Council, 430 N. Michigan Avenue, Chicago, Illinois 60611.

Downtown Idea Exchange. Downtown Research and Development Center, 1143 Broadway, Suite 1407, New York, New York 10010.

Economic Development Commentary. National Council for Urban Economic Development, 1730 K Street, N.W., Washington, D.C. 20006.

Economic Developments. National Council for Urban Economic Development, 1730 K Street, N.W., Washington, D.C. 20006.

Historic Preservation News. National Trust for Historic Preservation, 1785 Massachusetts Avenue, N.W., Washington, D.C. 20036.

Hotel and Motel Management. Edgell Communications, 7500 Old Oak Boulevard, Cleveland, Ohio 44130.

Journal of the American Institute of Architects. 1735 New York Avenue, N.W., Washington, D.C. 20004.

Journal of the American Planning Association. American Planning Association, 1313 E. 60th Street, Chicago, Illinois 60637.

Journal of Real Estate Development. Federal Reserve Press, 210 Lincoln Street, Boston, Massachusetts 02111.

Landscape. Blair Boyd, P.O. Box 7107, Berkeley, California 94707.

Landscape Architecture. American Society of Landscape Architects, 4401 Connecticut Avenue, N.W., 5th Floor, Washington, D.C. 20008.

Main Street. National Trust for Historic Preservation, National Main Street Center, 1785 Massachusetts Avenue, N.W., Washington, D.C. 20036.

Monitor. National Mall Monitor, Arbor Office Center, 1321 U.S. 19 South, Suite 500, Clearwater, Florida 33516.

Mortgage Banking. Mortgage Bankers Association of America, 1125 15th Street, N.W., Washington, D.C. 20005.

National Real Estate Investor. 6255 Barfield Road, Suite 100, Atlanta, Georgia 30328.

Nation's Cities Weekly. National League of Cities, 1301 Pennsylvania Avenue, N.W., 6th Floor, Washington, D.C. 20004.

The Parking Professional, 701 Kenmore Avenue, 2nd Floor, Fredericksburg, Virginia 22401.

PAS Memo. American Planning Association, 1313 E. 60th Street, Chicago, Illinois 60637.

Place. Partners for Livable Places, 1429 21st Street, N.W., Washington, D.C. 20036.

Planning. American Planning Association, 1313 E. 60th Street, Chicago, Illinois 60637.

Progressive Architecture. P.O. Box 95759, Cleveland, Ohio 44101.

Project Reference File. ULI–the Urban Land Institute, 625 Indiana Avenue, N.W., Suite 400, Washington, D.C. 20004.

Real Estate Finance. 2844 E. 3rd Street, Suite 106, Long Beach, California 90814.

The Real Estate Finance Journal. 210 South Street, Boston, Massachusetts 02111.

Real Estate Today. National Association of Realtors, 430 N. Michigan Avenue, Chicago, Illinois 60611.

Shopping Centers Today. 665 Fifth Avenue, New York, New York 10022.

Shopping Center World. 6255 Barfield Road, Atlanta, Georgia 30328.

Small Town. Small Town Institute, Third Avenue & Poplar Street, P.O. Box 517, Ellensburg, Washington 98926.

Stores. National Retail Merchants Association, 100 W. 31st Street, New York, New York 10001.

Transportation Quarterly. Eno Foundation for Transportation, Box 2055, Westport, Connecticut 06880.

Urban Affairs Quarterly. Sage Publications, 2111 W. Gillcrest Drive, Newbury Park, California 91320.

Urban Design International. Institute for Urban Design, 4253 Karensue Avenue, San Diego, California 92122.

Urban Land. ULI–the Urban Land Institute, 625 Indiana Avenue, N.W., Suite 400, Washington, D.C. 20004.

Waterfront World. Waterfront Center, 1536 44th Street, N.W., Washington, D.C. 20007.

Organizations

American Council for the Arts
1285 Avenue of the Americas
3rd Floor
New York, New York 10019
212-245-4510

American Institute of Architects
1735 New York Avenue, N.W.
Washington, D.C. 20006
202-626-7300

American Planning Association
1313 E. 60th Street
Chicago, Illinois 60637
312-955-9100

American Public Transit Association
1201 New York Avenue, N.W.
Suite 400
Washington, D.C. 20005
202-898-4000

Building Owners and Managers Association International
1201 New York Avenue, N.W.
Suite 300
Washington, D.C. 20005
202-408-2662

Downtown Research and Development Center
1143 Broadway
Suite 1407
New York, New York 10010
212-228-0246

Institute of Real Estate Management
777 14th Street, N.W.
Washington, D.C. 20005
202-628-4494

International Council of Shopping Centers
665 5th Avenue
New York, New York 10022
212-421-8181

International Downtown Association
915 15th Street, N.W.
Suite 900
Washington, D.C. 20005
202-783-4963

National Association of Home Builders
15th & M Streets, N.W.
Washington, D.C. 20005
202-822-0200

National Association of Housing and Redevelopment
 Officials
1320 18th Street, N.W.
Suite 500
Washington, D.C. 20036
202-429-2960

National Association of Realtors
430 N. Michigan Avenue
Chicago, Illinois 60611
312-329-8200

National Council for Urban Economic Development
1730 K Street, N.W.
Washington, D.C. 20006
202-223-4735

National League of Cities
1301 Pennsylvania Avenue, N.W.
6th Floor
Washington, D.C. 20004
202-626-3030

National Trust for Historic Preservation
1785 Massachusetts Avenue, N.W.
Washington, D.C. 20036
202-673-4254

Partners for Livable Places
1429 21st Street, N.W.
Washington, D.C. 20036
202-887-5990

Project Public Spaces
153 Waverly Place
Washington, D.C. 10014
212-620-5660

Society of Landscape Architects
4401 Connecticut Avenue, N.W.
5th Floor
Washington, D.C. 20008
202-686-2752

ULI–the Urban Land Institute
625 Indiana Avenue, N.W.
Suite 400
Washington, D.C. 20004
202-624-7000

INDEX

Abdus-Sabur, Muhammad, 117
Abraham & Strauss department store (New York), 162
Accelerated depreciation, 5, 227
Access: and convention/entertainment facilities, 208, 214–15, 216; and defining the downtown market, 134, 136, 139; and design, 146; and estimating market support, 141, 142; and festival marketplaces, 153; and housing, 183; and management, 170; and mixed-use projects, 163; and regional shopping centers, 158, 161; and requirements for downtown space, 165; and transportation/parking, 93; and waterfront development, 237–38, 242
Accountability, 16, 23
Adams Apartments (Seattle), 195–96
Adaptive use, 252, 254
Ad hoc committees, 17
Advertising. See Marketing.
Affordable housing: and approval process/building codes, 190, 192, 195, 197; and CBD evolution, 7; and condominium conversions, 192; federal programs for, 189–90; and future trends in downtown development, 247, 253; and historic preservation, 190, 191, 193; and housing trust funds, 190; and housing vouchers, 189; and housing zones, 195; incentives for, 178–79, 182, 186, 189, 190, 192, 193, 195, 196; and inclusionary zoning, 192; and linkage, 6, 190–91; opposition to, 198; and preservation of existing stock, 189, 190; and public/private partnerships, 190, 196–98; and rehabilitation, 179, 182, 189, 190, 191, 193, 196, 197; SROs as, 192–95, 196; state/local programs for, 190–96; and strategies/organization of downtown revitalization, 27, 31–32, 189–96; and surplus public land, 195; and TDRs, 27, 195–96
Air rights, 56, 92, 192, 208, 233–34
Alameda, Cal., 195
Alamo Plaza (San Antonio), 158
Albuquerque, 204
Alexandria, Va., 73, 235
Allied Stores Corporation, 157
Amenities: building, 25; cultural, 26; and cultural facilities, 218, 221–22; and future trends in downtown development, 247, 249; and housing, 175–76, 177, 183; and mixed-use projects, 108–9; and office space, 119, 120–25; and pedestrian, 25–26; and public financing techniques, 62; and retailing, 140–41; retailing as an, 162; and strategies/organization for downtown revitalization, 25–26; and transportation/parking, 95; and zoning, 25–26

American Institute of Architects, 18
American Planning Association, 18, 19, 195
America West Arena (Phoenix), 208–9, 210–11
Anaheim, Cal., 200–201
Anchors: and challenges to downtown retailing, 129; and convention/entertainment facilities, 210, 212, 215; and cultural facilities, 220; and defining the downtown market, 135, 138, 139, 140; and design, 147; and festival marketplaces, 152, 153; and future trends in downtown development, 251; and market studies, 142; and mixed-use projects, 162; and pedestrians, 95; and regional shopping centers/malls, 155, 156, 157, 159, 160, 162; and restructuring existing space, 150; and strategies/organization for downtown revitalization, 13; in the suburbs, 129
Annapolis, Md., 240–41
Appraisals, 67
Approval process: coordination of the, 56; and the development prospectus, 41; and downtown plans, 45–46; fast-track, 28, 48, 186, 188, 192, 195; and fees, 195; and housing, 175, 186, 188, 192, 195; and incentives, 186; and inclusionary zoning, 28; and initiation of projects, 45–48; and project conception, 37; and public financing techniques, 56; and retailing, 131; and strategies/organization of downtown revitalization, 28, 31
Aquariums, 254
Aquatic Lands Enhancement Account, 245
Architecture. See Design; Urban design.
Arco Arena (Sacramento), 208
Arenas, 140, 205–6, 208–9, 210, 212, 215
Arizona Center (Phoenix), 46–47, 63, 106, 107–8, 109, 210, 251, 254
Arizona State University, 221
Arthur Erickson Associates, 215
Arts District (Dallas), 176
Asheville, N.C., 60
A&S Plaza (New York), 162
Athens, Ga., 57–58
Atlanta: convention/entertainment facilities in, 133, 204, 206, 216–17, 251; downtown plans for, 22, 95; financing in, 133; and future trends in downtown development, 251, 254; historic preservation in, 224; office space in, 122; public/private partnerships in, 133; retailing in, 133, 154, 251; and strategies/organization for downtown revitalization, 17, 22; and transportation/parking, 95, 216; and urban design principles, 76; visitors in, 133
Atlantic Richfield Co., 208

Austin, Tex., 176, 195, 218
The Avenue (Cleveland), 135–36, 155

Back Bay (Boston), 27
Baltimore: and CBD evolution, 5; convention/entertainment facilities in, 204; downtown plans in, 249; historic preservation in, 224; hotels in, 201, 204; incentives in, 155; and the rationale for downtown revitalization, 2; rehabilitation in, 249; retailing in, 128, 129, 137, 138, 152, 155; transportation/parking in, 87; and urban design principles, 74; visitors in, 138; and waterfront development, 243. See also names of specific projects.
Bank of California (San Francisco), 80
Bank community development corporations, 51–52
Bank One Center (Dallas), 27, 81
Barton-Malow Company, 217
Battery (Charleston, S.C.), 242
Battery Park City (New York), 39, 109, 175, 176, 190, 239, 242
Battleship Building (Columbus, Ohio), 188
Beacon Companies, 38–39
Beckley, W.V., 114
Bedford, Va., 254
Beers, Inc., 217
Belk's department store (Charlotte, N.C.), 153
Bellevue Stratford Hotel (Philadelphia), 163
Bellevue, Wash.: and housing, 174, 175, 176; and quality of life, 250; transportation/parking in, 90, 91, 250–51; zoning in, 25, 29, 249
Benefit districts, 69
Benjamin Thompson & Associates, 226
Berkeley, Cal., 141
Board of directors, 16, 17–18, 30, 197, 248
Boeing Employees Good Neighbor Fund, 197
Bonds: and CBD evolution, 6; and convention/entertainment facilities, 208, 209; and incentives, 26; insurance for, 65; as a source of financing, 54, 62, 63, 64, 66; and strategies/organization for downtown revitalization, 16, 26. See also specific types of bonds.
Bonuses: and CBD evolution, 6; design review of, 29; and future trends in downtown development, 250; and housing, 174, 175, 178, 186, 190, 192; and mixed-use projects, 108–9; and office space, 121; and off-site improvements, 29; and public financing techniques, 55; and quality of life, 250. See also specific types of bonuses.
Boston: and CBD evolution, 5, 7; cultural facilities in, 191; design in, 17, 29, 73,

74, 79, 254; downtown plans in, 245, 248; and future trends in downtown development, 248, 249, 250, 252, 254, 255; historic preservation in, 38–39, 234; hotels in, 203; housing in, 176, 191, 195; incentives in, 155; linkage in, 191; mixed-use projects in, 106; office space in, 115–18, 191; public/private partnerships in, 38–39, 195, 248, 255; and the rationale for downtown revitalization, 2; rehabilitation in, 191, 195; retailing in, 138, 151, 152, 155, 191, 252; and strategies/organization for downtown revitalization, 15, 27, 29–30; transportation/parking in, 86, 89, 93, 96, 99, 100, 250; visitors in, 138, 152; waterfront development in, 238, 242, 245; zoning in, 29–30, 249

Boston Harbor Hotel, 203
Boston Housing Partnership, Inc., 196
Boulder, Colo., 151
Bourque, Linda, 27
Brackenridge, A. Bruce, 7
Brewery District (Columbus, Ohio), 188
Broadway Plaza (Los Angeles), 162
Brodie, M.J., 95
Brooklyn, N.Y., 194
Buffalo, N.Y., 59, 87
Building: color, 79–80, 84; entrances/windows, 78–79, 82
Building codes: and daycare facilities, 124; and financing, 56; and historic preservation, 235–36; and housing, 174, 186, 190, 197; and retailing, 131–32, 165
Building materials and cultural facilities, 218
Buildings: and design, 75, 79–80, 84; and future trends in downtown development, 251, 254; and historic preservation, 234, 235–36; and housing, 174, 181; and office space, 120, 251; and retailing, 147, 162
Bureau of Economic Analysis (U.S. Department of Commerce), 221
Burgee, John, 80, 120
Burlington, Vt., 151, 171
Business development, 171
Business development districts, 63
Business improvement districts, 19
Business/Industrial Development (BID) program, 59

Cabot Corporation, 7
California Plaza (Los Angeles), 219, 222, 250
Callahan Oaks (Orlando), 32
Camden, N.J., 252, 254
Campbell Soup Company, 252
Capital Management and Development, 167
Carnegie Library (Pittsburgh), 220
Car pools. See Ride sharing.
Carrier Dome (Syracuse, N.Y.), 208
Carr, Philip, 167
CBD. See Central business district.
CDBG. See Community Development Block Grants.

CDC. See Bank community development corporations.
Central Artery (Boston), 89, 238
Central business district: evolution of the, 2–8; methods for combatting decline of the, 4–6. See also Downtown revitalization.
Centralia, Wash., 15
Centralized retail management (CRM), 12, 13, 127, 166–72, 249–52
Central West End (St. Louis), 225
Century Freeway (Los Angeles), 89
Certificates of participation (COPs), 64–66, 102, 255
Chambers of commerce, 14, 17, 103, 166
Charitable donations, 17, 57
Charles Street (Baltimore), 249
Charleston, S.C., 242
Charlestown Navy Yard (Boston), 245
Charlotte, N.C.: convention/entertainment facilities in, 206; financing in, 52; office space in, 165; public/private partnership in, 153; regulations in, 165; retailing in, 153–54, 165; and transportation/parking, 90, 97, 98, 250–51; visitors in, 153; work force in, 153
Chattanooga, Tenn., 254
Cherry Creek (Denver), 156
Chicago: cultural facilities in, 218; and future trends in downtown development, 254; housing in, 134–35, 190; incentives in, 190; mixed-use projects in, 161, 163; and office space, 121; quality of life in, 249–50; retailing in, 134–35, 136, 160, 161, 162, 163; and transportation/parking, 86, 100–101; visitors in, 135; work force in, 135
Chicago Housing Partnership, 196
Chinatown district (Portland, Ore.), 182
China Trade Center (Boston), 252
Church Street Market (Orlando), 32, 33–36
Church Street Marketplace (Burlington, Vt.), 151
Church Street Station (Orlando), 251
Cincinnati: bonuses in, 29; convention/entertainment facilities in, 204; design in, 27, 29; hotels in, 204; housing in, 174, 176, 184; regulations in, 27, 47; retailing in, 130, 139; strategy/organization for downtown development in, 26; transportation/parking in, 97, 99
Citicorp Center (New York), 163
Citicorp Plaza (Los Angeles), 90
Cityfair (Charlotte, N.C.), 153–54
City Hall (Orlando), 254
City University of New York, 65
Civic Center (Cleveland), 55
Cleveland: cultural facilities in, 220; downtown plans in, 247; and financing, 55; and future trends in downtown development, 252, 254; hotels in, 203, 252; mixed-use projects in, 252; office space in, 132, 252; and the purpose of revitalization, 11; and the rationale for downtown revitalization, 1; retailing in, 132, 135–36, 137, 155; visitors in, 137

Cleveland Housing Network, Inc., 196
Clotfelter, Richard, 120, 121
Cognetics, Inc., 114
Coldwell Banker, 115
Coleman, Cathy, 130, 155
Colleges/universities, 220–21
Columbus, Ohio, 130, 187–88
Commercial banks, 50, 54
Commercial hotels, 199, 200, 202, 252
Community colleges, 220–21
Community Development Block Grants (CDBGs): and the CBD, 4–5; and historic preservation, 223, 228, 234; and hotels, 203; objectives of, 59; and Section 108 funds, 59; as a source of financing, 51, 59, 61; and strategies/organization for downtown revitalization, 11; uses for, 5, 59
Community housing partnerships, 189
Community Reinvestment Act, 14
Commuter assistance programs, 101
Commuting. See Parking; Transit systems; Transportation.
Concessions, 210, 212, 214
Condemnations, 64, 208
Condominium conversions, 192
Conference Board, 123
Construction: coordination of, 57; costs of, 131–32, 159, 250; loans for, 50, 51, 54
Consultants, 18–19, 29, 34, 35, 41, 42
Convention facilities/conventions: and access, 208, 214–15, 216; and anchors, 212, 215; as catalysts, 204, 205–6, 210, 213, 215, 216, 217; and concessions, 210, 212, 214; and design, 206–8, 210, 214, 216; determining need for, 205–6, 208; and downtown plans, 210; financing of, 208–9, 211, 215, 217; and historical preservation, 214; and hotels, 157, 199, 200–201, 202, 204, 208, 209, 214, 215, 216, 252; and land writedowns, 210; and management, 211–12, 214; and marketing, 211–12, 214–15; and mixed-use projects, 208; and office space, 209; operating budgets for, 209–11; and pedestrians, 210; planning/construction of, 206–8; and public spaces/plazas, 210; and retailing, 130, 133, 137, 142, 156, 158, 214; and safety/security, 213–14; sale/lease of name of, 208–9; and sites, 207–8, 210, 214, 216; and streetscaping, 210; and support facilities, 208; and tax abatements, 210; and transportation/parking, 207–8, 210, 211, 214–15, 216; and waterfronts, 214
Copley Place (Boston), 106, 118
COPs. See Certificates of participation.
Corning, N.Y., 79, 150
Corpus Christi, Tex., 254
Coty Building (New York), 81
Council on Urban Economic Development, 18
Coyle, Stephen, 116, 118
Crime, 7, 58. See also Safety/security.
Crow organization, 10
Cudahy (Milwaukee), 175
Cultural amenities, 26

Cultural districts, 219–21

Cultural facilities: and amenities, 218, 221–22; and anchors, 220; as catalysts, 218, 222; and cultural districts, 219–21; and design, 218; economics of, 221–22; and financing, 219; and future trends in downtown development, 247, 250, 252, 254; and hotels, 219, 221–22; and housing, 176; and mixed-use projects, 252; and office space, 219, 220, 221–22; overview of, 215, 218–22; and planning, 221; and public spaces/plazas, 218; and retailing, 133, 134, 135, 137, 140, 153, 218, 221–22; and streetscaping, 218

Dallas: cultural facilities in, 176, 220; entertainment facilities in, 251; examples of revitalization in, 10; financing in, 248; and future trends in downtown development, 248, 250, 251; and historic preservation, 176; hotels in, 203; and housing, 176; and mandated design features, 27; office space in, 122, 123, 124, 220, 248; quality of life in, 250; retailing in, 128, 251; site plan in, 68, 70; transportation/parking in, 96, 97; and urban design principles, 81

Dallas Arts District, 68, 70, 220

Dallas Museum of Art, 176, 220

Dallas Theatre Center, 176, 220

Daycare centers, 121–25, 208, 220

Day & Zimmermann, 158

Deal making. See Negotiations.

DeBartolo Corporation, 157, 159

Debt service, 45, 54–55, 185, 194

Deems, Lewis, McKinley (architects), 215

Deferred land payments, 64

DeGrilla, Robert J., 122

Demographics: and future trends in downtown development, 253; and housing, 183–84, 253; and retailing, 128–30, 132, 134, 135, 139, 154, 165

Demolition, 64, 158, 233, 234

Density: and design/development review, 28, 29; and housing, 174, 186, 190, 192, 195; and inclusionary zoning, 28; and infrastructure, 26; and public financing techniques, 55; and TDRs, 27; and transportation, 85; and urban design principles, 80

Denver: downtown plans in, 247; historic preservation in, 150; and office space, 115; retailing in, 150–51, 156, 162; and strategies/organization for downtown revitalization, 17; and transportation/parking, 88, 90, 97, 250–51

Department stores: and challenges to downtown retailing, 128–29, 130, 131; decline of, 128–29; and defining the downtown market, 135, 136–37, 138–39; and festival marketplaces, 153; and future trends in downtown development, 251, 252; and mixed-use projects, 162, 252; and regional shopping centers, 156, 157, 160; and

strategies for downtown retailing, 153, 156, 157, 160, 162

Design: basics of for retailing, 146–49; controls, 28–29, 116, 118, 181; and convention/entertainment facilities, 206–8, 210, 214, 216; and cultural facilities, 218; and defining the downtown market, 138, 139, 140; and festival marketplaces, 152, 153; and financing, 57, 254; and future trends in downtown development, 251, 254; and historic preservation, 227–28, 233, 234–35; and housing, 175, 181, 183, 186; and incentives, 186; and management, 169–70; mandated features in, 27; and mixed-use projects, 107–8, 162, 164, 254; and office space, 93, 116, 118, 119–20, 251; and public spaces, 254; and regional shopping centers, 158, 159, 162; and requirements for downtown space, 165; and restructuring existing space, 149–50; and strategies for downtown retailing, 145, 146–50, 152, 153; and street vending, 138; and transportation/ parking, 93; and vertical construction, 161; and waterfront development, 242–43. See also Urban design.

Design, project: competition for, 37

Des Moines, 184

Detroit, 3, 120, 122, 228–29

Developer fees, 2, 6, 7, 249

Developers, 40–43, 90–91, 101

Development: agreements, 43, 46–47; analysis, 43–45; authorities/commissions, 16; corporations, 16–17; process, 38; prospectus, 40–43

Dillard's department stores (San Antonio), 158, 159

Discovery Learning Centers, 124

Disney World. See Orlando.

Disposition and Development Agreement, 46–47

Dollars & Cents of Shopping Centers, 141, 145

Downtown Crossing (Boston), 99, 151

Downtown plans: approval of, 23, 25; and the approval process, 45–46; changes/amendments to, 20, 23, 25, 247–48; characteristics of good, 19; and convention/entertainment facilities, 210; example of, 23–24; and financing/management, 22–23; formalizing, 23; and future trends in downtown development, 247–49, 255; and goals/objectives/action plans, 22, 23–24; and guidelines for successful development, 11, 13; and housing, 178, 179, 182; implementation of, 248–49; and initiation of projects, 45–46; and market studies, 20–22; and mixed-use projects, 106–9; and the plan area, 22; and public/private partnerships, 255; purpose/functions of the, 19–20, 37; and retailing, 157, 158; and the RFP/RFQ, 43; and selection of developers, 43; steps in

developing a, 20–23, 25; and strategies/organization for downtown revitalization, 14, 19–25, 30, 249; and subplans, 25

Downtown residents, 134–35, 141, 144

Downtown revitalization: catalytic/incremental approach to, 9, 11, 249; history of, 2–8; indicators of, 7–8; initiation of, 37–48; management of, 9; and options for development, 37–48; purpose of doing, 11; rationale for, 1–2; strategies for, 9–36. See also Central business district.

Downzoning, 186;

Dragos, Stephen, 10

Duluth, Minn., 97, 103

Dunlop, Robert, 159, 160

Eagle Pass, Tex., 51

Easements, 57

East End (Washington, D.C.), 137, 177

Easy Streets program (Seattle), 169, 170

Eckstut, Stan, 71, 72

Economic adjustment grants, 59

Economic Development Administration, 59, 241

Economic development corporations, 61

Economic development grants, 209

Economic impact assessments, 45

Economic Recovery Tax Act (1981), 5, 228, 231, 236

Edmonton, Alberta, 96, 98

Ehrhardt, Paul, 96

Ellerbe-Becket, Inc., 211

ELS/Elbasani & Logan Architects, 131

Eminent domain, 11, 16, 56, 64, 185, 225

Emporia, Kan., 233

Emporium department store (San Francisco), 161

Enterprise zones, 6, 57

Entertainment facilities: and access, 208, 214–15, 216; and anchors, 212, 215; as catalysts, 204, 205–6, 210, 213, 215, 216, 217; and challenges to downtown retailing, 129–30; and concessions, 210, 212, 214; and defining the downtown market, 137, 139; and design, 210, 214, 216; determining need for, 205–6, 208; and downtown plans, 210; and festival/specialty marketplaces, 152, 214; financing of, 208–9, 211, 215, 217; and future trends in downtown development, 247, 250, 251, 252; and historic preservation, 214, 226; and hotels, 208, 209, 214, 215, 216; and housing, 176; and land writedowns, 210; and management, 211–12, 214; and marketing, 211–12, 214–15; and market studies, 144; and mixed-use projects, 107–8, 109, 165, 208, 252; and office space, 209; operating budgets for, 209–11; and opportunities for downtown retailing, 133; overview of, 204–15, 216–17; and pedestrians, 210; planning, design, and construction of, 206–8; and public spaces/plazas, 207, 210; and regional shopping centers, 156, 157, 158; and restructuring existing space, 150; and safety/security, 213–14; sale/lease of name of, 208–9; and sites, 207–8, 210, 214, 216; and streetscaping, 210; and support facilities, 208; and tax abatements, 210; and transportation/parking, 207–8, 210, 211, 214–15, 216; and waterfronts, 214

Environmental impact, 58, 99, 241

Environmental Protection Agency, U.S., 241

Equity, 50

Escondido, Cal., 154

European Community, 54

Evaluation committees, 43

Facades: and design, 79, 82, 84; and historic preservation, 234; and retailing, 145, 147–48, 158; and waterfronts, 243

Fairmont, W.Va., 114

Fairmont Hotel (San Jose, Cal.), 203–4

Fairmount Hotel (San Antonio), 158

Faison, Henry, 77

Faneuil Hall/Quincy Market (Boston), 5, 115, 152

Fannie Mae. See Federal National Mortgage Association.

Fan Pier master plan (Boston), 245

Farmers Home Administration, 59

Farmers' Market (Escondido, Cal.), 154

Farmers' markets, 154, 155

Faust, Kristin L., 193

Fayetteville, Ark., 220–21

Fayetteville, N.C., 17

FBI Building (Washington, D.C.), 76, 177

Feasibility: and the development prospectus, 40–41; and linkage fees, 191–92

Feasibility analysis, 18, 42, 43–45, 46–47, 140–45, 174, 177, 183–85, 206, 208. See also Market studies.

Federal government: and future trends in downtown development, 253; and historic preservation incentives, 224, 226–29, 230, 231–32; and housing, 185, 189–90, 253; and retailing, 160; as a source of financing, 58–59

Federal Highway Administration, 89, 157, 226

Federal Home Loan Mortgage Company (Freddie Mac), 190

Federal Housing Administration (FHA), 189, 190

Federal National Mortgage Association (FNMA), 190

Fees: and the approval process, 195; and future trends in downtown development, 254; and historic preservation, 228, 229; and housing, 186, 195; and incentives, 186; and strategies/organization for downtown revitalization, 16; waiver of, 192. See also specific types of fees.

Festival marketplaces: and CBD evolution, 5; and challenges for downtown development, 129, 130; characteristics of, 127; and defining the downtown mar-

ket, 138, 139; and market studies, 145; and opportunities for downtown development, 133, 134; overview of, 151–55; rents in, 145; as unsuccessful, 5

Fifth Avenue (New York), 136

Fiftieth Street Station (New York), 82

Financial feasibility. See Feasibility analysis.

Financial institutions, 14

Financial Institutions Reform, Recovery, and Enforcement Act (1989), 50

Financing: by ancillary parties, 56–57; change in vehicles for, 54; and convention/entertainment facilities, 208–9, 211, 215, 217; and cultural facilities, 219; and design, 254; developers as source of, 40; and development agreements, 43; difficulty in obtaining, 50; and downtown plans, 22–23; factors in considering, 50; and future trends in downtown development, 248, 251, 252, 254, 255; and historic preservation, 60; for hotels, 203–4; and housing, 178–82, 189–96, 197; and mixed-use projects, 106, 252; and office space, 114, 251; and parking, 101; private sources of, 50–54; and profit sharing, 60; and public financing techniques, 55–70; and public/private partnerships, 40, 255; reduction in availability of, 49; and retailing, 133, 154, 155; and the RFP, 42; and strategies/organization for downtown revitalization, 16, 22–23; and the suburbs, 248; takeout, 54; and tax reform, 49; and waterfront development, 243, 245. See also Incentives and specific types of incentives or specific cities.

First Interstate Bank Tower (Dallas), 81, 250

First Union Corporation, 153

Flats (Cleveland), 137

Flint, Mich., 155

Florida: COPs in, 66

Flynn, Raymond, 116

Fondersmith, John, 72

Foreign capital, 50, 53–54

Foreign trade zones, 57

Forest City Rental Properties, 69

Forest Fair Mall (Cincinnati), 139

Fort Collins, Colo., 51–52, 57, 62, 91

Foundation grants, 51, 56–57

Fox, Peter, 31

Freddie Mac. See Federal Home Loan Mortgage Company.

Front-end cash, 64

Galena, Ill., 224

Galleria (St. Louis), 251

The Galleries (Syracuse, N.Y.), 156

Gallery at Market East (Philadelphia), 92, 150, 156

Garn–St. Germaine Depository Institutions Act (1982), 50

Gaslamp Quarter (San Diego), 214

General obligation bonds, 63, 65, 69, 181, 209

Georgetown (Washington, D.C.), 141

Georgia Dome (Atlanta), 216–17

Georgia World Congress Center (Atlanta), 216

Gerald D. Hines Interests, 80, 119–20, 124, 125

Gerstenfeld, S. Jon, 167

Gheen Building (Shelby, N.C.), 12

Gilroy, Cal., 221

Ginnie Mae. See Government National Mortgage Association.

Globe Investment Pension Fund, 225

Golden West Hotel (Los Angeles), 193

Government buildings, 254

Government National Mortgage Association (Ginnie Mae), 190

Grand Avenue (Milwaukee), 131

Grand Central Station (New York), 223–24, 233–34

Grand Rapids, Mich., 184

Granville Island (Vancouver, B.C.), 244

Graphics, 77

Greyhound Bus Station (Washington, D.C.), 224

Grid system, 94

Griffin, John, 191–92

Ground leases, 49, 66–68, 209

Growth management, 6–7, 46, 191

Guthrie, Okla., 224

Habitat for Humanity (Austin, Tex.), 195

Hallidie Plaza (San Francisco), 161, 162

Handman, Arthur, 96

Harborpark District (Boston), 116

Harborplace (Baltimore), 5, 129, 138, 201, 243, 249

Harbourfront (Toronto, Ontario), 243

Hardin, Dan, 29

Harrisburg, Pa., 103

Harry Weese & Associates, 226

Hartford, Conn.: and the approval process, 47; and design review of bonus features, 29; entertainment facilities in, 165; and future trends in downtown development, 249, 250, 251–52; historic preservation in, 165; housing, 109, 174, 190–91, 195; incentives in, 165; mixed-use projects in, 109, 165; retailing in, 165; and strategy/organization of downtown development, 26; and transportation/parking, 96, 97, 103, 165, 250, 251; zoning in, 29, 109, 249, 251–52

Hartley's department store (West Virginia), 114

Hashimoto, Yutaka, 54

Heery/RFI/TVS, 217

Henri Bendel Building (New York), 81

Herald Center (New York), 161–62

High-occupancy-vehicle (HOV) lanes, 89, 101, 250

High Point, N.C., 100

High-rise construction. See Vertical construction.

Highway funds, 70

Highways, 86, 88–89

Hillsboro, Tex., 1, 21, 72, 224, 228

Hilton Hotel (Minneapolis), 204
Hilton hotels, 201, 204
Hines, Gerald D., 115. *See also* Gerald D. Hines Interests.
Historic districts, 57
Historic preservation: and building materials, 234, 235–36; as a catalyst, 228; and the CDBG, 223, 228, 234; and convention/entertainment facilities, 214, 226; and cultural facilities, 219; and defining the downtown market, 136; and demolition, 233, 234; and design, 77–78, 81, 149, 150, 227–28, 233, 234–35; and downtown plans, 21; and eminent domain, 225; and fees, 228, 229; and financing, 55–56, 60, 223, 225, 228; and future trends in downtown development, 252; guidelines/standards for, 223, 227–28, 229, 230, 231, 234, 235–36; and hotels, 224, 225, 252; and housing, 175, 176, 181, 182, 186, 190, 191; importance of, 77–78; incentives for, 5, 49, 186, 190, 223–33, 234; and insurance, 233; law cases about, 233–34; and maintenance, 233; management of, 38–39, 233–36; and mixed-use projects, 162, 165, 225, 226, 227; and the National Register, 229; and office space, 223–24, 228, 231–32, 233–34, 236; ordinances concerning, 233–36; organizations, 15; and parking/transportation, 102, 225, 226–27; and preservation easements, 232–33; and public/private partnerships, 38–39; and public spaces, 234–35; review process for, 230, 231, 234, 236; as a specialty, 236; and specialty/festival marketplaces, 152, 224, 227; and SROs, 193; and strategies/organization for downtown revitalization, 5, 12; and TDRs, 27, 55–56; and waterfront development, 240–41; and zoning, 26, 233. *See also* specific cities *or* properties.
Historic Preservation Fund, 229
Historic Sites Act (1935), 229
H.J. Russell Construction, 217
Holder Construction Company, 217
Holiday Inn Crowne Plaza (Memphis), 204
Home Buyer Program (Illinois Housing Development Authority), 190
HOME (Home Investment and Affordable Housing Partnership) program, 189, 253
Homeless, 7, 134, 193, 194, 195, 196, 198
Hoosier Dome (Indianapolis), 216
HOPE (Homeownership for People Everywhere) program, 189, 253
Horton Plaza (San Diego), 68, 106, 213, 218
Horton, Thomas P., 50
Hotel Crescent Court (Dallas), 203
Hotels: and convention/entertainment facilities, 200, 202, 204, 206, 208, 209, 214, 215, 216; and cultural facilities, 219, 221–22; and defining the downtown market, 137; demand for, 200; and festival marketplaces, 153; financing for, 203–4; and future trends in downtown development, 249, 252; and historic preservation, 224, 225, 252; and housing, 179, 181; importance of, 199–204; and incentives for development of, 203–4; and joint development revenues, 209; and land prices, 199; location by size of, 201; market mix of downtown, 203; and market studies, 141, 142, 143, 144; and mixed-use projects, 162, 167; and opportunities for downtown development, 133; and parking, 204; and public spaces, 201; and regional shopping centers, 157, 159; and renovation, 252; and safety/security, 199; sales per guest-day in, 204; and services, 201, 202; types of, 199; and waterfront development, 245; and zoning, 204. *See also* Mixed-use projects.
Hotson, Norton, 244
Housing: and capture rate, 184; conferences about downtown, 188; and cultural/entertainment facilities, 176; and demographics, 173, 183–84; difficulties in developing downtown, 174–75; and diversity, 175; and downtown plans, 21, 177, 178, 179, 182; and feasibility analysis, 174, 177, 183–85; and financing, 174, 178–82; and the four "P's," 184–85; and future trends in downtown development, 247, 252, 253; high-rise, 174, 185; and historic preservation, 175, 176, 181, 182, 186; and a livable downtown, 175–77; mix of, 175; and mixed-use projects, 105, 109, 177, 180–81, 252; multifamily, 178–79, 185; and a national housing policy, 253; and neighborhoods, 176; and office space, 173, 174, 179, 181, 182; and public improvements, 178–81, 186; and retailing, 178, 179, 180, 181, 182, 183; and services, 175, 186; socioeconomic factors affecting, 173–74; and strategies/organization for downtown revitalization, 31–32, 185–88; trust funds, 190; vouchers, 189. *See also* Affordable housing; Homeless; Single-room-occupancy units.
Housing Act (1949), 4
Housing and Community Development Act, 59
Housing and Urban Development, U.S. Department of, 189, 193, 241
Houston, 85–86, 94, 97, 122, 125, 202
Houstoun, Lawrence, 136
Hubert H. Humphrey Metrodome (Minneapolis), 208
Hutzler's department store (Baltimore), 137
Hyatt Hotel: in Cincinnati, 204; in St. Louis, 225; in San Diego, 214
Hyatt Regency: in Albuquerque, 204; in Cleveland, 55
Hyatt Regency hotels, 201

ICSC. *See* International Council of Shopping Centers

IDS Building (Minneapolis), 120
Illinois Center (Chicago), 218
Illinois Housing Development Authority, 190
IMAX theaters (San Antonio), 157, 158, 159
Impact fees, 191
Improvement districts, 63, 249
Incentives: and CBD evolution, 6; and cultural facilities, 219; factors to consider when offering, 55; and feasibility analysis, 44; and fees, 186; and financing, 25–26, 54, 55; and future trends in downtown development, 249, 250, 255; and historic preservation, 5, 186, 223, 224, 225, 226–29, 230, 231–33; for hotels, 203–4; and housing, 174, 178–81, 182, 185–86, 187–88, 189, 190, 192, 193, 195, 196; and mixed-use projects, 105; and organizational factors, 18; and public/private partnerships, 38–39, 255; for rehabilitation, 5; and retailing, 129, 130, 133, 139, 155, 171; and strategies/organization for downtown revitalization, 11, 25–26; and transportation/parking, 99, 101, 185; and waterfront development, 242; and zoning, 192. *See also* specific incentives.
Inclusionary zoning, 28, 186, 192
Indianapolis, 138, 216
Industrial development bonds (IDBs), 6, 63, 185
Industrial revenue bonds, 49, 69
Infill projects, 5, 78–80, 109, 176, 236
Infrastructure: and CBD evolution, 7; and density bonuses, 26; and financial feasibility analysis, 45; and future trends in downtown development, 247, 249, 250; and mixed-use projects, 105, 107; and public financing techniques, 64; and retailing, 158
Initiation of project, 37–48
Institute of Transportation Engineers, 93, 102
Insurance, 64, 65, 125, 152, 171, 233
Insurance companies, 52–53, 54
Interest. *See* Loans.
International Conference of Building Officials, 235–36
International Council of Shopping Centers, 136, 137, 141
International Downtown Association, 12, 18
Interstate Highway Act (1956), 3

Jackson Court (Orlando), 32
Jackson, Penrose, 151
Jacksonville, 61
Jacksonville Landing, 61
J.C. Penney department stores (West Virginia), 114
JCP Realty, Inc., 69
Jefferson, Tex., 51
Jensen, Hal, 222
John Hancock Tower (Boston), 116
John Jay College of Criminal Justice (New York), 65
Johnson, Philip, 80, 120
John Winthrop Apartments (Seattle), 197

Joint development revenues, 209
Joint ventures. *See* Public/private partnerships.
Joske Building (San Antonio), 157, 158, 159
J.P. Morgan & Company, 7

Kalamazoo, Mich., 99, 150
Kansas City, Mo., 11, 102–3, 175
Kemper Financial Services, 226
Key West, Fla., 234
Kickers, 54
Kids Building Boston, 116–17
Kids on the Mend (Houston), 125
Kids at Work (Dallas), 123, 124
Kifer, Ann, 120
Kingsport, Tenn., 103
Klugel Architectural Sheet Metal Works (Emporia, Kan.), 233
Kohler, Thomas R., 30
Kohn Pederson Fox, 81
Konomi, Masao, 53

Lacledes Landing (St. Louis), 11, 225
Lafayette Place (Boston), 74
Lakewood, Colo., 19
Land: banking, 64; conveyance, 195; surplus of public, 195; writedowns, 6, 64, 178–79, 180, 185, 210, 219
Land costs: and deferred land payments, 64; and future trends in downtown development, 250; and hotels, 199; and housing, 174, 185, 195; and office space, 7, 119; and retailing, 130–31, 155, 159, 160; and transportation, 250
Landfill, 239
Landscaping. *See* Streetscape.
Larimer Square (Denver), 150
La Salle Partners, Ltd., 226
Las Vegas, 200–201
Lazarus department store (Columbus, Ohio), 130
Leapfrogging, 73–74
Lenders, 44, 45, 50
Letters of credit, 54, 217
Leveraged buyouts, 54
Levinson, Herbert S., 93
Lexington, Mass., 192
Libraries, 220
LIHPRHA. *See* Low-income Housing Preservation and Resident Homeownership Act.
Lincoln Property Company, 33–35, 120
Linkage, 131, 156, 186, 190–91
Linkage fees, 6, 29–30, 116–17, 118, 186, 191, 249
Lipton Corporate Child Care Centers, 125
Loan pools, 6, 12, 51, 60, 185, 228, 233
Loans: bullet, 54, 194; and forward loan commitments, 54; and future trends in downtown development, 255; and housing, 178–79, 185, 188, 190, 194, 196; as an incentive, 185, 188; interest-free, 233; land development, 50; and loan guarantees, 60; and loan-to-value ratios, 53, 54; low-interest, 60–61, 165, 168, 171, 178–79, 185, 196; open-ended, 54; and public/private partner-

ships, 255; and standby loan commitments, 54
London, Eng., 147
Lord & Taylor (San Antonio), 158, 160
Los Angeles: approval process in, 195; cultural facilities in, 219, 222; housing in, 192, 193, 195; and quality of life, 250; retailing in, 162; and transportation/parking, 89, 90, 97, 250–51; UDAG in, 59; zoning in, 25
Loschsky, Marquardt & Nesholm (architects), 215
Louisville, 132, 234
Low-income housing/neighborhoods. *See* Affordable housing.
Low-income Housing Preservation and Resident Homeownership Act (1991), 189, 253
Luxury hotels, 199, 202–3

McClure, Glenda, 122, 124
McGarry, Dave, 116–17
Main Street Program (National Trust for Historic Preservation), 12, 18, 51, 150, 228, 233
Maintenance: and historic preservation, 233; and housing, 183; and retailing, 127, 130, 145, 150, 152, 159, 169; shared expenses for, 64
Malls. *See* Shopping centers/malls.
Management: and ad hoc committees, 17; and boards of directors, 16, 17–18, 30, 197, 248; centralized retail, 12, 13, 127, 166–72, 249–52; and challenges to downtown retailing, 130; and convention/entertainment facilities, 211–12, 214; decentralized, 130; and defining the downtown market, 138, 140; and design, 148, 149, 169–70; of development projects, 18; double line, 17; and downtown plans, 22–23; and festival marketplaces, 152; and future trends in downtown development, 247, 248, 249, 251, 252, 255; of historic preservation, 233–36; and marketing, 167–68, 170–71, 172; and market studies, 142, 167–68; and office space, 126; by one entity with full-time staff, 15–18; and opportunities for downtown retailing, 133–34; and private organizations, 17, 38; and public organizations, 16, 39; and public/private partnerships, 38–40, 255; and public spaces, 169; and quasi-public organizations, 16–17; and regional shopping centers, 157, 159–60; and special assessment districts, 150; and staff, 15–18, 248; and strategies for downtown retailing, 145, 148, 149, 150; and strategies/organization for downtown revitalization, 14, 15–18, 35; and traditional retailing, 127; and transportation, 250–51. *See also* Organizational factors.
Manhattan, Kan., 69–70, 234
Mardian Construction Co., 211

Marketing: and centralized retail management, 127, 167–68, 170–71, 172; and challenges to downtown retailing, 130; and convention/entertainment facilities, 209, 211–12, 214–15; and decentralized management, 130; and defining the downtown market, 140; and design, 148; and festival marketplaces, 152, 154; and future trends in downtown development, 252; and housing, 183, 186; and management, 127, 130, 167–68, 170–71, 172; and market studies, 145; and mixed-use projects, 162, 163, 164; and office space, 120–25; and opportunities for downtown retailing, 133–34; and regional shopping centers, 160; and restructuring existing space, 149–50; and services, 169–71; and strategies for downtown retailing, 145, 148, 149–50, 152; and traditional retailing, 127
Market Mohawk (Columbus, Ohio), 188
Market Street (Philadelphia), 150
Market studies: content of, 44; and the development prospectus, 40; and downtown plans, 20–22; and housing, 177, 183–85; importance of, 44; and the initiation of projects, 43–45; and lenders, 44; and management, 167–68; and office space, 114; and organizational factors, 18; purpose of, 44, 167–68; and retailing, 134–45, 157, 158, 165, 167–68, 170; and strategies/organization for downtown revitalization, 18, 20–22
The Market at Citicorp Center (New York), 163
Marriott Hotel: in Cleveland, 55; in San Antonio, 157, 158, 159; in San Diego, 214; in Washington, D.C., 137
Marriott Hotels, 201
Mason Square (Shelby, N.C.), 12
Massachusetts Bay Transportation Authority, 38–39
Massachusetts State Board of Building Regulations and Standards, 124
Matching funds, 58
May Company (San Antonio), 158
Megastructures, 81–82, 247
Melvin Simon and Associates, 162
Memphis, 186, 204
Menger Hotel (San Antonio), 157, 158, 159
Mercado (Phoenix), 108, 221, 252
Merchandising. *See* Marketing.
Merchants' associations, 17, 141, 166
Metropolitan residents, 135–36, 144–45, 156, 158, 160, 162
Metropolitan Square (Washington, D.C.), 125
Miami, 87, 190–91
Midtown Cultural District (Boston), 27, 191
Million, Rudy, 159
Milwaukee: downtown plans in, 247; examples of revitalization in, 10; financing in, 248; and future trends in downtown development, 248, 250; and housing, 175, 184; and public/private

ventures, 37; and quality of life, 250; retailing in, 131; and strategies/organization for downtown revitalization, 9, 10; and transportation/parking, 97; and urban design principles, 74

Milwaukee Repertory Theatre, 10

Miniperm financing, 51

Minneapolis, 97, 119–20, 204, 208

Mintz, Norman, 150

Missouri 353 corporations, 11, 56, 225, 233

Mixed-use projects: and amenities, 108–9; and the approval process, 46–47; and CBD evolution, 6; and convention/entertainment facilities, 165, 208, 252; and cultural facilities, 218, 221, 252; and design, 73, 107–8, 164, 254; and downtown plans, 106, 107–8, 109; and entertainment facilities, 107–8, 109; and financing, 106, 252; future of, 109; and future trends in downtown development, 252, 253, 254; and historic preservation, 165, 225; and hotels, 167, 203, 252; and housing, 105, 109, 177, 180–81, 252, 253; and incentives, 105, 108–9; and infrastructure, 105, 107; key features of, 106; and marketing, 164; and negotiations, 108–9; and office space, 109, 252; and pedestrians, 106, 107, 109; and rehabilitation, 163; and retailing, 107, 137, 142–45, 160, 162–65, 167, 252; and special districts, 109; and strategies/organization for downtown revitalization, 13; and transportation/parking, 85, 93, 94, 102, 105, 107, 109, 164–65, 252; and waterfront development, 242; and zoning, 105, 108–9

Montgomery County, Md., 192

Montreal, Quebec, 97

Moriarity, Tom, 150

Mortgage bond financing, 54

Mortgage guarantees, 6

Morton H. Myerson Symphony Center (Dallas), 176, 220

Multifamily housing, 49, 178–79, 185

Multilevel retailing. See Vertical construction.

Municipal parking authorities, 102–3

Museum of Contemporary Art (Los Angeles), 219, 222

Nashville, 204

National Affordable Housing Act (1990), 189–90

National Aquarium (Baltimore), 249

National Association of Industrial and Office Parks, 113

National Historic Preservation Act (1966), 229

National Main Street Center. See Main Street Program.

National Marine Fisheries Service, 241

National Park Service, 12, 223, 229, 230, 231, 241

National Place (Washington, D.C.), 107, 137

National Trust for Historic Preservation, 12, 18, 51, 150, 228. See also Main Street Program.

NCNB. See North Carolina National Bank.

Neenah, Wis., 168, 169, 171, 252

Negotiations: and consultants, 19, 42; and COPs, 66; and feasibility analysis, 44, 45, 46, 47; and financing techniques, 58, 66; and ground leases, 67; and housing, 190; and mixed-use projects, 108–9; and public disclosure statutes, 42; and questions developers should ask, 41; and steps in determining deals for cities, 54–55; and strategies/organization for downtown revitalization, 16, 17, 19, 34–36; and transportation/parking, 91; and waterfront development, 242

Neighborhoods, 15, 176. See also Affordable housing.

Net operating income (NOI), 45, 118

Net present value, 45

Newark, 220, 221

New Bern, N.C., 62

New Homes for Chicago, 190

New Jersey Performing Arts Center (Newark), 221

New Jersey State Aquarium (Camden), 252

New Orleans, 137, 201, 202, 206–7, 209, 254

Newport, R.I., 90

New Rochelle, N.Y., 16–17

New York City: air rights in, 233–34; and CBD evolution, 7; cultural facilities in, 220; and design principles, 81, 82; and future trends in downtown development, 252; historic preservation in, 81, 223–24, 233–34; hotels in, 201, 252; housing in, 175, 176, 190, 192; incentives in, 190, 192; mixed-use projects in, 161, 163; office space in, 223–24, 233–34; public/private partnerships in, 39, 190; and the rationale for downtown revitalization, 2; retailing in, 136, 137, 138, 147, 152, 161–62, 163; and transportation/parking, 86; visitors in, 137, 138, 152; waterfront development in, 239, 242; work force in, 132–33, 152; zoning in, 25, 109, 192. See also specific buildings.

New York State Dormitory Authority, 65

Niche markets, 130, 252

Nonprofit organizations, 18

Nordstrom department store (San Francisco), 160, 161

Norfolk, Va., 17, 155

North Carolina Main Street Center, 12

North Carolina National Bank (NCNB), 17, 52, 153

Northland Shopping Center (Detroit), 3

North Michigan Avenue (Chicago), 135, 136, 160

Norwalk, Conn., 254

Norwest Center (Minneapolis), 119–20

Oak Park, Ill., 168, 171, 252

O'Brien, Harry, 27

O'Connor, Joseph, 53

Off-budget debt financing, 64–66

Office of Coastal Zone Management, 241

Office space: and building materials, 251; and business growth by type, 118; and CBD evolution, 6, 7; and convention/entertainment facilities, 204, 209; and cultural facilities, 219, 220, 221–22; decline in demand for, 173, 174, 191, 249; and defining the downtown market, 135, 136–37, 138; and design, 147, 149, 251; determining supply and demand for, 114–18; factors affecting the market for, 111–12; and festival marketplaces, 153, 155; and financing, 114, 209, 251; future need for, 113–14; and future trends in downtown development, 249, 251, 252, 253; and historic preservation, 223–24, 228, 231–32, 233–34, 236; and housing, 173, 174, 179, 181, 182, 191, 253; importance of, 111; investment returns for, 119; and linkage, 191; and market studies, 145; metering, 115–18; and mixed-use projects, 109, 162, 252; and opportunities for downtown retailing, 132–33; and regional shopping centers, 156, 157, 158; and renovation, 251; and requirements for downtown space, 165, 166; and restructuring existing space, 150; and strategies for downtown development, 145, 147, 149, 150, 153, 155, 156; and transportation/parking, 85–86, 93; vacancy rates for, 115–18; and zoning, 249. See also Work force.

Office Worker Retail Spending, 141

Off-site improvements, 29

Oklahoma City, 220

Old Town district (Portland, Ore.), 182

Old Town Square (Fort Collins, Colo.), 62

Oliver Carr Company, 125, 167

Omni International Hotel (Orlando), 33

One Reading Center (Philadelphia), 92

125 High Street (Boston), 116–17

Open spaces, 6. See also Parks; Plazas.

Orange County, Cal., 147

The Oregon (Seattle), 197

Organizational factors, 14–15, 17–25, 37, 133–34, 245. See also Management *and* specific types of management.

Oriole Park at Camden Yards (Baltimore), 224

Orlando: and the approval process, 46; city commons in, 34–36; convention/entertainment facilities in, 208, 251; deal making in, 34–36; and design, 27; downtown plans in, 21, 248; and future trends in downtown development, 248, 251, 254; hotels in, 200–201, 202; housing in, 174, 176; incentives in, 33, 248; and initiation of project, 46; maintenance in, 169; office space in, 120, 121, 165; public/private partnerships in, 248; public spaces in, 169; regulations in, 165; retailing in, 165, 169, 251; and strategies/organization for downtown revitalization, 9, 16, 30–36; and transportation/parking, 100, 208, 251; zoning in, 33

269

Orlando Arena, 208
Ottawa, Ontario, 88
Overlay districts, 29, 109, 149, 174, 178
Overstreet Mall (Charlotte, N.C.), 98
Owners' associations. See Merchants' associations.

Pacific First Centre (Seattle), 121
Pacific First Federal (Seattle), 197
Palm Beach, Fla., 148
Parkersburg, W.Va., 114
Parking: and challenges to downtown retailing, 130, 132; and convention/entertainment facilities, 207–8, 211, 214–15, 216; cost/financing of, 100, 101, 102, 103, 104, 132, 185; and defining the downtown market, 139–40; and design, 76–77, 82–84, 147; determining needs for, 100–104; and downtown plans, 21; and feasibility analysis, 45; and festival marketplaces, 153; and future trends in downtown development, 252; garages, 153, 157, 159, 160, 252; and historic preservation, 102, 225, 226; and hotels, 204; and housing, 179, 182, 185, 186; and incentives, 185, 186; and land use, 102; and management, 169, 170; and market studies, 141; meters for, 104; and mixed-use projects, 102, 107, 252; off-street, 100, 101–2; on-site, 100, 101, 102; on-street, 83, 104; ordinances concerning, 101–2; and the parking generation report, 102; and parking validation programs, 103; permits for, 104; public downtown, 102–3; and regional shopping centers, 155, 157, 159, 160; and requirements for downtown space, 165–66; and restructuring downtown space, 150, 151; and safety/security, 83, 84; shared, 102, 211, 214; stand-alone facilities for, 100–101; and strategies/organization for downtown revitalization, 21, 32–33; structures, 83–84, 132; surface, 83, 95, 132, 147, 208; underground, 84, 157; and zoning, 29, 95, 100, 101
Parking management programs, 93
Parking validation programs, 103
Park Plaza (Asheville, N.C.), 60
Parks: and future trends in downtown development, 250; and housing, 176, 179, 181; and retailing, 140; and transportation/parking, 95
Participating mortgages, 54
Pasadena, Cal., 102
Paseo del Rio (San Antonio), 237
Paving materials, 95
Pedestrian malls, 95, 99–100, 140, 150–51
Pedestrians: amenities for, 25–26; and challenges to downtown development, 130; circulation of, 94–100, 245; and convention/entertainment facilities, 210; and defining the downtown market, 136, 140; and design, 74, 77, 148, 149; and festival market-

places, 153; and mixed-use projects, 106, 107, 109; and pedestrian malls, 95, 99–100, 140, 150–51; and regional shopping centers, 157, 158; and requirements for downtown space, 165–66; and transportation/parking, 85, 94–100; and waterfront development, 245
Pelli, Cesar, 120
Penn Central Transportation Company v. The City of New York (1978), 233–34
Pennsylvania Avenue Development Corporation (Washington, D.C.), 18, 22, 76, 95, 174, 177, 226
Pension funds, 53, 54
People places, 74, 247, 249–50
Performing Arts Center (Portland, Ore.), 181
Perini Corp., 213, 215
Perriello, Robert, 118
Philadelphia, 59, 86, 92, 150, 156, 163, 229
Phoenix: and convention/entertainment facilities, 208–9, 210–11; cultural facilities in, 221; and design, 254; downtown plans in, 210; entertainment facilities in, 107–8, 109, 251, 252; financing in, 63, 248; and future trends in downtown development, 248, 250, 251, 252, 254; mixed-use projects in, 106, 107–8, 109, 252; negotiations in, 46–47; and office space, 115; retailing in, 251, 252
Physical feasibility, 40
Pike Place Market (Seattle), 1, 136, 155
Pioneer Courthouse Square (Portland, Ore.), 182
Pioneer Place (Portland, Ore.), 106, 166, 182
Pittsburgh, 74, 87, 96, 128, 165, 220
Planning, 247–49. See also Downtown plans.
Playhouse Square (Cleveland), 220
Plaza of the Americas (Dallas), 122, 123
Plazas: and convention/entertainment facilities, 210; and cultural facilities, 218; and housing, 175, 181, 182; and transportation/parking, 96; and waterfronts, 243
Plumb, Pamela, 239
Portland, Me., 26, 191, 239
Portland, Ore.: and CBD evolution, 7; cultural facilities in, 181; and design principles, 72–73, 181, 247; downtown plan for, 21, 23–24, 109, 178, 179, 182, 247–48; financing in, 178–82; and future trends in downtown development, 247–48, 251; historic preservation in, 181, 182; hotels in, 179, 181; housing in, 109, 174, 176, 178–82, 192, 193, 195, 247–48; incentives in, 178–81; mixed-use projects in, 106, 109; office space in, 166, 179, 181, 182; and public improvements, 178–81; regulations in, 165–66; rehabilitation in, 179, 182; retailing in, 136, 165–66, 179, 180, 181, 182, 247, 251; safety/security in, 181; and strategies/organization for downtown

revitalization, 14, 21, 23–24, 26; streetscape in, 181; transportation/parking in, 87, 88, 97, 100, 103, 136, 165–66, 179, 181, 182; waterfront development in, 179, 180–81, 238–39, 242; zoning in, 26, 109, 178
Post Office Building (Shelby, N.C.), 12
Predevelopment, 61–62, 187–88
Presales of properties, 54
Preservation: easements, 57; of existing housing, 186, 189, 190. See also Historic preservation.
Private sector, 17, 38, 39–40, 49, 50–54, 141, 166, 190, 212. See also Public/private partnerships.
Privatization, 68, 138
Project conception, 37
Project reviews, 30–31, 37
Promotions. See Marketing.
Property taxes, 16
Proposition 13 (California), 65
Prudential Insurance Co., 221
Public affairs programs, 58
Public buildings, 64, 254
Public disclosure statutes, 42
Public grants, 60
Public housing, 190. See also Affordable housing.
Public improvements, 178–81, 186, 188
Public/private: definition of, 37
Public/private partnerships: and CBD evolution, 5; and city government questions, 41; and convention/entertainment facilities, 209; and developers' questions, 40–41; development process for, 38; and financing, 5, 133, 255; and future trends in downtown development, 247, 253, 254–55; and housing, 196–98, 253; importance of, 13, 196; and incentives, 255; interactions in, 40; management options for, 38–40; and retailing, 133, 153, 157, 160; and strategies/organization for downtown revitalization, 13; types of, 196. See also specific cities and specific projects.
Public sector, 16, 37, 39, 40, 49, 127, 212, 248. See also Financing; Public/private partnerships; and specific financing techniques.
Public spaces: and cultural facilities, 218; and design principles, 71, 82, 254; and downtown plans, 21; and future trends in downtown development, 249, 251, 252, 254; and historic preservation, 234–35; and hotels, 201; and housing, 176, 181; and management, 169; and retailing, 140, 141, 147, 162–63, 169; and waterfront development, 243
Public support, 14–15, 19, 40, 41, 208, 248
Public works grants, 59
Py-Vavra Development, Inc., 33

Quality Hill (Kansas City, Mo.), 11, 175
Quality of life, 249–54
Quasi-public management, 16–17, 212

Radisson hotels, 201, 202
Radisson Plaza Hotel (Orlando), 202
Rail transit. *See* Transit systems.
Ramada Renaissance Hotel (Washington, D.C.), 202
Raubeson, Andy, 193
Real Estate Credit Task Force, 50
Real estate investment trusts (REITs), 53
Real estate limited partnerships (RELPs), 53
Real Estate Research Corporation, 184
Real estate securities, 53
Recourse, 50
Rector Place (New York), 175
Regatta (New York), 239
Regional Industrial Multiplier System (RIMS), 221
Regional planning commissions, 14
Regulations. *See* Approval process; Building codes; *and* specific types of regulations.
Regulatory authority, 11
Rehabilitation: and future trends in downtown development, 251; and housing, 179, 182, 189, 190, 191, 195, 196, 197; incentives for, 5; and mixed-use projects, 163; and office space, 191; and retailing, 251; of SROs, 193, 196; and suburbs, 251; and tax reform, 49. *See also* Historic preservation; Renovation.
Relocation assistance, 64
Renovation, 149–50, 249, 251, 252
Rent, 55, 175. *See also* Retailing.
Request for Proposal/Request for Qualifications, 41–43
Resale/refinancing of project, 45
Resolution Trust Corporation (RTC), 50
Resort hotels, 200–201
Retailing: basic elements of, 141; and capture rate, 142, 144, 145; and CBD evolution, 7; challenges to downtown, 128–32; and comparison shopping, 146, 147, 163, 164; decline of downtown, 127, 128–29; and defining the downtown market, 134–40; and demand and supply, 140–45, 154; and downsizing, 130; and downtown residents, 134–35, 141, 144; drawing power of downtown, 139–40; and future trends in downtown development, 247, 249, 251–52, 255; ground-level, 165–66, 167; and housing, 178, 179, 180, 181, 182, 183; and leases/rents, 130, 141, 145, 152, 153, 155, 157, 158, 159, 161, 162, 164, 168–69, 171, 252; and market segments, 134; opportunities for downtown, 132–34; and parking, 83, 84; physical setting for, 130; and public support for revitalization, 14; regulations concerning, 165–66, 167; and restructuring/renovating existing space, 149–50; and sales/expenditures, 141–42, 143, 145, 152, 158, 164, 165, 166, 172, 252; and strategies/organization for downtown revitalization, 12, 13, 14,

33–36, 145–66; and target markets, 141–42; and taxes, 152; and trade areas, 141, 142, 144; and types of centers, 138–39; vacancy rates in, 252; and vertical construction, 131–32, 160, 161–62, 163. *See also* Department stores; Festival marketplaces; Shopping centers/malls; Suburbs.
Revenue bonds, 61, 63, 178–79, 186, 208, 209, 217
Richmond, Va., 128, 155, 233
Ride sharing, 89, 91, 93, 101, 102, 250
Ritz-Carlton Hotel (Cleveland), 55, 203, 252
Rivercenter (San Antonio), 156–60
RiverPlace (Portland, Ore.), 178, 179, 181, 242
Rizzoli Building (New York), 81
Roanoke, Va., 218
Robert, Joseph E., Jr., 50
Rochester, N.Y., 220
Rockefeller Center (New York), 162
Root, Marsha, 102
Rouse Company: and Baltimore revitalization, 129, 249; and Boston revitalization, 152; and Jacksonville revitalization, 61; and Milwaukee revitalization, 10, 131; and Norfolk revitalization, 155; and Phoenix revitalization, 46; and Portland, Ore., revitalization, 166, 182; and St. Louis revitalization, 225
Rouse, James, 155
Rowes Wharf (Boston), 117, 203, 242, 245, 254

Sacramento, 208
Safety/security: and convention/entertainment facilities, 213–14; and downtown plans, 21; and hotels, 199; and housing, 177, 181, 183, 193–94; and parking, 83, 84; and retailing, 130, 145, 147, 148, 150, 160, 169, 170; and urban design principles, 83, 84
St. Bartholomew's Church (New York), 223–24
St. Joseph's Hospital (Houston), 125
St. Louis, 11, 74, 224, 225, 228–29, 251
St. Paul, 97, 98
Saks Fifth Avenue (Portland, Ore.), 166, 182
Sales taxes, 19, 57–58, 255
Salisbury, N.C., 51
San Antonio, 77, 156–60, 218, 237
San Diego, 68, 87, 88, 106, 191, 192, 196, 213–15, 218
San Francisco: and design, 27, 80; downtown plans in, 247; and future trends in downtown development, 249, 250, 254; growth controls in, 6; and historical preservation, 162; hotels in, 202; housing in, 190–91, 192; linkage in, 191; office space in, 115, 191; regulations in, 162; rehabilitation in, 191; retailing in, 136, 138, 160, 161–62; and transportation/parking, 86, 100–101, 250; zoning in, 249
San Francisco Bay Area BRIDGE Housing Corporation, 196

San Francisco Bay Conservation and Development Commission, 242
San Francisco Shopping Centre, 138, 160, 161–62
San Jose, Cal., 203–4
Santa Clara, Cal., 209
Santa Fe, N.M., 235
Santa Monica, Cal., 190–91
Savings and loan institutions, 50
Schuman Lichtenstein Claman and Efron, 81
Scooter (Hartford, Conn.), 96, 97
Scottsdale, Ariz., 169
Seaport Village (San Diego), 214
Sears department stores (West Virginia), 114
Sears Tower (Chicago), 249–50
Seating, 95, 96, 175, 181, 209
Seattle: approval process in, 47; building codes in, 197; convention/entertainment facilities in, 207, 209; and design principles, 71; downtown plans in, 247; financing in, 197, 209; and future trends in downtown development, 250, 251, 252; growth controls in, 6; housing in, 174, 190–91, 192, 195–96, 197; incentives in, 192; and office space, 115, 121; public/private partnership in, 197; public spaces in, 251; and the rationale for downtown revitalization, 1; rehabilitation in, 197; retailing in, 136, 155, 169, 170, 171–72, 251, 252; streetscape in, 251; TDRs in, 195–96; transportation/parking in, 88, 100–101, 103, 169, 170, 250, 251; zoning in, 25, 29, 192
Seattle Foundation, 197
Seattle Housing Resources Group, 197
Secondary mortgage markets, 190
Secretary of the Interior's Standards for Rehabilitation, 227–28, 229, 230, 231, 234, 235
Section 8 Moderate Rehabilitation Program, 193, 194
Section 108 (Housing and Community Development Act), 59
Section 404 permits, 241
Section 504 loans (SBA), 59
Security Pacific Bank (Seattle), 197
Service fees, 19
Services: and feasibility analysis, 45; and future trends in downtown development, 252; and hotels, 201, 202; and housing, 175, 186; and retailing, 162, 169–71, 252
Setbacks, 79, 80, 82, 234, 254
712 Fifth Avenue (New York), 81
Sewer funds, 60
Shelby, N.C., 12
Sheraton hotels, 201, 252
Shoppers' goods, 128
Shopping centers/malls: community, 138–39, 142; and design, 72; distinctive identities of, 72; management of, 167; neighborhood, 127, 138, 142; operating characteristics of, 128; pedestrian, 95, 99–100; regional, 127, 128, 130,

131, 134, 139, 142, 146, 147, 150, 155–60; size of, 130; super regional, 127, 128, 142, 155, 170; types of, 142. *See also* Festival marketplaces; Pedestrian malls; Suburbs; Transit malls.

Sidewalks, 94, 95, 96

Signs, 76, 79, 147, 148, 149, 159, 160, 254

Single-room-occupancy (SRO) units, 6, 178, 182, 186, 192–95, 196

Sites: and convention/entertainment facilities, 207–8, 210, 214, 216; descriptions of, 42; and the development prospectus, 40; and housing, 174–75, 177, 183; and public financing techniques, 63–64; and retailing, 130–31, 153, 155

16th Street Mall (Denver), 97, 151

Sixth Street Marketplace (Richmond, Va.), 155

Skidmore district (Portland, Ore.), 182

Skidmore, Owings & Merrill, 82

Sklar, Louis, 124

Skyscrapers, 116, 117

Skywalks, 95, 97–99, 165–66

Small Business Administration, 59

Smith, Nancy, 197

Snow, Robert, 33

Solicitations for project, 41–43

South Coast Plaza (Orange County, Cal.), 147

Southern Building (Washington, D.C.), 167

South Park (Portland, Ore.), 178–79, 181

South Station (Boston), 38–39

South Street Seaport (New York), 152

Spaulding & Slye, 116–17

Special assessment districts, 12, 63, 150, 151

Special districts, 16, 28, 29, 109. *See also* types of districts.

Special funds, 26

Special taxes, 19, 63

Specialty retailing: and challenges to downtown development, 128–29, 131; and defining the downtown market, 134, 135–36, 137, 139; and festival marketplaces, 151, 152, 155; and future trends in downtown development, 247, 251; and historic preservation, 224; and market studies, 142; and mixed-use projects, 162, 163, 164; and regional shopping centers, 156, 157; and requirements for downtown space, 165

Speculation, 50

Spitzner, Peter, 29

SRO Housing Corp., 193, 194

Stadia, 140, 205–6, 208–9, 210, 212, 215

Stamford, Conn., 135, 155–56

State agencies, 241–42

State Thomas area (Dallas), 176

Station Square (Pittsburgh), 165

Stein and Company, 121

Storefronts. *See* Facades.

Stouffer Harborplace (Baltimore), 201, 204

Stouffer Hotel: in Cleveland, 55; in Nashville, 204

Street furniture, 218. *See also* Seating.

Streetscape: and CBD evolution, 6; and convention/entertainment facilities, 210; and cultural facilities, 218; and design principles, 75–76, 77, 83; and downtown plans, 21; and future trends in downtown development, 251, 252; and housing, 175, 181; and retailing, 140, 149, 157, 252; and strategies/organization for downtown revitalization, 31; and transportation/parking, 95; and zoning, 26

Street vending, 138

Stride Rite Corp., 125

Subdivision approvals, 46–47

Subsidies, 60, 145, 155, 156, 160, 190

Suburbs: and CBD evolution, 2–4; and financing, 248; and future trends in downtown development, 251; and office space, 114, 121; and rehabilitation, 251; retailing in the, 2–4, 127, 129, 134, 135, 137, 139, 160; and transportation/parking, 85, 86, 91, 94, 95–96, 103; and visitors, 139; work force in the, 139

SunBanks, 120

Superblocks, 46–47

Superdome (New Orleans), 206–7

Support. *See* Public support; Technical support.

Syracuse, N.Y., 45, 97, 156, 208

Tabor Center (Denver), 151, 162

Tampa, 121, 206, 254

Taos, N.M., 1

Task forces, 22

Tax abatements: and CBD evolution, 6; and convention/entertainment facilities, 210; and feasibility analysis, 47; as a form of financing, 49, 63; and historic preservation, 225; and housing, 178–79, 180, 185, 186, 188; and strategies/organization for downtown revitalization, 11, 26; and zoning, 26

Tax allocation bonds, 209

Tax credits, 49, 190, 191, 225, 228, 229, 231, 234

Tax deferrals, 6, 49, 188

Tax-exempt bonds, 6, 49, 190, 195

Tax-exempt financing, 114, 185, 208, 217. *See also* types of financing.

Tax incentives: and CBD evolution, 5; and historic preservation, 223, 226, 228, 229; and housing, 188, 190; as a public financing technique, 57–58. *See also* types of incentives.

Tax increment bonds, 6, 49

Tax increment financing: and convention/entertainment facilities, 209; and future trends in downtown development, 255; and housing, 178, 181, 182, 195; and incentives, 26, 49, 61, 62, 69; and parking, 102; and planning, 248; and public/private partnerships, 255

Tax Reform Act (1986), 5, 49, 59, 63, 185, 190, 191, 226, 228, 229, 231, 236

Technical support, 18, 19

Tenants, 50. *See also* Anchors; Retailing (and leases/rents).

Texas Main Street Program, 228

343 Sansome Building (San Francisco), 80

Toledo, Ohio, 155

Toronto, Ontario, 11, 97, 243

Touche Ross, 7

Tourists. *See* Visitors; Waterfronts.

Tower City Center (Cleveland), 203, 252

Town Center (Stamford, Conn.), 135, 155–56

Town Lake (Austin, Tex.), 176

Trainer, Steve, 122

Trammell Residential Company, 10

Transfer of air rights. *See* Air rights.

Transfer of development rights (TDRs), 6, 27, 55–56, 178, 192, 195–96

Transit malls, 99–100, 150–51, 170

Transit systems: and access, 93; and convention/entertainment facilities, 211, 216; and future trends in downtown development, 250, 251, 252; and housing, 176, 178, 181; and management, 169, 170, 250; and mixed-use projects, 164–65, 252; and parking, 101, 102; and pedestrians, 97; and retailing, 136–37, 150–51, 161, 163, 164–66, 169, 170; and solutions to transportation problems, 86–88; and transit malls, 99–100, 150–51, 170

Transportation: and access, 93; and CBD evolution, 2–3, 5; and construction costs, 250; and convention/entertainment facilities, 210, 211, 214, 216; and defining the downtown market, 136–37, 139–40; and density, 85; downtown as focus of, 86; and downtown plans, 21; and environmental impact, 99; and future trends in downtown development, 250–51, 252, 255; and the grid system, 94; and historic preservation, 226–27; and housing, 176, 178, 181, 182, 183, 184; and incentives, 99; and land costs, 250; and management, 89–93, 101, 169, 170, 250–51; and market studies, 141–42; misperceptions about, 85–86; and mixed-use projects, 105, 107, 109, 161, 163, 164–65, 252; ordinances about, 91; and parking validation programs, 103; and paving materials, 95; and pedestrian/vehicular circulation, 94–100, 245; and public/private partnerships, 91–93, 255; and regional shopping centers, 157, 160; and requirements for downtown space, 165–66; solutions to problems of, 86–93; and the streetscape, 95; and suburbs, 2–3; types of, 86; and waterfront development, 245; and zoning, 26, 95, 99. *See also* Transit systems.

Transportation management associations, 91

Transportation, U.S. Department of, 241

Trapper's Alley (Detroit), 228–29

Trenton Commons (New Jersey), 63

Trenton, N.J., 63, 220

Trip reduction ordinances, 91, 101

Trolley systems, 88, 102, 170, 176, 214

Trump Tower (New York), 161–62, 163

Tulsa, Okla., 17, 103, 168, 171

Turnkey tax-exempt transactions, 114
Tutor-Saliba Corp., 213, 215
222 Berkeley (Boston), 120

ULI–the Urban Land Institute: and housing, 135, 173, 191; Real Estate Credit Task Force, 50; and retailing, 128, 141, 145; as a source of information, 18; survey about downtown revitalization by, 7–8
Umscheid, Rudy, 118
Underground Atlanta, 133, 152, 154, 224, 251
Uniform Code for Building Conservation, 235–36
Union Square (San Francisco), 136
Union Station: in Hartford, Conn., 165; in St. Louis, 11, 224, 225, 228–29; in Washington, D.C., 164–65, 224, 226–27
Union wage requirements, 59
U.S. Army Corps of Engineers, 241, 245
U.S. Fish and Wildlife Service, 241
U.S. Navy Memorial (Washington, D.C.), 252
U.S. Post Office (Hillsboro, Tex.), 228
Universities, 220–21
University of Arkansas, 220–21
Urban design: and future trends in downtown development, 254; major new developments in, 80–81; and megastructures, 81–82; for office space, 116; principles of, 71–77; and retailing, 71, 81, 82, 83, 84, 145, 147, 169–70
Urban Design Group, 158
Urban Development Action Grants (UDAGs): and CBD evolution, 5, 6; and convention/entertainment facilities, 209; and future trends in downtown development, 255; and historic preservation, 223, 225, 228; and hotels, 203, 204; HUD study of, 59; and public/private partnerships, 5, 133, 255; repayments from, 59, 133, 203; and retailing, 133, 157, 158; as a source of financing, 59, 69; and strategies/organization for downtown revitalization, 11; uses for, 5
Urban Mass Transportation Administration, 86, 87–88, 165, 182
Urban redevelopment, 155
Urban renewal, 60, 178
US Bancorp (Seattle), 197

Vancouver, B.C., 102–3, 244
Vancouver, Wash., 104, 175, 176
Vertical construction, 131–32, 160, 161–62, 163, 174, 185
Vertical zoning, 29
Veterans Administration (VA), 3, 190
Vieux Carré (New Orleans), 137
Visibility, 141, 142, 146, 151, 164, 183, 207

Visitors: and defining the downtown market, 134, 135, 137–38, 139, 140; and festival marketplaces, 152, 153, 155; and future trends in downtown development, 247, 254; and market studies, 141, 142, 143, 144; and mixed-use projects, 162, 164–65, 167; and opportunities for downtown development, 133; and regional shopping centers, 157, 158, 159, 160; and regulations for downtown space, 167. *See also* Hotels; Waterfronts.
Visual continuity, 74–77

Walkways, 243
Wallick Development Company, 187
Washington, D.C.: COPs in, 66; and downtown plans, 22; entertainment facilities in, 164–65, 167, 226; and future trends in downtown development, 252; historic preservation in, 224, 226–27, 234; hotels in, 137, 167, 202; housing in, 177, 195, 252; incentives in, 129; metropolitan residents in, 164; mixed-use projects in, 107, 161, 164–65, 167, 252; office space in, 115, 125, 137, 224; public spaces in, 252; regulations in, 165; retailing in, 107, 129, 136, 137, 141, 161, 164–65, 167, 226; and strategies/organization for downtown revitalization, 18, 22; and transportation/parking, 86, 136, 164–65, 226–27; and urban design principles, 76; visitors in, 164–65, 167; and waterfront development, 239, 245; work force in, 164–65. *See also* Pennsylvania Avenue Development Corporation.
Washington State Convention and Trade Center (Seattle), 197, 207
The Waterford (Columbus, Ohio), 188
Waterfront Center (Washington, D.C.), 239
Waterfronts: and access, 237–38, 242; complexity of developing, 237–38; and convention/entertainment facilities, 214; and design, 242–43; and financing, 243, 245; functions of the, 239–41; future development of, 245; and future trends in downtown development, 250; and geographic location, 238–39; and hotels, 245; and housing, 176, 179, 180–81; jurisdictional responsibility for, 242; and land characteristics, 238–39, 243; and office space, 245; and the regulatory process, 237, 240, 241–42, 243, 245; and retailing, 136, 138, 152, 156–60; and transportation, 245
Water funds, 60
Waterside (Norfolk, Va.), 155
Water Tower Place (Chicago), 155, 160, 161, 162, 163

Wellhoefer, Jon, 10
Wentworth Institute (Boston), 116
West End Historic District (Dallas), 176, 251
Whelan, Bill, 118
Whyte, William, 169
Willard Hotel (Washington, D.C.), 167
Williams Jackson Ewing, 226
Williamsport, Pa., 233
Williams Realty Corporation, 157
Williams, Roy, 152, 165
Wisconsin Partnership for Housing Development, Inc., 196
Work force: and challenges to downtown development, 130; and defining the downtown market, 134, 135, 136–37, 139; and design, 147; and festival marketplaces, 152, 153; and future trends in downtown development, 253; and housing, 176–77, 183–84, 253; and marketing, 171; and market studies, 141, 142, 143; and mixed-use projects, 162, 164–65, 167; and opportunities for downtown development, 132–33; and regional shopping centers, 156, 160, 162; and regulations for downtown space, 167; and restructuring existing space, 151; and services, 169
World Trade Center (New York), 22, 239
Worldwide Plaza (New York), 82
Wright Runstad and Company, 195–96

Yamhill district (Portland, Ore.), 182
Yankee Hill (Milwaukee), 10

Zeckendorf Company, 82
Zoning: and amenities, 25–26; changes in the 1990s, 29–30; and design/development review, 28–29; and downtown plans, 22, 23; and financing techniques, 55, 56; and future trends in downtown development, 249, 251–52; and historic preservation, 26, 233; and hotels, 204; and housing, 26, 174, 178, 186, 188, 192, 198; and incentives, 25–26, 174, 178, 186, 188, 192; inclusionary, 28, 186, 192; and initiation of projects, 45, 46–48; and mandated design features, 27; and mixed-use projects, 105, 108–9; and office space, 116, 121, 249; and project conception, 37; purpose of, 25–26; regulatory relief from, 56; and retailing, 131–32, 140–41, 165; and special districts, 29, 109; and strategies/organization for downtown revitalization, 25–30; and TDRs, 27; and transportation/parking, 95, 99, 100, 101; vertical, 29; and waterfront development, 242